Cognitive Approaches to Neuropsychology

HUMAN NEUROPSYCHOLOGY

COGNITIVE APPROACHES TO NEUROPSYCHOLOGY
Edited by J. Michael Williams and Charles J. Long

A Continuation Order Plan is available for this series. A continuation order will bring delivery of each new volume immediately upon publication. Volumes are billed only upon actual shipment. For further information please contact the publisher.

Cognitive Approaches to Neuropsychology

Edited by

J. Michael Williams

Hahnemann Medical University
Philadelphia, Pennsylvania

and

Charles J. Long

Memphis State University and
University of Tennessee Center for the Health Sciences
Memphis, Tennessee

PLENUM PRESS • NEW YORK AND LONDON

Library of Congress Cataloging in Publication Data

Memphis Conference on Human Neuropsychology (5th: 1987) Cognitive approaches
to neuropsychology.

(Human neuropsychology)
"Proceedings of the Fifth Memphis Conference on Human Neuropsychology, held
May 15–16, 1987, in Memphis, Tennessee" — T.p. verso.
Includes bibliographies and index.
1. Neuropsychology—Congresses. 2. Cognition—Congresses. I. Williams, J.
Michael, 1954–   . II. Long, Charles J., 1935–   . III. Title. IV. Series. [DNLM:
1. Cognition—congresses. 2. Neuropsychology—congresses. WL 103 M533c 1987]
QP360.M365   1987   152   88-25178
ISBN 0-306-43024-X

Proceedings of the Fifth Memphis Conference on Human Neuropsychology,
held May 15–16, 1987, in Memphis, Tennessee

© 1988 Plenum Press, New York
A Division of Plenum Publishing Corporation
233 Spring Street, New York, N.Y. 10013

Printed in the United States of America

Contributors

Geri R. Alvis, Department of Psychology, Memphis State University, Memphis, TN

Seija Äystö, Department of Psychology, University of Jyvaskyla, 40100 Jyvaskyla, Finland

Peggy P. Barco, Head Injury Resource Center, Irene W. Johnson Institute of Rehabilitation, St. Louis, MO

William W. Beatty, The Neuropsychiatric Institute, 700 First Ave. South, Fargo, ND

Fredda Blanchard-Fields, Psychology Department, Louisiana State University, Baton Rouge LA

Jill Booker, Amnesia and Cognition Unit, Department of Psychology, University of Arizona, Tucson, AZ

Teresa C. Brobeck, Head Injury Resource Center, Irene W. Johnson Institute of Rehabilitation, St. Louis, MO

Jen Y. Chang, Baumritter Institute of Nuclear Medicine, Mount Sinai Medical Center, Miami Beach, FL

Wayne Cowart, Department of Linguistics, Ohio State University, Rm 204 Cunz Hall, 1841 Millikin Rd., Columbus OH

Bruce Crosson, Department of Neurology and Neurological Surgery, Washington University School of Medicine, St. Louis MO

Walter F. Daniel, Department of Psychology, Memphis State University, Memphis TN

Kathleen B. Fitzhugh-Bell, Departments of Psychiatry and Neurology, Indiana University School of Medicine, Indianapolis IN

Wm. Drew Gouvier, Psychology Department, Louisiana State University, Baton Rouge LA

Arthur C. Graesser, Department of Psychology, Memphis State University, Memphis TN

Helen J. Kahn, Department of Psychology, University of North Dakota, Grand Forks, ND

Kathleen C. Kirasic, Department of Psychology, University of South Carolina, Columbia, SC

Susan Kotler-Cope, Psychology Department, Louisiana State University, Baton Rouge LA

David A. Loewenstein, Wien Center for Memory Disorders, 4300 Alton Road, Miami Beach Florida & Department of Psychiatry, University of Miami School of Medicine, Miami, FL

Debra L. Long, Department of Psychology, Memphis State University, Memphis TN

Charles J. Long, Department of Psychology, Memphis State University, Memphis, TN

Robert L. Mapou, Greenery Rehabilitation Center, 99 Chestnut Hill Ave, Brighton MA

Kurt A. Moehle, Department of Psychology, Purdue University at Indianapolis, 1125 E. 38th Street, P.O. Box 647, Indianapolis IN

Sam B. Morgan, Department of Psychology, Memphis State University, Memphis TN

Murry G. Mutchnick, Department of Psychology, Memphis State University, Memphis TN

Randolph W. Parks, Department of Psychiatry, University of British Columbia, 2255 Wesbrook Mall, Vancouver, BC , Canada V6T 2A1

Michael I. Posner, Department of Neurology, Box 8111, Washington University School of Medicine, 660 S. Euclid, St. Louis MO

Robert L. Pusakulich, Department of Psychology, VA Medical Center, Memphis TN

Jeffrey L. Rasmussen, Department of Psychology, Purdue University at Indianapolis, 1125 E. 38th Street, P.O. Box 647, Indianapolis IN

Jennifer Sandson, Department of Neurology, University of Maryland School of Medicine, 22 S. Greene, Baltimore MD

Daniel L. Schacter, Amnesia and Cognition Unit, Department of Psychology, University of Arizona, Tucson, AZ

Craig A. Velozo, Head Injury Resource Center, Irene W. Johnson Institute of Rehabilitation, St. Louis, MO

Jeannette P. Ward, Department of Psychology, Memphis State University, Memphis, TN

J. Michael Williams, Department of Mental Health Sciences, Hahnemann Medical University, Philadelphia, PA

Preface

Since its early development, neuropsychology has examined the manner in which cognitive abilities are mediated by the brain. Indeed, all of neuropsychology, and especially clinical neuropsychology, could be subsumed under this general investigation. However, a variety of factors impeded the close association of neuropsychologists and cognitive/experimental psychologists. These factors were prominent influences in both camps, which kept the study of cognition away from a consideration of biological foundations and kept neuropsychology theoretically impoverished. In recent years, these factors have diminished and "cognitive neuropsychology" has become a popular term to describe the new movements to join the study of cognition with the study of brain function.

The factors which kept these areas separate were manifestations of historical trends and represent a social distance which largely happened by accident. The first and perhaps most important factor was that early investigators of cognition and brain function were not psychologists. Most were neurologists or other neuroscientists who were excellent observers of behavior following brain injury but had virtually no theoretical context of cognitive psychology, which would allow them to expand and deepen their understanding of the behavior they were observing. As more psychologists who have such a context have observed the consequences of brain disorders, especially aphasia and amnesia, the study of them has become far more comprehensive as theories of language and memory derived from cognitive psychology have been incorporated into the investigations.

A second major factor was that early psychologists specializing in neuroscience or experimental neuropsychology focused on brain structure and were essentially reductionistic. Almost all were heavily involved in animal models of brain function. As a consequence, they focused on brain functions which animals and humans have in common, such as sensory systems, especially vision, and basic memory and motor functions. As groups of these investigators became interested in brain-injured humans, most notably after the world wars, they began to view the neurological disorders in humans within the context of cognitive theories developed by their colleagues in psychology. Clinical human neuropsychology also emerged from this group and this further interest in the complex behavioral manifestations and everyday problems of brain-injured people highlighted the void in understanding human brain function. Many of the findings of cognitive neuropsychology have come from the clinical development and application of neuropsychological test batteries.

Other major influences are derived from the cognitive psychology camp. In the early years of cognitive psychology, investigators were more concerned with establishing their discipline and fending off attacks from behaviorism rather than breaking into new areas of mutual interest with neuropsychologists. There was also a notion held by many cognitive psychologists that the brain represented a common medium for any cognitive system and consequently, the cognitive psychologist need not develop an understanding of brain structure and function in order to understand cognition. Certainly the findings of modern neuropsychology have laid this notion to rest.

These factors and many others kept neuropsychologists and cognitive psychologists apart until recent years. Now, the intellectual climate for cognitive psychology could not be better and investigations of brain function have matured to include many sophisticated cognitive constructs. Now, there are major movements in cognitive psychology which attempt to include and explain the neuropsychology findings. These are most prominently represented by the new cognitive models which include parallel processing (see Long, Graesser and Long, this volume).

Given this new interest, the Mid-South Conference on Human Neuropsychology decided to focus on a variety of approaches to neuropsychology which have been influenced by cognitive psychology. These include neuropsychological assessment (e. g. Mapou, Williams), the cognitive constructs themselves (e. g. Booker & Schacter), and even clinical neuropsychological decision-making (e. g. Long, Graesser & Long). There are certainly many other areas of interaction which we have not covered. Cognitive neuropsychology is growing by great leaps and bounds; it is one of the most vigorous and theoretically important areas of neuropsychology. We look forward to these chapters becoming quickly outdated and having an opportunity to host another conference on this topic in the future.

J. Michael Williams and Charles J. Long

Memphis, Tennessee

Contents

Cognitive Approaches to Neuropsychology

1

Four Computational Models for Investigating Neuropsychological Decision-making

Debra L. Long, Arthur C. Graesser and Charles J. Long

Neuropsychological decision-making in the clinical setting can be investigated from the perspective of different computational models derived from cognitive science. In this chapter, we focus on four of these models: Multivariate analyses, expert knowledge-based systems, exemplar-based reasoning models, and connectionist models. All presuppose that neuropsychological decision-making is essentially a complex pattern recognition task. For example, the neuropsychologist might attempt to recognize the locus of a lesion on the basis of a pattern of symptoms, test scores, and historical data. The four models in this chapter provide substantially different solutions for this complex pattern recognition problem.

The four models have been applied to other pattern recognition problems, such as speech perception (Coles & Rudivicky, 1983; Erman & Lesser, 1980; Klatt, 1980; McClelland & Elman, 1986; Reddy, Erman, Fennell & Neely, 1973; Stevens & Blumstein, 1981). Multivariate analyses have revealed the phonemic features that are important for speech perception, such as burst amplitude, left and right context, vowel onset, and vowel duration (Klatt, 1980; Salasoo & Pisoni, 1985). Researchers in artificial intelligence have developed knowledge-based systems to account for the effect of contextual information on speech perception, such as semantic and grammatical context (Erman & Lesser, 1980; Reddy, Erman, Fennell & Neely, 1973). Speech perception has been simulated by sophisticated parallel computational models. The connectionist model, called TRACE, is an example of one of these models (McClelland & Elman, 1986). Connectionist models attempt to account for the errors of human perceivers, in addition to the mechanisms that generate correct pattern recognition. Finally, exemplar-based reasoning models are the state of the art for commercial speech recognition systems.

Just as in speech perception, the neuropsychologist arrives at decisions on the basis of patterns of information. The neuropsychologist gathers and evaluates information in patients' test profiles and history in order to identify patterns associated with various cerebral dysfunctions (Long, 1985). A particular patient's profile is composed of information from a variety of sources.

Long, D. L., Graesser, A. C., & Long, C. J. (1988). Four computational models for investigating neuropsychological decision-making. In J. M. Williams and C. J. Long (Eds.), *Cognitive approaches to neuropsychology*, New York: Plenum.

Neuropsychologists initially interview and observe the patient and family in order to obtain descriptive information about neurological symptoms, levels of cognitive and emotional functioning, occupational factors, and situational factors. The neuropsychologist subsequently obtains information from neuropsychological assessment batteries, such as the Halstead-Reitan Neuropsychological Battery (Halstead, 1947; Reitan, 1966). This battery is composed of tests which measure strengths and weaknesses in various cognitive functions. The patient's test performance profile can be used to determine the presence and extent of dysfunction and whether the dysfunction is generalized, lateralized or focal. Finally, neuropsychologists often have access to medical information, such as EEGs, CAT Scans, and surgical data that are useful in confirming the decision-making process.

Table 1

Information from a Patient Profile

Symptoms	Subset of test scores:
Memory difficulties	Verbal IQ = 86
Language comprehension difficulty	Performance IQ = 94
Feels depressed and anxious	Finger agnosia
Situational Factors	Aphasia screening=7 errors
Caring for an elderly mother	Impaired rhythm perception
Significant job stress	Normal TPT test scores

A patient profile specifies the patient's strengths and weaknesses on a number of dimensions. Table 1 contains a subset of the information that neuropsychologists analyze when they describe or diagnose particular cerebral dysfunctions. A great deal of information was obtained during the initial interview with this particular patient. The patient was experiencing memory deficits and had substantial difficulty in understanding spoken language. The patient explained that she had recently moved in with her elderly mother, who requires a significant amount of daily care. She complained about feeling anxious and depressed. The patient was subsequently administered a neuropsychological test battery. Her test scores indicated that her performance IQ was better than her verbal IQ. She was experiencing significant right-sided weaknesses (e.g., two errors on finger agnosia with the right hand). The test scores also indicated that she was significantly impaired on language related skills (e.g., seven errors on aphasia screening).

The neuropsychologist then searches for patterns in such patient profiles. In the profile described above, there is a pattern indicative of left hemisphere impairment. Performance involving the right side of the body was consistently worse than performance involving the left side. In addition, the available indicators suggested a focal rather than a global impairment. Furthermore, the patient's overall level of functioning was too high for the deficits to be associated with a rapidly developing or global lesion.

The pattern recognition process for neuropsychological decision-making is very complicated and we therefore believe that multiple computational models are necessary to obtain a complete picture. The four models discussed in this chapter have a history in cognitive psychology. However, we acknowledge that there may be other computational models equally well suited for this endeavor.

Multivariate Analyses

Neuropsychologists are most familiar with multivariate analyses as a computational foundation for investigating decision-making. There are a variety of multivariate techniques that have been pursued, such as multiple regression, factor analysis, and discriminant analysis (Crockett, Klonoff & Bjerning, 1969; Cureton, Elder, Fowler & Morra, 1962; Goldstein & Shelly, 1972, 1973; Swiercinsky & Hallenback, 1975; Wheeler, Burke, & Reitan, 1963; Wheeler & Reitan, 1963). We have chosen one particular technique, called obverse factor analysis. Obverse factor analysis provides an exploratory method for discovering profiles that are associated with particular cerebral dysfunctions. A major goal of the analysis is to cluster subjects who are similar, and who are maximally dissimilar from other subgroups. We were specifically interested in how subjects, as opposed to variables, are associated with latent factors. Latent factors represent subjects of a given "type". For example, a factor may represent localized brain dysfunction (e.g., a left temporal lobe lesion) or a psychological dysfunction (e.g., language impairment). Our application of obverse factor analysis can be captured by six major assumptions, which are listed and described below.

(1)   There exists a set of dysfunction indicators (I_1, I_2,...I_n). The indicators come from the patient profile and can range from demographic information (e.g., age, sex) to test information (e.g., scores on the WAIS, sensory-motor tests, or the MMPI).

(2)   There exists a set of patients (P_1, P_2,...P_m). Each patient has a vec-

tor of n values associated with n indicators. In other words, each indicator (e.g., sex, IQ) has a value associated with it (e.g., sex = female, IQ = 85) for each subject.

(3) The indicators are weighted equally. If an indicator is included in the analysis for one patient it is included for all patients. Also, each indicator is assumed to be equally important as a predictor of the dysfunction. If an indicator is associated with a particular dysfunction in one patient, then it is assumed that the indicator will be associated with all patients who share that dysfunction. For example, if a patient with a left anterior lesion is exhibiting contralateral hemiparesis, and this is strongly associated with this type of lesion, then it is expected that all patients with left anterior lesions should exhibit the same pattern on tests that are sensitive to motor function on the right side.

(4) Patients are selected on the basis of a set of P a priori dysfunctions (D_1, D_2,...D_p). These dysfunctions, and the groups of patients, are mutually exclusive. For example, 4 patients with a left temporal lobe lesion and 4 patients with a right temporal lobe lesion may be selected for analysis based upon an independent measure of dysfunction. It should be noted that the measure used to categorize patients according to their dysfunction must not be an indicator included as data in the analysis. Figure 1 is a pictorial representation of groups of patients associated with particular dysfunctions.

(5) A matrix of correlations is computed for all possible pairs of patients. Each correlation is performed on the two vectors of standardized indicator values for a pair of patients. This is just the reverse of standard factor analysis where correlations are computed for all pairs of variables across subjects. Patients who exhibit similar profiles will be highly correlated.

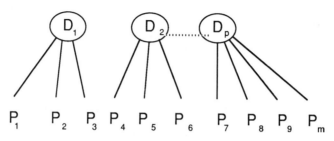

Figure 1. A representation of groups of patients (P_1, P_2,...P_m) associated with various dysfunctions (D_1, D_2,...D_p).

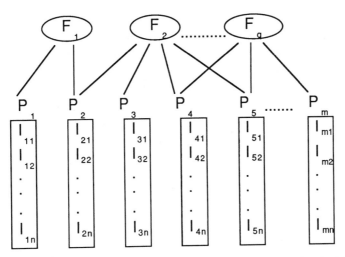

Figure 2. A representation of groups of patients (P$_1$, P$_2$,...P$_m$) associated with a set of factors (F$_1$, F$_2$,...F$_q$). Each patient has dysfunction indicators (I$_1$, I$_2$,...I$_n$).

(6) A set of latent factors (F$_1$, F$_2$,...F$_q$) is statistically discovered by grouping together patients that are intercorrelated. Patients load upon these factors to the extent that they are similar to other patients who load upon the same factor. It should be noted that patients may load upon more than one factor, so the factors are not mutually exclusive. Figure 2 contains an example of a pattern of factor loadings. There is a group of patients (P$_1$, P$_2$,...P$_m$) who load upon a set of factors (F$_1$, F$_2$,...F$_q$). Again, patients have dysfunction indicators (I$_1$, I$_2$,...I$_n$) associated with them.

These factors were interpreted in two ways. First, we examined how the apriori dysfunction classifications map onto the factors. In other words, do patients who load on a common factor share the same dysfunction? If all patients with a left anterior lesion and no patients from any other group load on a single factor, we can assert that the factor represents the profile of the "ideal" left anterior lesion patient. Second, we examined how the indicators associated with the patients map onto the factors. Do patients who load on the same factor share a common subset of indicators? For example, two patients in different dysfunction groups may load on a common factor because they have similar MMPI profiles. We can assert that the factor represents an "ideal" patient with that particular MMPI profile.

We have conducted several obverse factor analyses to determine if we could extract interpretable factors from a sample of patients. The data in our analyses were test scores from a modified Halstead-Reitan neuropsychological test battery. This battery included the Wechsler Adult Intelligence Scale, the Wechsler Memory Scale, tests of language production and perception (e.g., aphasia screening), and tests of sensory-motor abilities (e.g. Finger Tapping). Also included were tests of emotional functioning (e.g., the MMPI and the Cornell Index).

One discrimination made by neuropsychologists is a lateralizing distinction, that is, discriminating left hemisphere versus right hemisphere dysfunctions. In our first analysis, we attempted to find a pattern indicative of the lateralizing distinction. We classified patients into three dysfunction groups: eight left hemisphere impaired patients, eight right hemisphere impaired patients, and eight patients with generalized impairment. Patients were selected according to medical indicators such as EEG, CAT Scan, and surgery information. We were interested in the extent to which these three subgroups had distinctive patterns of indicators associated with their classified dysfunction. In other words, would all patients within a subgroup (e.g., left hemisphere impairment) load on a common factor?

In our analysis of these three subgroups, we found a seven-factor solution that was not a good fit to the data ($X^2 = 246.8$, $p < .0001$). In general, the factor loadings were low (.01-.60). When we attempted to map the indicators to the apriori classification of dysfunctions, we concluded that for this set of patients there did not appear to be distinct patterns of indicators associated with the three subgroups. We hypothesized that these results occurred because our subgroups of left, right, and generalized patients were not homogeneous. In other words, the profile of test scores exhibited by a patient with a left anterior lesion may be very different than the set of scores exhibited by a patient with a left posterior lesion. If this is the case, it would not be surprising that the test scores of patients within a subgroup (e.g., left hemisphere impaired) were not highly correlated.

Subsequent analyses were conducted in an attempt to get an improvement in our fit to the data if we separated our patients into more focal lesion groups (i.e., if we made our subgroups more homogeneous). One analysis was conducted for groups of patients with left anterior, left medial, and left posterior dysfunctions. A separate analysis was conducted for groups of patients with right anterior, right medial, and right posterior dysfunctions. For the three subgroups of left hemisphere impairments we got a fit to the data with seven factors ($X^2 = 139.8$, p = .24). For the three subgroups with right hemisphere impairments, we failed to get a solution to converge.

Although we got a fit to the data in our analysis of the group of left hemisphere impaired patients, the fact that a 7 factor solution was needed to explain the intercorrelations among 24 subjects is less than impressive. An examination of the intercorrelation matrix revealed that the correlations within our left hemisphere subgroups were relatively low (.01-.46). The obvious conclusion to be made from these analyses is that patients within the subgroup (e.g., left anterior impairment) were not very similar. We also found that the within-group correlations among our right hemisphere subgroups were extremely low. This explained our failure to get a solution to converge. Overall, the results suggest that if there are profiles in the test data associated with particular cerebral dysfunctions, they will most likely be found in very focal lesion groups in left hemisphere impaired patients. This is probably due to patterns of language deficits associated with left hemisphere impairment.

There are several reasons the results of our analyses did not suggest a strong association between patterns in the test data and particular dysfunctions. One obvious reason is that this was an artifact of our particular population of patients. In general, our patients had relatively high levels of functioning. Patients functioning at very low levels were unable to complete the entire test battery. These patients were not included in the analyses because they had too many missing test scores. When patients are at high levels of functioning, their profiles of strengths and weaknesses may primarily reflect individual differences rather than group differences. Missing data can be a serious problem in multivariate analyses.

Other reasons for a lack of relationship between indicators and dysfunctions reflect shortcomings of the computational foundation of multivariate analyses. Some of the indicators included in our analysis may not be relevant for every patient in a given subgroup. For example, one patient may exhibit severe language deficits with no right-sided motor impairment. Another patient may exhibit severe right-sided motor weaknesses with no language impairment. Whereas both patterns are indicative of left hemisphere dysfunction, language indicators are predictive of the dysfunction in one patient but not in the other. When we include irrelevant or inconsistent indicators in the analysis of a patient, we increase unexplained variance in the multivariate analysis and we mask similarities due to a common dysfunction.

Multivariate analyses rest heavily on a quantitative foundation. However, many important variables do not naturally lend themselves to quantification. For example, neuropsychologists often consider qualitative information about symptoms. While it is certainly possible to assign one numeric value to describe a sharp pain and another numeric value to describe a dull pain, it is doubtful that qualitative subtleties are well represented in such a scheme.

Finally, and perhaps most importantly, the neuropsychologist needs to consider carefully which indicators should be included in the analyses. Readily quantified information, such as test battery scores, is easily analyzed. However, there may be other important information to be considered. The clinical neuropsychologist may identify patterns associated with various dysfunctions based upon information that is not in a test battery. Neuropsychologists may hypothesize about the nature of a patient's cerebral dysfunction based upon information they gather from the family and observations of the patient during the interview. The test data may be a means of confirming the neuropsychologist's hypothesis when the test information is consistent with the hypothesis. Alternatively, it may reduce the neuropsychologist's confidence in the hypothesis when the test data are inconsistent with the hypothesis.

Multivariate analysis is very useful as a discovery method or as a confirmatory technique. However, in practice, it is limited to use with quantified variables and with variables that do not interact in antagonistic or asymetrical ways. We have turned to expert systems (or knowledge-based systems) in order to investigate complex interactions and features of neuropsychological decision-making that are not represented in our test battery data.

Expert Systems

An expert system is an intelligent, interactive computer system that uses a large body of knowledge and a set of inference procedures to make decisions that require significant human expertise (Barr, Cohen & Feigenbaum, 1981; Harmon & King, 1985; Hayes-Roth, 1984; Hayes-Roth, Waterman, & Lennet, 1983). The system consists of a set of facts, rules and heuristic control processes. Facts are static entities, such as object properties, attributes and relations. Rules are usually expressed in the form of IF <state> THEN <action> statements. Heuristic control processes are the way that rules are combined to operate on facts and generate new facts.

It is the job of the knowledge engineer (the designer of the system) to extract the knowledge and reasoning strategies from the expert so that the expert's knowledge and actions can be translated into rules or information structures (Hayes-Roth, Waterman, & Lennet, 1983; Winston & Prendergast, 1984). There are several knowledge engineering techniques. The expert can be trained to think aloud while problem solving. Alternatively, the expert can be probed with questions about how and why the expert arrived at certain conclusions. Knowledge engineering is an ongoing process. The knowledge engineer continually expands and modifies the system's knowledge base while the expert system is developed. An expert system for neuropsychological decision-making would have the following features.

(1) There is a set of *relevant* dysfunction indicators $(I_1, I_2,... I_n)$. There is again a set of dysfunctions $(D_1, D_2,...D_p)$. A different set of indicators may be relevant for different types of cases. The goal of the system is to classify a new (or target) case as belonging to one, or a small set, of dysfunction categories.

(2) There is a knowledge base consisting of a set of rules. The rules are extracted from experts through knowledge engineering techniques. Rules are expressed in the form of <if...then> statements:

$$IF <I^*> THEN <I_j>$$

$$IF <I^*> THEN <D_k>$$

According to the top expression, if a particular boolean combination of indicators (I^*) occurs, then the system generates an additional indicator (I_j). According to the bottom expression, if a boolean combination of indicators occurs, then the system converges on a particular dysfunction (D_k).

(3) Expert systems have inference procedures. Rules are chained together in a way that allows the system to consider a set of hypothesis and attempt to confirm each hypothesis in the set. Confirming a hypotheses involves implementing decision rules. A decision rule is a rule that contains the goal in the conclusion statement (e.g., if $<I^*>$ then $<D_k>$). Table 2 contains an example of such rule chaining. The system begins with rule #2 and attempts to confirm the first premise of the rule, <u>if the patient has a lateralized deficit.</u> The system searches for any rule that has this expression as a conclusion statement, <u>the patient has a lateralized deficit.</u> Notice that rule #1 has this statement in its conclusion. The system then attempts to confirm the first premise statement of rule #1 (<u>if the patient has (standardized) score for verbal IQ</u>) by searching

through the knowledge base. At some point the system may query the user for information (e.g., <u>What is the patient's (standardized) verbal IQ score?</u>). This process continues until the system can confirm one or more decision rules and eventually converge on a solution.

(4) Decisions are products of a dialogue between the computer and the neuropsychologist user. The user inputs values of relevant indicators as they are requested by the system. In addition, indicators can be supplied by the rules or chains of rules. In the previous example (Table 2), the value for the first premise statement, <u>if the patient has a lateralized deficit (true or false)</u>, is supplied by applying rule #1. If the values needed to apply rule #1 (verbal and performance IQ scores) are not present in the database, the values are requested from the user.

Table 2

An Example of Rule Chaining

Rule #1
IF   [the patient has (standardized) score for verbal IQ &
the patient has (standardized) score for performance IQ &
verbal IQ $\neq$ performance IQ &
the (absolute value) verbal IQ - performance IQ > 1]
THEN   [the patient has a lateralized deficit]

Rule #2
IF [the patient has a lateralized deficit &
verbal IQ < performance IQ]
THEN [the deficit is left hemisphere]
ELSE [the deficit is right hemisphere]

A diagram of the user-computer dialogue is displayed in Figure 3. The user inputs indicator start values. These start values are ordinarily indicators that are associated with most patients (e.g., demographic information, test scores). The system searches its knowledge base to generate whatever additional indicator values it needs to apply a decision rule. If the system cannot find values for additional indicators in the knowledge base, it requests the information from the user. Again, the process continues until the system can converge on a set of likely dysfunctions.

(5) Indicators have confidence factors associated with them. As users input information, they can assign a value to the information to indicate how certain they are that the indicator value is true. For example, the system may query the user with the following question: Is the patient's educational background consistent with his/her scores on the WAIS? The user may answer "yes" and assign an 80% confidence factor to the input. This indicates how confident the user is that the patient's IQ scores are indeed consistent with his/her years of education. In addition, rules have probabilities associated with them.

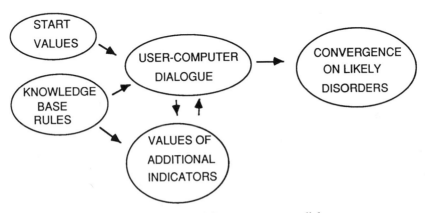

Figure 3. A diagram of the user-computer dialogue.

Consider the following rule:

IF [IQ scores are less than would be expected from years of formal education]

THEN [there is evidence of cognitive impairment]

[Confidence = 85%]

The assumption here is that IQ scores and cognitive abilities are positively correlated. It is convenient to view the confidence factor as a probability or frequency index. The probability associated with this rule indicated that 85% of the time there is no cognitive impairment when years of education are consistent with IQ test performance. However, 15% of the time the rule does not hold true. For example, in some cases occupation may be a better corre-late with cognitive abilities than is formal education (e.g., the self-educated individual). The system combines these probabilities and certainty factors according to some quantitative metric in order to converge on a decision.

(6) When the expert system converges on a dysfunction, the dysfunction may have certainty factors associated with it. These factors indicate the system's confidence in the decision. Often the system will converge on a set of likely dysfunctions, with a certainty factor associated with each dysfunction.

In order to explore this model of decision-making, we designed a small prototype expert system. This system was developed in part to discover additional information about neuropsychological decision-making. The ideal expert system would divide neuropsychological services into three tasks: describe neurological dysfunctions, identify neurological dysfunctions, and make recommendations for treatment. At times the specific neural pathology is identified through medical procedures (e.g., surgery, CAT Scan). In this case, the neuropsychologist's task is to describe the patient's level of functioning (e.g., the patient's profile of cognitive strengths and weaknesses). Alternatively, medical indices may be ambiguous or missing and the neuropsychologist's task is to identify the dysfunction from the pattern of indicators. Finally, neuropsychologists are asked to make recommendations, such as whether the patient should return to work or seek psychological counseling.

We decided to concentrate on the identification task in our first version of the expert system. We conceptualized the identification problem as the analysis of information about four factors. These factors are displayed in Figure 4. the neuropsychologist gathers information about the patient's symptoms (e.g., course and onset of illness), situational factors (e.g., occupation, financial situation, lifestyle), emotional factors (e.g., depression, anxiety), and cognitive factors (e.g., intelligence, memory). The neuropsychologist must then consider the way in which these factors interact.

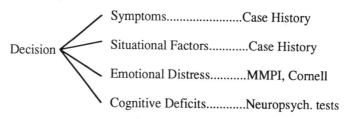

Figure 4. Factors involved in the neuropsychological identification problem.

Table 3

An Example of a User-System Dialogue

INPUT THE PATIENT'S STANDARDIZED VERBAL IQ

.2

INPUT THE PATIENT'S STANDARDIZED PERFORMANCE IQ

1.3

IS THE DISCREPANCY BETWEEN VERBAL IQ AND PERFORMANCE
IQ DUE TO OCCUPATIONAL FACTORS?

WHY

IF [the patient has a lateralized deficit & verbal IQ < performance IQ &

the discrepancy is not due to occupational factors]

THEN [the deficit is left hemisphere]

Note. User responses are underlined.

The example in Table 3 illustrates the interaction of two of these factors. The rule at the bottom of the table takes into account an interaction between cognitive and situational factors. A discrepancy between verbal and performance IQ should not be attributed to a neurological dysfunction if the discrepancy can be explained by other factors, such as occupation. For example, mechanics may have higher performance IQ scores than verbal IQ scores due to the spatial demands of their occupation. Our system handles the interactions among the four factors and decides if the patient is impaired. If the patient is impaired, it also decides whether the impairment is associated with the left or the right hemisphere.

We believe that the expert systems approach for the investigation of neuropsychological decision-making has several advantages. Indeed, we have identified seven advantages over multivariate analyses.

First, expert systems only request or compute values of *relevant* indicators. For example, our expert system requests indicator values for stress, only if information about stress is relevant to the hypothesis the system is considering. In contrasts, the indicators in multivariate analyses are not entered according to their relevance or predictive value; all indicators are considered equally in most multivariate analyses.

Table 4

An Example Indicator Interaction

Rule 1: IF [stress indicators=high & cognitive indicators = high] THEN [neural impairment = low]	Rule 3: IF [stress indicators=low & cognitive indicators = high] THEN [neural impairment=low]
Rule 2: IF [stress indicators= high & cognitive indicators = low] THEN [neural impairment = ?]	Rule 4: IF [stress indicators=low & cognitive indicators = low] THEN [neural impairment=high]

Second, expert systems can handle very complex interactions among indicators. For example, expert systems can handle cases where indicators combine antagonistically or asymmetrically. As a simplified example of an asymmetric interaction, consider the four rules in Table 4.

Because we know that stress may augment cognitive deficits, it is difficult to attribute any observed cognitive deficits to neural impairment when stress factors are high. It is only when cognitive indicators and stress are both high, or when cognitive indicators are high and stress is low, that one can diagnose the presence or absence of a neural impairment. Low levels of cognitive functioning are only relevant indicators when stress is low. This is the type of case in which a pattern is difficult to detect via a multivariate approach because stress values would be computed on all cases. Asymmetries like the one described in Table 4 are easily handled by rule-based systems.

Third, knowledge engineering techniques can be used to identify relevant indicators. As experts consider the information they use while decision-making, they can identify indicators that are useful in discriminating one dysfunction from another. These indicators can be qualitative. As mentioned before, qualitative information is often not easily scaled or quantified. For example, symptom information, such as the quality of pain experienced by the patient (e.g., shooting, burning, stabbing, aching, etc.) is less easily scaled than quantitative information, such as the intensity of pain. Multivariate techniques rest on a psychometric tradition and have been designed to reliably handle quantified information. The typical database for these analyses include tests, such as the Halstead-Reitan neuropsychological battery, that have been assessed for reliability and validity. An expert system handles this type of quantified information in addition to the qualitative information that is identified through knowledge engineering techniques. Moreover, new indicators may then be added to the pre-existing database as needed.

Fourth, low frequency events are better represented in expert systems than in multivariate databases. Indeed, low frequency events are often excluded from multivariate analyses. However, low frequency, salient events are important in the pattern recognition process. For example, visual field cuts are low frequency occurrences. However, visual field cuts are certain indicators of neural dysfunction. This type of low frequency event can be represented in an expert system by a single rule.

Fifth, an expert system can trace its reasoning by virtue of its symbolic representation. Table 3 contains an example of how a user can ask the system to trace its reasoning. The rules are represented symbolically, in natural language and are easily interpreted by the user. The user can then examine the rules that the system is assessing as it attempts to confirm hypotheses. In contrast, the computational rules used in multivariate analysis are statistical and are less valuable to a user who is trying to trace the reasoning behind a particular output.

Sixth, an expert system can query the user for additional information or recommend the administration of additional tests. As the system considers each rule it checks the existing database for information. If the information is not present in the database, the system requests the information from the user. Thus, the system can make the user aware of any critical missing information.

Seventh, expert systems can converge on a solution in spite of missing data. We mentioned earlier that missing data is a problem in multivariate analyses. We speculated that this constraint produced a selection bias in our analysis of patients with left hemisphere versus right hemisphere impairment. Those patients who had complete data sets were at relatively high levels of functioning; this masked differences between dysfunction groups and emphasized individual differences within a dysfunction group. A rule-based system can often converge on a solution in spite of missing data. Alternatively, it can notify the user if a piece of missing data is critical for identifying the dysfunction.

Expert systems are receiving substantial attention in fields such as medicine (Atkins, Kunz, Shortliffe & Fallat, 1984; Buchanan & Shortliffe, 1984; Clancey & Shortliffe 1984; Pople, 1982). Many of these systems are based on a diagnosis-prescription model. The expert system, MYCIN, diagnoses and recommends treatment for infectious diseases. Consequently, there are existing tools and procedures that may be eminently suitable for designing systems which embody neuropsychological decision-making.

The expert systems approach may be an important clinical support tool. If the expert system arrives at the same conclusion as the neuropsychologist, the neuropsychologist can feel confident in the decision. If the expert system arrives at a different conclusion than the neuropsychologist, the neuropsychologist can trace the system's reasoning. In some cases the system arrives at a faulty conclusion. In other cases the system needs additional information or rules to make a similar conclusion as the neuropsychologist. In yet other cases the neuropsychologist will discover his or her own error in reasoning.

Exemplar-based Reasoning Models

Recently there has been considerable interest in models that produce decisions by matching a target problem to all previous specific cases or episodes, called "exemplars". These models, called exemplar-based reasoning models, involve comparing a target case to specific cases in memory in order to find the most similar case (Cheeseman, 1983; Lebowitz, 1986; Stanfill & Waltz, 1986). If the target case is very similar to a case in the database, the same decisions are applied to the new case. If there are no similar cases, the model indicates that there are no good matches in memory. This type of decision-making, called "reasoning from memory", may approximate the neuropsychologist's reasoning process. That is, the neuropsychologist may access specific cases from memory to compare to the current case. If the cases are very similar, the neuropsychologist will apply the same decision to the current case. Current decision-making is directly guided by the decisions associated with previous specific cases.

In one of these models, a similarity-based reasoning model, accessing specific memory episodes involves several operations (Stanfill & Waltz, 1986).

(1) The first operation is to count the number of times that features or combinations of features occur in association with various decisions. In the domain of neuropsychological decision-making, features correspond to the dysfunction indicators we have discussed previously ($I_1, I_2,...I_n$). For example, we may want to know how often errors on aphasia screening occur in combina-

tion with a left temporal lobe lesion. It is important to note that all (n) indicators must be represented in the database.

(2) The second operation involves using the feature counts to produce metrics. One of the simplest metrics used in these systems is an dissimilarity metric. A dissimilarity metric is a measure of dissimilarity between two patterns (P_1 and P_2). Each pattern is composed of a vector of indicators.

$$P_1 = [I_{12}, I_{11},...I_{1n}]$$

$$P_2 = [I_{21}, I_{22},...I_{2n}]$$

In addition, each indicator has an associated indicator value.

$$\text{Indicator values for } P_1 = [V_{11}, V_{12},...V_{1n}]$$

$$\text{Indicator values for } P_2 = [V_{21}, V_{22},...V_{2n}]$$

The dissimilarity between P_1 and P_2 is computed according to the following formula.

$$\text{Dis } (P_1, P_2) = \sum_{i=1}^{n} F(V_{1i}, V_{2i})$$

$$\text{if } V_{1i} = V_{2i} \text{ then } F = 0$$

$$\text{if } V_{1i} \neq V_{2i} \text{ then } F = 1$$

That is, the dissimilarity (Dis) between P_1 and P_2 is the number of features (F) for which P_1 and P_2 have different values. The value of F increases as a function of the dissimilarity between P_1 and P_2.

(3) There are also metrics for weighting features. It is sometimes critical to separate important features from unimportant ones (Stanfill & Waltz, 1986). Features which are strongly associated with one decision and no other are weighted heavily. Features that are associated with several different decisions are not good discriminators and receive lower weights.

(4) There are additional metrics for calculating value similarity. It is often too strict to base a similarity match on the precise equality of two features; different values of a feature may be functionally equivalent. For example,

there may be a range of IQ scores (e.g., 50 - 60) that it is practical to equate. Two cases in the database with IQ features in this range would be judged as matched on the IQ feature. In a dynamic model, all of the metrics in the model are recomputed after each additional exemplar is added to the database. Thus, the model is immediately sensitive to new information that accumulates in the database.

We believe that exemplar-based reasoning models may have several advantages for investigating neuropsychological decision-making. As mentioned above, reasoning from memory may be an important strategy employed by neuropsychologists when decision-making. A computer model, such as the one described here, can exhaustively and tirelessly search the database for a match. Because information is never lost or distorted in the system's memory, these models should be an important clinical support tool.

Exemplar-based reasoning models can form hypotheses on the basis of a single case in memory, although with a small database it is likely that the system will tell you that there are no good matches in memory. Rule-based systems operate much differently. Rules are induced from regularities in the cases (Stanfill & Waltz, 1986) or a special rule has to be formalized to handle every irregular case. If there are very many exceptional cases, it can become cumbersome to add a rule to handle each irregular case. In addition, adding or deleting rules in an expert system can have a profound effect on the response of the system. The rules are very intricately chained, ordered, and organized in these systems. Therefore, the system designer must be very careful to assure that a change in the rule base does not effect the model's response to cases that it already handles appropriately.

Like rule-based systems, exemplar-based reasoning models can account for low frequency information. The system just needs one exemplar in memory to find a good match to the target case. As discussed previously, multivariate models rely on many instances of an indicator-dysfunction association before it can identify a pattern.

Connectionist Models

The final computational model is the connectionist model, or parallel distributed processing model. Recently, there has been increasing interest in parallel distributed models that learn to produce "outputs" from repeated experiences with a corpus of input and output pairs (Feldman, 1986; Feldman & Ballard, 1982; Feldman & Ballard, 1983; McClelland & Rummelhart, 1986).

The additional computational power of the parallel processing computer has made research involving these models more feasible. These models are particularly suited to pattern recognition problems (Ballard & Sabbah, 1983; Feldman, 1985; McClelland & Rummelhart, 1986; Rummelhart & McClelland, 1986; Zisper, 1986). Connectionist models have several distinctive features, which are specified below.

(1) Connectionist models are composed of a large number of units. The units can be segregated in the manner depicted in Figure 5. First, there is a set of input units. The input units are displayed at the bottom of Figure 5. In our neuropsychological application, input units would correspond to the set of dysfunction indicators (I_1, I_2,...I_n) we have discussed previously. Second, there is a set of output units, displayed at the top of Figure 5. The output units correspond to the dysfunction classification (D_1, D_2,...D_p). Finally, there is a set of hidden units, corresponding to the middle layer of units in Figure 5. The hidden units will come to represent latent features that are predictive of the dysfunction. Units have activations associated with them. An activation is ordinarily a real number that indicates the extent to which the unit is excited when a specific input is evaluated. Information is represented in the system by a pattern of activation across input, output and hidden units.

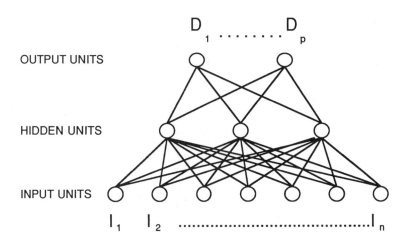

Figure 5. The units in a connectionist model. The lines between units indicate connections. Each connection is weighted.

(2) All units in these models are connected by links indicated by the lines in Figure 5. Each link has a weight associated with it (W_1, W_2,...W_r). Weights between nodes influence the units' activations and determine how the system will respond to an input presentation. These weights change as the system learns the domain representation.

(3) Learning, in these networks, involves adjusting connection weights to new values after presentations of input and output pairs. There are several different learning algorithms. The simplest algorithm involves first presenting the model with an input. For example, the model may be presented with a pattern of indicators associated with a particular dysfunction. If the model produces the correct output (the unit corresponding to the correct dysfunction activates) all weights connected to the correct output unit are incremented and all other weights are decremented. If the output is incorrect (the incorrect dysfunction unit is activated), all weights connected to the incorrect output unit are decremented and all other weights are incremented. The input and output pairings occur over many trials. The model has learned when it consistently produces the correct output in response to a pattern of inputs.

We presently do not know whether connectionism provides a viable model of neuropsychological decision-making. However, we do know that in principle these models have several advantages. The knowledge acquisition process in a connectionist model is automatic. (This also applies to the exemplar-based reasoning model.) Moreover, the performance of the system does not depend on the expertise of a knowledge engineer, which is the case in expert systems. It is important to point out that the knowledge engineer must be skilled at extracting information from the expert, as well as skilled at formally representing this knowledge. It is a major challenge to represent an expert's knowledge in the form of rules, and then to appropriately order and chain the rules. In addition, the system designer must constantly monitor the system to be sure that rule probabilities are combined properly so that erroneous conclusions do not result. It is possible that, in some cases, experts will have difficulty articulating their decision-making strategies. A connectionist model discovers the associations between indicators and dysfunctions without the system designer as an intermediary.

An important advantage of connectionist models is that they can account for high-order interactions. Previously, we discussed the problems that multivariate analyses have with asymmetrical or antagonistic interactions and how expert systems are able to handle these types of interactions. However, very high-order interactions, such as four- or five-way interactions can only be handled by an expert system if they are identified during the process of knowledge engineering. We know that it is difficult to conceptualize a three-way interaction; the difficulty is compounded with higher-order interactions. If an interaction is difficult for the system designer to interpret, it is almost impossible for the interaction to be written into the rule base. Connectionist systems can represent these types of interactions because there is no intermediary (system designer) who must first interpret the representation. Of course, it will still be difficult to explain a higher-order interaction in a connectionist model. Nevertheless, the model's response will be appropriately determined by the representation.

In connectionist models, hidden units represent features of the indicators that are predictive of the dysfunction. There is some chance that we can discover and label these features (Hinton, 1986). One feature discovery technique involves selectively deleting hidden units and subsequently observing changes in the model's response to patterns of inputs. This gives us information about the function of the deleted units. However, it should be noted that the more complex the domain representation is, the less likely it is that individual units represent any individual feature. Instead, it is the activation of clusters of units that determine feature representations.

Final Comments

We do not advocate the exclusive use of any one of the computational models we have discussed. The purpose of this paper has been to introduce these models as an ensemble of computational tools that can be used in the investigation of neuropsychological decision-making. Multivariate techniques have been the traditional approach. They provide very useful data summary and reduction techniques. Even negative results are helpful because they provide the impetus to reconceptualize the problem. Based on the results of our multivariate analyses, we have turned the focus of our investigation to features of patient profiles that are not represented in the test battery information (e.g., symptom and observational information).

Modeling neuropsychological decision-making through expert systems, exemplar-based reasoning models, and connectionist models will hopefully provide us with new insights about expert neuropsychological decision-making. We have identified several advantages of these alternative approaches. Some of these advantages include systems that can (1) simulate the neuropsychologist's decision strategies and act as clinical support tools, (2) handle antagonistic or asymetrical interactions, (3) represent low frequency events, (4) trace its reasoning, (5) converge on solutions in spite of missing data, (6) form hypotheses on the basis of a single case, (7) discover relevant features of indicator-dysfunction relationships, and (8) employ automatic knowledge acquisition techniques. Used in combination, these computational models may provide us with a sophisticated foundation for understanding brain-behavior relationships.

References

Atkins, J.S., Kunz, J.C., Shortliffe, E.H., & Fallat, R.S. (1984). PUFF: An expert system for interpretation of pulmonary function data. In B.C. Clancey & E.H. Shortliffe, *Readings in medical artificial intelligence: The first decade*. Reading, Mass.: Addison-Wesley.

Ballard, D.H., & Sabbah, D. (1983). View-independent shape recognition. *IEEE Trans on Pattern Analysis and Machine Intelligence, 5*, 6, 653-660.

Barr, A., Cohen, P. R., & Feigenbaum, E.A. (Eds.) (1981). *The handbook of artificial intelligence*: Vol. 1 and 2. Los Altos, CA William Kaufman.

Buchanan, B.G., & Shortliffe, E.H. (Eds.) (1984). *Rule-based expert systems*. Reading, Mass.: Addison-Wesley.

Charniak, E. (1983). The Bayesian basis of common sense medical diagnosis. In *Proceedings of the 3rd National Conference on Artificial Intelligence* (Washington D.C. Aug. 22-26). American Association for Artificial Intelligence, Menlo Park, CA, pp. 70-73.

Cheeseman, P.A. (1983). A method for computing Bayesian probability values for expert systems. In *Proceedings of the 8th International Joint conference on Artificial Intelligence*. (Karlsruhe, West Germany, Aug. 8-12) 168-202.

Clancey, D.C., & Shortliffe, E.H. (Eds.) (1984). *Readings in medical artificial intelligence: The first decade*. Reading, Mass.: Addison-Wesley.

Coles, R.A., & Rudivicky, A. (1983). What's new in speech perception? The research and ideas of William Chandler Bagley, 1894-1946. *Psychological Review, 90*, 94-101.

Crockett, D., Klonoff, H. & Bjerning, J. (1969). Factor analyses of neuropsychological tests. *Perceptual and Motor Skills, 29*, 791-802.

Cureton, E.E., Elder, R.F., Fowler, R.C., & Morra, M.A. (1962). Perseveration factor. *Science, 135*, 794.

Erman, L.D., & Lesser, U.R. (1980). The Hearsay-II speech understanding system: A tutorial. In W.A. Lea (Ed.), *Trends in speech recognition*. Englewood Cliffs, NJ: Prentice-Hall.

Feldman, J.A. (1985). Four frames suffice: A provisional model of vision and space. *The Behavioral and Brain Sciences, 8*, 265-219.

Feldman, J.A. (1986). Neural representation of conceptual knowledge. *Technical Report* 189, June.

Feldman, J.A., & Ballard, D.H. (1982). Connectionist models and their properties. *Cognitive Science, 6*, 205-254.

Goldstein,, G., & Shelly, C. H. (1972). Statistical and normative study of the Halstead Neuropsychology Test Battery relative to a neuropsychiatric hospital setting. *Perceptual and Motor Skills, 34,* 603-620.

Goldstein, G., & Shelly, C.H. (1973). Univariate vs. multivariate analyses in neuropsychological test assessment. *Cortex, 9,* 204-216.

Halstead, W.C. (1947). *Brain and intelligence: A quantitative study of the frontal lobes.* Chicago: University of Chicago Press.

Harmon, P., & King, D. (1985) *Artificial intelligence in business.* New York: John Wiley & Sons.

Hayes-Roth, F. (1984). Knowledge-based expert systems: The technological and commercial state of the art. *Computer,* Aug.

Hayes-Roth, F., Waterman, D., & Lennet, D. (Eds.) (1983). *Building expert systems.* Reading, Mass.: Addison-Wesley.

Klatt, D. H. (1980). Speech perception: A model of acoustic-phonetic analysis and lexical access. In R. Cole (Ed.), *Perception and production of fluent speech.* Hillsdale, NJ: Erlbaum.

Lebowitz, M. (1986). Not the path to perdition: The utility of similarity-based learning. In *Proceedings of the 5th National Conference on Artificial Intelligence.* (Philadelphia, PA, Aug. 11-15). American Association for Artificial Intelligence. Menlo Park, CA, p. 533-537.

Long, C.J. (1985). Neuropsychology in private practice: Its changing focus. *Psychotherapy in Private Practice, 3,* 45-55.

McClelland, J. L., & Elman, J. L. (1986). The TRACE model of speech perception. *Cognitive Psychology, 18 ,* 1-86.

McClelland, J. L., & Rummelhart, D. E. (Eds.) (1986). *Parallel distributed processing: Explorations in the microstructures of cognition: Volume 1: Foundations.* Cambridge, Mass.: The MIT Press.

Pople, H.E. (1982). Heuristic methods for imposing structure on ill-structured problems: The structuring of medical diagnostics. In P. Szolovits (Ed.), *Artificial intelligence in medicine.* Boulder, CO: Westview Press.

Reddy, D.R., Erman, L.D., Fennell, R.D., & Neely, R.B. (1973). The Hearsay speech understanding system: An example of the recognition process. *Proceedings of the International Conference on Artificial Intelligence,* 185-194.

Reitan, R.M. (1966). A research program on the psychological effects of brain Lesions in human beings. IN H.R. Ellis (Ed.), *International review of research in mental retardation* (Vol. 1). New York: Academic Press.

Rummelhart, D.E., & McClelland, J.A. (Eds.) (1986). *Parallel distributed processing: Explorations in the microstructure of cognition: Volume 2: Psychological and biological models.* Cambridge, Mass.: The MIT Press.

Salasoo, A., & Pissoni, D.R. (1985). Interaction of knowledge sources in spoken word identification. *Journal of Memory and Language, 24,* 210-231.

Stanfill, C., & Waltz, J.D. (1986). Toward memory-based reasoning. *Communications of the ACM, 29*(12), 1213-1228.

Stevens, D., & Blumstein, S. (1981). The search for invariant acoustic correlates of phonetic features. In P.H. Eimas & J.L. Miller (Eds.), *Perspectives on the study of speech.* Hillsdale, NJ: Erlbaum.

Swiercinsky, D.P., & Hallenback, E.C (1975). A factorial approach to neuropsychological assessment. *Journal of Clinical Psychology, 31*, 610-618.

Winston, P.H., & Prendergast, K.A. (Eds.) (1984). *The AI business: The commercial uses of artificial intelligence.* Cambridge, Mass.: MIT Press.

Wheeler, L., Burke, C., & Reitan, R. M. (1963). An application of discriminant functions to the problem of predicting brain damage using behavioral variables. *Perceptual and Motor Skills, 16*, 417-440.

Wheeler, L, & Reitan, R. M. (1963). Discriminant functions applied to the problem of predicting cerebral damage from behavioral tests: A cross-validation study. *Perceptual and Motor Skills, 16,* 681-701.

Zipper, D. (1986). Biologically plausible models of place recognition and goal location. In D.E. Rummelhart & J.L. McClelland (Eds.), *Parallel distributed processing: Explorations in the microstructures of cognition, Volume 1: Foundations.* Cambridge, Mass.: The MIT Press.

2

Acalculia: Multiplication Fact Retrieval in Normal and Impaired Subjects

Helen J. Kahn

Psychologists such as Binet and Galton were among the first scholars to characterize the range of arithmetic ability among individuals (Fancher, 1979). Galton focused on measurement issues and the mechanisms by which heredity and cultural factors influenced the ability to handle numbers (Galton,1908). Binet, in contrast, developed instruments based on group norms that measured intellectual abilities, including numerical aptitude, so that predictions could be generated on the capability of children to succeed in school. Binet along with Simon published the first scale of intelligence in 1905. Their test, of course, is the predecessor for the Stanford-Binet Intelligence Test, still in use today.

History of Research on Acalculia

Historical aspects of acalculia have been reviewed by Boller and Grafman (1983) and Levin (1979). Solomon Henschen, a neurologist from the early part of this century is credited with coining the term acalculia (Henschen, 1919, cited in Boller & Grafman, 1983). Acalculia refers to a condition arising from brain damage in which a patient is unable to calculate, read or write numbers. The common etiology for acalculia includes cerebral vascular accident, head injury, or brain tumor. In 1926, Henschen published the first complete discourse on acalculia. He argued that calculation could be localized to specific centers in the brain, that these centers were isolated from those of language, and that disorders of calculation could occur independent from disorders of language. Henschen theorized that left hemisphere visual factors played a primary role in calculation. The term "cipher blindness" followed from his view that the disorder was one of the visual system. It was proposed by Henschen that the pronunciation of numbers, and the reading and writing of numbers could be localized to cortical centers, such as the angular gyrus.

In 1933 a Festschrift for Henschen was published and among the manuscripts was the first case study of acalculia. Singer and Low (1933) reported a patient with diffuse cerebral injury from carbon monoxide poisoning. The patient was unable to perform the simplest of subtraction and division

Kahn, H. J. (1988). Acalculia: Multiplication fact retrieval in normal and impaired subjects. In J. M. Williams & C. J. Long (Eds.), *Cognitive approaches to neuropsychology,* New York: Plenum.

problems even though he had received several months of instruction. For addition, he could reach a correct answer if the sum was the number 10 or less. Multiplication products were somewhat preserved although he made more errors than correct responses. Particularly noteworthy is that Singer and Low (1933) included an "Analysis of Mistakes" in their discussion. These included: 1) substitution of one operation for another (e.g. subtraction for addition); 2) substitution of counting for calculation (14 + 15 = 16); 3) the reversal of digits (10 + 2 = 21). The authors speculated that their patient's difficulty was in recognizing and comprehending numbers, not in retention. Thus, the patient had the math facts but could not perform the correct operations with them.

One of the most important contributions to the early literature on acalculia came from Hans Berger, also the discoverer of the EEG (Berger, 1926, cited in Boller & Grafman, 1983). Like his predecessors, Berger was interested in localization of calculation but was probably the first individual to generate a classification of the disorder. He pointed out the existence of two forms of acalculia. Secondary acalculia occurred in patients who were impaired in attention, had a loss of immediate or delayed memory, or a language disturbance including aphasia, alexia, or agraphia for numbers. Primary acalculia was pure acalculia and was not related to any other cerebral disturbances. Primary or pure acalculia was reported to be less frequent than secondary acalculia. Berger essentially agreed with Henschen (1926) that acalculia could occur in isolation or as a concomitant to other disorders.

Hecaen, Angelergues and Houillier (1961) studied 183 patients who became acalculic following retrorolandic lesions. They classified their patients into three groups:

1) Digit alexia and agraphia with or without alexia and agraphia for words.

2) Spatial acalculia in which the spatial arrangement of numbers was disturbed. This included rules for setting written digits in their proper order and position, inverted numbers or reversal errors.

3) Disorders in the procedure of arithmetic operations not included in any of the above subgroups. This would include errors in the calculation of numbers such as an incorrect addition sum.

Grewel (1969, 1952) provided a classification scheme for acalculia that not only took both psychological and anatomical dimensions of the disorder into account but also added a new dimension, semiotics, the study of generative symbol systems. In order to use semiotics in reading, writing numbers and calculation, the elements (numbers) and the rules of combining the elements must be known. Grewel proposed that calculation is carried out according to syntactic rules. Number notations can be placed one under the other in a vertical arrangement, tens by tens, or in a horizontal arrangement. The vertical arrangement for addition and subtraction is preferred since it allows the numerical units to be "brought into relation with each other", e.g., tens with tens, hundreds with hundreds. The consequence is that certain functions can be performed in a logical manner such as "carrying over" or regrouping. If the sequence has been performed properly, the result will be the number notation or product of the required number. Grewel (1969) stated that in order for calculation to proceed smoothly, the addition and multiplication tables must be memorized and available for the generative system to be used.

According to Grewel (1969) disorders of calculation associated with cerebral injury cannot be explained by localization theory alone and instead require that an analysis of the disorder itself be performed. It is not enough to consider the correctness or incorrectness of a particular problem, but rather the researcher must "find out which of the many links in the performance is missing or deranged" (Grewel, 1969, p.183). This approach predates modern cognitive neuropsychological methods of analyzing calculation deficits (McCloskey, Caramazza, & Basili, 1984) in which a single patient is studied, errors are analyzed and "lesion(s)" are proposed to account for a disruption in the normal cognitive system. Unlike modern cognitive neuropsychology, Grewel was interested in a classification system that utilized both of the theories of early researchers in acalculia and the neuroanatomical correlates of the disorder.

Like Berger (1926) and Henschen (1926), Grewel used a system of primary and secondary types with primary acalculia representing the pure disorder and secondary acalculia representing an expression of the disorder in relation to other neuropsychological disorders. Among the primary acalculias were:

1) Asymbolic acalculia: The patient is unable to differentiate between or among arithmetic symbols. The asymbolia can occur for both digits and signs, such as the "+" sign for addition and the "x" sign for multiplication.

2) Asyntactic acalculia: The breakdown of the symbolic-syntactic system used in calculation. Specific disorders here might include the failure to

treat a complex number as a unity, failure to use the number zero in its different functions and a disorder of written arithmetic, such as beginning addition problems on the left side rather than the right.

Secondary acalculia may be related to aphasia, memory disorders or dementia and were not further differentiated by Grewel (1969). The secondary form of acalculia was instead considered as only one symptom of a syndrome, such as aphasia. For instance, Grewel (1969) surmised that in some forms of aphasia, computation disorders can occur but they are the result of the aphasia, not an acalculic disorder. In a patient with a memory disorder, the forgetting of immediate information can interfere with written as well as verbal arithmetic.

Grewel further differentiated acalculia by functional localization. This included, among others, temporal acalculia which was associated with the specific inability to identify sounds and numbers, and parietal acalculia where constructional apraxia may give rise to an inability to organize spatial relations on paper.

From this brief historical review it can be seen that early papers reported the presence of acalculia and attempted to localize the disorder (Henschen, 1926) while later papers attempted to work out classification schemes (Grewel, 1969; Hecaen, et al., 1961; Berger, 1926). With the traditional classification or syndrome model, a list of observed symptoms was generated, then compared to a list of symptoms associated with the disorder. The presence or absence of particular symptoms were noted, and a decision made in favor of the disorder if enough symptoms were present. The syndrome method was based on a medical model often used in clinical situations, but considered inaccurate for research investigations. In recent years, researchers have chosen to downplay localization and extend the classification paradigm. The course has been to describe acalculia in terms of the psychological processes that are disrupted and contribute to the disorder. Localization has not been altogether abandoned, since neurological information on subjects is often reported but the classification emphasis has shifted.

Current emphasis has been placed on the convergence between the disciplines of cognitive psychology and clinical neuropsychology. The aim is to establish a relationship between normal cognitive function and the symptoms associated with disordered cognitive function in brain-injured patients. Coltheart (1984) outlined some ways in which this can be accomplished: 1) A paradigm can first be established with normal subjects in a cognitive psychology investigation and then extended for use with the investigation of neuropsychological patients; 2) Paradigms in cognitive psychology and clinical neuropsychology can develop independently and later converge; 3) A paradigm can first be developed in clinical neuropsychology and then applied to the investigation of normal functioning of cognitive processes. Recent research in acalculia is beginning to adopt some of Colheart's (1984) approaches.

Recent Studies of Acalculia

Over the past two decades, studies on acalculia have examined the relationship between mathematics and laterality (Jackson & Warrington, 1986; Annett & Kilshaw, 1982; Katz, 1980), and the co-occurrence of acalculia with other disorders, e.g., Gerstmann's Syndrome (Dahman, Hartje, Bussing & Strum, 1982; Spellacy & Peter, 1978; Benson & Denckla, 1969). Other studies have attempted to describe the components of the disorder (Benson & Weir, 1972; Warrington, 1982; Grafman, Passafiume, Faglioni & Boller, 1982). Warrington (1982) used a method common to cognitive neuropsychology, that is, a model of normal functioning reported in the cognitive psychology literature applied to an acalculic patient. The patient, a physician, was intact for reading and writing numbers but was unable to execute addition, multiplication and subtraction problems without error. The patient was accurate in executing the steps of an addition or subtraction problem but was unable to retrieve the correct answer for single digit problems. For instance, the patient might respond with the sum of 6 for the addition problem, 4 + 3 while clearly understanding that the operation was addition. Warrington concluded that her patient had a selective disturbance in the arithmetic long term memory store. She asserted that calculation disorders could be "fractionated" into components that could be described according to cognitive mechanisms, and that each component of the calculation system could be selectively disrupted. She concluded that her data was best explained by a model of normal retrieval proposed by Groen and Parkman (1972). When her patient was unable to retrieve the correct answer from long term store, he used a procedure explained by the "counting" model (Groen and Parkman, 1972, for explanation of model see below). However, the patient's employment of the "counting" procedure was not always accurate and resulted in errors.

McCloskey, Caramazza and Basili (1985) extended Warrington's (1982) fractionation thesis and outlined a model explaining the number processing/calculation performance of both normal and cognitively impaired subjects. They reported on patterns of errors from impaired individuals and provided a theoretical framework for interpreting the deficits. The model demonstrates that impaired performance can be interpreted as reflecting the functioning of a cognitive system in which one or more components have been damaged. Recently, McCloskey and colleagues (McCloskey et al., 1986) have reported case studies of patients who had selective disruptions in the production of verbal numbers.

Other recent studies of acalculia include those of Deloche and Seron (Seron & Deloche, 1984; Seron & Deloche, 1983; Deloche & Seron, 1982a; Deloche & Seron, 1982b) Their focus has been on transcoding, a linguistic task in which numbers are converted from digit to the corresponding lexical representation or the reverse. Patients with linguistic impairments, most often aphasia, were given transcoding tasks. It was found that the patients systematically made two classes of errors: lexical or syntactic. Lexical errors were described as the accessing of a substitute number (e.g., 6 for 8) much like a paraphasic error. Syntactic errors, on the other hand were in the serial organization of the numbers.

An Acalculia Exam (Table 1) has been designed that considers both the historical perspectives on the disorder as well as recent advances (Kahn & Konewko, 1986). Instead of simply determining the presence or absence of

Table 1
The Acalculia Examination

Digit Magnitude: 1 - 9   473 - 734

Lexical Magnitude:
Ten   Zero
Five Thousand Thirteen   Four Thousand Six Hundred Fifty Eight

Transcoding Lexical To Digit Errors:
Seven Thousand -> 740
Three Thousand Six Hundred Fifty Nine -> 3269

Multiple Choice Multiplication: 3 x 8 = A. 24 B. 26 C. 22

---

acalculia, it presupposes that the disorder is comprised of separate components, any of which can break down and have minimal, maximal or no effect on the other components. The exam enables both the researcher and clinician to identify impaired patients, and isolate the individual components that contribute to the disorder. To investigate whether the disorder is modality specific, the patient is tested in more than one modality (e.g., written, visual, and auditory) in both lexical and digit form. Components addressed in the exam are: 1) magnitude judgment of digits in written and oral and lexical representation; 2) ordering numbers sequentially; 3) counting numbers; 4) identifying, copying, reading, and writing to oral dictation; 5) transcoding in both directions (lexical to digit and digit to lexical representation); 6) Addition, subtraction and multiplication problems in production and multiple choice tasks (written and auditory presentation). Our acalculia examination (Kahn & Konewko, 1986) is especially useful in analyzing data from single subjects. Reported below is one such study.

Case Study of KH

KH presented with a left frontal-parietal lesion and right hemiparesis from a cerebral vascular accident. Our acalculia exam (Kahn & Konewko, 1986) was administered and it was determined that number processing was intact but errors in calculation were evident. KH was able to execute the calculation procedures correctly, understood the arithmetic operations but was selectively impaired for math facts, particularly in multiplication. For instance, when multiplying single digit numbers, he frequently produced responses such as $7 \times 8 = 64$.

Tests of verbal production for numbers as well as auditory and visual tests were administered independent of the acalculia exam. These he performed free of errors. Thus, it cannot be assumed that a deficiency in verbal processing or production contributed to the arithmetic errors.

KH was presented with a large number of multiplication problems in a variety of modalities. He was asked to provide responses to problems that were auditorially presented, to write answers to visual problems and verify products to multiplication problems that were were both auditorially and visually presented. All problems were single-digit with multiplicands 1 through 9. Ten was eliminated from the study because the algorithm for problems with a multiplicand of 10 may be to simply add 0 to the other multiplicand and thus is not a retrieval procedure. Table 2 shows the percentage correct across the tasks in all modalities.

It is evident that the degree of retrieval difficulty is not the same for all of the facts. For example, for the problem 3 x 9, KH was accurate 75% of the time and for the problem 7 x 8 he was accurate 50% of the time. The deficit was less severe for facts that occurred in the left half of the table than for the right and was most severe in the lower right quadrant of the table, i.e., those products with the larger multiplicands and products. There were times that KH was unable to retrieve a product. In these instances he used a backup procedure similar to the method used by Warrington's (1982) patient. If KH was unable to retrieve the product for 8 x 6, for instance, he might first figure the problem 8 x 5 = 40 then add 8 to produce a response of 48 (8 x 5 = 40 + 8 = 48). Like Warrington's (1982) patient, KH's back-up procedure did not always result in correct responses.

When KH's errors were coded according to whether his response could be found *on* the multiplication table (e.g., 7 x 8 = 63) as opposed to *off* the

Table 2
Multiplication Fact Retrieval for Patient KH

	1	2	3	4	5	6	7	8	9
1	-	-	-	-	-	-	-	-	-
2	-	-	-	-	-	-	87	87	87
3	-	87	75	-	-	87	87	87	75
4	-	-	-	-	87	87	87	75	87
5	-	-	-	-	-	-	87	-	87
6	-	87	73	-	-	-	75	78	0
7	-	-	-	87	62	75	87	50	-
8	-	-	-	75	-	-	50	10	62
9	-	87	78	-	-	50	87	88	0

Note. Figures represent percentage correct. Hyphen indicates 100% accuracy.

Table 3
Multiplication Fact Errors for KH

On-Table Errors	Off-Table Errors
2 x 7 = 16	4 x 6 = 26
5 x 7 = 40	7 x 6 = 46
7 x 8 = 63	

multiplication table (e.g., 7 x 6 = 46), it was evident that 91% of the errors were products that occurred on the multiplication table (Table 3). In other words, the incorrect answers that KH produced were not random. It was clear that he was retrieving products from a mental representation of the multiplication facts. This pattern of errors cannot be explained by assuming that KH calculated each answer individually.

KH's performance raises some issues that are not easily explained in the acalculia literature. First, how can KH's difference in error rate be explained? There were more errors in the right lower quadrant of the multiplication table than any other place on the table. Or stated another way, is retrieving the product of 3 x 2 the same or a different process than retrieving the product for 9 x 8? Second, KH's errors were often products related to the correct product. For instance, KH produced errors such as 7 x 9 = 56 and not 7 x 9 = 64. Both products can be found on the multiplication table, yet KH was more likely to respond with a product related to one of the multiplicands. Finally, most of the incorrect answers corresponded to tabled products. For instance, a likely error that KH might make would be 8 x 4 = 36. An unlikely error would be 8 x 4 = 37.

One can proceed in a variety of ways in developing a model of normal cognitive functioning for calculation based on the above case study. Adopting the McCloskey et al. (1985) approach, the single case alone is used to formulate a model that makes inferences about normal multiplication fact retrieval. There is an alternative, however, that requires less inference because it makes use of real data from normal subjects and neuropsychological patients. In this method, the error data from neuropsychological investigations is used to develop hypotheses about normal cognitive processing and the hypotheses are put to test in an experiment with normal individuals. It is the alternative method that provides the best validation of the original observation in the case study.

Studies of Calculation in Cognitive Psychology

In the cognitive psychology literature, studies of normal individuals have resulted in two types of models that explain the retrieval of math facts in addition and multiplication. The first, the counting model, assumes that each sum or product is individually computed each time a problem is encountered unless the problem is a tie (e.g., 5 + 5). In the case of ties, math facts are directly retrievable from memory (Parkman & Groen, 1971). The second model, stored representation, assumes that because it takes time to retrieve math facts with some problems taking longer than others, the facts are stored in a specific memory representation (Stazyk, Ashcraft & Hamann, 1982). The distance travelled through the stored representation predicts the length of time it takes to retrieve a particular math fact.

The first chronometric study of calculation was published by Parkman and Groen in 1971. College students were tested on a series of simple addition problems in which they decided if the presented sum was correct or incorrect. This task is typically referred to as a verification task, because the subject is not required to produce the answer but to verify or confirm if the presented answer is correct or not. In Parkman and Groen's (1971) study, true decisions yielded faster response times than false decisions and the reaction time for decision was positively correlated with the smaller addend. For example, for 3 + 6, reaction time would be correlated with the addend of 3. It was proposed that addition followed a counting procedure. An internal counter is set to the larger addend, and then an incrementation takes places equal to the smaller addend until a sum is obtained. This model is sometimes referred to as the "min" model because the counting procedure takes place according to the size of the minimum or smaller addend. Parkman (1972) extended the model to multiplication. He speculated that response time could be predicted by the sum of the two multiplicands. For instance, in the problem 2 x 3, an estimate of response time would be obtained by adding together 2 and 3 and arriving at the sum of 5. For the problem, 6 x 2, the sum of the multiplicands is 8, thus the problem 2 x 3 can be solved faster than the problem 6 x 2.

Ashcraft and Battaglia (1978) tested the counting model (Groen & Parkman, 1972; Parkman & Groen, 1971) with a single digit addition verification task. It was found that the response times could be best predicted by the square of the correct sum. The predictive value of a squared sum is virtually the same as the sum (Parkman & Groen, 1971) since squaring is a simple transformation. The major distinction between the Ashcraft and Battaglia (1978) study and the one done by Parkman and Groen (1971) is the interpretation of results. While Parkman and Groen (1972) proposed a counting model to explain their results, Ashcraft and Battaglia (1978) speculated that the correct sum for simple addition is obtained through retrieval from a memory network of addition facts. In the network, the sum of any two numbers is stored at the intersection of a column and row. For example, to retrieve a sum for the problem 5 + 4, the 5 node and 4 node would be located and an inward spread would be made until the intersection is reached. Ashcraft and Stazyk (1981) refined the model by proposing that spreading activation theory (Collins & Loftus, 1975) might be the process for the actual retrieval of facts. The time it took for a fact to be retrieved was assumed to be a function of the distance traveled through the network by spreading activation. Thus, it takes longer to reach the sum of 17 for 9 + 8, than for the sum of 9 for the problem 5 + 4.

Further research by Stazyk, Ashcraft and Hamann (1982) showed that the network model could be extended to multiplication. They speculated that product size would predict reaction time in much the same way that sum size in addition predicted response time. Multiplication facts are stored in a table and can be accessed, like addition, by proceeding to the corresponding node that represents the multiplicands in the problem. The time it takes a subject to respond to a problem is reflected in the distance from the nodes to the intersection where the product is located.

An Explanation of Acalculia Derived from Neuropsychology

The cognitive literature supports the observation that patient KH's multiplication fact retrieval errors were systematic because they arise from a specific memory representation (Geary, Widaman & Little, 1986; Stazyk, Ashcraft & Hamann, 1982). However, there are some aspects of KH's performance that are not explained by the cognitive literature. For instance, KH made infrequent errors on verification and production tasks in which the response could not be found on the addition or multiplication network, e.g., off-table. Since the studies reviewed thus far only used verification tasks and not production tasks, it is not known if normal subjects would produce an off-table product. Further, in the verification tasks used by Parkman (1972) and Stazyk, Ashcraft and Hamann (1982), off-table products were not controlled but were presented in the same experimental conditions as on-table products.

The Stazyk, Ashcraft, and Hamann (1982) study was extended by Kahn (1986) to determine whether differences in response time could be found when subjects verified false multiplication problems that were assigned products not found in the multiplication table, e.g., off-table. If an interrelated network of multiplication facts predicts response time according to product size (Stazyk, Ashcraft & Hamann, 1982), then off-table products should produce a different pattern of response times than on-table products. In Kahn's (1986) study subjects verified true and false multiplication problems presented in single digit form (e.g., 2 x 3 = 6). False problems differed from their true counterpart by ± 1 - 8 and were assigned to either the on-table or off-table condition. For instance, the problem 3 x 8 = 25 was assigned to the on-table condition because a difference of 1 was added to the true product of 24 and the false product, 25, can be found on the multiplication table. The problem 6 x 3 = 11 was assigned to the off-table condition because a difference of 7 was subtracted from the true product of 18 and the false product of 11 is not found on the multiplication table or is off-table. The major finding in this study was that the pattern of response times was significantly different for on-table than for off-table products (Figure 1).

True products were verified faster than false products which replicated Stazyk, Ashcraft and Hamann (1982). Additionally, both true and false problems showed a problem size effect. Problems with larger products took longer to verify than problems with smaller products. This follows from the

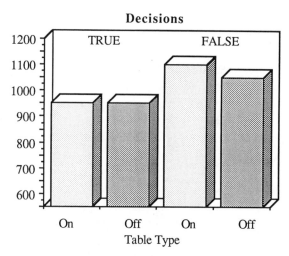

Figure 1. Mean reaction times (msec) for multiplication fact retrieval by Decision and Table.

Stazyk, Ashcraft and Hamann (1982) observation that multiplication retrieval time can be predicted by product size or the location of the product in the network. Products that are farther out in the network from their multiplicand nodes take longer to verify than products that are close in distance to their nodes. The next fastest verifications were the off-table false products followed by the on-table false products. This demonstrated that there is a difference between verifying on-table false problems vs. off-table false problems. When a subject was presented with an on-table multiplication product, true or false, retrieval in the multiplication network was necessary before the subject responded. When an off-table problem was encountered the subject seems to have decided that the answer was not a multiplication product, and retrieval was not necessary. For off-table products, the retrieval step was eliminated, resulting in faster negative decisions.

One last issue that so far has not been addressed in this review of the cognitive literature is the observation that KH produced multiplication errors that were related to one of the multiplicands, e.g., 7 x 9 = 56. Campbell (1987) recently reported a study on network interference in multiplication that accounts for the basis of such acalculic errors.

Campbell (1987) used a production paradigm rather than the standard verification paradigm. The advantage of a production paradigm for this type of study is that the experimenter can directly investigate the source of error. This is in contrast to a verification study in which the experimenter hopes to keep error rate low so that the speed of response time will not be sacrificed for accuracy. Also, in verification paradigms, errors are routinely eliminated from the data analysis. In Campbell's (1987) experiment, subjects were given a practice set of multiplication problems to study, then an interference set of problems. For each problem in the interference set, there was at least one problem in the practice set of problems that had a multiplicand in common with the practice set. Campbell's aim was to induce the transfer of practice effects from the first set of problems to the interference set of problems. The results showed that errors committed during the interference set were related to the problems practiced in the first set. Campbell (1987) referred to this phenomenon as error priming. That is, if the practice set included the problem 7 x 8 for which the subject produced the correct response of 56, it was likely that 56 was also produced when the interference set included the problem 7 x 9. This is because both problems have the multiplicand of 7 in common and the response in the practice set primed the response for the interference set. Campbell suggests that the concept of a multiplication network means that when a multiplication problem is encountered each problem can become linked to a set of possible answers and each answer may be linked to several problems. When the subject encodes a multiplication problem in a practice set, a set of possible responses are activated and each response gets activated according to its acquired strength. In the example given above, 56 can be thought of as a strong false associate of 7 x 9 because 56 is linked through the network to 7 x 8. Retrieving a product through one problem increases the probability that the product will be retrieved in error to another problem.

The Construction of a Model with Evidence from Cognitive Psychology and Neuropsychology

The cognitive studies that deal with multiplication (Campbell, 1987; Kahn, 1986; Stazyk, Ashcraft & Hamann, 1982) have important implications for understanding the nature of multiplication errors in acalculia. When the findings of these studies are integrated, it becomes clear that acalculic errors are systematic because they arise from an interrelated network of multiplication products that can become associated with one another. The few errors that are off-table arise because an individual is not retrieving from the network but is using a back-up procedure that has failed.

A revision of the multiplication network model is proposed according to both the normal data and the acalculic case study. When an individual has a multiplication problem to solve the nodes that correspond to the multiplicands are first located. How nodes are accessed or located is not altogether clear as yet. Next, there is a directed search or spread inward which intersects at the correct product on the multiplication table. However, the correct product is strongly associated with other products in close proximity, particularly those products associated with one or both of the multiplicands of the problem. Therefore it might be possible for an individual to select an incorrect product because the incorrect products are strongly activated for selection along with the correct product.

A Classification of Fact Retrieval Errors

The data from patient NM provides an illustration of how errors in multiplication fact retrieval can be classified according to the model discussed above.

NM's multiplication fact retrieval errors were similar to patient KH. There were few off-table errors and the majority of the errors were associated with one of the multiplicands. NM's errors can be categorized according to

Table 4

Proposed Classification of Multiplication Fact Errors from Patient NM

Within-class, on-table	Between-class, on-table	Off-table
9 x 8 = 81	7 x 4 = 30	6 x 9 = 53
3 x 9 = 24	6 x 6 = 28	
4 x 2 = 6		

Note. Within-class, on-table: Error related to one multiplicand, product found on the multiplication table. Between-class, on-table: Error not related to either multiplicand, product found on the multiplication table. Off-table: Product not found on the multiplication table.

class with class referring to multiplicand (Table 4). For instance, all the products associated with the multiplicand of 6 would comprise one class while the products associated with the multiplicand of 8 would comprise another class. 9 x 8 = 81 is an in-class, on-table error because 81 is a product related to one of the multiplicands. On-table refers to products that are found on the multiplication table and 81 is an on-table product. This is in contrast to the problem 7 x 4 = 30, a between-class, on-table error. Neither multiplicand, 7 nor 4, are related to the incorrect product of 30, yet 30 is an on-table product. An off-table error would be an incorrect product that is not found on the multiplication table such as 6 x 9 = 53. In-class, on-table errors are the most frequent type of error followed by between-class, on-table errors which are less frequent. Off-table errors are the least frequent of all.

Conclusions

Both cognitive psychology and neuropsychology studies have provided evidence for a network representation that is used for the retrieval of multiplication facts. Products that are strong false associates of the correct answer set up an interference effect. In cognitive priming studies of normals, this causes an increase in the probability of errors. In acalculic patients, retrieval errors follow the same pattern: the errors are most often within-class, on-table products with an occasional between-class, on-table error. Off-table errors seldom occur.

With information from both cognitive and neuropsychological investigations, a more definitive model of multiplication retrieval has been proposed. The model is clearly preferable to one based only on neuropsychological evidence or normal subject evidence alone. It is not necessary to make inferences on what normal performance might be like, for instance, because the experimenter has both cognitive and neuropsychological data. This is not to say that any inferences made about normal performance based on neuropsychological evidence will necessarily be incorrect. Direct evidence will always have more credibility. Neuropsychological evidence can be used to pose questions or make predictions about normal performance, but it cannot replace the evidence that directly confirms such predictions.

References

Annett, M. & Kilshaw D. (1982). Mathematical ability and lateral asymmetry. *Cortex, 18,* 547-568.

Ashcraft, M.H. & Battaglia, J. (1978). Cognitive arithmetic: Evidence for retrieval and decision processes in mental addition. *Journal of Experimental Psychology: Human Learning and Memory, 4,* 527-538.

Ashcraft, M.H. & Stazyk, E.H. (1981). Mental addition: A test of three verification models. *Memory and Cognition, 9,* 185-196.

Benson, D.F. & Denckla, M.B. (1969). Verbal paraphasia as a cause of calculation disturbances. *Archives of Neurology, 21,* 96-102.

Benson, D.F. & Weir, W.F. (1972). Acalculia: Acquired anarithmetia. *Cortex, 8,* 465-472.

Boller, F. & Grafman, J. (1983). Acalculia: Historical development and current significance. *Brain and Cognition, 2,* 205-223.

Campbell, J.I.D. (1987). Network interference and mental multiplication. *Journal of Experimental Psychology: Learning, Memory and Cognition, 13,* 109-123.

Collins, A.M. & Loftus, E.F. (1975). A spreading-activation theory of semantic processing. *Psychological Review, 82,* 407-428.

Coltheart, M. (1984). Editorial. *Cognitive Neuropsychology, 1,* 1-8.

Dahman, W., Hartje, W. Bussing. A. & Strum.W. (1982). Disorders of calculation in aphasic patients--spatial and verbal components. *Neuropsychologia, 20,* 145-153.

Deloche, G. & Seron, X. (1982a). From one to 1: An analysis of a transcoding process by means of neuropsychological data. *Cognition, 12,* 119-149.

Deloche, G. & Seron, X. (1982b). From three to 3: A differential analysis of skills in transcoding quantities between patients with Broca's and Wernicke's aphasia. *Brain, 105,* 719-733.

Fancher, R.E. (1979). *Pioneers of Psychology.* New York: W.W. Norton & Company.

Galton, F. (1908) *Memories of My Life.* London: Methuen.

Geary, D.C., Widaman, K.F. & Little, T.D. (1986). Cognitive addition and multiplication: Evidence for a single memory network. *Memory and Cognition, 14,* 478-487.

Grafman, J., Passafiume, D., Faglioni, P. & Boller, F. (1982). Calculation disturbances in adults with focal hemispheric damage. *Cortex, 18,* 37-50.

Grewel, F. (1969). The acalculias. In P.J. Vinken and G.W. Bruyn (Eds.), *Handbook of Clinical Neurology.* Amsterdam: North-Holland, Vol.4, 181-196.

Grewel, F. (1952). Acalculia. *Brain, 75,* 397-407.

Groen, G.J. & Parkman, J.M. (1972). A chronometric analysis of simple addition. *Psychological Review, 79*, 329-343.

Hecaen, H., Angelergues, R. & Houillier. S. (1961). Les varietes cliniques des acalculies au cours des lesions retrorolandiques: Approche statisque du probleme. *Revue Neurologique, 105*, 85-103.

Henschen, S.E. (1926). On the function of the right hemisphere of the brain in relation to the left in speech, music and calculation. *Brain, 49*, 110-123.

Jackson, M. & Warrington, E.K. (1986). Arithmetic skills in patients with unilateral cerebral lesions. *Cortex, 22*, 611-620.

Kahn, H.J. (1986). Individual differences in cognitive processes: Calculation and semantic memory. Unpublished master's thesis, University of North Dakota, Grand Forks, N.D.

Kahn, H.J. & Konewko, P. (1986). An exam for acalculia.

Katz, A.N. (1980). Cognitive arithmetic: Evidence for right hemispheric mediation in an elementary component stage. *Quarterly Journal of Psychology, 32*, 69-84.

Levin, H.S. (1979). *The acalculias*. In K.M. Heilman and E. Valenstein (Eds.) *Clinical Neuropsychology*. New York: Oxford University Press. 128-140.

McCloskey, M. Caramazza, A. & Basili, A. (1985). Cognitive mechanisms in number processing and calculation: Evidence from dyscalculia. *Brain and Cognition, 4*, 171-196.

McCloskey, M., Sokol, S. & Goodman, A. (1986). Cognitive processes in verbal-number production: Inferences from the performance of brain-damaged subjects. *Journal of Experimental Psychology: General, 115*, 307-330.

Parkman, J.M. (1972). Temporal aspects of simple multiplication and comparison. *Journal of Experimental Psychology, 95*, 437-444.

Parkman, J.M. & Groen, G.J. (1971). Temporal aspects of simple addition and comparison. *Journal of Experimental Psychology, 89*, 335-342.

Seron, X. & Deloche, G. (1984). From 2 to two: An analysis of a transcoding process by means of neuropsychological evidence. *Journal of Psycholinguistic Research, 13*, 215-236.

Seron, X. & Deloche, G. (1983). From 4 to four: A supplement to "From three to 3". *Brain, 106*, 735-744.

Singer, H.D. & Low, A.A. (1933). Acalculia (Henschen): A clinical study. *Archives of Neurology and Psychiatry, 29*, 476-498.

Spellacy, F. & Peter, B. (1978). Dyscalculia and elements of the developmental Gerstmann Syndrome in school children. *Cortex, 14*, 197-206.

Stazyk, E.H., Ashcraft, M.H. & Hamann, M.S. (1982). A network approach to mental multiplication. *Journal of Experimental Psychology: Learning, Memory and Cognition, 8*, 320-335.

Warrington, E.K. (1982). The fractionation of arithmetical skills: A single case study. *Quarterly Journal of Experimental Psychology, 34*, 31-51.

3

Attentional Imbalances following Head Injury

Jennifer Sandson, Bruce Crosson, Michael I. Posner, Peggy P. Barco,
Craig A. Velozo and Teresa C. Brobeck

Unilateral left and right hemisphere lesions produce numerous well documented neuropsychological consequences (DeRenzi, 1982). Some of these sequelae are attentional, involving anatomical systems related to the selection of information for conscious detection (Nissen, 1986; Posner & Rafal, 1986). Such attentional deficits can often be demonstrated in tasks involving conflicts between stimuli (Posner & Presti, 1987). For example, patients with left hemisphere lesions have difficulty selecting a verbal input when it conflicts with a simultaneous spatial command. Patients with right hemisphere damage show the reverse pattern (Walker, Friedrich, & Posner, 1983). Similarly, patients with parietal lobe lesions often have great difficulty when an event in the contralesional visual field is in conflict with one in the ipsilesional field. In severe cases these patients may be completely unaware of contralesional targets while in milder cases the target may be detected but with longer latency (DeRenzi, 1982; Posner, Walker, Friedrich & Rafal, 1984).

These findings from patients with focal unilateral lesions demonstrate the value of cognitive tests for the precise measurement of attentional deficits related to hemisphere imbalance (Posner & Rafal, 1986). The conflicts tasks, for example, detect residual attentional imbalance well after standard neurological methods suggest that the patient's performance is normal (Posner, et al, 1984).

Clinical neurology has long used imbalances between the two eyes as a means of detecting subtle insults to the cranial nerves at the level of the midbrain (Mesulam, 1981). In recent years, there has been much evidence of the specialization of the two cerebral hemispheres in the performance of higher level cognitive and emotional activity (Mesulam, 1985). It seems likely that imbalances between the two cerebral hemispheres, as reflected by cognitive tasks involving conflict may be of similar benefit in clinical neuropsychology. To explore this hypothesis, it is important to measure these imbalances and to relate them to everyday behaviors likely to be differentially mediated by the two cerebral hemispheres.

Sandson, J., Crosson, B., Posner, M. I., Barco, P. P., Velozo, C. A., & Brobeck, T. C. (1988). Attentional imbalances following head injury. In J. M. Willliams & C. J. Long (Eds.), *Cognitive approaches to neuropsychology*, New York: Plenum.

It is now common for patients recovering from closed head injury to spend an extended period of time in a rehabilitation program, often supervised by a clinical psychologist. The opportunity for extended detailed observation of their classroom and extracurricular performance makes patients participating in such programs ideal subjects for relating attentional imbalances to disturbances in everyday behaviors.

As a step toward investigating this relationship, six patients undergoing therapy at the Head Injury Resource Center of Washington University were tested with several standard neuropsychological tests and three special attentional paradigms sensitive to attentional deficits in patients with unilateral lesions. We then examined clinical ratings of their academic performance and social interaction to determine if imbalances found in our tests might relate to aspects of everyday life involving attention. Because of the limited sample size this study serves primarily to provide validation of our tests to individual brain injured patients and as pilot data toward the goal of relating attentional imbalances to natural performance.

Cognitive Attention Tasks

Covert orienting of visual spatial attention (Task 1) (Posner & Presti, 1987; Posner et al, 1984). This task involved the detection of a target stimulus (an asterisk) which occurred within one of two boxes located five degrees to the left or right of a fixation cross (Figure 1). Trials were either cued (80%) or uncued (20%). Cues consisted of a brightening of one of the two peripheral boxes and remained present until target detection. The majority of cued trials (80%) were valid, with the targets occurring on the brightened side. The remaining 20% of the cued trials were invalid, with the target occurring on the side that was not brightened. Inter-trial interval was 1000 msec for cued and uncued trials. The interval between brightening of a peripheral box and target onset was either 100 or 800 msec for the cued trials (valid and invalid). Uncued targets occurred 1100 or 1900 msec following previous target onset.

Subjects received three blocks of 254 trials. Instructions were to fixate on the control cross and to press the single response key with the index finger of the dominant hand as rapidly as possible following target detection. Subjects were informed that most trials would be cued and that most cues would be valid.

Covert Orienting of Spatial Attention with Central cues (Task 2) (Posner, 1980; Posner, et al, 1984). The purpose of this task was to study ori-

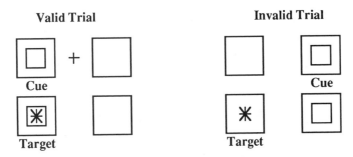

Figure 1. Cue conditions for Task 1. Valid trials are ones in which the target occurs on the cued side. Invalid trials are ones in which the target occurs on the opposite side of the cue.

enting from central rather than peripheral cues. With the exception of cue location, the design was very similar to that of Task 1. Cues consisted of either a directional arrow (80% valid) or a neutral plus sign. Subjects were explicitly instructed to shift their attention, but not their eyes, in the direction indicated by the arrow. Targets followed cue onset at intervals of 100, 500, 800, or 1000 msec.

Selective Attention to Linguistic and Spatial Information (Task 3) (Posner & Henik, 1982; Walker, Friedrich & Posner, 1983). As described above, this task involved selective attention to a specified stimulus mode (spatial or linguistic). For each block, subjects were instructed to attend to one of two types of information (arrow or word). They had to press one of two keys depending on whether the instructed stimulus mode indicated 'left' or 'right'. The attended stimulus was presented in one of three conditions: either alone, or with redundant information or conflicting information from the unattended modality. Redundant and conflicting stimuli were centered on the CRT and arrayed vertically (Figure 2). These three stimulus conditions were randomly mixed within a 96 trial block. Blocks were presented within an ABBA/BAAB design (A = attend arrow, B = attend word).

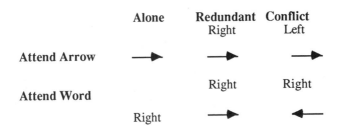

Figure 2. Stimulus conditions for arrow/word task.

Table 1

Mean Reaction Times (and Percentage Errors) for the Arrow/Word Task

	Arrow			Word			
	Alone	Redundant	Conflict	Alone	Redundant	Conflict	
RH	700 (10)	800 (5)	878 (44)	738 (5)	760 (2)	801 (3)	N=6
LH	591 (6)	666 (5)	654 (7)	666 (5)	652 (1)	748 (28)	N=3
C	507 (1)	533 (1)	558 (3)	541 (2)	541 (1)	575 (3)	N=12

Note. RH=Right hemisphere; LH=Left Hemisphere; C=Controls.

Although never published, we had studied unilateral stroke patients on a task similar to 3 (Walker, Friedrich & Posner, 1983). Since the current version was slightly different, we ran 12 normal subjects, six patients with unilateral right hemisphere lesions (from strokes) and three patients with unilateral left hemisphere lesions (from strokes) to validate our previous results. The results conformed well to our previous findings and are shown in Table 1. For the normal subjects, there was no significant difference in RT between the attend arrow and the attend word instructions and the two conditions yielded approximately equivalent interfering effects when placed in conflict. In contrast, the patients with right hemisphere lesions were slower and made many more errors when attending to an arrow in the conflict situation than when attending to the word. Several found the conflict task so difficult that they responded incorrectly (i.e. on the basis of the conflicting stimulus mode) more than correctly. The left hemisphere damaged patients showed good performance on the arrow condition, but were very slow and made many errors in the word condition. Errors were most common in the word conflict condition. Despite the small sample size, these findings were confirmed with parametric statistical tests.

Subjects

Subjects were six clients, four male and two female, recruited from the Head Injury Resource Center. All subjects received a formal neuropsychological evaluation as part of the admissions procedure. All were involved in an intensive program of daily therapy and rehabilitation. Both formal neuropsychological and less formal treatment notes were thus available for comparison with cognitive test results. Demographic information pertaining to the six subjects is presented in Table 2.

Table 2

Six Head-injured Subjects

---

1. Male, Age 28, Years of Education=12, 1 year post injury
Sensory Deficit: color blindness; right ear conductive hearing loss; impaired visual tracking with the left eye in the nasal direction
Neurological Information: rt. frontal hemorrhage; EEG showed abnormal LH activity; lengthy period of post traumatic amnesia and agitation generalized cerebral impairment

2. Male, Age 20, Years of Education=12, 18 months post injury
Sensory Deficit: None
Neurological Information: hemorrhage in left sylvian fissure; lucency in left peripheral thalamus and left temporal lobe; lucency in right basal ganglia; craniotomy with evacuation of right temporal hematoma

3. Male, Age 24,Years of Education=12, 1 Year post injury
Sensory Deficit: right homonymous hemianopsia
Neurological Information: left occipital skull fracture; diffuse region of low density in left temporal/parietal occipital area; region of low density in right frontal lobe; right temporal contusion with craniotomy; left to right midline shift

4. Female, Age 24, Years of Education=16, 9 months post injury
Sensory Deficit: None
Neurological Information: depressed left frontal skull fracture; left frontal contusion; right occipital/parietal contusion; left frontal craniotomy with debridement

5. Female, Age 24, Years of Education=16, 9 years post injury
Sensory Deficit: None
Neurological Information: bilateral intracerebral hematomas; frontal & basal ganglia contusions; right frontal subdural hematoma

6. Male, Age 57, Years of Education=14, 2 1/2 years post injury
Sensory Deficit: 5th, 6th, 7th nerve palsy
Neurological Information: basilar skull fracture; right temporal lobe atrophy

---

Group Data

The brain injured subjects were compared to twelve normal controls on tasks one and three. The group data for these tasks are shown in Figures 3 and 4. Figure 3 displays median reaction times in Task 1 for valid and invalid trials at the 100 msec cue to target interval. Contamination of the data by eye movements is impossible at this short delay. Non cue trials are from the two delays combined. Inspection of the control data reveals the expected pattern, with valid cues facilitating performance in comparison to invalid cues in both visual fields. The most striking aspect of the grouped head injury data is how closely it resembles the normal pattern. Although slower than controls by approximately 100 msec, the head injured subjects generate the expected pattern of facilitation and inhibition.

Figure 4 shows group data for the arrow/word decision (Task 3). Control subjects tend to respond faster to an arrow than to a word and show slightly, but not significantly, more interference of the arrow in the attend word conflict trials than of the word in the attend arrow conflict trials. This pattern is replicated in a slower and exaggerated fashion by the head injured subjects.

Although many studies have considered patients with closed head injury as a homogeneous group, it is clear that differences due to lesion size and loca-

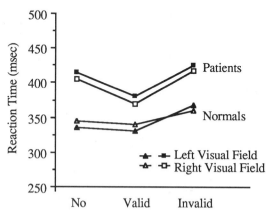

Figure 3. Mean Reaction Time as a function of cue condition for Task 1. Data are from valid, invalid and no cue trials for 6 closed head injury patients and 12 normal controls. All cued data are from the 100 msec cue to target condition.

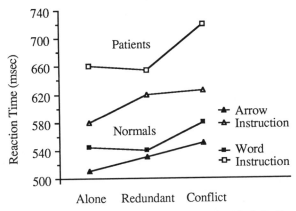

Figure 4. Mean Reaction Time as a function of condition for Task 3. Data are for 6 closed head injury patients and 12 normal controls.

tion may affect task performance. Combining the data of our six subjects is misleading because differences between subjects are obscured by averaging. It is not surprising then that the resulting pattern differs only in speed from that of healthy controls. It is more useful to look at the patterns of performance of the three tasks in individual subjects, and to attempt to relate these patterns to neuropsychological and observational parameters.

Individual Subjects

Individual patient scores for the three cognitive tests are given in Tables 3, 4 and 5. To simplify the presentation we again present reaction times for valid and invalid trials at the 100 msec interval only. The results for each subject are discussed individually below.

Subject 1: Subject 1 shows a pattern of attentional deficits that is consistent across the tasks. At the 100 msec delay, Subject 1 shows a pattern of covert orienting on Task 1 very similar to that seen in patients with left parietal lesion (See Table 3). This pattern is characterized by particular difficulty in shifting attention contralesionally when there has been an ipsilesional cue. It is reflected in very long reaction times to invalidly cued targets in the right visual field. On Task 2 (Table 4), Subject 1 is slower to respond to targets in the right visual field at the 100 msec delay. In addition, the validity effect appears to be larger for right than left sided targets.

Table 3

Median RTs (msec) for Brain Injured Subjects in Task 1 As a Function of Visual Field and Validity

Subject	Valid		Invalid	
	Left	Right	Left	Right
1	422	440	458	590
2	370	380	455	431
3	412	432	504	430
4	637	593	629	621
5	380	322	395	347
6	344	343	421	398

Note. Measurements are for 100msec interval.

Subject 1 evidences a large advantage of the arrow over the word on the task of selective attention (Table 5). Moreover, the word shows a much larger interference effect from the arrow in the conflict condition than the arrow shows from the word.

In summary, the cognitive tests converge to suggest that Subject 1 may have an attention deficit that is left hemisphere predominant. Neuropsychological test results are consistent with this hypothesis. In particular, performance on language measures tapping naming, comprehension, and repetition are well within the aphasic range, indicating significant left-hemisphere dysfunction. Lateralizing measures were somewhat more suggestive of left than right hemisphere dysfunction. Additionally, clinical observations are notable for problems caused by poor memory, inflexibility, and concreteness. These problems are most severe when they interact with linguistic demands. It is worth noting that memory problems were accompanied by confabulation when the patient first entered the program. In addition to the effects on recent memory, the patient's basic fund of knowledge (semantic memory) and remote memory for events (episodic memory) were both impaired. For example, he sometimes was unable to demonstrate any knowledge about the characteristics or uses of familiar objects, and he sometimes was unable to remember significant events in his life as far back as his childhood. Although memory had improved substantially by the end of treatment, evidence of intrusion

Table 4

Median RTs for Brain Injured Subjects in Task 2 As a Function of Visual Field and Validity

Subject	Valid		Invalid	
	Left	Right	Left	Right
1	596	631	652	704
2	403	392	441	404
3	504	567	576	783
4	581	512	608	560
5	476	417	545	492
6	373	382	409	388

Note. Measurements are for 100 msec interval.

was still present on formal testing. Subject 1 was consistently unaware of the extent of his deficits and in particular, their implications. Interestingly, on the other hand, he shows a strength in his ability to maintain a focus of attention in structured and repetitive tasks, and this proved to be an asset vocationally for him.

Subject 2: Subject 2 obtained a pattern of cognitive test results that is almost the opposite of Subject 1 and appears to exemplify a right hemisphere attentional imbalance. This effect is rather weakly demonstrated on Task 1 (Table 3) in which the left visual field was systematically worse than the right only in the invalid condition, but the trend is confirmed on Task 2 (Table 4) where performance was generally worse in the left visual field. Subject 2 is the only subject for whom word processing on Task 3 was faster than arrow processing (Table 5). Interference effects appear to be approximately equal for the arrow and the word.

In spite of severe bilateral injury on acute CT scans, neuropsychological test results are most consistent with the right hemisphere deficit hypothesis suggested by the cognitive tasks. Subject 2 obtained a WAIS-R Performance IQ 15 points below his Verbal IQ of 113. Of note, finger tapping is within normal limits for the right index finger but severely impaired for the left. Informal observations, in fact, suggest that subject 2's areas of greatest functional impairment are not in attention but in organization and memory. Although memory tests were generally within normal limits by the end of the program, the pre-program testing had shown a pattern consistent with a consolidation deficit in verbal memory. It is of further interest that Subject 2 often remembers a fact or happening but cannot associate such information with the context in which it occurs. He had difficulty recognizing the memory problem and the implications of this problem, and thus, is not consistent in compensating for this deficit. Finally, he is often noted to show irritability and difficulty with temper control.

Subject 3: Subject 3 shows the most complex pattern of the head injured group on cognitive testing. On Task 1 (see Table 3), Subject 3 was slower to respond to invalid stimuli in the left visual field. On closer inspection, however, the advantage of cues for targets in the left visual field appears to be normal. Targets in the right visual field, in contrast, failed to show a validity effect at the 100 msec delay. Task 2 data (Table 4) provide confirmation of a left rather than a right hemisphere deficit, as detection of right visual field stimuli is much slower than of left visual field stimuli, especially for invalid trials. Performance on the arrow/word task further supports a left hemisphere attentional imbalance with slower processing for the word and a greater interference effect of the arrow (Table 5).

Table 5

Median RT and Number of Errors for Brain Injured Subjects in Task 3 as a Function of Condition and Conflict

	ARROW			WORD		
	Alone	Redundant	Conflict	Alone	Redundant	Conflict
1.	514 (1)	570 (2)	581 (1)	658 (4)	659 (2)	736 (11)
2.	586 (1)	602 (1)	627 (2)	531 (0)	544 (1)	555 (1)
3.	609 (1)	634 (0)	647 (0)	902 (0)	868 (0)	978 (2)
4.	642 (0)	671 (0)	688 (1)	671 (0)	679 (0)	708 (0)
5.	557 (1)	589 (0)	585 (3)	596 (0)	562 (0)	671 (3)
6.	563 (0)	632 (0)	628 (5)	614 (1)	598 (0)	629 (0)

Note. Number of errors is in parentheses.

Neuropsychological data for Subject 3 are consistent with the cognitive test results. Although not grossly aphasic, Subject 3 shows deficits in many realms of verbal functioning. Like Subject 1, he was impaired in naming and auditory-verbal comprehension, and is especially impaired with repetition. Phoneme and rhythm discrimination were also notably disturbed. There was a right homonymous hemianopsia and indications of a right visual neglect. Although the left-hemisphere injury is obvious from testing, it is worth noting that this subject had a partial right temporal lobectomy. During functional activities in therapies, he does show slowed ability to learn secondary to verbal memory and auditory processing deficits. Yet this patient demonstrates good nonverbal skills, excellent orientation to his surroundings, and good interpersonal/social skills. In spite of comparatively severe deficits, he demonstrates strengths in his awareness of and ability to compensate for deficits.

Subject 4: Subject 4 shows slightly longer RTs toward stimuli in the left visual field at 100 msec on Task 1 (Table 3). In addition, the data reveal difficulty in orienting attention to the left side (no validity effect). Task 2 also reveals a reduced validity effect on the left (Table 4). These results suggest a right hemisphere deficit that involves attention. Data from the arrow/word task (Table 5) show a minimal advantage of spatial over linguistic processing and the symmetric nature of the interference effects are compatible with a slight deficit in right hemisphere processing.

While neuropsychological testing of Subject 4 indicated some evidence of anterior left hemisphere dysfunction (i.e., Visual Naming and Controlled Oral Word Association were below the 12th percentile), the pattern was generally supportive of right hemisphere predominant dysfunction. For example, her performance IQ was 13 points below her verbal IQ of 91. Although Subject 4 showed a relative strength in block design, she demonstrated deficits in attention to visual detail, visual sequencing, puzzle construction, and psychomotor speed. During initial evaluation, she also demonstrated a scanning deficit, omitting items on the left side of the page. These results are consistent with the left frontal injury caused by depressed skull fracture and the posterior right hemisphere contusion visualized on the CT scan. Clinically, residual visual-spatial deficits were apparent in affecting her attention to surroundings and her ability to integrate visual details into an organized whole. Difficulties were also present in mental flexibility, concreteness, interpretation of nonverbal signals, and comprehension of subtleties/humor. Additionally, Subject 4 demonstrated lack of awareness of the deficit areas, as well as their implications in her life. Like Subject 1, Subject 4 was able to sustain attention during structured tasks.

Subject 5: Subject 5 stands out on Tasks 1 and 2 in showing a slower RT to left visual field stimuli, thus a right hemisphere deficit that does not interact with cue type and thus does not appear to be attentional in our sense. Performance on Task 3 was better for the arrow than for the word alone. In addition, while word processing was considerably slowed by the presence of conflicting arrows, arrow processing was uninfluenced by the presence of conflicting words.

Subject 5 showed very few deficits on formal neuropsychological evaluation, and has obtained a Bachelor of Science Degree since her injury. Fine motor coordination was slow bilaterally, more so for the left hand than for the right. The most striking aspect of the neuropsychological examination was a severe deficit on the Tactual Performance Test with the left hand. This latter pattern of performance is generally considered to be suggestive of right parietal dysfunction. Clinically, Subject 5 was characterized by susceptibility to distraction, concreteness, and impulsivity. Her most severe functional deficits, however, were in the areas of social and interpersonal skills, including difficulty recognizing the emotions of others and monitoring appropriate verbal output. Additionally, Subject 5 was unaware of her deficits and their implications into her life. She also was characterized by an inability to experience negative affect. This reduced the likelihood that effective response to confrontation would result in behavior change.

Subject 6: Subject 6 shows no evidence of hemispheric imbalance. Performance on the two spatial orienting tasks is largely symmetric. Reaction times for Task 3 are faster for the arrow than the word alone. Arrow processing, though, was inhibited in both redundant and conflict conditions by the presence of the word while word processing was facilitated by the arrow in the redundant condition and inhibited by the arrow in the conflict condition.

In contrast to the weak results on cognitive testing, neuropsychological test results from Subject 6 are compatible with a deficit that is right hemisphere predominant. This is most strikingly indicated by a significantly lower Performance IQ, as compared to Verbal IQ. Testing revealed both verbal and nonverbal memory deficits, with greater visual memory impairment apparent than verbal. This pattern of memory impairment would be consistent with the right temporal lobe atrophy on CT scan, although this atrophy may have preceded the injury. Left hand finger tapping was mildly impaired in comparison to the right. Clinically, attentional problems were evident, including attention to detail, attention to surroundings, and concentrating on several items simultaneously. Additional difficulties were observed in organization, integration of parts into the whole, and in recognition of faces. Subject 6 demonstrated excellent awareness of his deficit areas, as well as good ability to compensate for them.

Discussion

The goal of this project was twofold: 1) to determine if attentional imbalances could be measured in head injured patients using cognitive tasks and 2) to relate attentional imbalances between the hemispheres to formal and less formal neuropsychological measures. Although our small sample size precludes firm conclusions, several interesting findings emerged.

Hemispheric imbalances were found in five of the six brain damaged subjects (all but subject 6) suggesting that such imbalances may be quite frequent following closed head injury. In our sample, four of the patients with hemispheric imbalances probably had an attentional component to their deficit as evidenced by an interaction between cue type and hemispheric asymmetry on the task of covert spatial orienting.

Performance on the arrow/word attention task was consistent with the covert orienting task in all four subjects with attentional imbalances. We treated the arrow/word task as attentional because the unilateral patients (see Table 1) had so much more trouble in the conflict situation. An alternative is that the deficit arises in the difficulty of patients in processing the word or arrow condition even when it is not presented with conflicting information. This appears to be particularly true of patient 3.

These attentional imbalances occurred in the presence of bilateral injury in all four cases. Some factor such as the comparative location or volume of injury most likely accounts for the imbalance. The presence of both right and left hemisphere imbalances in different patients further demonstrates the importance of considering each patient individually rather than as a homogeneous group.

These preliminary data raise the issue of whether the imbalances found in the cognitive task are greater than one might expect from the normal population. We have only a little data on this issue. Three of the patients had an imbalance based primarily upon right-left differences in the invalid cue condition of Task 1. These differences are 132, 74 and 48 milliseconds respectively. Of thirty normal subjects run in this test only three had differences in this condition as large as 50 milliseconds. At least two of the patient values do seem quite large to be normal. One subject was diagnosed primarily on the lack of a validity effect in one field but not the other. This pattern was detected in only three of our 30 normals. Finally, one patient was diagnosed largely on the reversal of the normal pattern in the arrow/word study and this pattern was larger than we found in any of the twelve normals studied. These findings suggest that the differences found in our patients were the result of the cerebral injuries but further work would be necessary to establish the general validity of the testing methods.

Two of the four patients with attentional imbalance were hypothesized to have greater left hemisphere dysfunction. Both performed well within the aphasic range on several language parameters, and had neuropsychological evaluations consistent with a primary left hemisphere deficit. The remaining two patients with attentional imbalances on cognitive testing were hypothesized to have predominant right hemisphere dysfunction. In addition to other neuropsychological indications of a primary right hemisphere deficit, both patients suffered from social/emotional adjustment problems and depression. A third subject with evidence of greater right hemisphere dysfunction without an attentional imbalance (Subject 5) suffers from serious social and interpersonal difficulties. This relation may suggest an important link between the imbalance found in cognitive tasks and observational ratings of behavior and personality during therapy.

Our three tasks appear to converge on the side of primary deficit in most of the head injury patients. In addition, it appears that they relate well to patterns of lateralization in neuropsychological evaluation. It remains to be determined if these tests provide a sufficiently sensitive measure of imbalances to be useful as a tool for diagnosis and recovery. In addition, we need to know much more about the relationship of such imbalances to performance outside the laboratory.

A useful step would be to relate performance on cognitive tasks over time to neuropsychological and functional measures of recovery. There is some evidence (e.g. Morrow & Ratcliffe, 1987) that the size of the validity effect on the peripheral orienting task correlates with clinical recovery from left sided visual neglect. Replication and expansion of this result would serve as further evidence for the usefulness of simple cognitive measures in the evaluation of attentional deficits and their remediation.

This research was supported by the Office of Naval Research Contract N-0014-86-0289.

References

DeRenzi, E. (1982) *Disorders of Space Exploration and Cognition.* New York: John Wiley.

Mesulam, M. (1985) Mental state assessment of young and elderly adults in behavioral neurology. In M. Mesulam (Ed.) *Principles of Behavioral Neurology*, New York: F.A. Davis Company.

Mesulam, M. (1981) A cortical network for directed attention and unilateral neglect. *Annals of Neurology, 10,* 309-325.

Morrow, L.A. & Ratcliffe, G. (1987) Attentional mechanisms in clinical neglect. *Journal of Clinical and Experimental Neuropsychology., 9,* (Abstract).

Nissen, M.J. (1986) Neuropsychology of attention and memory. *Journal of Head Trauma Rehabilitation 1,* 13-21.

Posner, M.I. (1980) Orienting of attention. The 7th Sir F.C. Barlett Lecture. *Quarterly Journal of Experimental Psychology, 32,* 3-25.

Posner, M.I. & Henik, A. (1983) Isolating representational systems. In J. Beck, B. Hope and A. Rosenfeld (Eds.), *Human and Machine Vision,* New York: Academic Press.

Posner, M,I. and Presti, D. (1987) Selective attention and cognitive control. *Trends in Neuroscience, 10,* 12-17.

Posner, M.I. and Rafal, R.D. (1986). Cognitive theories of attention and the rehabilitation of attentional deficit. In R.J. Meir, L. Diller, and A.C. Benton (Eds.), *Neuropsychological Rehabilitation.* London: Churchill-Livingston.

Posner, M.I., Walker, J.A., Friedrich, F. and Rafal, R. (1984) Effects of parietal lobe injury on covert orienting of visual attention. *Journal of Neuroscience, 4,* 1863-1874.

Walker, J.A., Friedrich, F. & Posner, M.I. (1983) Spatial conflict in parietal lesions. Paper presented to International Neuropsychological Society, San Diego.

4

Toward a Cognitive Neuropsychology of Complex Learning

Jill Booker and Daniel L. Schacter

The cognitive neuropsychology of memory has grown rapidly during the past several years. This trend is reflected by the appearance of interdisciplinary volumes concerned with memory and amnesia that contain contributions from both cognitive psychologists and neuropsychologists (e.g., Cermak, 1982; Roediger & Craik, in press; Squire & Butters, 1984), the widespread use of cognitive paradigms in neuropsychological investigations (e.g., Cermak, Talbot, Chandler, & Wolbarst, 1985; Charness, Milberg, & Alexander, in press; Cohen & Squire, 1980; Johnson, Kim, & Risse, 1985; Moscovitch, 1982; Nissen & Bullemer, 1987; Schacter & Graf, 1986b), and the growing importance of neuropsychological observations concerning amnesia in cognitive theories of memory (e.g., Jacoby, 1984; Johnson, 1983; Mandler, 1980; Schacter, 1987b; Tulving, 1985). This vigorous interaction between cognitive psychology and neuropsychology contrasts sharply with the relative lack of communication between the two fields during much of the past century (Schacter & Tulving, 1982).

The purpose of the present chapter is to discuss an area of research that we believe can be, though it has not yet been, pursued profitably within an interdisciplinary, cognitive neuropsychological context: the nature of the processes involved in complex learning. The phrase "complex learning" refers to learning in relatively rich knowledge domains (e.g., computer programming, text editing, physics/math problems, chess playing) that require the acquisition of various kinds of information, such as items, concepts, relations, and conditional associations. Although there has been some neuropsychological research on complex learning in amnesic patients, and cognitive psychologists have studied the phenomenon extensively in non-impaired populations, little cross-disciplinary interaction exists concerning the issue. Our main objective is to set the stage for such an interaction by discussing relevant research from both cognitive psychology and neuropsychology, and delineating issues that can be usefully studied within a cognitive neuropsychological framework.

Booker, J., & Schacter, D. L. (1988). Toward a cognitive neuropsychology of complex learning. In J. M. Williams and C. J. Long (Eds.), *Cognitive approaches to neuropsychology*, New York: Plenum.

61

The chapter is divided into two main sections. The first examines studies of preserved learning in amnesic patients with particular attention to recent experiments that have begun to explore complex learning processes. The second section outlines cognitive research on complex learning and suggests ways in which these studies can contribute to, and benefit from, neuropsychological analyses of amnesic patients.

Preserved Learning in Amnesic Patients

The idea that it is useful to study complex learning in amnesic patients may at first seem somewhat perplexing. After all, the amnesic syndrome is typically defined by serious difficulties in remembering recent experiences and acquiring even the simplest kinds of new information (e.g., Whitty & Zangwill, 1977). However, this idea becomes more palatable when considered in the context of recent research that has shown that even severely amnesic patients have some preserved learning abilities (for review and discussion, see Parkin, 1982; Schacter, 1987a, 1987b; Shimamura, 1986; Squire, 1987). Several different lines of research have demonstrated that despite amnesic patients' inability to show conscious or *explicit memory* for their recent experiences, they can show *implicit memory* for those experiences through facilitation of performance on various tests that do not require intentional recollection of any prior episode (Graf & Schacter, 1985; Schacter, 1987a, 1987b). For example, amnesic patients can acquire various perceptual and motor skills, even though they lack explicit memory for the experience of learning the skills (e.g., Brooks & Baddeley, 1976; Cohen & Squire, 1980; Milner, Corkin, & Teuber, 1968). In addition, amnesic patients have shown robust repetition priming effects: After studying a list of familiar items, such as common words or idioms, amnesics exhibit a normal facilitation of performance on such implicit tests as word stem completion (Graf, Squire, & Mandler, 1984; Warrington & Weiskrantz, 1974), free association (Schacter, 1985; Shimamura & Squire, 1984), and lexical decision (Moscovitch, 1982).

An important question for the present purposes concerns the extent to which amnesic patients' preserved implicit memory abilities can support the acquisition of *new* associations, concepts, and other kinds of information that are involved in complex learning. If amnesic patients can show implicit memory for newly-acquired information -- even though they may not explicitly remember having learned it -- then there would be some basis for suggesting that the study of complex learning in amnesic patients represents a useful research direction. Several recent studies have used implicit tests to examine the acquisition of various kinds of new knowledge by amnesic patients.

In a series of studies, Graf and Schacter (1985) developed a paradigm for investigating implicit memory for new associations. New associations between previously unrelated words represent a more complex form of knowledge than the single words used in repetition priming. In the new associations experiments, subjects were shown pairs of unrelated words (e.g. ,WINDOW-REASON). For each pair, subjects created a sentence that related the words in a meaningful way. In the implicit memory test, subjects saw a cue that consisted of one word plus three letters that form the stem of the target (e.g. WINDOW-REA___). The subjects were asked to complete the stem with the first word that came to mind. The word accompanying the stem was either the same word with which the target was previously presented (same context condition, e.g., WINDOW-REA____), or a new word (different context condition, e.g., SHIP-REA___). Graf and Schacter (1985) argued that, if the proportion of completions of the fragment was higher in the same context condition that in the different context, an association between the two previously unrelated words had been formed. That is, a new association had been acquired and could be detected with an implicit memory task. The experimental results showed that normal subjects did indeed form new associations that were expressed on an implicit test. The experiments were then repeated with mildly and severely amnesic patients (Schacter & Graf, 1986b). In this case, the mildly amnesic patients showed normal implicit memory for the new associations, but the severe amnesics did not. Mild amnesics, then, were able to form new associations, that is, they were able to create new, albeit simple, organizations of existing information. Severely amnesic patients in this study showed no evidence for having formed such new information structures. However, Cermak, Blackford, O'Connor and Bleich (in press) have observed evidence of implicit memory for new associations in a severely amnesic patient using the Graf and Schacter paradigm. Similarly, Moscovitch, Winocur and McLachlan (1986) reported evidence of associative influence on implicit memory with a task that required patients to read and re-read degraded word pairs.

Using yet another implicit memory task, McAndrews, Glisky and Schacter (1987) found that even severely amnesic patients could acquire new associations. In this study, subjects were shown sentences that were difficult to understand (e.g., The haystack was important because the cloth ripped) and asked to explain the meaning of each sentence. If they failed to explain a sentence, subjects were told a word that made the meaning of the sentence clear (for the example above, the word was parachute). After a delay, the old sentences were presented again, along with some new sentences. The severely amnesic patients did not explicitly remember seeing the old sentences before, but nevertheless showed an increased rate of comprehension of the old sentences. This suggests that the severely amnesic patients had acquired a unit of complex information that associated the sentences with the words and could later express this information implicitly.

The foregoing studies examined implicit memory for new associations following a single study trial. Other experiments have shown that amnesic patients can acquire rather more complex associations following extensive repetition. Nissen and Bullemer (1987), for instance, studied responses in a serial reaction time task. In this task, a light appeared on each trial and the subject was required to press the key that was below that light. Subjects either responded to random sequences of lights, or to a repeating 10-trial light sequence. Normal subjects' reaction times improved across encounters with the repeated sequences, but stayed constant with random stimulus patterns. The subjects always reported that they had noticed the repeated sequence. Korsakoff's patients, although their reaction times were generally slower than those of controls, showed a similar pattern of responses to normal subjects: their reaction times improved across repeated presentations of the 10-light sequence. None of the amnesic patients, however, were aware that they had seen repeated patterns. The improvements in response times showed that the amnesics had acquired a complex piece of information, the sequence of the lights, in such a way that their knowledge could be demonstrated implicitly but not explicitly.

In a study that examined learning of a more cognitive nature, Charness, Milberg and Alexander (in press), reported teaching a Korsakoff's patient an algorithm for squaring two-digit numbers. During the first few training sessions, the patient performed the squaring task while the formula to be used was available for him to refer to as needed. After a few sessions the display was removed, although the experimenters continued to prompt the patient when he required assistance. At the end of seven days of training, the patient mentally squared numbers using the algorithm as quickly as age-matched controls. His error rate was not significantly different from that of the controls. The patient's success in learning the cognitive skill occurred in spite of his inability to explain the procedure he was using to perform the task.

Complex Learning in Amnesic Patients: Acquisition of Computer Skills

The demonstrated success of amnesics in learning new information and associations provides reason for cautious optimism that patients might be able to learn the kinds of complex information that would be useful to them in everyday life. Glisky, Schacter and colleagues (Glisky & Schacter, in press-a, in press-b, 1988, 1987; Glisky, Schacter & Tulving, 1986a, 1986b) have investigated this possibility in a series of studies in which they taught computer skills to amnesic patients. The choice of the computer as the domain to be taught arose from the belief that computers could prove to be useful tools for amnesics. Computers could be used, for instance, to store new information and keep track of appointments. Before attempting to train patients to operate a computer, Glisky et al first tried to teach the patients computer vocabulary.

To tap the patients' implicit memory abilities, Glisky, Schacter and Tulving (1986a) devised a technique they called "the method of vanishing cues". A series of definitions was presented to the subjects on a computer screen (e.g., to transfer a program from storage to computer: LOAD). When a definition appeared, subjects tried to complete the definition with the appropriate computer vocabulary word. If they failed, they were prompted with the first letter of the word as a cue. If they still did not complete the word correctly, one letter at a time was added to the cue until the patient gave the right answer or the whole word was provided by the computer. On the next trial for that definition, the definition was presented along with a cue that was one letter shorter than the cue required for successful completion on the last trial. Thus, the cue "vanishes", one letter at a time, until the subject can complete the definition without a cue. The results of the experiment demonstrated that, after a large number of trials, even severely amnesic patients could learn the computer vocabulary although they had little conscious recollection of the learning experience. The vanishing cues technique, then, successfully built on preserved abilities to produce new learning.

Having demonstrated that amnesic patients could learn a new vocabulary, Glisky, Schacter and Tulving (1986b) went on to investigate whether patients could learn to operate a computer and write simple programs in BASIC. Again using the method of vanishing cues, patients were taught nine commands that could be used to load and store programs on disk, print on the screen, and create and edit programs. After extensive training, four head-injured patients were able to learn all nine commands and use them to write, edit, run and save simple BASIC programs. Further, the patients' newly acquired skills were retained for several months.

The next step in this research, reported by Glisky and Schacter (1987), explored whether amnesic patients' abilities to learn simple computer skills in a laboratory setting could be extended to teach a real-world computer job to a severely amnesic patient, H.D. The job required H.D. to extract information from cards and enter it onto a multi-column computer display. Using the vanishing cues method, H.D. was taught the location of relevant information on the cards, where the items were to be entered on the computer screen, the meaning of coded columns on the screen, and the mappings between the cards and the screen -- many of which were not straightforward. After extensive training in the laboratory, H.D. learned the task, albeit at a rather slow rate. She then began working in the actual work setting and performed the job as accurately and quickly as experienced employees doing the same job. In addition, H.D. successfully learned a second job in which she transferred printed records to microfilm (Glisky & Schacter, in press-a). This job required learning the mechanical skills to operate the camera as well as the necessary vocabulary and procedures.

In a recent extension of this work, Glisky and Schacter (in press-b) demonstrated that H.D. could acquire the knowledge necessary to perform a far more complex data-entry task that required learning how to enter information from eleven different document types onto the computer. Successful performance of this task required learning a complex set of rules for discriminating among documents as well as a set of procedures for extracting various kinds of information from each of the document types and entering it into the appropriate coded column on the computer. Despite the complexity of this task, which required learning over 250 discrete items of information, H.D. eventually learned to perform it accurately and quickly after several months of training. She now works at the company on a full-time basis performing this job.

The critical point of the foregoing studies is that H.D. -- a severely amnesic patient -- was able to learn complex information in several new domains and apply it in a real-world environment. Nevertheless, many questions remain about the nature of complex learning by amnesic patients. First, further research is required to determine whether complex, job-related knowledge and skills can be acquired by patients with various etiologies and severities of amnesia. Second, amnesic patients' learning processes are clearly not normal.

For instance, in the computer vocabulary experiment, amnesics required many more trials to learn the information than did normal subjects. This suggests that, without explicit memory, new information might only be obtainable at a slow rate. An interesting challenge for cognitive psychologists would be to devise methods to speed up this rather slow learning process.

Third, the learning of the amnesic patients seems to be qualitatively different from that of normal subjects, even apart from the dimension of explicit awareness. Glisky, Schacter and Tulving (1986a) have characterized the amnesics' learning as "hyperspecific": The new knowledge seems strongly bound to the cues with which it was learned. Although the extent of the hyperspecificity has not been assessed experimentally, patients seem unable to express their knowledge if they are not prompted in a way that is very similar to that in which they originally learned it. Since amnesic patients presumably rely largely on implicit memory for their new learning, hyperspecificity suggests the need for further study of the role of context in implicit memory.

Research in cognitive psychology can follow up on some of the issues identified in the study of complex learning by amnesic patients. Implicit memory research, for instance, can address questions about the organization of information with respect to cues and context, and the speed at which information can be acquired. As neuropsychology continues to provide clues for research in cognition, developments in cognitive psychology can in turn suggest approaches for neuropsychology. In the next section, we present a summary of some current cognitive trends in the study of complex learning processes, and indicate how their findings suggest directions for neuropsychological research to pursue.

Cognitive Psychology and Complex Learning

Complex learning is studied from a variety of perspectives in cognitive psychology. Some researchers, for instance, are particularly interested in the acquisition of complex knowledge and its organization; others study methods of helping novices learn new domains; still others concentrate on the utilization of knowledge in problem-solving. We believe that this research represents a valuable source of techniques, ideas and data for neuropsychological investigations of complex learning in amnesic patients. For example, although the neuropsychological studies discussed above have demonstrated some successes in teaching amnesic patients complex information, amnesics' skills must be characterized more precisely before further attempts can be made to enhance their performance. Consideration of the neuropsychological data in light of cognitive research could provide a framework for formulating more precise descriptions of the nature of amnesics' learning abilities. In this section, we consider five areas of study that we think are relevant to, and may have direct implications for, neuropsychological research: 1) the representation of complex information as mental models, 2) qualitative differences in expert and novice performance, 3) the use of analogy in learning, 4) the role of remindings in acquiring complex knowledge, and 5) the role of examples in learning.

Mental Models

A mental model has been defined as "a psychological representation of the environment and its expected behavior" (Holyoak, 1984, p. 193). It is a representation of a person's current understanding of a domain that is developed as the person works with the domain (Norman, 1983). The mental model provides the basis for giving explanations and making predictions within the domain (Young, 1983).

Gentner and Gentner (1983) investigated the use of mental models in solving problems about electrical circuits. People are often taught to think about electricity in terms of a moving-crowd model or a hydraulics model. The hydraulics model describes the flow of electricity through a circuit by comparing it to the flow of water through pipes. Thinking of electricity this way provides a good description of the behavior of electricity in combinations of batteries. The crowd-flow model, on the other hand, compares electrical flow to the motion of people in a crowd. This description lends itself well to explanations of electricity in combinations of resistors. In an experiment, subjects who reported that they used one or the other of these mental models were asked questions about current and voltage in simple circuits composed of resistors or of batteries. Since the hydraulics model was more suited to the battery problems, subjects who used that model would be expected to solve battery problems more accurately than resistor problems. The reverse should hold for subjects who used the crowd-flow model. This result was obtained, and supported the idea that mental models are employed for reasoning in a domain.

In a second experiment, subjects were explicitly taught one of the two models and then tested on the circuit problems. Subjects who were taught the hydraulics model performed more accurately on the battery problems than on the resistor problems. Subjects taught the crowd-flow model showed the opposite patten of results. These results showed that subjects were able to make use of models that they were taught.

Evidence for the development of a mental model during learning was reported by Williams, Hollan and Stevens (1983). They analyzed protocols of a subject learning about a heat exchanger. During the session, the subject was found to use three different models. When an existing model did not contain the information that would allow him to explain a conclusion he had reached, the subject produced a new model that could account for the new situation. For example, his final model was essentially a combination of two earlier models, neither of which was sufficient on its own to explain the domain. Experience with problems about the heat exchanger helped the subject understand the relations among the elements of the domain and incorporate them into a more useful model.

Development of a mental model was also suggested in a study in which a subject learned to solve the Tower of Hanoi problem (Anzai & Simon, 1979). The subject's protocol revealed that she initially thought out moves one piece at a time, but eventually began to refer instead to groups of pieces. This grouping of pieces suggested that, after some experience, the subject understood the relations among the individual items, and acted on these groups rather than the single entities. From this change in performance, the development of a more refined model can be inferred.

Mental models do not always accurately reflect the operation of a domain. One example of this non-veridicality was reported by Mayer (1985). Novice programmers were able to write programs reasonably well in spite of an inaccurate understanding of the way in which many BASIC statements operate. The subjects apparently understood the syntax and general purpose of the commands well enough to use them in a program, but they did not understand what was occurring in the computer when the command was executed. That is, they did not have a veridical mental model of the programming language.

Since novices do not always develop useful mental models while they learn, experiments have been performed to determine whether subjects can be taught a useful model. Mayer (1975) taught novices a model of a computer in which, for instance, the data stack and memory of the computer were described in terms of scoreboards and ticket counters. The subjects were then taught FORTRAN statements and their operation in terms of the model. This training was expected to lead to a good understanding of the relational information of the computer domain, i.e., to a well-developed mental model. Control subjects, who did not receive the model, were not expected to be able to understand the computer as well, and so would not be expected to develop as good a mental model. Compared to the controls, subjects in the model groups correctly answered more items on complex problem-solving tasks. The controls were more accurate than the model group on simple tasks in which the problems closely resembled the information they had read.

There are several points to be noted from the above studies (for a more detailed discussion, see Booker, 1987). First, in the studies in which models were presented to subjects, the study phase ensured that the subjects related the new material to the model. In Mayer's (1975, 1985) programming studies, this was accomplished by explanations of the programming language statements in terms of the model. A second point is illustrated by Mayer's (1985) BASIC study in which novices were able to write some programs in spite of an imperfect understanding of the BASIC statements. Ability to perform a task only assesses the content of the mental model with respect to that goal. In learning a complex domain, the global aim is to be able to perform a variety of tasks within the domain, so the mental model would ideally provide a representation of the domain that is useful for all of those tasks. Assessment of a mental model of a domain, then, must include various measures such as tests of conceptual knowledge as well as skill in simple task performance. Finally, the foregoing studies have demonstrated that novices' ability to perform tasks successfully was restricted to those tasks that did not require complex conceptual knowledge.

If normal learning of complex domains can be characterized in terms of mental model development, an important question for neuropsychologists to investigate is whether amnesic patients develop mental models when they learn complex knowledge. When normal subjects learn, they revise their mental models in accordance with a) the facts they acquire, b) recognition of the relations among them, and c) the outcome of practice in the domain. Much of the revision presumably occurs at a conscious or explicit level. Severely amnesic patients, who lack explicit memory, will likely rely on implicit memory for their learning. A critical research issue, then, is whether mental models will develop without explicit memory. Data suggestive of this possibility have been provided by studies of implicit learning that appear to indicate that subjects can acquire complex rules (e.g., Lewicki, Czyzewska, & Hoffman, 1987) even though they cannot explicitly articulate the rules, and by related studies that indicate that subjects can learn to perform tasks that involve mastery of complex input-output relations that cannot be verbalized explicitly (e. g., Berry & Broadbent, 1987). It would be extremely interesting to determine whether amnesic patients can achieve mastery of complex tasks through implicit learning processes, and to compare the resulting "implicit models" of a domain to fully articulated explicit models.

If implicit memory and learning processes cannot support the development of mental models, amnesics will probably not be able to acquire the advanced knowledge organization that is necessary for complex, conceptual problem-solving. Instead they, like novices, would only have a set of rote-learned, unconnected facts that would severely limit their ability to apply their knowledge to new problems. We will discuss this issue further after a more detailed consideration of expert and novice performance differences.

Expert/Novice Performance Differences

In addition to studying the development of mental models in non-expert populations, cognitive psychologists have also studied learning and organization of complex knowledge by comparing the performance of expert and novice subjects. Two general task types have been employed in investigations of novices' and experts' performance: free recall and problem-solving ability. Studies that employed recall tasks will be considered first.

Chase and Simon (1973) investigated chess masters' and novices' memory for the location of pieces on a chessboard. Subjects were shown an arrangement of chess pieces on a chessboard and then asked to recreate the board. Some of the patterns presented were positions that could actually occur in a chess game; others were random arrangements of pieces on the board. The masters showed superior recall, but only for those arrangements of the chess pieces that could occur within a game. When meaningless configurations were used, masters' recall was no better than that of novices. Rather than having a global memory advantage, the experts demonstrated a different organization of memory for chess positions. During recall, the masters chunked pieces together according to their strategic relationship. The chunks, in turn, lead to the higher recall on the part of the masters. Novices' understanding of chess was not as well developed and so the novices were unable to make use of the strategic groups of pieces to form chunks.

Adelson (1981) studied novices' and experts' representations of computer programs. In one experiment, lines of code from three programs were presented in random order to novices and experts. Subjects were then asked to recall the code. Experts tended to group the code into program units during recall, whereas novices tended to recall in groups of items that were similar syntactically. As in Chase and Simon's (1973) study of chess masters, experts were able to organize the information presented to them into higher-level conceptual groups, but novices could only use superficial information as the basis for their organization.

In a subsequent study, Adelson (1984) investigated abstract and concrete representations of programs, where abstract was defined as what the program did and concrete as how the program worked. Subjects first studied either an abstract or concrete flowchart of a program to induce an abstract or concrete mental set. They were then shown the program and asked either a concrete or abstract question about it. Based on an analysis of error rates, Adelson concluded that, although subjects could use either induced mental set, novices' preferred representation was concrete whereas experts used an abstract representation.

Subjects' ability to detect structure has also been demonstrated in problem-solving tasks. Larkin (1981, 1983) demonstrated the poor ability of novices to form appropriate representations of physics problems. Novices' problem representations contained only the surface details of the problem and familiar objects and events. For instance, in a problem dealing with forces applied to carts, one novice reasoned in concrete terms such as pushing on the cart and wind resisting the motion of the cart. Experts, in contrast, detected the underlying principles that applied to the problem, such as "uniformly-accelerating frames" and "pseudo-forces". Like chess masters and expert programmers, the experts were released from reliance of surface content and were able to see patterns in the problem that were relevant to finding the solution.

The foregoing studies illustrate the differences in performance shown by novices and experts on domain-related tasks. Experts were able to discover meaningful structure in the information presented to them, and could thus chunk items for recall and successfully solve problems. Novices could only work with superficial details that were not relevant to the conceptual structure of the domain.

The context-specificity of novices' learning resembles in certain respects the apparent hyperspecificity of amnesic patients' learning discussed previously. Amnesic patients, like novices, seem to be highly dependent on surface features (i.e., the cues present during training) to perform successfully in complex domains. The amnesics who were trained in the laboratory, however, did not have extensive experience at their tasks, so it could be that the specificity would be reduced with practice. Unless their context dependence is reduced, amnesic patients cannot be said to have gained expertise in a domain.

Another possible area of investigation for neuropsychology concerns whether amnesic patients eventually come to "chunk" information with extensive practice in a task -- a key hallmark of expertise. One possibility would be to assess chunking with standard organization measures (e.g., Adelson, 1984). However, amnesic patients' serious difficulties on free recall tasks might preclude such an approach. An alternative and as yet unexplored possibility would be to design implicit measures that can detect the formation of chunks (c.f. Nissen & Bullemer, 1987). More generally, it would be intriguing to determine whether amnesic patients' preserved learning abilities can support the acquisition of what might be called "implicit expertise": Expert knowledge about a domain that can be expressed in performance, but not articulated explicitly. As noted earlier, studies of implicit learning (Berry & Broadbent, 1987; Lewicki et al., 1987) suggest that this kind of process occurs in normal subjects. An important challenge for future research on complex learning in amnesia will be to determine whether patients can become "implicit experts", despite poor explicit knowledge of a domain. Indeed, some of Glisky and Schacter's research on computer learning (Glisky et al., 1986b; Glisky & Schacter, 1987, in press-b) is suggestive of such a phenomenon.

Analogy and Transfer

A number of investigators have examined the role of analogy in the learning of complex new material (for review, see Booker, 1987; Holyoak, 1985). Holyoak (1984) considers an analogy to provide a basis for a mental model of the target domain via mappings that are established from elements of the analogy to the target. The initial mapping is likely to be incomplete because the critical points of correspondence between the analogy and target are difficult to identify at an early stage of learning. As more information is acquired the mapping can be refined and extended.

The process of analogical transfer - the use of mappings between the base and target to aid problem solution - has been studied extensively by Gick and Holyoak (1983). They investigated the ability of subjects to utilize analogies spontaneously when solving word problems. Subjects in these experiments first read a story that described a problem and its solution. Then the critical problem, whose solution could be simply derived by analogy to the first story, was presented. Without an analogy, about 10% of subjects solved the critical problem. After seeing the analogy this number rose to about 30%. When subjects were given an explicit hint to use the analogy, however, about 75% produced the solution. Subjects were able to apply the analogy when it was pointed out to them, but they often failed to recognize the analogy spontaneously. Further experiments revealed that subjects were more likely to notice the analogy to the critical problems if they initially read and compared two stories which described similar problems and their solutions. Gick and Holyoak suggested that the comparison lead the subjects to construct a generalized representation of the type of problem illustrated in the stories. The generalized representation could then be identified as a model of the target to provide a basis for a mental model of the target problem and applied to find the solution.

A further result illustrates the strong influence of surface similarities on recognition of an analogy. Holyoak (1985) presented subjects with a story about a problem and its solution prior to asking them to solve an analogous target problem. He found that subjects were more likely to recognize an analogy spontaneously when the topics of the stories they read were similar. The superficial aspects of the problems, rather than the actual structure of the problems, seem to determine whether subjects realize that an analogy is available.

The foregoing studies indicate that use of analogies during learning requires explicit processing of the analogy and the target domain to establish mappings between the two. Because of the necessity for the explicit availability of the analogical information, it seems unlikely that amnesic patients will be able to benefit from analogies when learning in complex domains, at least under the experimental conditions typically used in studies of college students. If, however, the components of the analogy were taught individually, perhaps with a procedure such as the vanishing cues technique, amnesic patients might be able to learn them. But it is not clear whether they would be able to use the analogies to structure acquisition of new knowledge. Since normal subjects are unlikely to notice analogies spontaneously, there is no reason to expect amnesics to be any different. The question, then, is whether patients could make use of analogy if its relation to the target problem were explicitly pointed out to them. If the analogy were drawn to something that the amnesics already knew about, they could at least explicitly access the analogy for processing. The crucial problem becomes whether they could apply the analogy successfully. Because it may be difficult to accomplish this explicitly, it would be interesting to investigate whether a newly-learned analogy could in some way be accessed implicitly for help in problem-solving.

Remindings and Learning

When people try to solve problems, the current problem will often remind them of problems they have previously encountered. These memories of similar instances have been called remindings (Ross, 1984, in press). Once a reminding has occurred, the memory of the prior solution can be applied to the current problem. Ross expected remindings to occur more frequently during early stages of learning and when problems are difficult, because these are the situations in which subjects do not immediately know the answer and must search for a solution. In one experiment reported by Ross (1984), subjects were taught two methods for each of several operations in a text editor. Each editing method was illustrated on a piece of text with a distinctive topic. For instance, the text used to demonstrate one method of deleting words was a restaurant review. The other method was shown on a bibliography. Subjects were then asked to think aloud while they edited a document. Examination of the protocols revealed that subjects experienced remindings, that is, they recalled task-relevant information from a specific prior problem. Moreover, once a reminding occurred, the subjects' choice of solution method for the current problem was consistent with that used in the first instance. Remindings were also found to be more common during difficult tasks than during easier tasks.

In view of Ross' results, presentation of a rich set of examples during learning would seem valuable as a source for later remindings. One drawback, however, is the importance of surface similarities for the occurrence of reminding. Remindings in Ross' (1984) study, for instance, were triggered by the topic of the text in the editing task, rather than by the type of change to be made with the editor. The editing operation to be performed is, of course, the critical factor for solving the problem. This observation indicates that, although examples form a source for later remindings, they may lead to the wrong solution if they match the target on surface appearance but not on problem type.

In normal subjects, remindings are explicit memories of a prior instance. Although amnesic patients have serious difficulties recalling previous instances, it would be interesting to investigate whether presentation of appropriate cues in a problem-solving task could involuntarily trigger a previously-acquired piece of knowledge. The knowledge might become explicitly accessible (although it would not likely be recognized as a previous instance) and thus be available for guidance in problem-solving. Alternatively, activated knowledge might not be explicitly available, but perhaps could guide problem-solving at an implicit level. The possibility of an "implicit reminding" effect on problem-solving performance has not yet been investigated, but may merit exploration with amnesic patients.

Role of Examples in Learning

In view of the previously noted importance of examples as sources of re-mindings, it is useful to consider how to structure the presentation of examples during learning of a complex task in order to optimize their effectiveness.

Nitsch (1977; see also DiVesta & Peverly, 1984) studied the use of examples in a concept-learning task. Subjects were taught definitions of concepts (e.g., crinch - to make someone angry by performing an inappropriate act) and a context in which that term arose (crinch was said to have been created by waitresses who referred to people who failed to leave tips as "crinches"). Subjects were then given practice examples of the concepts. Examples were either set in the same context as that given in the definition, or in varied contexts. Subjects were then tested on their ability to apply the concepts to new examples. The use of varied context examples was expected to lead to decontextualization of the concept, i.e., the concept should be freed of association to a particular context, and thus should be easy to apply in any context. With examples from only one context, on the other hand, the definitions of the concepts would likely remain tied to that context, and so could not easily be applied to new context. The results supported these hypotheses: study with varied context examples lead to more accurate identification of new examples of concepts than did practice in the same context. Thus, varied examples lead to improved ability to apply knowledge to novel situations.

A further result is also worth considering, however. Nitsch (1977) found that subjects who received same context examples learned the concepts to criterion on the practice task much faster and with less confusion than did those who received the varied examples. It seems, then, that varied examples produce more flexible knowledge, but at the cost of initial difficulty in learning. A further experiment found that the problem of learning from varied contexts could be eased by presenting "hybrid" examples. In this procedure, subjects first studied a set of same-context examples that helped them to establish the concept easily, and then received varied-context examples to decontextualize the information. Subjects who received hybrid training were able to learn the information without too much confusion, and still performed the test task as well as the varied example group, who rated themselves as confused.

These studies of examples and context could prove important to the study of the hyperspecificity of amnesic patients' learning. The role of varied examples in decontextualization suggests one way to try to reduce amnesic patients' strong contextual dependence. For amnesics, it could be that the entire learning context rather than just the context of the examples should be varied. The critical issue is whether varied examples in fact reduce context dependence, given that the patients are relying largely on implicit memory. Moreover, it would also be important to determine whether the varied contexts increase the initial difficulty in learning to the point that the cost associated with this procedure outweighs any possible benefits.

Concluding Comments

The main purpose of the present chapter was to discuss the empirical basis of, and delineate possible directions for, a cognitive neuropsychological approach to complex learning. The research that we have considered suggests that such an approach is likely to be well worth pursuing. On the neuropsychological side, the finding of implicit memory for new associations in some amnesic patients (Cermak et.al., in press; Graf & Schacter, 1985; McAndrews et.al., 1987; Moscovitch et.al., 1986; Nissen & Bullemer, 1987; Schacter & Graf, 1986b), and the demonstration that a variety of memory-impaired patients can acquire complex computer-related knowledge (Glisky & Schacter, 1987, 1988; Glisky et.al., 1986a,b), indicates that further investigation of complex learning in amnesic populations is justified and even demanded. Such research can have practical as well as theoretical consequences: If patients with memory disorders can learn to perform complex tasks in vocational and educational domains, the negative impact of memory impairment on everyday life could be significantly reduced (for further discussion, see Glisky & Schacter, 1987; Schacter, Glisky, & McGlynn, in press).

On the cognitive side, the existence of a wealth of experimental paradigms and conceptual frameworks for exploring such phenomena as development of mental models, acquisition of expertise, and the role of analogies, remindings, and examples in complex learning provides useful analytic tools for neuropsychological research. In addition, cognitive analyses can benefit from studies of complex learning in amnesic patients. For example, understanding whether severely amnesic patients, like normal subjects, can develop organized mental models when learning complex tasks -- despite their lack of explicit memory for having performed the tasks -- should shed light on the processes involved in model development. Similarly, investigation of the related issue of whether amnesic patients can truly become "experts" in a complex domain will likely provide insight into mechanisms underlying acquisition of expertise in non-impaired populations. For all of these reasons, we believe that exploration of complex learning in amnesic patients represents one of the more exciting frontiers in the cognitive neuropsychology of memory.

Preparation of this chapter was supported by a University of Arizona Biomedical Research Support Grant to D. L. Schacter.

References

Adelson, B. (1984). When novices surpass experts: The difficulty of a task may increase with expertise. *Journal of Experimental Psychology: Learning, Memory and Cognition, 10*, 483-495.

Adelson, B. (1981). Problem solving and the development of abstract categories in programming languages. *Memory & Cognition, 9*, 422-433.

Anzai, Y. & Simon, H.A. (1979). The theory of learning by doing. *Psychological Review, 86*, 124-140.

Berry, D. C., & Broadbent, D. E. (1987). The combination of explicit and implicit learning processes in task control. *Psychological Research, 49*, 7-15.

Booker, J. (1987). The role of consistent and varied analogies in the development of a mental model of a computer database. Unpublished master's thesis, University of Toronto.

Brooks, D.N. & Baddeley, A.D. (1976). What can amnesic patients learn? *Neuropsychologia, 14*, 111-122.

Cermak, L.S. (1982). *Human memory and amnesia.* Hillsdale, NJ: Erlbaum Associates.

Cermak, L.S., Blackford, S.P., O'Connor, M. & Bleich, R.P. (in press). The implicit memory abilities of a patient with amnesia due to encephalitis. *Brain & Cognition.*

Cermak, L.S., Talbot, N., Chandler, K. & Wolbarst, L.R. (1985). The perceptual priming phenomenon in amnesia. *Neuropsychologia, 23*, 615-622.

Charness, N., Milberg, W., & Alexander, M.P. (in press). Teaching an amnesic a complex cognitive skill. *Brain & Cognition.*

Chase, W.C. & Simon, H.A. (1973). Perception in chess. *Cognitive Psychology, 4*, 55-81.

Cohen, N.J. & Squire, L.R. (1980). Preserved learning and retention of pattern-analyzing skill in amnesia: Dissociation of "knowing how" and "knowing that". *Science, 210*, 207-209.

DiVesta, F.J. & Peverly, S.T. (1984). The effects of encoding variability, processing activity, and rule-examples sequence on the transfer of conceptual rules. *Journal of Educational Psychology, 76*, 108-119.

Gentner, D. & Gentner, D.R. (1983). Flowing waters or teeming crowds: Mental models of electricity. In. D. Gentner & A.L. Stevens (Eds.). *Mental models*. Hillsdale, NJ: Erlbaum.

Gick, M.L. & Holyoak, K.J. (1983). Schema induction and analogical transfer. *Cognitive Psychology, 15*, 1-38.

Glisky, E.L. & Schacter, D.L. (1988). Long-term retention of computer learning by patients with memory disorders. *Neuropsychologia, 26*, 173-178.

Glisky, E.L. & Schacter, D.L. (in press-a). Acquisition of domain-specific knowledge in patients with memory disorders. *Journal of Learning Disabilities*.

Glisky, E.L. & Schacter, D.L. (in press-b). Extending the limits of complex learning in organic amnesia: Computer training in a vocational domain. *Neuropsychologia*.

Glisky, E.L. & Schacter, D.L. (1987). Acquisition of domain-specific knowledge in organic amnesia: Training for computer-related work. *Neuropsychologia, 25*, 893-906.

Glisky, E.L., Schacter, D.L., & Tulving, E. (1986a). Learning and retention of computer-related vocabulary in amnesic patients: Method of vanishing cues. *Journal of Clinical and Experimental Neuropsychology, 8*, 292-312.

Glisky, E.L., Schacter, D.L., & Tulving, E. (1986b). Computer learning by memory-impaired patients: Acquisition and retention of complex knowledge. *Neuropsychologia, 24*, 313-328.

Graf, P. & Schacter, D.L. (1985). Implicit and explicit memory for new associations in normal and amnesic subjects. *Journal of Experimental Psychology: Learning, Memory and Cognition, 11*, 501-518.

Graf, P., Squire, L.R., & Mandler, G. (1984). The information that amnesic patients do not forget. *Journal of Experimental Psychology: Learning, Memory and Cognition, 10*, 164-178.

Holyoak, K.J. (1985). The pragmatics of analogical transfer. *The psychology of learning and motivation, 19*, 59-87.

Holyoak, K.J. (1984). Mental models in problem solving. In J.R. Anderson & S.M. Kosslyn (Eds.). *Tutorials in learning and memory*. San Francisco: W.H. Freeman.

Jacoby, L.L. (1984). Incidental versus intentional retrieval: Remembering and awareness as separate issues. In L.R. Squire & N. Butters (Eds.), *Neuropsychology of memory*. New York: Guilford Press.

Johnson, M. (1983). A multiple-entry, modular memory system. In G.H. Bower (Ed.), *The psychology of learning and motivation* (Vol. 17). New York: Academic Press.

Johnson, M. K., Kim, J.K., & Risse, G. (1985). Do alcoholic Korsakoff's syndrome patients acquire affective reactions? *Journal of Experimental Psychology: Learning, Memory and Cognition, 11*, 27-36.

Larkin, J. (1983). The role of problem representation in physics. In D. Gentner & A.L. Stevens (Eds.). *Mental models*. Hillsdale, NJ: Erlbaum.

Larkin, J. (1981). Enriching formal knowledge: A model for learning to solve textbook physics problems. In J.R. Anderson (Ed.). *Cognitive skills and their acquisition.* Hillsdale, NJ: Erlbaum.

Lewicki, P., Czyzewska, M., & Hoffman, H. (1987). Unconscious acqisition of complex procedural knowledge. *Journal of Experimental Psychology: Learning, Memory and Cognition, 13*, 523-530.

Mandler, G. (1980). Recognizing: The judgment of previous occurrence. *Psychological Review, 87*, 252-271.

Mayer, R.E. (1985). Learning in complex domains: A cognitive analysis of computer programming. *The psychology of learning and motivation, 19*, 89-130.

Mayer, R.E. (1975). Different problem-solving competencies established in learning computer programming with and without meaningful models. *Journal of Educational Psychology, 67*, 725-734.

McAndrews, M.P., Glisky, E.L. & Schacter, D.L. (1987). When priming persists: Long-lasting implicit memory for a single episode in amnesic patients. *Neuropsychologia, 25*, 497-506.

Milner, B., Corkin, S., & Teuber, H.L. (1968). Further analysis of the hippocampal amnesic syndrome: 14 year follow-up study of H.M. *Neuropsychologia, 6*, 215-234.

Moscovitch, M. (1982). Multiple dissociations of function in amnesia. In L.S. Cermak (Ed.), *Human memory and amnesia.* Hillsdale, NJ: Erlbaum.

Moscovitch, M., Winocur, G. & McLachlan, D. (1986). Memory as assessed by recognition and reading time in normal and memory-impaired people with Alzheimer's disease and other neurological disorders. *Journal of Experimental Psychology: General, 115*, 331-347.

Nissen, M.J. & Bullemer, P. (1987). Attentional requirement of learning: Evidence from performance measures. *Cognitive Psychology, 19*, 1-32.

Nitsch, K. (1977). Structuring decontextualized forms of knowledge. Doctoral Dissertation, Vanderbilt University.

Norman, D.A. (1983). Some observations on mental models. In D. Gentner & A.L. Stevens (Eds.). *Mental models.* Hillsdale, NJ: Erlbaum.

Parkin, A. (182). Residual learning capability inorganic amnesia. *Cortex, 18*, 417-440.

Roediger, H.L. & Craik, F.I.M. (in press). *Varieties of memory and consciousness: Essays in honor of Endel Tulving.* Hillsdale, NJ: Erlbaum.

Ross, B.H. (in press). Remindings in learning and instruction. In S. Vosniadou & A. Ortony (Eds.). *Similarity, analogy and thought.*

Ross, B.H. (1984). Remindings and their effect in learning a cognitive skill. *Cognitive Psychology, 16*, 371-416.

Schacter, D.L. (1987a). Implicit expressions of memory in organic amnesia: Learning of new facts and associations. *Human neurobiology, 6*, 107-118.

Schacter, D.L. (1987b). Implicit memory: History and current status. *Journal of Experimental Psychology: Learning, Memory, and Cognition, 13*, 501-518.

Schacter, D.L. (1985). Priming of old and new knowledge in amnesic patients and normal subjects. *Annals of the New York Academy of Sciences, 444*, 41-53.

Schacter, D.L. Glisky, E.L. & McGlynn, S.M. (in press). Impact of memory disorder on everyday life: Awareness of deficit and return to work. In D. Tupper & K. Cicerone (Eds.), *The neuropsychology of everyday life.* Boston: Martinus Nijoff.

Schacter, D.L. & Graf, P. (1986a). Effects of elaborative processing on implicit and explicit memory for new associations. *Journal of Experimental Psychology: Learning, Memory and Cognition, 12,* 432-444.

Schacter, D.L. & Graf, P. (1986b). Preserved learning in amnesic patients: Perspectives from research on direct priming. *Journal of Clinical and Experimental Neuropsychology, 8,* 727-743.

Schacter, D.L. & Tulving, E. (1982). Memory, amnesia, and the episodic/semantic distinction. In R.L. Isaacson & N.E. Spear (Eds.). *The expression of knowledge.* New York: Plenum Press.

Shimamura, A.P. (1986). Priming effects in amnesia: Evidence for a dissociable memory function. *Quarterly Journal of Experimental Psychology, 384,* 619-644.

Shimamura, A.P. & Squire, L.R. (1984). Paired-associate learning and priming effects in amnesia: A neuropsychological study. *Journal of Experimental Psychology: General, 113,* 556-570.

Squire, L.R. (1987). *Memory and brain.* New York: Oxford University Press.

Squire, L.R. & Butters, N. (1984). *Neuropsychology of memory.* New York: Guilford Press.

Tulving, E. (1985). How many memory systems are there? *American Psychologist, 40,* 385-398.

Warrington, E.K. & Weiskrantz, L. (1974). The effect of prior learning on subsequent retention in amnesic patients. *Neuropsychologia, 12,* 419-428.

Whitty, C.M.W. & Zangwill, O. (1977). *Amnesia.* London: Butterworths.

Williams, M.D., Hollan, J.D., & Stevens, A.L. (1983). Human reasoning about a simple physical system. In D. Gentner & A.L. Stevens (Eds.). *Mental models.* Hillsdale, NJ: Erlbaum.

Young, R.M. (1983). Surrogates and mappings: Two kinds of conceptual models for interactive devices. In D. Gentner & A.L. Stevens (Eds.) *Mental models.* Hillsdale, NJ: Erlbaum.

5

Aging and Spatial Cognition: Current Status and New Directions for Experimental Researchers and Cognitive Neuropsychologists

Kathleen C. Kirasic

It is quite common for us humans to find ourselves in new and unfamiliar environments. Whether we encounter these environments by choice (e. g. traveling to a new city or country) or by accident (e. g. becoming lost), we attempt to make sense of the spatial arrangement of that large-scale environment and navigate successfully within it. The cognitive mechanisms employed in the task of spatial wayfinding and orientation, whether it be a novel or familiar environment, has been a topic of study for many years (see Hart & Moore, 1973 and Siegel & White, 1975 for reviews). The majority of the empirical investigations have focused on the development of these skills in children or on the components of these skills in young adult populations (Cohen, 1985). The bulk of this work relied upon table top models of spatial arrays or paper and pencil measures of spatial knowledge (Horn & Cattell, 1966; Huttenlocher & Presson, 1973; Pick & Rieser, 1982). Only over the past 10 years has there been a concerted effort put forth to exam macrospatial (or large-scale) knowledge and behavior (Evans, Brennan, Skorpanich, & Held, 1984; Kirasic & Allen, 1985; Kirasic, in press; Walsh, Krauss, & Regnier, 1981). Again, however, most researchers in this area have worked with children and/or young adults (Allen, 1981; Cornell & Heth, 1982; Cohen & Cohen, 1982). Changes or lack of changes in macrospatial ability and macrospatial performance that accompany increasing age has only recently become an area of interest and study in cognitive psychology. It is the purpose of this chapter to provide a summary of what is known about spatial cognitive changes with age. Five major areas will be reviewed: 1) findings from the psychometric and experimental literature; 2) the spatial activities commonly engaged in by elderly adults; 3) the research focusing on spatial behavior in macrospatial environments; 4) the applicable neurological literature; and 5) some conclusions, implications, and questions for future research.

Kirasic, K. C. (1988). Aging and spatial cognition: Current status and new directions for experimental researchers and cognitive neuropsychologists. In J. M. Williams & C. J. Long (Eds.), *Cognitive approaches to neuropsychology,* New York: Plenum.

Psychometric and Experimental Research Findings

The psychometric study of spatial abilities has had a long history (Guilford, 1967). Numerous batteries of spatial tests have been developed. One comprehensive and frequently used series of spatial tasks are found in the Kit of Factor-Referenced Cognitive Tests (Ekstrom, French, & Harman, 1976). The typical finding stemming from standardized psychometric instruments reflects evidence of a general age-related decrement in cognitive and perceptual-motor functioning. The greatest decrements are reliably found on tasks requiring flexibility in the face of novel, abstract tasks. This decrement, in what has been called fluid intelligence (Horn & Cattell, 1966), has been attributed largely to problems in maintaining concentration and in apprehending organization which are expressed in short term memory and speeded performance. Figure 1 summarizes effectively the points of interest with regard to this research area.

Examination of these data reveals the greatest decline during this period to be Spatial Orientation (approximately a 19% decline), followed by Speed of Closure (11% decline), Visualization (6% decline), and finally Flexibility of Closure (5% decline) (Cattell, 1963; Horn & Cattell, 1967). The general conclusion to be drawn from the Psychometric domain is to expect a drop in spatial ability and spatial competence with increasing age.

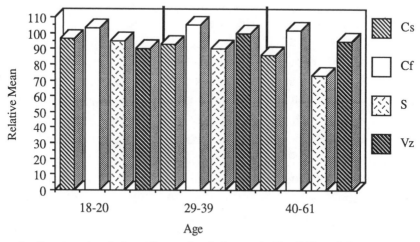

Figure 1. Cross-sectional view of age-related changes in Flexibility of Closure (Cf), Speed of Closure (Cs), Visualization (Vz), and Spatial Orientation (S) provided by the psychometric method (Horn and Cattell, 1966).

A review of the experimental research indicates that the literature can be broken down into the following areas of study: 1) Spatial perception via visuospatial illusions; 2) Applications of spatial concepts; 3) Mental rotation of spatial stimuli; 4) Spatial memory; and 5) Macrospatial cognition (see Kirasic & Allen, 1985 for review). By and large, the general finding, again, is an age related decline in all of the above areas of spatial performance.

However, over the past few years, researchers have suggested that the decline observed in many of these studies may reflect the esoteric nature of many of these tasks or stimuli (Jacewicz & Hartley, 1979; Kirasic, 1981; Krauss, Awad, & McCormick, 1981; Ohta, 1981). More recently, studies that have been designed using familiar stimuli and situations have demonstrated no or markedly smaller age-related declines.

A study conducted by Waddell and Rogoff (1981) serves a good example of this current research. Two test environments were employed in this project. Participants were asked to recall the location of test items in either a neighborhood-like panorama setting or in a partitioned-off cubical setting.

Results from the analyses of the number of objects correctly placed are shown in the next figure and indicate that performance of the elderly adults is poorer in the cubical setting. Similar patterns of finding were found in other dependent measures.

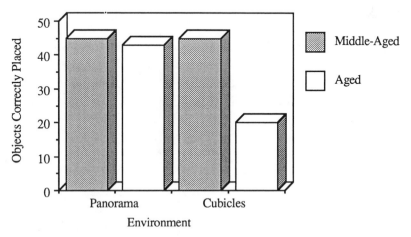

Figure 2. Number of objects correctly placed as a function of contextual setting.

Recently, Craik (1987) explained similar findings using the term "environmental support". The panorama, in this case, provided more "environmental support" or context in organizing the spatial relationships between objects in the array. Meaningfulness of the stimuli, familiarity of the task, and how closely the task approximates real world spatial behavior and activities appear to have a positive effect on the performance of elderly adult to a greater extent than it does to a younger adult (Kirasic, 1981; Waddell & Rogoff, 1981). These findings, however, do not necessarily negate the considerable psychometric or traditional experimental findings. Rather, the two approaches, traditional psychometric/experimental and contextual /ecological, complement each other in providing a more complete picture of the competencies, capabilities, and compensations made by elderly adults in various tasks.

Spatial Activities of Elderly Adults

It is accurate to say that for most psychometric and experimental spatial research very little attention is given to the nature of the spatial activities in which elderly adults actually engage. While the reductionist approach of the psychometricians or the tightly controlled and constrained work of the traditional experimentalist has their place in contemporary psychology, it can be argued that time has come to take our experimental tools out into the world and investigate the actual behaviors of individuals in the environment. One way to do this, is to get an idea of the spatial activities in which elderly adults actually engage and distill that information into reasonable questions for investigation purposes.

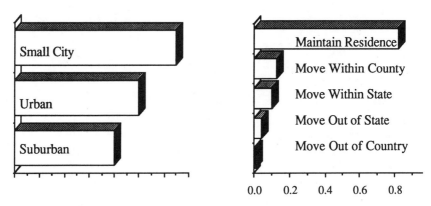

Figure 3 (Left). Proportion of the population aged 65 and over in these three settings.
Figure 4 (Right). Trends in mobility for elderly adults. Numbers indicate proportion of total.

An investigation of recent census data resulted in the identification of three data bases than may be of primary concern to spatial researchers. Those areas focus on the 1) residential distribution and mobility of elderly adults, 2) trends in labor force participation and occupations, and 3) transportation utilization. The data represented in Figures 3-6 provide information on the healthy, noninstitutionalized elderly adults in our country. A review of these figures provides an interesting picture of today's elderly adults. Figures 3 and 4 provide an idea of the residential distribution and diversity that characterizes the elderly adults' lifestyles.

By far, most older individuals have been in the same residence for a relatively long period of time, presumably with well established patterns of spatial behavior involving trips to work and other necessary destinations (e.g. physician, bank, etc.). There are, however, a considerable number of elderly adults who face adjusting to a new residence and establishing new patterns of travel to necessary and desired locations. The data further indicate that older adults are still quite active in the labor force both, full time and part time, and are the primary source of their own transportation. Those who do not drive, utilize other sources for their transportation.

In all, these data suggest that elderly adults are active participants in and users of their environment. However, it is important to note that certain spatial activities may be assumed to be common to individuals across lifestyles and age range. Everyone is faced with the task of navigating to and from neces-

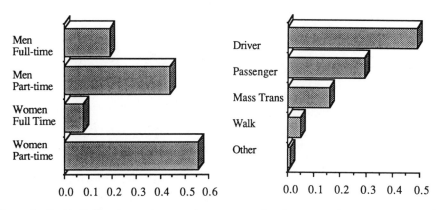

Figure 5. (Left) Full and part-time employment standing by men and women over age 65.
Figure 6. (Right) Modes of transportation utilized by elderly adults and the percentage of use for each mode listed.

sary and desired destinations using some means of transportation, and everyone must rely on spatial memory for the day-to-day activity of locating objects in the home or place of work. These problems represent reasonable foci for researchers interested in studying the role of spatial cognition in the daily lives of elderly adults.

Macrospatial Cognition

Macrospace or large-scale space has been defined as a space so large such that its entirety cannot be perceived from a single vantage point within that space (Kuipers, 1978). Two processes that appear critical in the study of macrospatial cognition in elderly adults are memory for spatial location and maintenance of spatial orientation. While these processes are not unique to elderly adults, it is important to note that too little is known about the effects of normal aging on the processes involved in these activities and in solving problems inherent to them.

Very few psychologists studying macrospatial cognitive processing actually investigate the phenomena of their interest in the environment or real world itself. The ventures that have attempted to capture the large scale environment in their labs or that have conducted their investigations in macrospatial settings are indeed ambitious endeavors.

The seminal piece of macrospatial research was conducted by an interdisciplinary research team at the Andrus Gerontology Center in California (Walsh, Krauss, & Regnier, 1981). The purpose of the study was to examine the relationships among spatial abilities which included experimental as well as paper and pencil measures of spatial abilities, macrospatial knowledge as defined as neighborhood knowledge resulting from map construction tasks, and neighborhood use, referring to the use of goods and services by the subjects. An extensive data set was accumulated. However, the one pertinent finding, with regard to this discussion, indicated that the tests of spatial abilities via experimental and psychometric assessment were, in fact, significant predictors of neighborhood knowledge. Not surprisingly, it was also found that neighborhood knowledge was a significant predictor of use of goods and services in the neighborhood. However, central to all of this was the finding that the relationship between spatial abilities and neighborhood use was found not to be significant. These findings suggest that performance on traditional experimental and psychometric measures of spatial abilities may not represent the actual macrospatial competence of the individual. In light of these findings, it is important to temper inferences regarding extant macrospatial abilities using the results from laboratory based spatial measures alone.

In line with this approach to the study of spatial competence in healthy elderly adults, a series of were conducted by Kirasic. The result of three studies, in particular, supports the previous contention that no experimental or psychometric findings regarding spatial abilities are sufficient in and of themselves in ascribing spatial competence to elderly adults.

Studies by Kirasic and her colleagues (Ackerman, Kirasic, & Haggerty, 1987; Bernicki & Kirasic, 1987; Kirasic, 1981; Kirasic, in prep) have indicated that familiarity with the environment has a significant influence on elderly adults' performance of macrospatial cognitive tasks. Specifically, in one experiment it was found that young, middle-aged, and elderly residents of a small city were equally accurate in a perspective-taking task that required subjects to produce direction and distance estimates to a number of locations in their home town (Figure 7). When the same task demands involved a number of locations learned in a laboratory setting, the performance of the same elderly subjects was worse than that of young adults in the lab setting and worse than their own performance when hometown locations had been used in the task.

A second study conducted in supermarkets that were either familiar or unfamiliar to young and elderly subjects further documented the effect of fa-

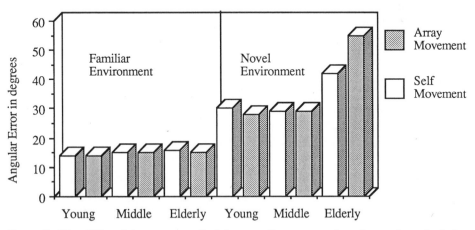

Figure 7. The ability of three groups of adults to perform two modes of mental manipulation utilizing landmarks in familiar and novel environments.

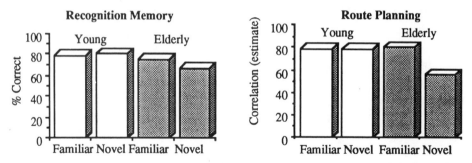

Figure 8. (Left) Recognition memory performance by young and elderly adults in a familiar and novel environment.
Figure 9. (Right) A comparison of routes planned by two groups of adults in two different environments to the most efficient route in each environment.

miliarity on the spatial performance of older adults. After a brief tour of the unfamiliar supermarket, young and elderly adults showed equivalent performance on a recognition test involving scenes from the stores (Figure 8). However, elderly adults were better at planning routes and identifying specific item locations in the familiar supermarket than in the novel store. Environment familiarity did not affect the performance of young adults on these two tasks (Figure 9).

Kirasic has also investigated the predictive validity of psychometric and experimental spatial tasks for elderly adults' performance on macrospatial tasks in real-world settings. The aforementioned study involving tasks in novel and familiar supermarkets revealed no significant correlations between psychometric tests of spatial abilities (i.e., visualization, spatial relations, and visual memory) and older adults' performance in either supermarket setting (Kirasic, in prep). A second study has substantiated the finding of low correlations between psychometric measures of spatial abilities and measures of performance on real-world tasks. However this larger study has also revealed that performance on experimental tasks that involve components of real-world situations may be significant predictors of everyday macrospatial performance. Specifically, elderly adults' performance on a task in which they selected effective landmarks from a slide sequence portraying a walk through an actual neighborhood has been found to be correlated significantly with their performance on a behavioral efficiency task. The search for additional statistical relationships among experimental measures, psychometric measures, and measures of performance in actual environments is continuing as this study progresses.

Neurological Implications for Spatial Performance

One area of research that is rarely included in a review or discussion of elderly adults' macrospatial cognitive abilities is that of the neuropsychological implications of aging to spatial cognition. A review of the literature implicates a number of different neurological sites as being responsible for spatial/wayfinding abilities. The area of the brain that have been highlighted as playing some role in spatial performance are the right temporal neocortex, the right frontal lobe, the right parietal, the amygdala of the right hemisphere, and the right hippocampus. A considerable amount of work in this area has focused on the contribution of the right hippocampus to spatial performance. Despite disagreement regarding the extent of the role the hippocampus plays in spatial functioning, the majority of researchers attribute the hippocampus as being a major contributor to the coordination and consolidation of spatial information.

Over the past 10 years, significant progress has been made toward localizing the area or areas of the brain responsible for spatial abilities in the general sense. The work of a number of researchers (e.g. O'Keefe & Nadel, 1978; Olton, 1982, 1986; Olton, Becker, & Handelmann, 1979; Smith & Milner, 1981, 1984) doing human and animal studies have provided some insights in two major categories of interest in large scale spatial research, namely, memory for spatial location and spatial orientation.

In the study of memory for spatial location, Smith and Milner (1984) focused on the impact of temporal lobectomies in either the left or right hemisphere. The two temporal lobectomy groups and a group of normal controls were tested on the incidental recall of objects and their locations in an array both immediately and after a 24hr-delay. The results of the Object recall task are shown in Figure 10. As can be seen, the only group showing impairment on the task was the left temporal lobe group in the delay condition. Results for the recall of absolute location task are shown in Figure 11. Analyses indicated that in both recall conditions, immediate and delayed, only the right temporal group demonstrated deficits. By breaking the groups down further into subgroups reflecting degree of excision (either > or < 1.5cm), it was shown that the right temporal, large excision subgroup manifested considerable deficits (Figure 12). This group was impaired relative to all others in immediate recall and significantly worse than the controls and both left temporal subgroups in the delay condition.

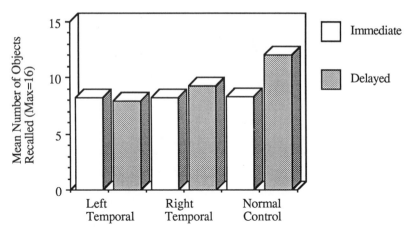

Figure 10. Performance by controls and two different lesion groups on an object naming task immediately after presentation and after a 24-hour delay.

In a similar study, but with a delay of only 4 minutes, Smith and Milner (1981) demonstrated the same dramatic results (Figure 13). These results support the notion that lesions of the right temporal lobe will result in impairments of recall of spatial location. This appears to be especially true if there is severe damage to the right hippocampal region.

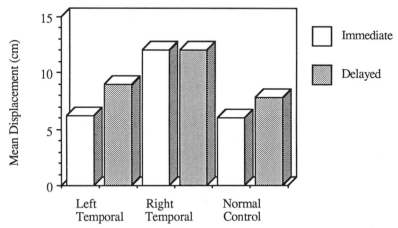

Figure 11. Performance by controls and two lesion groups on an object placement task, immediately and after 24-hour delay.

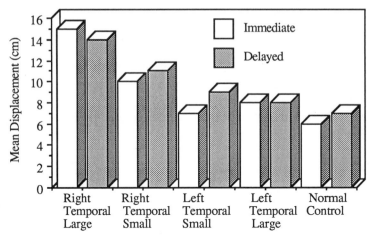

Figure 12. Performance by normal controls and four lesion groups, categorized by location and extent of excision, on an immediate and 24-hour delayed object placement task.

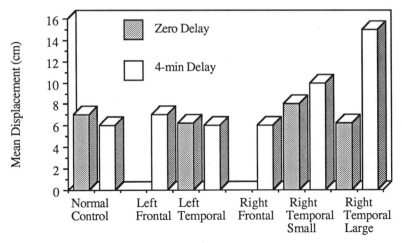

Figure 13. Performance by normal controls and five lesion groups in an immediate and 4-minute delayed object placement task.

One particular study by Ungerleider and Mishkin (1982) in which primates were to learn the location occupied by a particular object point to the hippocampus as the coordinator of spatial locational information. These researchers have identified two, what they refer to as, multisynaptic cortico-cortical pathways in the primate visual system; an occipitotemporal pathway and an occipitoparietal pathway. They hypothesize that the ventral, occipitotemporal pathway is specialized for object perception. Whereas, the pathway from the occipital to the parietal lobe is concerned with the perception of location and of spatial relations among objects. In their analyses, the authors suggest that memory for a location occupied by a particular object requires the association of the separately stored representation of the object in the temporal cortex and the separately stored representation of the spatial location in the parietal cortex. Ungerleider and Mishkin (1982) and others (O'Keefe & Nadel, 1978; Gaffan & Saunders, 1985) suggest that the hippocampus is the structure that mediates this association.

In reviewing the area of spatial orientation, De Renzie (1982) provides a comprehensive review of disorders in topographical memory. However, much of the research cited reflects performance by patients on pencil and paper tests or table top models. Similarly, the majority of the clinical accounts of disorders in large-scale spatial navigation describe the nature of the problem or compensations made by individuals in order to way find successfully.

However, one exception to this is a recent study conducted by Van Der Linden and Seron (1986). In their examination of a patient showing a right cortico-subcortical fronto-parietal lesion, the authors were able to demonstrate the selective breakdown in configurational knowledge (global, organized, integrated information regarding the relationship of locations in an euclidian space) to the maintenance of route knowledge (knowledge pertinent to a particular pathway) in this individual. The primary difference between these two types of spatial knowledge lies in the fact that the relationship of multiple paths is not necessary for route knowledge thereby serving as the critical point of departure from configurational knowledge.

A series of tasks were devised that would allow for the dissociation between these two kinds of spatial knowledge. The tasks as well as the patient's performance on them are shown in Table 1. It is shown that performance on route knowledge tasks yield relatively accurate performance while extremely poor performance is shown for configurational knowledge. This evidence suggests that the distinction between route knowledge and configurational knowledge, which has been incorporated into a number of conceptual frameworks for spatial cognition, has some basis in neurophysiology.

While it has been shown, in this limited discussion of the neurophysiology of spatial cognition, that the nature of specific spatial deficits can be associated with particular sites of trauma or lesion, very little can be said regarding the normal course of brain-behavior functioning as it applies to spatial abilities in the "healthy" independent living elderly adult. The one exception

Table 1

Findings of Patient with Right Frontal-Parietal Lesion

Route Knowledge	Accuracy
Descriptions	Good
Responses to direct questions	83%
Detection of false routes	84%
Detection of errors along routes	100%

Configural Knowledge	Accuracy
Direction estimation	26%
Distance estimation	27%
Map placement	20%
Detection of road distortions	10%
Map Drawing	Poor

to this, is a study conducted by Stern and Baldinger (1983). In this study, the notion of "preferred modes of information processing" as indexed by lateral eye movements was investigated employing tasks of fluid (spatial) or crystalized (verbal) intelligence. Young and elderly adults were first identified as either right movers (left hemisphere people) or left movers (right hemisphere people). The tasks and results are found in Figure 14.

The results suggest differential declines in information processing abilities as a function of preferred mode of information processing in older subjects. Old right movers perform significantly better than old left movers on tasks tapping both fluid and crystalized intelligence. Old left movers perform significantly more poorly on these tasks when compared to young left movers, while no differences between young and old right movers were obtained. What these data tend to suggest is a selective impairment in right hemisphere function as a result of aging. These results further suggest that those who place greater reliance on the use of this hemisphere will show greater deficits in all aspects of intellectual performance than those with a preference for using their left hemispheres.

While this study lacks precision in pinpointing selective cortical changes in the elderly left movers (right hemisphere people), there are three aspects to

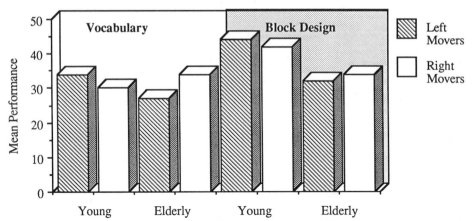

Figure 14. Effect of "preferred mode of information processing" in young and elderly adults on verbal and spatial tasks.

this study that make it particularly useful and informative for the researcher studying normal aging. First, it did not employ a clinical population. Secondly, it focused on relatively healthy, independent living elderly adults. Finally, it employed an albeit crude, but in this case, a successful non-invasive technique to evaluate "information processing preference" and subsequent performance on verbal and spatial tasks. The results of this study are interesting and point the way to future efforts in this area.

Direction for Future Work

Thus far, the emphasis and focus of this chapter has been on the role of the right hippocampus and right hemisphere in the processing of spatial information. However, it appears from some literature that further study of the right hemisphere may provide some insights into normal cognitive changes accompanying aging. It has been suggested by Poon (personal communication, February 1987) that the question of differential age-related decline in the functioning of the two cerebral hemispheres has not been adequately addressed.

Two studies should be noted with regard to this particular issue. Klisz (1978) found that subtests on the Halstead-Reitan Battery that are indicators of right hemisphere damage discriminate middle-aged controls from older controls better than subtests that are indicators of either left hemisphere or diffuse brain damage. Furthermore, in a survey of the evidence by Albert and Kaplan (1980), it was stated that there is evidence for both frontal and right hemisphere decline with normal aging.

The task ahead then is to investigate the validity of these conclusions. Collaborative efforts, consisting of a cognitive neuropsychologist and an experimental cognitive researcher, would be a profitable pairing of expertise in approaching this particular question. By working together, this team could more efficiently and more completely identify and evaluate whether or not there are confounding problems in the psychometric instruments employed or in the theoretical postulations that led to the conclusions.

The legitimacy of these conclusions of age-related differential hemispheric decline could be evaluated in a multi-step procedure that would 1) examine the theoretical postulations of hemispheric asymmetrical decline in the psychological and biological literature, 2) tease apart the psychometric instruments and the various functions they measure and 3) tease apart controlled laboratory experiments that examine age differences. Substantive conclusions could then be made as a result of the combination of this tripartite procedure.

The implications of the age and hemispheric asymmetry question would be to determine *why* and *how* this differential decline in the right hemisphere occurs. Additionally, from a life span developmental perspective the question of *when* could also be added to the investigation. Numerous other questions would then, as a result of these initial efforts, emerge to expand our understanding.

By working together on tasks of this type both the cognitive neuropsychologist and the experimental psychologist would benefit from the results. The field of psychology, itself, would gain from these types of unified efforts in that a broader and more comprehensive understanding of the basis of brain/behavior relationships, as they occur in a normal aging population, would be obtained.

During the preparation of this chapter, the author was supported by Grant AG05169-02 from the National Institute on Aging and awarded to Old Dominion University, Norfolk, VA. The author also wishes to thank the Department of Psychology at the University of South Carolina for its support in the preparation of this manuscript.

References

Ackerman, K.M., Kirasic, K.C.,& Haggerty, D. (1987). *Macrospatial cognitive abilities in young and elderly adults: A comparison of experimental and self-assessment measures*. Presented at the meetings of the Eastern Psychological Association, Crystal City, MD.

Albert, M.S. & Kaplan, E. (1980). Organic implications of neuropsychological deficits in the elderly. In L. Poon et al. (Eds.), *New Directions in Memory and Aging*. Hillsdale, NJ.: Erlbaum.

Allen, G.L. 1981. A developmental perspective on the effects of "subdividing" macrospatial experience. *Journal of Experimental Psychology: Human Leaning and Memory*. 7, 120-132.

Bernicki, M.R. & Kirasic, K.C. (1987). *An investigation of temporospatial integration abilities in elderly adults*. Presented at the meetings of the Gerontological Society, Washington, DC.

Catell, R.B. (1963). Theory of fluid and crystallized intelligence: A critical experiment. *Journal of Educational Psychology*. 54, 1-22.

Cohen, R. 1985. *The development of spatial cognition*. Hillsdale, NJ: Lawrence Erlbaum Associates.

Cohen, S. & Cohen, R. (1982). Distance estimates as a function of type of activity in the environment. *Child Development*. 53, 834-837.

Cornell, E.H. & Heth, C.D. (1983). Spatial cognition: Gathering strategies used by preschool children. *Journal of Experimental Child Psychology*. 35, 93-110.

Craik, F. (1987). *Overview and theoretical issues*. Presented at the First Cognitive Aging Conference, Atlanta, GA.

De Renzi, E. (1982). *Disorders of space exploration and cognition*. New York: John Wiley & Sons.

Ekstrom, R., French, J.W., & Harman, H. (1976). *Manual for kit of factor-referenced cognitive tests*. Princeton, NJ: Educational Testing Service.

Evans, G.W., Brennan, P.L., Skorpanich, M.A., & Held, D. (1984). Cognitive mapping and elderly adults: Verbal and location memory for urban landmarks. *Journal of Gerontology*. 39, 452-457.

Gaffan, D. & Saunders, R.C. (1985). Running recognition of configural stimuli by fornix-transected monkeys. *Quarterly Journal of Experimental Psychology*. 37, 452-457.

Guilford, J.P. (1967). *The nature of human intelligence*. New York: McGraw-Hill.

Hart, R.A. & Moore, G.T. (1973). The development of spatial cognition: A review. In R. Downs & D. Stea (Eds.), *Image and environment*. Chicago: Aldine.

Horn, J.L. & Cattell, R.B. (1966). Age differences in primary ability factors. *Journal of Gerontology, 21*, 277-299.

Huttenlocher, J. & Presson, C.C. (1973). Mental rotation and the perspective problem. *Cognitive Psychology, 4*, 277-299.

Jacewitz, M.H. & Hartley A.A. (1979). Rotation of mental images by young and old college students: The effects of familiarity. *Journal of Gerontology*. 34, 396-403.

Kirasic, K.C. (1981). Studying the "hometown advantage" in elderly adults' spatial cognition and spatial behavior. Paper presented as part of the symposium, *Spatial cognition in older adults: From lab to life*, at the meetings of the Society for Research in Child Development, Boston, MA.

Kirasic, K.C. (1986). *Macrospatial cognition in young and elderly adults.* Presented at the meetings of the Gerontological Society, Chicago, IL.

Kirasic, K.C. *Spatial cognition: A comparison of psychometric, experimental, and environmental assessments.* In preparation.

Kirasic, K.C. (in press). Acquisition and utilization of spatial information by elderly adults: Implications for day-to-day situations. To appear in L. Poon, D. Rubin, & B. Wilson (eds.), *Everyday cognition in adulthood and late life: Proceedings of the Third George Talland Memorial Conference.*

Kirasic, K.C. & Allen, G.L. (1985). Aging, spatial performance, and spatial competence. In N. Charness (Ed.), *Aging and performance.* London: John Wiley and Sons.

Klisz, D. (1978). Neuropsychological evaluation of older persons. In M. Storandt, E.C. Siegler, & M.F. Elias (Eds.), *The clinical psychology of aging.* New York: Plenum Press.

Krauss, I.K., Awad, Z.A., & McCormick, D.J. (1981). Learning, remembering, and using spatial information as an older adult. Paper presented as part of the symposium *Spatial cognition in older adults: From lab to life*, at the meetings of the Society for Research in Child Development, Boston, MA.

Kuipers, B.J. (1978). Modeling spatial knowledge. *Cognitive Science. 2*, 129-153.

Ohta, R.J. (1981). Spatial problem solving: The response selection tendencies of young and elderly adults. *Experimental Aging Research. 7*, 81-84.

O'Keefe, J. & Nadel, L. (1978). *The hippocampus as a cognitive map.* Oxford: Clarenden Press.

Olton, D.S. (1982). Spatially organized behaviors of animals: Behavioral and Neurological Studies. In M.Potegal (Ed.), *Spatial Abilities: Development and Physiological Foundations.* New York: Academic Press.

Olton, D.S. (1986). Temporally constant and temporally changing spatial memory: Single unit correlates in the hippocampus. In P. Ellen and C. Thinus-Blanc (Eds.), *Cognitive Processes and Spatial Orientation in Animal and Man.* Dordrecht, Netherlands: Martinus Nyhoff.

Olton, D.S., Becker, J.T., & Handelmann, G.E. (1979). Hippocampus, space and memory. *The Behavioral and Brain Sciences. 2*, 313-365.

Pick, H.L. Jr. & Rieser, J.J. (1982). Children's cognitive mapping. In M. Potegal (Ed.), *Spatial abilities: Development and physiological foundations.* New York: Academic Press.

Siegel, A.W. & White, S.H. (1975). In H.W. Reese (ed.), *Advances in Child Development and Behavior, vol. 10.* New York: Academic Press.

Smith, M.L. & Milner, B. (1981). The role of the right hippocampus in the recall of spatial location. *Neuropsychologia. 6*, 781-793.

Smith, M.L. & Milner, B. (1984). Differential effects of frontal-lobe lesions on cognitive estimation and spatial memory. *Neuropsychologia. 22*, 697-705.

Stern, J.A. & Baldinger, A.C. (1983). Hemispheric differences in preferred modes of information processing and the aging process. *International Journal of Neuroscience. 18*, 97-106.

Ungerleider, L.G. & Mishkin, M. (1982). Two cortical visual systems. In D.J. Ingle, M.A. Goodale, & J.J.W. Mansfield (eds.), *Analysis of Visual Behavior*. Cambridge, MA: The MIT Press.

Van Der Linden, M. & Seron, X. (1986). A case of dissociation in topographical disorders: The selective breakdown of vector-map representation. In P. Ellen and C. Thinus-Blanc (eds.), *Cognitive Processes and Spatial Orientation in Animal and Man*. Dordrecht, Netherlands: Martinus Nyhoff.

Waddell, K.J. & Rogoff, B. (1981). The effect of contextual organization on the spatial memory of middle aged and older women. *Developmental Psychology*. *17*, 878-885.

Walsh, D.A., Krauss, I.K., & Regnier, V.A. (1981). Spatial ability, environmental knowledge, and environmental use: The elderly. In L. Liben, A. Patterson, & N. Newcombe (Eds.), *Spatial Representation and Behavior Across the Life Span*. New York: Academic Press.

6

An Integrated Approach to the Neuropsychological Assessment of Cognitive Function

Robert L. Mapou

Historically, results of neuropsychological assessment have been used to determine the presence and location of brain damage. As neurodiagnostic technology has advanced, the focus of assessment has begun to shift from localization to delineation of cognitive function. Cognition, however, is an internal process and cannot be observed. In contrast, performance on a neuropsychological test is observable. According to Kaplan (1983), neuropsychological tests are instruments which are used to elicit behavior which the examiner may observe. From these observations, the experienced neuropsychologist may then make inferences about the patient's cognition.

This chapter will present an approach to neuropsychological assessment, the primary focus of which is to delineate cognitive strengths and weaknesses. Several issues will be addressed. First, the components of an evaluation which are needed to develop inferences about cognition will be discussed. It will be shown that some current assessment methods frequently do not include all of these components. The cognitive neuropsychological and Boston process approaches to assessment will be presented as attempts to surmount these difficulties. The strengths and limitations of each approach will be discussed, and from these discussions, an approach to neuropsychological evaluation, which integrates the strengths of these two approaches, will be developed.

Developing Inferences About Cognitive Functioning

To develop inferences about a patient's cognitive functioning, several components, at minimum, are needed. First, a model of cognition should be used to guide assessment. This issue will be discussed further below. A second requirement is the use of hypothesis-testing to develop and test inferences about cognition. By beginning an evaluation with specific hypotheses about the patient's cognitive strengths and weaknesses, and by then using test performance to generate new hypotheses and to select subsequently administered measures, neither strengths nor weaknesses will be missed. In contrast, battery-based approaches, in which the same tests are administered to every pa-

Mapou, R. L. (1988). An integrated approach to neuropsychological assessment of cognitive function. In J. M. Williams & C. J. Long (Eds.), *Cognitive approaches to neuropsychology*, New York: Plenum.

tient regardless to etiology, are weak since they do not allow the clinician to go beyond the battery and assess other functions. Many of the tests may be irrelevant to the difficulties that the patient is having, while failing to assess particular areas of difficulty. For example, the Halstead-Reitan Neuropsychological Test Battery (Reitan & Wolfson, 1985) includes neither an adequate assessment of memory functioning nor an adequate assessment of reading skills. For patients suffering disorders of memory or reading, this battery will be incomplete.

Hypothesis-testing is based upon behavioral responses to administered procedures since, as noted, cognitive processes cannot be observed. Because these procedures are multi-factorial, however, and require multiple cognitive processes for performance (Kaplan, 1983; Walsh, 1985), it is usually impossible to draw conclusions about cognition from a single measure. Thus, a third requirement of this type of evaluation is the inclusion of different measures, the results of which, when examined together, converge upon a conclusion about a particular cognitive function. Again, a battery-based approach will usually not provide enough different sources of information to be able to draw these types of conclusions.

Problems in Current Research and Practice

Although models of various cognitive processes have been developed and verified empirically (cf, Anderson, 1983; Coltheart, Job, & Sartori, 1987; Coltheart, Patterson, & Marshall, 1980; Deloche & Seron, 1987; Ellis & Young, 1987; Patterson, Marshall, & Coltheart, 1985; Posner, Walker, Friedrich, & Rafal, 1984; Roeltgen, 1985; Squire & Butters, 1984), the application of these models to clinical practice tends to be the exception rather than the rule. Most clinical neuropsychologists have their own models of cognition which guide assessment. These models may be specified either explicitly or implicitly. Although there are similarities among models, terms used by one clinician may be used differently by another. Thus, one clinician reading the report of another may have to refer to the tests themselves in order to interpret the findings. Imagine, for a moment, what it would be like if every physician had a different model of physiological functioning which he or she used to interpret diagnostic findings! In some ways, the present state of clinical neuropsychology suffers exactly from this problem.

Paralleling the lack of a standardized model is disagreement about definitions of cognitive functioning. When comparing reports of neuropsychological evaluation or of empirical work, it is often the case that different terms may be used to refer to the same function, or that the same term may be used to refer to different functions. For example, this author has observed that the Block Design subtest of the Wechsler Adult Intelligence Scale-Revised (WAIS-R; Wechsler, 1981) may be variously referred to as a measure of visuospatial skills, visuomotor skills, visuoconstructional skills, visuospatial constructional skills, nonverbal intellectual skills, nonverbal problem-solving skills, nonverbal planning skills, nonverbal organizational skills, and so on.

Another difficulty is the way in which multi-factorial tests are applied and interpreted. Although ideally tests should be designed to assess individual cognitive functions, both the lack of knowledge about individual functions and the fact that any behaviorally-based task will always require many cognitive components for completion makes this unlikely. Thus, performance on any test requires multiple cognitive skills, and it cannot automatically be assumed that a poor test performance by one patient occurs for the same reason as a poor test performance by another patient. Unfortunately, in both clinical practice and research, performance on a single task may be equated with a particular cognitive function, and it may be concluded that a poor performance reflects a breakdown in that particular function, rather than in the contributing component functions.

Clinical and research reports may also lack information about the performance itself. This is particularly true of battery-based approaches, in which performance may be characterized by score only. For example, Kaplan (1983) has shown that patients with right hemisphere lesions tend to make errors on visuospatial constructional tasks which reflect difficulty reproducing figure contour or configuration, but patients with left hemisphere lesions make errors which reflect difficulty reproducing inner details. Thus, the same score on the Block Design subtest of the WAIS-R may be associated with two entirely different patterns of performance. Information about the way in which a patient has solved or has failed to solve a problem is essential to understanding which cognitive functions are impaired. It is this type of information which is most frequently lacking in research reports, where data are presented in terms of group analyses of test scores.

Analysis of group data also obscures differences among individual patterns of performance, which can result in drawing incorrect conclusions about spared and impaired cognitive functions. Caramazza (1986), Marshall and Newcombe (1984), Shallice (1979), and Wilson (1987) have all discussed the problems associated with analysis of group data in neuropsychological research. All have argued for single-case research designs, with a focus on delineation of cognitive function and an emphasis on hypothesis-testing. More recently, Kay, Ezrachi, and Cavallo (1986) and Kay, Ezrachi, Cavallo, and Newman (1987) have directly shown that group analysis of data can result in a failure to identify subgroups of patients with very different patterns of performance.

In summary, the lack of empirically validated models of cognition, disagreement about definitions of terms describing cognitive functioning, equation of test performance with cognition, analysis of test scores without examination of performance, and analysis of group data rather than single-case data are all problems which characterize many current approaches to neuropsychological assessment. These difficulties may be found in both clinical practice and research. In order to improve the ability to delineate a patient's cognitive strengths and weaknesses, an approach to assessment is needed which surmounts all of these problems.

There are two current approaches to assessment which appear to offer solutions to many of these difficulties. The first, the cognitive neuropsychological approach, builds and tests theoretical models of cognitive processes through use of multiple measures which converge on specific aspects of cognitive functioning. The second, the Boston process approach, derives conclusions about spared and impaired functions through use of multi-factorial tests, collection of qualitative data, and testing limits to examine cognitive components of the composite test performances. Each approach will now be examined.

Cognitive Neuropsychology

The basic aim of cognitive neuropsychology is to show the relationship between theories of normal cognitive functioning and the behavior of people in whom cognitive functioning has been impaired by brain damage (Coltheart, 1985; McKenna & Warrington, 1986; Shallice, 1979). Analysis of a particular cognitive process proceeds as follows. First, based upon clinical findings, a modular, information-processing model of the cognitive process is developed. From the model, predictions are made about how impaired subjects should perform in the laboratory. These hypotheses are tested directly, and the model is modified and retested. The model is evaluated in terms of the extent to which it can explain the impairments and preservations in people suffering various forms of disorder of the same cognitive process. A disorder can be explained in a theoretical way by demonstrating that the pattern of impairments and preservations is what would be expected if certain components/modules were damaged while others remained intact.

Cognitive Neuropsychological Analysis of a Reading Disorder

To illustrate application of this approach, an example of the assessment of a reading disorder will be presented. This is, perhaps, the most well-known illustration of cognitive neuropsychological assessment, since much empirical data have been collected to verify and modify the model of reading (Coltheart, 1985; Coltheart, Patterson & Marshall, 1980; Patterson, Marshall, & Coltheart, 1985). Similar types of analyses have been applied to assessment of mathematical disabilities (Deloche & Seron, 1987), language disorders (Coltheart, Job, Sartori, 1987; Roeltgen, 1985), and other specific aspects of cognitive functioning (Ellis & Young, 1987).

The theoretical model of reading used to guide evaluation is illustrated in Figure 1. In addition to analysis of the reading process itself, other components of cognition must also be assessed. Language comprehension must be examined, to rule out the possibility that the reading disorder is secondary to a failure to comprehend language in general. Visuospatial perceptual functioning must also be evaluated, to rule out the possibility that the patient is simply unable to perceive the written word. Finally, the ability to read and identify single letters and the ability to integrate letters into the word form are assessed. Once it has been determined whether a patient is able to perceive and read the written word, and extract information from auditory presentations of

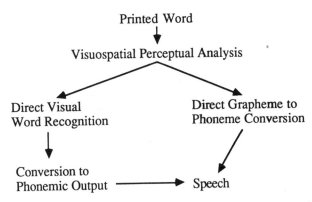

Figure 1. Schematic model of the ability to read single words aloud.

single words, the evaluation continues with assessment of spared and impaired functions as defined in the model.

Grapheme-to phoneme conversion is the decoding of the written word into its phonemic components, to develop an auditory representation. In the model, this representation provides one route to extract meaning from the written word. This component of the model is assessed by having the patient read aloud single words which can be read by application of regular grapheme-to-phoneme conversion rules (e.g., same, shop) and nonsense words which must be sounded out through application of these rules (e.g., wull, boad).

A second route used to extract word meaning is through direct visual recognition of the word form without auditory analysis. Visual word recognition skills are assessed by having the patient read aloud single words which are irregular and cannot be sounded out, but must be recognized (e.g., give, shoe). The relative intactness of grapheme-to-phoneme conversion skills and visual word recognition skills may then be compared by examining the accuracy for each type of word (regular vs. irregular) or nonsense word.

In addition to these comparisons, the ability to read single words aloud as a function of word length, word frequency, and word type (e.g., abstract vs. concrete, parts of speech) must also be evaluated. Differences as a function of these characteristics also have implications for diagnosis of the subtype of reading disorder.

Finally, reading comprehension is evaluated. This should include evaluation of the ability to derive meaning from single words, sentences, and paragraphs.

Throughout the evaluation, error analysis is used to understand the pattern of impaired processes. For example, an error in which grapheme-to-phoneme conversion rules are misapplied (e.g., *tool* read as "two-ole") must be differentiated from an error in which the word produced has a visual similarity to the presented word (e.g., *tool* read as "took"). Comparison with normative data is much less important than comparison of performance among tasks.

There are many strengths to the cognitive neuropsychological approach. Assessment is based upon a theoretical model. Cognitive processes are defined explicitly, definitions are agreed upon among researchers, and predictions from the model are verified empirically. Tests are designed to be single-factored (to the degree that this is possible) and to tap a minimum of cognitive processes. Information about performance, including error analysis, is used to develop an understanding of spared and impaired component skills. Finally, single-case studies allow examination of individual patterns of performance, which would be lost in analysis of group data.

There are, however, a number of weaknesses of this approach. In general, this is an empirical and not a clinical approach. Most of this work has been conducted in the laboratory and not by the clinician. Further, because the approach is empirically based, the availability of tests is limited (Lezak, 1987; White, 1987). Measures are frequently created within the laboratory for a specific study. This also means that normative data, frequently necessary for the clinician, are usually unavailable. The development of these types of measures requires the manipulation of many parameters, as discussed above. Not only does such development take time, it also requires a thorough understanding of the cognitive process under investigation. In sum, although providing a systematic and empirically-based method for assessment of cognitive functioning, the cognitive neuropsychological approach may not be easily applied by the clinician.

The Boston Process Approach

The basic aim of the Boston process approach to neuropsychological assessment is to understand which impaired processes have led to a breakdown on a particular neuropsychological measure and then to use this information diagnostically (Kaplan, 1983; Milberg, Hebben, and Kaplan, 1986). Unlike the theoretically-based cognitive neuropsychological approach, the process approach is clinically-based and better suited to the practitioner. An assessment typically proceeds as follows.

A series of standardized measures are administered. These include typically non-neuropsychological measures, such as the WAIS-R (Wechsler, 1981) and the Wechsler Memory Scale (WMS; Wechsler, 1945) or Wechsler Memory Scale-Revised (Wechsler & Stone, 1987), and neuropsychological measures such as the Rey-Osterrieth Complex Figure Test (ROCF; Lezak, 1983), the California Verbal Learning Test (CVLT; Delis et al., 1987), the Boston Naming Test (BNT; Kaplan, Goodglass, & Weintraub, 1983), the Cookie Theft Picture description from the Boston Diagnostic Aphasia Examination (BDAE; Goodglass & Kaplan, 1983), the Hooper Visual Organization Test (HVOT; Western Psychological Services, 1983), and others (see Milberg,

Hebben, & Kaplan, 1986). Modifications are often made in administration of these measures to provide additional information which will help determine spared and impaired cognitive functions. For example, time limits may be extended or eliminated, additional stimuli or task items may be added, or patients may be asked questions about responses. Task performance is examined closely, and additional data are gathered about performance (e.g., verbal responses are recorded verbatim, drawings are flow-charted by the examiner). Creative limit testing may be used to determine what facilitates and what hinders performance. From performance on initial measures, hypotheses about spared and impaired functions are developed and tested using additional measures. Finally, using performance information, test scores, and knowledge about premorbid functioning, conclusions are drawn about the pattern of spared and impaired functions and the probable diagnosis.

Process Analysis of a Visuospatial Constructional Disorder

To illustrate application of this approach, an example of assessment of a visuospatial constructional disorder will be presented. Such a disorder is characterized by difficulty with motoric reproduction or manipulation of visual stimuli. The presence of the disorder may have emerged during initial testing (e.g., on WAIS-R, WMS, or ROCF), but may also have been discovered during observation of difficulties with activities of daily living and/or independent living skills. Application of the Boston process approach to assess this disorder would include evaluation of at least the following component cognitive skills.

Evaluation of visuospatial perceptual skills is performed to determine whether presented stimuli are being perceived correctly. Assessment could include use of the Visual Form Discrimination Test (Benton et al., 1983), the Judgement of Line Orientation Test (Benton et al., 1983), visuospatial perceptual tasks from Luria's Neuropsychological Investigation (Christensen, 1979), and matching of figures using Kaplan's adaptations of the WMS (Milberg, Hebben, & Kaplan, 1986). Also examined are the types of responses produced on other measures requiring perception of complex visual stimuli, but not necessarily having assessment of perceptual functioning as the primary goal. Such measures include WAIS-R Picture Completion and Picture Arrangement and the BNT.

Gross and fine motor functioning must be assessed, to rule out the contributions of these factors. Assessment may use the Strength of Grip Test (Reitan & Wolfson, 1985), Finger Tapping (Reitan & Wolfson, 1985), Purdue

(Purdue Research Foundation, 1948) and/or Grooved Pegboards (Matthews & Kløve, 1964), and tasks such as WAIS-R Digit Symbol with Kaplan's symbol copy addition (Milberg, Hebben, & Kaplan, 1986) and the Symbol-Digit Modalities Test (Smith, 1973). Object manipulation on writing and drawing tasks and on constructional tasks such as WAIS-R Block Design and Object Assembly is also observed.

Visuospatial constructional skills are assessed directly using the WAIS-R Block Design and Object Assembly subtests, copy of the ROCF, drawings-to-command and copy from the Boston Spatial Quantitative Battery (Borod, Goodglass, & Kaplan, 1980), and copy of the Visual Reproduction designs on the WMS, as adapted by Kaplan (Milberg, Hebben, & Kaplan, 1986).

Throughout the evaluation, speed of performance, attention to task, and maintenance of the required response set are observed. During visuospatial constructional tasks, observation is made of where designs are started and in which direction the patient works (e.g., left-to-right vs. right-to-left), along with the overall style of reproduction, in particular, how the configuration and the details are reproduced and interrelated. Additional manipulations typically include extending task time limits, increasing or decreasing the number of stimuli present (e.g., by having nine or twelve blocks available during Block Design), and providing verbal or nonverbal cuing.

There are many strengths of the Boston process approach. Terms used to describe performance are defined and applied in a standardized fashion. The approach uses commonly available tests and instruments and may be applied to any instrument. The multi-factorial nature of most tests is explicitly recognized, and methods are provided for extracting component skills. Hypothesis testing is used to rule in and rule out explanations of performance. Information about performance and error analysis is used to understand strengths and deficits. Finally, the approach is oriented towards single-case studies.

There are, however, several weaknesses to the approach. There is no empirically-validated model of cognition which is used to guide assessment, such as those developed within the cognitive neuropsychological approach. Instead, assessment and interpretation are based upon clinical data and knowledge which have been collected by Kaplan and her associates over the years. Additionally, the approach was developed to understand the effects of various lesions and diseases on neuropsychological functioning, rather than having as its goal the understanding of cognition. The approach also utilizes standardized measures in non-standardized ways, rendering normative data less than useful. In sum, in contrast to the cognitive neuropsychological approach, the Boston process approach has its basis in clinical practice and is lacking, in some degree, a more empirical base.

An Integrated Approach to Neuropsychological Assessment

Because of the ways that the cognitive neuropsychological approach and Boston process approach complement one another, it would seem desirable to develop an approach to neuropsychological assessment which draws on the strengths of the two approaches while avoiding some of the weaknesses. Such an approach will now be presented, along with an illustration of its application.

The components and assessment procedures include the following. Assessment is guided by a framework of cognition proposed by Cohen (Cohen, 1985; Cohen & Mapou, 1988), but based upon prior research by others, and modified by this author (See Table 1). Terms in the framework are defined and used to interpret results of the evaluation.

Each neuropsychological measure is task-analyzed, in terms of the framework, and a description is developed of those aspects of cognition which appear to be required for successful task performance. For example, Block Design from the WAIS-R requires adequate arousal and attentional functioning, gross and fine upper extremity motor functioning, visuospatial perceptual skills, nonverbal planning, sequencing, and organizational skills, and visuospatial constructional skills. Breakdown of any component skill may lead to a poor performance.

A wide range of standardized and non-standardized measures is employed to provide multiple avenues of assessment of particular functions. The evaluation is patient-centered, and measures are selected depending upon the diagnostic question. Nevertheless, the evaluation is also comprehensive. In each evaluation, assessment of six areas, from the framework, is always included: (1) Arousal and Attentional Functioning, (2) Executive Functioning, (3) Language Functioning, (4) Visuospatial Functioning, (5) Reasoning and Problem-Solving Abilities, and (6) Learning and Memory Functioning.

Hypothesis-testing is used to answer questions about an individual's cognitive strengths and deficits. As in the Boston process approach, subsequent test selection is guided by the results of an initial assessment. Assessment of a particular function can be terminated when it is believed that a clear understanding of that function has been developed. Information about performance and errors is collected continuously and contributes to hypothesis-testing. Limit testing is used to determine what facilitates and what hinders performance.

Table 1

Framework of Cognition to Guide Neuropsychological Evaluation

Arousal and Attentional Functioning	Number and symbol writing
Low Level Functions	Number fact retrieval
Alertness/Tonic Arousal	Basic and complex operation abilities
Orienting/Phasic Arousal	Visuospatial Functioning
Selective Attention	Simple visual perception
Shifting Attention	Complex visual form perception
Sustained Attention	Spatial orientation and awareness
Speed of Processing	Visuospatial constructional ability
High Level Functions	Reasoning, and Problem-Solving Abilities
Span of Attention	Abstract reasoning
Resistance to Interference	Analogical reasoning
Mental Manipulation	Deductive reasoning
Executive Functioning	Inductive reasoning
Establishing, maintaining, and shifting response set	Memory Functioning
Initiating, monitoring, and modulating or regulating the production of planned sequences of action	Anterograde learning of episodic, declarative information
	Retrograde remembering of episodic, declarative information
Sustaining effort	Retrograde remembering of semantic information
Resistance to perseveration and/or stimulus-bound behavior	Priming
Responsive and spontaneous temporal and spatial sequencing	Procedural (skill) learning
Organizing thought processes and behaviors	Emotional Information Processing
Auditory Perceptual Functioning	Comprehension, repetition, naming, and generation of emotional information
Nonspeech-sound discrimination	Initiation, monitoring, and modulation of emotional expression
Speech-sound discrimination, analysis, repetition, and synthesis	Motor Functioning
Speech/Language Functioning	Handedness
Spoken language comprehension	Grip strength
Speech production	Speed and persistence of motor responses
Repetition	Dexterity
Naming	Sequential alternation of motor responses
Spoken language generation	Execution of a complex motoric sequence
Reading, Writing	Somesthetic Functioning
Calculational Abilities	Simple unimodal perception
Number and symbol reading	Complex unimodal perception

In comparison to the two approaches presented, there are several commonalities. All three approaches utilize hypothesis-testing, are patient-centered, and consider performance and error analyses as essential. All are also single-case study approaches and consider comparison among tasks from an individual patient as frequently more important than comparison to normative data. The approach uses a model of cognition to guide assessment, a strength of the cognitive neuropsychological approach, but a weakness of the Boston process approach. Finally, the approach uses many standardized measures which are available and which have normative data, a strength of the process approach, but a weakness of the cognitive neuropsychological approach. In sum, the best features of the two presented approaches are included, while some of the weaknesses are avoided.

Analysis of an Inability to Learn and Remember Verbal Information

A model of verbal learning and memory functioning is shown in Figure 2. It is an integration of two frameworks of memory functioning, one in which learning and memory is broken into the steps of encoding, storage or consolidation, and retrieval (Cermak, in press; Milberg, Hebben, & Kaplan, 1986; Squire, 1986), and a second in which the cognitive skills required at initial learning and retrieval are broken down into attentional functions, organizational functions, and memory functions (Cohen & Mapou, 1988; Mack, 1986). Although simplified as compared to many current theories of memory (cf, Squire & Butters, 1984) and partially lacking in empirical validation, the model has been found useful when conceptualizing and treating the types of memory disorders encountered in patients in a rehabilitation center (Cohen & Mapou, 1988).

Of primary importance in this model is the distinction between attentional functioning and memory functioning. Attention refers very specifically to the ability to maintain information in mind from moment to moment, without reference to later recall or recognition. As such, measures of immediate memory, for example, digit span, sentence repetition, and immediate recall of prose passages, would be conceptualized as measures of attention, since these include no indication of what can be retrieved after a delay. In contrast, memory refers to the ability to access information after a delay, without maintaining the information consciously in mind. Thus, delayed recall and recognition measures are the only types of measures which would be considered measures of memory. The distinctions among attention and memory are

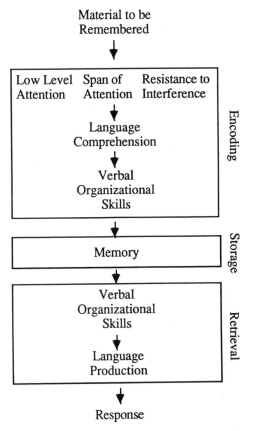

Figure 2. Schematic model of ability to learn and remember new verbal information

important because disorders at each level will have different implications for treatment.

The evaluation is guided directly by the model, although the sequence of assessment may vary. Nevertheless, attentional functioning should be examined first, since any decrement in the ability to attend to information initially will result in recall of less than normal amounts of information at a later time. For this reason, many disorders of memory are actually disorders of attention (Wood, 1987). First, the patient's level of arousal and alertness, ability to orient to presented stimuli, ability to focus attention on presented stimuli, degree of distractibility, and ability to shift attention among stimuli (Low Level Attentional Functions) should be observed. At present, there are no standard neuropsychological tests which measure these functions, so measurement relies upon observation alone.

The length of time that the patient is able to sustain attention without fatigue or performance decrement should also be noted. This may be assessed directly using vigilance or continuous performance tasks (Parasuraman, 1985). Information about sustained attention may also be obtained by comparison of performance (speed and/or accuracy) during the first and second halves of lengthy, non-graded tasks.

Next, the patient's immediate span of attention, the amount of information which can be held consciously in mind at any one moment, should be assessed. This will indicate any limitations in attentional capacity at initial processing stages (Saffran & Marin, 1975; Squire, 1986). Tasks used could include WAIS-R or WMS Digit Span-Forwards, Verbal Sequencing Span Tests[1], sentence repetition (cf, Goodglass & Kaplan, 1983; Spreen & Benton, 1969), and measures of immediate recall of prose and word lists. Of interest is the relationship between the number of words recalled on each trial of a list learning procedure and the patient's digit span. When these two are approximately equal and reduced, this frequently indicates that the patient is limited in the ability to attend to information initially.

Also important to assess is resistance to interference, or the ability to maintain access to small amounts of information following performance of a short, interpolated task. When information which has just been attended to disrupts attention to new information (a type of proactive interference) or when attention to new information limits access to information which has been processed just before (a type of retroactive interference), then a patient's ability to attend to and encode verbal information initially will be limited. This may be assessed best by using a consonant trigrams measure or Peterson-Brown task (Brown, 1958; Peterson & Peterson, 1959), or one of its variants such as the Verbal Primary Memory with Interference Test[1].

Disorders of spoken language comprehension and production may also produce what appears to be a memory disorder. An aphasic patient, for example, may fail to reproduce verbal information either because the information was not comprehended initially or cannot be reproduced verbally. Thus, assessment of language functioning is a critical component of any evaluation of learning and memory. Spoken language comprehension may be evaluated through use of the Peabody Picture Vocabulary Test-Revised (Dunn & Dunn,

1981), the Vocabulary subtest of the WAIS-R, any number of versions of the Token Test (DeRenzi & Vignolo, 1962; Lezak; 1983; Spreen & Benton, 1969), and other measures of syntactic comprehension such as the Active-Passive Test (Dennis & Kohn, 1985). Language comprehension may also be observed in the context of the testing session. Language production may be evaluated using structured measures of naming such as the BNT or Picture Naming Test (Oldfield & Wingfield, 1965), word list generation utilizing letters or categories (Lezak, 1983; Spreen and Benton, 1969) and descriptions of complex visual material, such as the Cookie Theft Picture of the BDAE (Goodglass & Kaplan, 1983). It is also important to record observations of the patient's spontaneous speech and language productions in regard to fluency, grammatical structure, and word finding skills, since impairment in any of these can contribute to problems with verbal recall.

Disorders of organizational abilities are pervasive following head trauma and are quite common after other types of brain damage (Malec, 1983; Wood, 1987). Although these disorders are easily labelled, they may be less easily described in terms of cognitive or behavioral components, and a variety of cognitive difficulties may be classified as organizational. At one level, problems in organizational skills may be reflected in a patient's inability to perform a sequence of steps necessary to initiate and complete a task, such as an activity of daily living. Even when provided with the steps, the patient may still have difficulty performing the task in sequence. Attentional difficulties may also contribute to the loss of sequence (Wood, 1987). An organizational disorder may also be reflected in poorly organized language productions, which may be characterized by tangentiality or irrelevance. At another level, an organizational disorder may produce difficulty with identification of the inherent organization or structure of presented verbal material. For example, a patient may fail to perceive that words on a long list fall into several categories. Even if a patient is aware of organizational structure or structure is more explicit, as in a prose paragraph, the patient may fail to use such structure when learning material. Recall of a word list may be by rote or recall of a paragraph may be out of order, with elements recalled from end to beginning to middle. Unlike the ability of neurologically-intact individuals to use context and organization to facilitate recall, the brain-damaged person may be oblivious to the organization or may be unable to use it effectively.

Organizational skills, then, are an essential component of normal initial learning and encoding of verbal material and subsequent recall. Whether organization takes place during initial encoding (e.g., as the person is attending to the material) or occurs upon initial recall (e.g., person uses categories to cue self) will not be debated here. Suffice to say that an evaluation of organizational skills is an important part of an evaluation of a memory disorder.

An inability to organize language productions may result in poor spontaneous recall of prose material. This ability may be assessed directly by noting organization of verbal descriptions produced spontaneously and in response to structured tasks (e.g., BDAE Cookie Theft Picture Description).

The ability to recognize inherent organization of verbal information, including categorical or analogical relationships among words or stimuli, may be assessed by a variety of measures including WAIS-R Similarities, the Woodcock Reading Mastery Test: Word Comprehension subtest (Woodcock, 1973), the Wisconsin Card Sorting Test (Grant & Berg, 1948; Lezak, 1983), or the Visual Verbal Test (Feldman & Drasgow, 1976).

The way that organization is used to facilitate spontaneous recall should also be evaluated. Various aspects of the reproduced material may be examined. For example, are words on a categorized word list clustered by category or recalled in sequential order? Is the number of words recalled on each learning trial equivalent to the patient's span for unrelated information, or are more words recalled because the patient uses semantic clustering? Are sentences recalled more readily than digits because information is interrelated? Is a prose paragraph recalled from beginning to end, or are details interwoven, sometimes resulting in distortion of the original material? Comparisons between spontaneous recall and cued recall, using semantic cues, or open-ended, forced-choice or multiple-choice recognition questions also provide evidence of organizational problems interfering with spontaneous recall. A patient with a "pure" organizational disorder, for example, may recall little information spontaneously, but may be totally accurate on a forced-choice recognition task. Thus, any memory measure should include both recall and recognition assessment.

Finally, the ability to retain information over time, or memory functioning, should also be assessed. As can be seen already, many other cognitive difficulties can produce what the patient or others describe as a "memory problem," and assessment of these factors must often come before the assessment of memory functioning itself. Measures of memory which make less demand on attentional functioning (e.g., by slowing presentation rate), which make no demand on organizational skills (e.g., by using unrelated material), and which require only recognition should be included. These include the Auditory Verbal Recognition Memory Test[1], the Recognition Memory Test

(Warrington, 1984), and continuous recognition memory tests, such as the verbal Continuous Paired Associate Test (Newton & Brown, 1985).

In the course of evaluation, the ability to learn and retrieve different types of verbal information should be evaluated. The ideal measure of learning and remembering is one which is developed from an empirically-based model of memory, and allows discrimination among aspects of cognition already described. Probably the one measure satisfying these criteria (Loring & Papanicolaou, 1987) is the CVLT. Other measures of list learning abilities include selective reminding tests (Buschke, 1973; Hannay & Levin, 1985), Verbal List Learning with Categorical Clustering[1], and Associative Learning from the WMS (with Kaplan's adaptations for reversed recall and delayed free and cued recall; Milberg, Hebben, & Kaplan, 1986) or WMS-R. Measures of the ability to learn and remember prose include Logical Memory from the WMS (with Kaplan's adaptations for delayed free recall, cued recall, and recognition; Milberg, Hebben, & Kaplan, 1986) or the WMS-R, the California Discourse Memory Test (Delis, Kramer, & Kaplan, 1984), and Prose Passage Recall[1].

Comparisons among different data obtained are essential for determining the source of the memory difficulty. Comparisons should be made among the type of material used: Is there a difference between learning of a word list and learning of a prose passage? What are the characteristics of the learning curve over several trials of a word list? Are there primacy and/or recency effects? Is there evidence of proactive interference? Does the order in which words are recalled change over trials, for example, from sequential recall to recall clustered by categories? Finally, the differences between immediate and delayed recall and recognition will indicate whether or not actual forgetting, the hallmark of a true memory disorder, has taken place.

Testing of limits may help to determine how performance may be facilitated or hindered. For example, the organization of a word list may be increased or decreased by manipulating the degree to which words are interrelated. The similarity of presented material to the types of material the patient has to learn in real situations may also be manipulated.

In sum, a memory disorder may be produced by dysfunction in any of the cognitive systems described above. The contributing factors of deficits in attentional functioning, language, verbal organizational abilities, and retention of material over time must be thoroughly assessed. The process is far from brief, but allows the clinician to draw conclusions about cognitive strengths and weaknesses which form the basis of the patient's performance in real situations. These conclusions may then allow the clinician to make more effective recommendations for treatment and management of the memory disorder (cf, Cohen & Mapou, 1988; Tankle, 1988).

Conclusions

The integrated approach to assessment which has been developed and described addresses many of the problems in current neuropsychological research and practice which were discussed. Assessment is guided by a framework of cognition, in which cognitive processes are explicitly defined. Commonly available, multi-factorial instruments may be utilized, in addition to procedures designed to assess narrower aspects of cognition, an approach now advocated by others (Brooks, 1987). The approach provides a way of task-analyzing multi-factorial procedures, to allow the determination of cognitive components which contribute to the final outcome on a task. The method may be easily applied to new tests. The approach is patient-centered, and hypothesis-testing is used to develop conclusions and to guide assessment. Data are constantly collected about the performance itself, and both these data and final scores are used to reach conclusions about cognitive functioning.

There are still several weaknesses to the approach. Portions of the framework of cognition have not yet received validation. Additional research is needed to demonstrate the hypothesized relationships among proposed cognitive variables. Some of the procedures used are still not widely available. Finally, the process requires considerably more time and patience to complete than some more popular approaches and may not appear practical to many clinicians. Yet, it is the opinion of this author that this type of assessment is essential to developing a full understanding of brain-based disorders of cognition and, as such, is well worth the time. Further, such an approach is more likely to lead to specific and more effective treatment recommendations (Cohen and Mapou, 1988; Tankle, 1988).

Knowledge of cognitive function has advanced considerably in the past 20 years. In some ways, less progress has been made in the practical application of his knowledge to the clinical assessment of cognition. As technology has improved and neuropsychological assessment is needed less to diagnose the presence or location of brain damage, there is more opportunity and reason for clinical neuropsychology to become more cognitively-based (Loring & Papanicolaou, 1987; Mapou, 1988). The proliferation of quick and easily-administered assessment instruments has done little more than provide additional ways of diagnosing brain damage. What is needed now is more careful clinical analysis of the cognitive disorders leading to such a diagnosis. The clinical neuropsychologist, in the role of scientist and practitioner, is in the ideal position to apply what is known about cognitive functioning to assessment of disorders of cognition. The integrated approach described provides a way of evaluating cognitive functioning, a method for developing more specific treatment recommendations based upon neuropsychological evaluation, and it is hoped, a direction for future clinical assessment of brain-based disorders.

[1]These measures were developed and standardized in the neuropsychology laboratory of James L. Mack. Information about these measures may be obtained by writing to Dr. Mack at the Department of Neurology, University Hospitals, 2074 Abington Rd., Cleveland, OH 44106.

The preparation of this paper was supported by Greenery Rehabilitation and Skilled Nursing Center, Boston, MA. The author would like to thank Ronye Cornblatt and J. Daniel Eubanks for their helpful comments during its preparation.

References

Anderson, John R. (1983). *The architecture of cognition*. Cambridge, MA: Harvard University Press.

Benton, A. L., Hamsher, K. deS., Varney, N. R., & Spreen, O. (1983). *Contributions to neuropsychological assessment*. New York: Oxford University Press.

Borod, J. C., Goodglass, H., & Kaplan, E. (1980). Normative data on the Boston Diagnostic Aphasia Examination, Parietal Lobe Battery, and the Boston Naming Test. *Journal of Clinical Neuropsychology,. 2*, 209-216.

Brooks, D. N. (1987). Measuring neuropsychological and functional recovery. In H. S. Levin, J. Grafman, & H. M. Eisenberg (Eds.), *Neurobehavioral recovery from head injury* (pp. 57-72). New York: Oxford University Press.

Brown, J. (1958). Some tests of the decay theory of immediate memory. *Quarterly Journal of Experimental Psychology, 10*, 12-21.

Buschke, H. (1973). Selective reminding for analysis of memory and behavior. *Journal of Verbal Learning and Verbal Behavior, 12*, 543-550.

Caramazza, A. (1986). On drawing inferences about the structure of normal cognitive systems from the analysis of patterns of impaired performance: The case for single-patient studies. *Brain and Cognition, 5*, 41-66.

Cermak, L. S. (in press). Encoding and retrieval deficits of amnesic patients. In E. Perecman (Ed.), *Integrating theory and practice in clinical neuropsychology*.

Christensen, A.-L. (1979). *Luria's neuropsychological investigation. Text* (2nd ed.). Copenhagen: Munksgaard.

Cohen, R. F. (1985, November). Hypothesis-testing approach to neuropsychological assessment for treatment planning. Paper presented at the Boston Neuropsychological Foundation conference, *Neurological syndromes: Pathophysiology, neuropsychological assessment, and treatment,* Boston, MA.

Cohen, R. F., & Mapou, R. L. (1988). Neuropsychological assessment for treatment planning: A hypothesis-testing approach. *Journal of Head Trauma Rehabilitation, 3 (1),* 12-23.

Coltheart, M. (1985). Cognitive neuropsychology and the study of reading. In M. I. Posner & O. S. M. Marin (Eds.), *Attention and performance XI* (pp. 1-37). Hillsdale, NJ: Lawrence Erlbaum Associates.

Coltheart, M., Job., R., & Sartori, G. (Eds.). (1987). *The cognitive neuropsychology of language.* London: Lawrence Erlbaum Associates.

Coltheart, M., Patterson, K. E., & Marshall, J. C. (Eds.). (1980). *Deep dyslexia.* London: Routledge & Kegan Paul.

Delis, D., Kramer, J. H., & Kaplan, E. (1984). *The California Discourse Memory Test.* San Diego: Authors.

Delis, D., Kramer, J. H., Kaplan, E., Ober, B. A. (1987). *California Verbal Learning Test* (Research ed.). San Antonio: The Psychological Corporation.

Deloche, G., & Seron, X. (Eds.). (1987). *Mathematical disabilities: A cognitive neuropsychological perspective.* Hillsdale, NJ: Lawrence Erlbaum Associates.

Dennis, M., & Kohn, B. (1985). The Active-Passive Test: An age-referenced clinical test of syntactic comprehension. *Developmental Neuropsychology, 1,* 113-137.

De Renzi, E., & Vignolo, L. A. (1962). The Token Test: A sensitive test to detect disturbances in aphasics. *Brain, 85,* 665-678.

Dunn, L. M., & Dunn, L. M. (1981). *Peabody Picture Vocabulary Test-Revised.* Circle Pines, MN: American Guidance Service.

Ellis, A. W., & Young, A. W. (1987). *Human cognitive neuropsychology.* Hillsdale, NJ: Lawrence Erlbaum Associates.

Feldman, M. J., & Drasgow, J. (1976). *The Visual-Verbal Test.* Los Angeles: Western Psychological Services.

Goodglass, H., & Kaplan, E. (1983). *The assessment of aphasia and related disorders* (2nd ed.). Philadelphia: Lea & Febiger.

Grant, D. A., & Berg, E. A. (1948). A behavioral analysis of degree of reinforcement and ease of shifting to new responses in a Weigl-type card-sorting problem. *Journal of Experimental Psychology, 38,* 404-411.

Hannay, H. J., & Levin, H. S. (1985). Selective reminding test: An examination of the equivalence of four forms. *Journal of Clinical and Experimental Neuropsychology, 7,* 251-263.

Kaplan, E. (1983). Process and achievement revisited. In S. Wapner & B. Kaplan (Eds.), *Toward a holistic developmental neuropsychology* (pp. 143-156). Hillsdale, NJ: Lawrence Erlbaum Associates.

Kaplan, E., Goodglass, H., & Weintraub, S. (1983). *The Boston Naming Test.* Philadelphia: Lea & Febiger.

Kay, T., Ezrachi, O., & Cavallo, M. (1986, August). Plateaus and consistency: Long term neuropsychological changes following head trauma. Paper presented at the 94th annual meeting of the American Psychological Association, Washington, D.C.

Kay, T., Ezrachi, O., Cavallo, M., & Newman, B. (1987, August). Analysis of neuropsychological change within one year following head trauma. Poster presented at the 95th annual meeting of the American Psychological Association, New York, NY.

Lezak, M. D. (1983). *Neuropsychological assessment* (2nd ed.), New York: Oxford University Press.

Lezak, M. D. (1987). Making neuropsychological evaluation relevant to head injury. In H.S. Levin, J. Grafman, & H. M. Eisenberg (Eds.), *Neurobehavioral recovery from head injury* (pp. 116-128). New York: Oxford University Press.

Loring, D. W., & Papanicolaou, A. C. (1987). Memory assessment in neuropsychology: Theoretical considerations and practical utility. *Journal of Clinical and Experimental Neuropsychology, 9*, 340-358.

Mack, J. L. (1986). Clinical assessment of disorders of attention and memory. *Journal of Head Trauma Rehabilitation, 1(3)*, 22-33.

Mapou, R. L. (1988). Testing to detect brain damage: An alternative to what may no longer be useful. *Journal of Clinical and Experimental Neuropsychology, 10*, 271-278.

Marshall, J. C., & Newcombe, F. (1984). Putative problems and pure progress in neuropsychological single-case studies. *Journal of Clinical Neuropsychology, 6*, 65-70.

Malec, J. (1983). Training the brain-injured client in behavioral self-management skills. In B. A. Edelstein & E. T. Couture (Eds.), *Behavioral assessment and rehabilitation of the traumatically brain-damaged* (pp. 121-150). New York: Plenum Press.

Matthews, C. G., & Kløve, H. (1964). *Instruction manual for the Adult Neuropsychology Test Battery*. Madison, WI: University of Wisconsin Medical School.

McKenna, P., & Warrington, E. K. (1986). The analytical approachy to neuropsychological assessment. In I. Grant & K. M. Adams (Eds.), *Neuropsychological assessment of neuropsychiatric disorders* (pp. 31-47). New York: Oxford University Press.

Milberg, W. P., Hebben, N., & Kaplan, E. (1986). The Boston process approach to neuropsychological assessment. In I. Grant & K. M. Adams (Eds.), *Neuropsychological assessment of neuropsychiatric disorders* (pp. 65-86). New York: Oxford University Press.

Newton, N. A., & Brown, G. G. (1985). Construction of matched verbal and design continuous paired associate tests. *Journal of Clinical and Experimental Neuropsychology, 7*, 97-110.

Oldfield, R. C., & Wingfield, A. (1965). Response latencies in naming objects. *The Quarterly Journal of Experimental Psychology, 17*, 273-281.

Parasuraman, R. (1985). Sustained attention: A multifactorial approach. In M. I. Posner & O. S. M. Marin (Eds..), *Attention and performance XI* (pp. 493-511). Hillsdale, NJ: Lawrence Erlbaum Associates.

Patterson, K. E., Marshall, J. C., & Coltheart, M. (1985). *Surface dyslexia: Cognitive and neuropsychological studies of phonological reading*. London: Lawrence Erlbaum Associates Limited.

Peterson, L. R., & Peterson, M. J. (1959). Short-term retention of individual items. *Journal of Experimental Psychology, 24*, 394-405.

Posner, M. I., Walker, J. A., Friedrich, F. J., & Rafal, R. D. (1984). Effects of parietal injury on covert shifts of attention. *Journal of Neuroscience, 4*, 1863-1874.

Purdue Research Foundation. (1948). *Examiner's manual for the Purdue Pegboard*. Chicago: Science Research Associates.

Reitan, R. M., & Wolfson, D. (1985). *The Halstead-Reitan Neuropsychological Test Battery: Theory and clinical applications.* Tucson: Neuropsychology Press.

Roeltgen, D. (1985). Agraphia. In K. M. Heilman & E. Valenstein (Eds.), *Clinical neuropsychology* (2nd ed.) (pp. 75-96). New York: Oxford University Press.

Saffran, E., & Marin, O. S. M. (1975). Immediate memory for word lists and sentences in a patient with deficient auditory short-term memory. *Brain and Language, 2*, 420-433.

Shallice, T. (1979). Case study approach in neuropsychological research. *Journal of Clinical Neuropsychology, 1*, 183-211.

Smith, A. (1973). *Symbol Digit Modalities Test.* Los Angeles: Western Psychological Services.

Spreen, O., & Benton, A. L. (1969). *Neurosensory Center Comprehensive Examination for Aphasia.* Victoria, BC: Neuropsychology Laboratory, Dept. of Psychology, University of Victoria.

Squire, L. (1986). The neuropsychology of memory dysfunction and its assessment. In I. Grant & K. M. Adams (Eds.), *Neuropsychological assessment of neuropsychiatric disorders* (pp. 268-299). New York: Oxford University Press.

Squire, L. R., & Butters, N. (Eds.). (1984). *Neuropsychology of memory.* New York: The Guilford Press.

Tankle, R. S. (1988). Application of neuropsychological test results to interdisciplinary cognitive rehabilitation with head-injured adults. *Journal of Head Trauma Rehabilitation, 3 (1)*, 24-32.

Walsh, K. (1985). *Understanding brain damage: A primer of neuropsychological investigation.* Edinburgh: Churchill Livingstone.

Warrington, E. (1984). *Recognition Memory Test.* Windsor, Berkshire: NFER-Nelson.

Wechsler, D. (1981). *Wechsler Adult Intelligence Scale-Revised.* San Antonio: The Psychological Corporation.

Wechsler, D. (1945). A standardized memory scale for clinical use. *Journal of Psychology, 19*, 87-95.

Wechsler, D., & Stone, C. P. (1987). *Wechsler Memory Scale-Revised.* San Antonio: The Psychological Corporation.

Western Psychological Services. (1983). *Hooper Visual Organization Test.* Los Angeles: Author.

White, R. F. (1987). Review of Neuropsychological Assessment of Neuropsychiatric Disorders (Eds.: I Grant and K. M. Adams). *The Clinical Neuropsychologist, 1*, 267-273.

Wilson, B. (1987). Single-case experimental designs in neuropsychological rehabilitation. *Journal of Clinical and Experimental Neuropsychology, 9*, 527-544.

Wood, R. L. (1987). *Brain injury rehabilitation: A neurobehavioral approach.* Rockville, MD: Aspen Publishers.

Woodcock, R. W. (1973). *Woodcock Reading Mastery Tests.* Circle Pines, MN: American Guidance Service.

7

Everyday Cognition and the Ecological Validity of Intellectual and Neuropsychological Tests

J. Michael Williams

The notions of ecological validity and everyday cognition emerged predominantly from three sources in psychology. These were the study of practical intelligence in cognitive psychology (Sternberg, 1977; Neisser, 1982), the study of everyday cognition in gerontology (Acker, 1986; Poon, 1986; West, 1985) and the prediction of everyday functioning in neuropsychological rehabilitation settings (Chelune & Moehle, 1986; Hart & Hayden, 1986). Movements in all of these areas were at least partially motivated by a reaction to the general psychometric, trait-oriented theories of intelligence and the arcane style of intellectual and neuropsychological tests which had developed largely since the second world war. The following is a very brief history of these movements, a review of the current ideas subsumed under the term ecological validity and a future program of test development which will presumably combine these new ideas with the best from the past.

The Construction of Clinical Intelligence Tests

As every introductory psychology student knows, clinical or applied intelligence testing began in 1902 with the Binet-Simon test battery, developed to evaluate and place children in school. Other investigators had previously invented tests which could have practical applications, but the Binet-Simon tests were the first to have an applied mission from the inception of the test battery. Binet developed a set of tasks and a format for presenting them which laid the groundwork for virtually all intellectual test batteries which were to follow. The basic design strategy was to choose a group of tasks for the foundation of the battery which were already developed and had some support among clinicians and investigators. These tests were often then modified and standardized. New tasks invented by the developers were then added to this foundation group. The battery was then administered to clinical groups and further modifications were made based upon such pilot studies. Although Binet and Simon had fewer previously developed tests for possible inclusion in their battery, by the time of Wechsler's intelligence scales (see Wechsler,

Williams, J. M. (1988). Everyday cognition and the ecological validity of intellectual and neuropsychological tests. In J. M. Williams & C. J. Long (Eds.), *Cognitive approaches to neuropsychology*, New York: Plenum.

1958), many tests were available and this style of test development was widely accepted without qualification among test developers and clinicians.

The notion of building new batteries from the good tests currently available probably represents an adequate, common sense approach to test development. It also enhances the use of the test among clinicians because the subtests are usually known to the potential market. However, this general approach stands in contrast to procedures used in developing methods to experimentally examine intellectual constructs, such as memory, language and problem-solving. Here, the investigator begins with a theory of the construct and then develops methods to test hypotheses based upon the theory. There is a close, necessary connection between a theoretical idea of the construct and the assessment methodology. Probably as a result of clinical expediencies, current test developers have been, and still are, allowed to invent intellectual and neuropsychological tests without first explaining the constructs the tests were designed to measure.

From the very beginning, intellectual batteries designed for clinical use have had only cursory face validity and fit into models of cognition that were very global and nonspecific. For example, in the words of Binet and Simon (1916), intelligence is, ". . . judgement, otherwise called good sense, practical sense, initiative, the faculty of adapting one's self to circumstances. To judge well, to comprehend well, to reason well, these are the essential activities of intelligence". Wechsler's (1958) definition presented 39 years later was similarly vague: "The aggregate or global capacity of the individual to act purposefully, to think rationally and to deal effectively with the environment".

It is unfortunate that these definitions of intelligence which clearly stress ecological validity notions, such as environmental adaption and practical knowledge, led to test batteries which were so abstract and arcane. One must wonder at the ability of some of the Wechsler Adult Intelligence Scale subtests, such as digit Span, or Digit Symbol, to measure one's ability "to act purposefully, to think rationally and to deal effectively with the environment". Although Wechsler and others certainly recognized the practical aspects of intellectual skills, the test batteries themselves were not developed from a theoretical basis of practical intelligence. The batteries were simply constructed by gathering together tasks already known to clinicians and roughly validating them with clinical populations.

Another major influence on test development is "test inertia". This is represented by the familiar resistance to new test developments and an over-reliance on traditional assessment instruments, usually those acquired in the process of graduate training. Every discipline relies on traditional methods to some extent, but psychologists appear more prone to this than others, largely because of our relatively conservative stance toward new technologies of assessment. This conservative tendency probably arises from the uncertainty inherent in psychological assessment and our understandable reluctance to make liberal assessment decisions based on measures of overall low to moderate reliability and validity. Also, as clinicians, we sometimes develop a romantic attachment to our tests or battery and healthy change is constrained by this attitude. How many neuropsychologists claim with pride that they are devotees of the "Halstead-Reitan school", or the "process approach" to assessment, as if these designations represent something more profound than simply an approach to the technology of assessment. A similar absurdity would be for a neurologist to claim allegiance to the "CT-scan" vs the "neurological examination" school of neurological diagnosis. Such romantic notions and a basic conservative posture both work to produce test inertia. Numerous examples of test inertia can be found in the area of personality assessment as well. The almost religious attachment some psychologists have to the Rorschach inkblot test and the Minnesota Multiphasic Personality Inventory are further examples of this phenomenon.

The overall result of these trends is an impediment of the growth of new assessment technology in psychology and an over-reliance on outdated, often poorly constructed tests from the past. One of the clearest examples of this is apparent in the history of the Wechsler Memory Scale. This scale was originally published in 1945 and has had a long history of use as a clinical memory test. However, criticisms of the test mounted, and by the late 70's, the drawbacks of the scale were obvious to clinicians and researchers alike, and criticisms were broadcast through the professional literature (e.g., Erickson and Scott, 1977; Prigatano, 1978). Symposia on memory assessment were conducted at conferences and many suggestions for improved measures were made in the literature. However, very little was done until 1986-1987, when the Psychological Corporation finally redesigned and published a new version of the scale. Perhaps clinicians will adopt the new scale in another five to ten years, once clinical programs train another generation of practitioners.

The final major influence on test development is the tendency of test inventors to use techniques developed in the experimental laboratory without adapting the method to the clinical setting. This factor more than any other has probably determined the obtuse style of current test batteries. Among the techniques available to test developers are a variety of measures derived from methodologies used in research. Often, these methods were never intended to be used as clinical tests and are usually so specific to the research study that they require substantial modification before they can possibly find a place in the usual clinical setting. However, many are taken and placed in clinical test batteries with little accommodation to a possible clinical use for the test. Some procedures used in animal laboratories have even been modified for use as clinical tests (e.g., Albert & Moss, 1984). This results in overly specific and abstract tests which are not necessarily useful in predicting or measuring everyday cognitive abilities.

The reader can easily see how these influences will impede the development of new assessment techniques which incorporate everyday cognition. If clinicians remain inappropriately attached to their old tests, and test developers do not explain the theoretical foundation of the tests and manner in which items or tasks were constructed, then tests will not improve by incorporating any positive innovation, including everyday cognition. These theoretical explanations must also include a clear description of the clinical applications of the test and how they are to be accomplished. If a test is supposed to predict everyday abilities, then this relationship should be explained at a theoretical level as well as established through empirical investigations whenever possible. These investigations should be deemed as important as the standardization and normative studies. In order to invent new tests and conduct such investigations, test developers must first turn to the emerging theoretical basis of practical intelligence.

Practical Cognition

One prominent movement in the development of cognitive psychology was the emergence of a variety of theories which stressed information processing as a general model of cognition. The information processing movement gave rise to some extremely reductionistic, abstract models of memory, language and other cognitive abilities. These in combination with tests of "academic intelligence" were criticized as impractical and conceptually distant from explanations of cognition in everyday life (Neisser, 1979). The emerging reaction to this strict information processing point of view has been loosely described as the study of everyday cognition. This approach always examines some practical ability, usually within the context of traditional cognitive theories. One clear example is the study of eyewitness testimony (Loftus & Palmer, 1974; Buckout, 1974). Here, an everyday domain was chosen for analysis using theories of memory function largely developed in the laboratory.

The everyday cognition movement also represents a departure from traditional methods used in cognitive psychology. In the practical cognition framework, methods reflect the complexity, comprehensiveness and uncertainty of everyday cognition. In contrast, experimental methods invented in the laboratory usually isolate and control for numerous influences which are extraneous to the specific relationships under study. Experimental methods were not intended to be comprehensive or to have an applied utility. In contrast, everyday measures cover a wide variety of constructs and variability may be accounted for by a variety of factors, many of which are unknown to the investigator. For example, memory for eyewitness testimony is influenced by such complex social factors as the degree of empathy perceived by the witness for people in the scene the witness observes (Buckout, 1974). Likewise, the complex role of confabulations and reconstructions in eyewitness recall represent a further manifestation of the complexity and uncertainty present in the study of everyday memory skills. Such complex interactions and multiple factors are usually partialed out of experimental studies so that simple relationships between them are clarified.

Although Sternberg (1985), Neisser (1979) and others proposed that the practical cognition movement began as a reaction to "academic" intelligence, which is presumably that embodied in most intelligence tests, and the testing movement's impoverished theoretical development, it also probably represents the simple infusion of pragmatism into cognitive psychology. Many investigators in the practical cognition movement do not necessarily view their efforts as the study of "intelligence". Many are involved in simply examining an applied skill or some everyday domain without referring to a general model of intelligence and all such a term implies. The testing movement itself represents one applied area of cognitive psychology. Unfortunately, the testing movement developed and gained momentum before there were sophisticated theories of cognition. If the current level of sophistication in theories of cognition were available to Binet or Wechsler, intelligence tests would probably be much more sophisticated.

Everyday Cognition and Aging

The practical cognition movement in cognitive psychology has greatly influenced the study of cognition and aging. Many gerontologists are psychologists trained in academic, psychology departments in the areas of developmental and cognitive psychology. For some, interests in gerontology emerged from the study of development across the life span (Baltes, 1973).

There has now emerged a gerontology movement which includes every branch of the social sciences. There is a strong clinical/professional group emerging among gerontologists who are establishing geriatric clinical services in hospitals, community mental health centers, nursing homes and rehabilitation facilities. This movement will grow more pronounced as the population continues to age and more emphasis is placed on enhancing the quality of life of older people.

The gerontology movement has prompted numerous studies of cognitive abilities and aging. Early investigations of these relationships revealed pronounced cognitive declines over the life span. These early declines were substantially qualified by later studies (Salthouse, 1985; Schaie, 1983; Poon, 1986). In addition to these qualifications of functional levels, many of these investigators observed that many conventional measures of cognitive abilities were arcane and unrelated to the subject's apparent high level of everyday adjustment. Although the older subjects performed worse on conventional tests, they were not correspondingly unsuccessful in the cognitive demands of everyday life. All these concerns led to a strong ecological validity emphasis in gerontology.

Cognitive Rehabilitation

The final relevant setting in which everyday cognition has become prominent is rehabilitation. Here there is strong interest in the ability of intellectual tests to predict functioning in everyday life. This interest has emerged over a time of greatly expanding rehabilitation services for brain-injured patients. As these services have moved from the acute hospital to outpatient and community transitional programs, it has become increasingly apparent that conventional tests are greatly limited in assessing brain-injured patients for rehabilitation purposes.

The basic assessment task of the rehabilitation setting is to predict the patient's post-injury functional levels in occupational, school and home environments (Williams, 1987). This task is daunting, given the assessment tools available and lack of prediction studies. The neuropsychological batteries may be adequate in predicting everyday abilities but there are no current studies which allow the clinicians any reliable basis for such predictions.

All of these factors and interests have worked to produce a high degree of discontent among rehabilitation psychologists and a strong need for a practical assessment technology. In partial response to this need, a variety of rehabilitation-oriented rating scales, inventories and short neuropsychological batteries have been developed (e.g. Prigatano et al., 1984). However, these measures are still tentative and in their early developmental stages.

The rehabilitation, gerontology and practical cognition movements have all worked to strongly influence the development of new assessment tools. Each has contributed a host of criticisms of current intellectual and neuropsychological tests (see Erickson and Scott, 1977; Poon, 1986). Consistent with the practical cognition movement, these criticisms often focus on the predictive utility of the tests. There are large gaps in knowledge concerning the relationship between conventional intellectual tests and adjustment to occupational, school and home environments. Although the clinician may know that a patient's IQ is reliably near 85, this knowledge may not reduce the uncertainty in predicting whether this patient can work at a certain occupation, or function independently at home.

Such prediction considerations make up one clear juncture for all of these applied movements. All are grappling with such basic validity issues. In the context of developing new, pragmatic approaches, some familiar intellectual constructs have been substantially modified, some new ones have emerged. Overriding these modifications are the terms, "everyday cognition", and "ecological validity". these terms form the groundwork of the new practical theorizing. Although they have been recently studied and discussed in the context of superficial empirical studies, they have not been the subject of much theoretical development. Certain fundamental questions need pondering in order for future studies to have a coherent theoretical basis. What is the distinction between an "everyday" skill, and any other skill? What is the role of the environment in "ecological" validity? Must intellectual tests be invented, or modified to actually measure and everyday skill, or is it sufficient simply to be able to predict everyday functional levels using tests already developed?

The Nature of Everyday Skills

Everyday cognition is a general term which refers to a variety of skills, knowledge structures and reasoning strategies which apply to a particular class of environmental settings. Each setting in which we function has cognitive demands, such as memory for required facts and performance skills, which specifically apply to the setting and may or may not apply to another. For example, the venerable profession of bartending requires a knowledge of drink ingredients, the skills to combine the ingredients quickly and efficiently (in case the bar becomes active), fluent social skills in starting and maintaining conversations, basic academic skills (e.g. arithmetic ability) and a variety of other cognitive skills which an expert bartender could enumerate. Of course, many of these skills are required for successful functioning only in the bar-room setting. Skill in making drinks is not required for successful functioning at home. However, many other abilities, such as social skills and basic academic skills are common to many work environments.

These clusters of environment-specific skills make up the required sets of skills needed by each person. Each person has a "profile" of necessary skills that are organized according to the settings in which competent performance is required. Often the term "everyday skill" is used to refer to skills used only in the home environment. This use is especially characteristic of rehabilitation professionals and gerontologists. Many disabled people are attempting return to the home environment when rehabilitation services are provided. In the case of gerontologists, many older people are not working and everyday skills are those required to live independently at home.

An important distinction is between a set of everyday skills which may be considered generic and those which are very specific to certain environmental settings (Table 1). Generic everyday skills are usually simple, basic skills, often referred to as Activities of Daily Living (ADL; Hart & Hayden, 1986). These are skills required of everyone, such as dressing, maintaining personal hygiene and feeding oneself. They are generic because they are fundamental to successful functioning in virtually all environments. They are also foundation skills for all others. Geriatric and rehabilitation settings, especially inpatient settings, often refer only to these generic abilities when describing the everyday abilities of their patients. This occurs because patients in these settings are usually coping with the reacquisition of these basic skills while in the very restricted hospital setting.

The other major type of everyday skills are those specific to individual environments, typically work settings. These represent very specific task demands which an individual masters in order to successfully adjust to the setting. As a rule of thumb, specific skills are usually more complex and difficult to learn and teach than are generic skills.

This generic-specific distinction is an important bridging structure for the entire everyday cognition domain. For example, most inpatient brain-injury rehabilitation programs spend their resources training the patients in generic everyday skills, such as ambulation, dressing, cooking, and the like.

Table 1

Some Everyday Skills Required of Psychologists

Generic:	Specific:
Clean, dress and care for self	Report writing skills
Driving a car or engaging public transport	Interviewing skills
Basic communication skills	Test interpretation skills
Basic arithmetic	Psychotherapy skills

Outpatient rehabilitation programs typically train generic *and* specific skills. The transitional nature of outpatient programs compels rehabilitation efforts to include specific environments and consequent specific skills training, such as job-related skills. The more individualized and specific outpatient programs become, the more successful will be their efforts at integrating patients into community-based settings.

The generic-specific distinction also accounts for the trouble in predicting post-morbid cognitive function from neuropsychological test batteries. This dilemma of clinical prediction is often informally expressed thusly:

"This patient was an accountant before his closed head injury, sustained in an automobile accident. Now, nine months later, his IQ is 102, and his other test findings are essentially in the unimpaired range. I feel confident that many of his cognitive abilities have fallen below premorbid levels because I guess that accountants probably need a higher level of intellectual ability than that measured for this patient. However, what cognitive skill levels must accountants have to function, and on which skills? How can I predict the success or failure of this patient in accountancy without knowing this? What I need is a neuropsychological battery for accountants or at least some idea of how the average, garden variety accountant scores on my battery of tests."

How often have the clinicians reading this uttered this sentiment or heard it expressed by colleagues? Usually the specific skills of such occupations as accountancy are unknown to the evaluating neuropsychologist unless he or she has had some personal experience as an accountant. In such clinical situations, the neuropsychologist is confined to a very uncertain prediction of specific performance in such work environments. Such predictions are often based on idiosyncratic rules of thumb, or common sense, rather than an empirical relationship established between the neuropsychological tests and the specific everyday skill levels. An interesting research endeavor would be to ferret out these heuristics using the techniques developed by cognitive psychologists (see Long, Graesser & Long, this volume).

However, generic skills are much easier to predict because they represent much lower levels of ability and the neuropsychologist is presumably very familiar with performing them. For example, it is much easier to predict whether a patient will be able to dress independently rather than predict whether a patient can keep payroll accounts. Keeping payroll accounts requires skills which are far too specific to have direct referents among neuropsychological test batteries. Also, the neuropsychologist has personal experience with dressing and can perform an informal, qualitative appraisal of the required skills. This subjective context is missing for any setting that is personally unfamiliar to the neuropsychologist making predictions.

There is some precedent for the prediction of such specific job skills. Our colleagues in vocational rehabilitation and general vocational counseling often grapple with this problem. At present, the gains in this area are subsumed within evaluation systems like the General Aptitude Test Battery (GATB; U. S. Department of Labor, 1979). The GATB includes a variety of tests of generic vocational skills, such as basic clerical and arithmetic skills. Specific occupational skills are assessed using a job task analysis, which includes a combination of informal observations of people in the job setting and formal specifications of tasks which compose the job activities (Anchor, Sieveking, Peacock, & Presley, 1979). Unfortunately, these task analyses are most often applied to simpler, physical occupations that do not have complex cognitive components. There are essentially no task analyses performed for such complex occupations as accountants or managers. However, the general model of job task analysis is one which could be developed to help in solving one aspect of the everyday prediction problem in rehabilitation. The job task analyses could be related to neuropsychological tests and the clinician would have a much more substantial, empirical basis for the prediction of everyday vocational skills.

Neuropsychological Studies of Everyday Skills

Activities of Daily Living

There have been a variety of studies examining the utility of neuropsychological tests in predicting basic activities of daily living. Almost all of these studies examined head trauma or stroke patients originally treated in inpatient rehabilitation settings. ADL's were measured at some follow-up time after discharge and neuropsychological assessments performed while the subjects were inpatients were used to predict the ADL's. In general, conventional neuropsychological and intellectual tests predict simple activities of daily living at a low to moderate level (Chelune & Moehle, 1986; Hart & Hayden, 1986; Heaton & Pendleton, 1981). Apparently patients who perform at low levels on neuropsychological tests likewise have difficulty executing simple everyday living skills.

The predictive utility of neuropsychological tests are constrained in this setting for two major reasons. First, many ADL's involve basic sensory and motor skills which are not adequately measured by neuropsychological batteries. Such skills as walking, dressing or bathing among brain-injured populations probably contain a strong component of sensorimotor coordination and strength in the extremities, which are not carefully assessed by cognitively oriented neuropsychological tests.

Second, ADL measures are not scaled in the above average to superior range, whereas many neuropsychological tests are scaled across the average to superior range. Many severely impaired patients have great difficulty responding to many neuropsychological tests but will demonstrate a range of function on ADL scales. For example, patients who cannot dress themselves may be completely untestable on the Tactual Performance Test, a conventional part of the Halstead-Reitan battery. As a consequence, this neuropsychological test will not appear predictive of ADL's due to this contrast in scaling.

The Use of Neuropsychological Tests to Predict Employment Status

The neuropsychologist in the outpatient setting is often faced with the straight-forward question of whether a patient can return to former employment. If that is determined to be impossible, then the neuropsychologist is often asked to specify which occupations are now reasonable expectations for the patient. Although this prediction task has become extremely important in outpatient and rehabilitation oriented neuropsychology, very few studies have examined the prediction of actual employment skills using neuropsychological tests. Most studies in this area have simply predicted employment status rather than specific occupational skills.

A number of these studies have in fact validated the use of neuropsychological tests in the prediction of simple employment status (Dikman & Morgan, 1980; Heaton, Chelune & Lehman, 1978; Newnan, Heaton & Lehman, 1978). The strength of this relationship is apparently low to moderate. This characterization is tentative, however, because most of the studies performed thus far have used only mean comparisons to establish this relationship and virtually no study used regression techniques to make predictions of employment status. Typically, employed and unemployed patients are compared on neuropsychological tests. Unemployed patients have been observed to have significantly lower neuropsychological test scores. Although such comparisons indicate that some relationship between these variables exist, the strength of such relationships cannot be established with such simple designs.

A very few studies have examined the relationship of neuropsychological tests to actual job-related skills. These have also found a low to moderate relationship between the test findings and the job skills (Chelune & Moehle, 1986). It is apparent from these studies that job skills are extremely specific and make up skill clusters which neuropsychological tests may predict only in very general terms. For patients who have borderline impairment, this situation results in great uncertainty for the prediction of job success. Our pilot research on this "reasoning under uncertainty" (Kahneman Slovic & Tversky, 1982) suggests that neuropsychologists develop idiosyncratic rules of thumb and systematic biases in their reasoning concerning relationships of the tests to job skills (Williams, 1987). In general, neuropsychologists believe their tests are more reliable and the predictive relationships between tests and job skills are more robust than research would suggest. For example, many neuropsychologists had strong beliefs about the ability of the Tapping test to predict motor skills in job areas, such as assembly line work.

Miscellaneous Skills

The final domain of interest involves the prediction of general everyday skills which are more sophisticated than ADL's and not specific to occupational environments. This includes a few studies which have used intellectual and neuropsychological batteries to predict driving skills, everyday memory skills (e.g. remembering phone numbers) and the like. These studies are often not presented as validity studies per se. They are often presented as part of a general rehabilitation study. Consequently, these relationships are somewhat obscured. Among these studies, there has been an almost exclusive focus on two everyday skill domains: driving skills and everyday memory skills. The driving studies are usually performed in brain-injury rehabilitation settings, the everyday memory studies are performed by gerontologists who typically examine normal elderly volunteers.

Driving is certainly a generic skill which is important for successful functioning in most occupational, educational and home environments. The few prediction studies using neuropsychological tests strongly suggest that the tests are predictive of the cognitive aspects of driving (Golper, Rau, & Marshall, 1980; Gouvier, Webster, & Blanton, 1986). Certainly the basic motor and sensory aspects of driving are best predicted by physical strength and dexterity assessment devices and driving simulators. Neuropsychological tests appear especially useful in predicting the visuospatial components of driving (Gouvier & Warner, 1987).

In the memory assessment arena, numerous gerontologists have criticized conventional memory tests because they are not "ecologically valid". This criticism arises from the simple observation that elderly adults who are functioning competently in the home environment can score poorly on memory and intellectual tests. There is an apparent discrepancy between their tested vs. everyday ability. This basic discrepancy has led to studies examining everyday competencies among the elderly, prediction studies using conventional tests, and the development of new assessment devices (Crook, 1986; Eisdorfer, 1986; Little, Williams, & Long, 1986). For all the criticism of the tests, very few studies have actually examined the relationships of memory function to everyday skills. Most test the relationship of memory skill self-report to memory test performance. These indicate that tests are moderately related to self-report (Gilewski & Zelinski, 1986). However, one study cast considerable doubt on the reliability and validity of self-report as a measure of everyday ability. Little, Williams and Long (1986) discovered that certain areas of memory function are better observed by elderly adults than others. For example, subjects were much better at assessing their own memory for reading material than their memory for phone numbers or new names. Most subjects underestimate their ability to remember names and other common information, presumably because errors in memory for this material are often noticed in everyday life. Consequently, subjects reported that their ability level was low. Williams, Little, Scates and Blockman (1987) also discovered that memory self-report is also strongly influenced by depression.

When other criteria are used, such as actual everyday skills (e.g. a test of memory for names and faces), the correlations between tests and everyday abilities rise (Little, Williams, & Long, 1986). However, most everyday skills cannot be formatted into a test as such, and when they are, they appear more like memory tests and not like their everyday referents. For example, once a name and faces memory test is constructed, it appears more like a paired associates memory test rather than the ecologically rich, complex task it is in everyday life.

Summary of Everyday Skill Studies

The general findings of these studies has been restated throughout. The relationship of everyday skills to neuropsychological tests is low to moderate. Although this area suffers from too few studies and other methodological shortcomings, this overall characterization has been repeatedly sustained. There is no study which indicates that neuropsychological tests are strongly predictive of any everyday functional skill. Certainly patients who do very poorly, or are untestable, will have great problems at home and will not be able to function in any job. However, we do not have the clinical or experimental evidence to support predictive statements that are any stronger, even if we are identified as the most likely professional to make such predictions.

Although a trend has developed in the overall findings, these studies suffer from methodological problems and considerable gaps in the conceptualization and coverage of everyday skill areas. First, and most important, are the conceptualization and design of what are termed the everyday skills. Most researchers and clinicians probably have a very reliable conceptualization of everyday skills. These are the skills used in home, school and occupational environments. Such abilities include remembering new names and faces, driving a car, washing the clothes and using the telephone. There is little controversy over defining these skills as in the province of the "everyday", and any test measuring or predicting them would certainly embody "ecological validity".

There are currently grave problems in translating this simple idea into a clinical assessment strategy or research study. On the clinical application side, most clinical neuropsychologists wish to keep their tried and true assessment batteries, either ones they have pasted together or the formal batteries. The idea of altering the tests is unpalatable. Such clinicians would certainly prefer to see prediction studies which show that their tests predict everyday skills at moderate to high levels. If such were demonstrated, then the clinicians would keep their tests intact and feel confidant in their clinical predictions.

On the side of research, it is very difficult to construct an everyday task which actually assesses the full complexity of the everyday task. For example, suppose an experimenter wishes to construct a name and faces memory test. One simple, straight-forward strategy would be to show subjects unfamiliar faces and pair them with names. Recall can be tested by later showing the subject the faces and requesting them to produce the name. Another strategy would be to present the subject with a videotape of someone giving a name and an introduction. The subject could then be showed the videotape without the sound and asked to recall the associated name and other pertinent information about the person on the tape. It is apparent that such tasks do not completely represent the full complexity and richness of the memory for names and faces which exist in the everyday world. The more one attempts to create a "test" of everyday function, the less ecological relevance is embodied in the task.

This problem of objectifying everyday tasks in order to design a test varies from task to task. Certain everyday skills are more amenable to direct measurement than others. For example, a name and faces test is relatively easy to construct and is similar enough to the task in everyday life. However, many everyday social skills and abilities required of certain occupations would probably be impossible or impractical to develop, both because they are too specific and complex; any test would consequently be very distant from the real-life tasks. For example, many skills required of a factory supervisor would be very difficult to standardize and still have the test resemble the everyday activities.

Another approach to gathering information pertinent to success in everyday tasks is to use self-report or significant other questionnaires of everyday abilities (Little, Williams, & Long, 1986; McDonald, 1986; Williams, Klein, Little, & Haban, 1986; Williams, Little & Haban, 1987). They rely on observations and inferences made either by the patient or a reliable observer of the patient, such as a family member. These measures are attractive because of their ease of administration. They are constrained by the relative unreliability of such observations and the limited coverage of possible content areas. Many everyday skills are difficult for patients or family members to rate. Many occupational tasks have not even been attempted at the time the questionnaire is administered.

A Prospectus for New Tests

There are two possible mechanisms by which ecological validity may influence the development of new tests. The first is by compelling test designers to choose more or less traditional tasks and rating scales which predict everyday abilities. The advantage of this approach is that current tests need not change remarkably and new tests can have the comfortable look and feel of the older tests. Test developers and publishers must simply include studies of ecological validity as well as reliability and normative studies. If a tests is represented by developers as an instrument for the prediction of rehabilitation outcome or independence among the elderly and the like, then these validity studies should be held in as great esteem by the developers as normative studies.

The second approach is to actually modify tests to include everyday tasks whenever possible. Such innovations would probably result in a great increase in the ability of clinical evaluations to predict everyday functioning. Many content areas can be directly assessed using tasks which are very similar to their everyday referents. Some of these have been already invented but only a few have been incorporated into commercially available test batteries. The development of new everyday tasks should be part of a creative new movement in the invention and marketing of psychological tests.

The major constraint on the incorporation of everyday skills into clinical batteries is the specificity of many skills needed for occupational and everyday living environments. This problem will probably not be overcome by developing new and better tests. The format of present tests is just too limited to assess many of these skills. Such specific skills as supervisory ability, skilled craftwork and the like are either far too complex or logistically impossible to assess directly. Most of the logistical problems arise because the examiner cannot construct a facsimile of the environment in which the skill is conducted. However, many everyday skills, such as memory for reading or everyday arithmetic skills, can be easily measured using a test. The ideal test battery would consequently include a mix of traditional and everyday tasks. For example, an improved memory battery would include traditional list-learning paradigms along with a test of memory for names and faces. Such a battery would presumably have a greater potential for predicting levels of similar skills in everyday environments.

In order for these inventions and innovations to come about, some headway must be made against the test inertia mentioned in the early parts of this chapter. The dogmatic feelings and attachments clinicians have concerning their favorite tests will impede the development of any new tests, including those invented to measure everyday skills. In order to combat this tendency, test users must reframe their activities as the application of assessment technology rather than the combination of science and art that is fostered in graduate training. If clinicians accept this point of view then they will create a market demand for the development of new tests. This demand will fuel improvements of all sorts, ranging from improved normative studies to the inclusion of everyday tasks.

References

Acker, M.B. (1986). Relationship between test scores and everyday life functioning. In B. Uzzell and Y. Gross (Eds.), *Clinical neuropsychology of intervention*, New York: Martinus Nijhoff.

Albert, M., & Moss, M. (1984). The assessment of memory disorders in patients with Alzheimer's disease. In L. R. Squire and N. Butters (Eds.), *Neuropsychology of memory*, New York: Guilford.

Anchor, K., Sieveking, N., Peacock, C., & Presley, B. (1979). Work behavior sampling in vocational assessment: Applications for neuropsychological methodology. *Clinical Neuropsychology, 1*, 51-53.

Baltes, P. B. (1973). Prototypical paradigms and questions in life-span research on development and aging. *Gerontologist, 13,* 458-467.

Binet, A., and Simon, T. (1916). *The development of intelligence in children.* (E.S. Kit, trans.), Baltimore, MD: Williams and Wilkins.

Buckout, R. (1974). Eyewitness testimony. *Scientific American, 231*, 23-31.

Chelune, G., & Moehle, K. (1986). Neuropsychological assessment and everyday functioning. In D. Wedding, A. M. Horton & D. Webster (Eds.), *The neuropsychology handbook*, New York: Springer.

Crook, T. (1986). Overview of memory assessment instruments. In L. Poon (Ed.), *Handbook for clinical memory assessment of older adults.* Hyattsville, MD: American Psychological Association.

Dikman, S., & Morgan, S. F. (1980). Neuropsychological factors related to employability and occupational status in persons with epilepsy. *Journal of Nervous and Mental Disease, 168,* 236-240.

Eisdorfer, C. (1986). Conceptual approaches to the clinical testing of memory in the aged: An introduction to the issues. In L. Poon (Ed.), *Handbook for clinical memory assessment of older adults.* Hyattsville, MD: American Psychological Association.

Erickson, R. C., & Scott, M. L. (1977). Clinical memory testing: A review. Psychological Bulletin, 84, 1130-1149.

Gilewski, M. J., & Zelinski, E. M. (1986). Questionnaire assessment of memory complaints. In L. Poon (Ed.), *Handbook for clinical memory assessment of older adults.* Hyattsville, MD: American Psychological Association.

Golper, L., Rau, M., & Marshall, R. (1980). Aphasic adults and their decision on driving: An evaluation. *Archives of Physical Medicine and Rehabilitation, 61*, 34-40.

Gouvier, W. D., & Warner, M. S. (1987). Treatment of visual imperception and related disorders. In J. M. Williams and C. J. Long (Eds.), *The rehabilitation of cognitive disabilities*, New York: Plenum.

Gouvier, W. D., Webster, J. S., & Blanton, P. D. (1986). Cognitive retraining with brain damaged patients. In D. Wedding, A. M. Horton & D. Webster (Eds.), *The neuropsychology handbook*, New York: Springer.

Hart, T., & Hayden, M. E. (1986). The ecological validity of neuropsychological assessment and remediation. In B. Uzzell and Y. Gross (Eds.), *Clinical neuropsychology of intervention*, New York: Martinus Nijhoff.

Heaton, R. K., & Pendelton, M. G. (1981). Use of neuropsychological tests to predict adult patients' everyday functioning. *Journal of Consulting and Clinical Psychology, 49*, 807-821.

Heaton, R. K., Chelune, G. J., & Lehman, R. A. (1978). Using neuropsychological and personality tests to assess likelihood of patient employment. *Journal of Nervous and Mental Disease, 166*, 408-416.

Kahneman, D., Slovic, P., & Tversky, A. (1982). *Judgement under uncertainty: Heuristics and biases*. New York: Cambridge University Press.

Little, M. M., Williams, J. M., & Long, C. J. (1986). Clinical memory tests and everyday memory. *Archives of Clinical Neuropsychology, 1*, 323-333.

Loftus, E. F., & Palmer, J. C. (1974). Reconstruction of automobile destruction: An example of the interaction between language and memory. *Journal of Verbal Learning and Verbal Behavior, 13*, 585-589.

McDonald, R. S. (1986). Assessing treatment effects: Behavior rating scales. In L. Poon (Ed.), *Handbook for clinical memory assessment of older adults*. Hyattsville, MD: American Psychological Association.

Neisser, U. (1979). The concept of intelligence. *Intelligence, 3*, 217-227.

Neisser, U. (1982). *Memory observed: Remembering in natural contexts*. San Francisco: W. H. Freeman.

Newnan, O. S., Heaton, R. K., & Lehman, R. A. (1978). Neuropsychological and MMPI correlates of patient's future employment characteristics. *Perceptual and Motor Skills, 46*, 635-642.

Poon, L. W. (1986). *Clinical memory assessment of older adults*. Washington, DC: American Psychological Association.

Prigatano, G. P. (1978). The Wechsler Memory Scale: A selective review of the literature. *Journal of Clinical Psychology, 34*, 816-832.

Prigatano, G. P., Fordyce, D. J., Zeiner, H. K., Roueche, J. R., Pepping, M., & Case Wood, B. (1984). Neuropsychological rehabilitation after closed head injury in young adults. *Journal of Neurology, Neurosurgery, and Psychiatry, 47*, 505-513.

Salthouse, T. A. (1985). *A theory of cognitive aging*. Amsterdam: North Holland.

Schaie, K. W. (1983). *Longitudinal studies of adult psychological development*. New York: Guilford.

Sternberg, R. J. (1977). *Intelligence, information processing, and analogical reasoning: The componential analysis of human abilities*. Hillsdale NJ: Erlbaum.

Sternberg, R. J. (1985). *Beyond IQ: A triarchic theory of human intelligence*. New York: Cambridge University Press.

Sternberg, R. J., & Wagner, R. K. (1986). *Practical intelligence*. New York: Cambridge University Press.

United States Department of Labor. (1970). *Manual for the USES General Aptitude Test Battery,* Washington, DC: U. S. Government Printing Office.

Wechsler, D. (1958). *The measurement and appraisal of adult intelligence* (4th ed.), Baltimore, MD: Williams and Wilkins.

West, R. (1985). *Memory fitness over 40.* Gainseville, FL: Triad Publishing Company.

Williams, J. M. (1987). *The neuropsychologist's personal model of cognition.* Paper presented at the annual meeting of the Tennessee Psychological Association, Nashville, TN.

Williams, J. M., Klein, K., Little, M., & Haban, G. (1986). Family observations of everyday cognitive impairment in dementia. *Archives of Clinical Neuropsychology*, 1, 21-28.

Williams, J. M., Davis, K., Little, M. & Haban, G. (1987) *The Cognitive Behavior Rating Scale,* Odessa, Florida: Psychological Assessment Resources.

Williams, J. M. (1987). The role of cognitive retraining in comprehensive rehabilitation. In J. M. Williams and C. J. Long (Eds.), *The rehabilitation of cognitive disabilities*, New York: Plenum.

Williams, J. M., Little, M., Scates, S., & Blockman, N. (1987). Memory complaints and abilities among depressed older adults. *Journal of Consulting and Clinical Psychology*, 55, 595-598.

Zelinski, E. M., Gilewski, M. J., & Thompson, L. W. (1980). Do laboratory tests relate to self-assessment of memory ability in the young and old? In L. Poon, J. L. Fozard, L. S. Cermak, D. Arenberg, & L. W. Thompson (Eds.), *New directions in memory and aging* (pp. 519-544). Hillsdale, N. J.: L. Erlbaum.

8

Psychometric Confirmation of Neuropsychological Theory

Kurt A. Moehle, Jeffrey L. Rasmussen and Kathleen B. Fitzhugh-Bell

Although North American clinical neuropsychology has been traditionally data-based and empirical (Beaumont, 1983; Luria & Majovsky, 1977; Russell, 1986), the need for theoretical direction is evidenced by the eagerness with which many neuropsychologists have embraced recent hypotheses in theory-rich cognitive psychology (Szekeres, Ylvisaker, & Holland, 1985) and past hypotheses in neurological theory (e.g., Luria, 1980). Many see neuropsychology and cognitive psychology as compatible and complimentary areas (Gazzaniga, 1984) and propose that a wedding of knowledge from the two areas might lead to new insights about brain functioning and cognition.

The utility of theory in the scientific examination of brain-related abilities should be clear to neuropsychologists trained in academic psychology. An examination of theories and systems in psychology and their role in science is part of the typical doctoral training experience. Academically-trained psychologists are taught that theories are useful because they: (1) clarify the description of the *possible* world in ordinary language, (2) summarize existing knowledge, (3) mediate applications of knowledge to new systems, and (4) stimulate fruitful lines for experimental inquiry (Marx & Hillix, 1963).

Theories can serve either a descriptive function by summarizing a large amount of data, or an explanatory function by generating testable predictions (Arnoult, 1972). Their crucial function is to guide research and organize facts (Wood, 1977). It has been noted that "a mere accumulation of facts without some frame of reference for the interpretation of such facts would be chaos, or blind belief, and not science" (Chaplin & Kraviec, 1960, p. 2). Scientific activity is partially defined by the fact that theory figures prominently in any scientific activity. On the applied side, the practical significance of theories stems from their utility in generating novel procedures, such as new treatment procedures for the head-injured.

Moehle, K. A., Rasmussen, J. L., & Fitzhugh-Bell, K. B. (1988). Psychometric confirmation of neuropsychological theory. In J. M. Williams & C. J. Long (Eds.), *Cognitive approaches to neuropsychology*, New York: Plenum.

Incagnoli and Newman (1985) recently reviewed target areas for cognitive rehabilitation intervention. A brief examination of the areas (e.g., inappropriate social behavior, attention and motivation, etc.) reveals what we will call a "pragmatic" approach to development of new treatments rather than a theoretical approach.

These techniques and target areas appear to have sprung from the clinical experience of frontline service providers, using a cornucopia of techniques borrowed from the various training backgrounds of clinicians (e.g., social work, counseling, occupational therapy, speech therapy, etc.). This approach is an unsystematic one in which the rehabilitationist targets a problem through unspecified means and uses whatever technique he or she happens to be familiar with to solve it. Little thought is given to how one targets and prioritizes problem areas or how one chooses techniques.

In applied human neuropsychology, and cognitive rehabilitation in particular, such an approach appears to have outstripped a carefully reasoned approach based on theories of brain function and recovery. Such nonsystematic experimentation with human patients is fraught with risk for the patient and is detrimental to the field of rehabilitation neuropsychology. Knowledge is not being gathered and communicated in an organized cumulative way through research dissemination and independent replication by other investigators.

Instead of this pragmatic approach, prevailing neuropsychological and cognitive theory could be used to help formulate more effective, innovative, and specific intervention strategies (e.g., see Oliver, Shaller, Majovski, & Jacques, 1982, regarding stroke patients). Knowledge and working hypotheses could be generated in the four areas Diller (1976) has identified as important in designing a rehabilitation program: (1) determining the patient's problem, (2) determining how to diagnose it, (3) determining how to treat it, (4) and determining if the treatment is effective.

Characteristics of Theories.

Given that theory is important, some attention should be given to what constitutes a theory. A theory should possess an adequate structure, delineating an empirical area through explicit data language, clear theoretical concepts, and clearly derived relations between constructs and experimentally-derived variables. A theory should have methodological characteristics of quantitativeness and should lend itself to formal derivations of theoretical constructs. Specific predictions should flow from the theory. Constructs and tenets should be stated as clearly and unequivocally as possible since deductions or hypotheses about different subject matter will vary in the precision of their statements depending upon the clarity of the theory and its language (Marx & Hillix, 1963).

In psychology, many of the structures or schemas around which we organize our data are actually "models" rather than theories (Marx & Hillix, 1963). A model might be viewed as a subclass of theory. Boring (1957) notes that, whereas the theory states its version of reality in the "as" form (that is, making the assumption its tenets are true), the model is a convenient device that uses the "as if" (that is, meaning it is just a temporary, convenient heuristic that can guide activity for the moment, but which may be readily discarded if it seems not to fit the facts). A model does not seriously attempt to organize reality in a strongly defensible way. In applied human neuropsychology these models often take the form of simple neuropsychological explanations of isolated phenomena such as stuttering (Webster, 1985) or movement responses on the Rorschach (Paneth, 1981).

While the use of models is convenient, it can also be needlessly reductionistic. At the other end of the spectrum lies the "system," a much broader structure in which theories are often couched. A system is composed of accumulation of facts and theories which organize and explain a body of data (Chaplin & Kraviec, 1960). An example of this might be the learning theory framework within clinical psychology and psychiatry. This is a powerful framework for evaluating data, and numerous similarly-oriented theoretical viewpoints can flourish within this framework of system.

In neuropsychology, such systems might consist of an anterior-posterior or sensory-motor division of brain functions (Howes, 1965; Luria, 1980), lateralization of function (Benton, 1965; Penfield & Roberts, 1959; Wada & Rasmussen, 1960), and hierarchical organization of brain functions (Jackson, 1958; Luria, 1980; MacLean, 1970). The current methodological argument between behavioral neurologists and clinical neuropsychologists (Heilman & Valenstein, 1985; Rourke & Brown, 1986) might also be seen as the clash of two systems.

Although a few were mentioned above, there are actually few systems within the field of clinical neuropsychology. Rather there exists a growing corpus of "facts" or, in many cases, "assumptions" about brain-related abilities and their treatment or rehabilitation, with no general system to help pull the data together and little organizing theory to guide investigation and assist in development of the field. As Woodruff and Baisden (1986) have noted, the influence of theory in neuroscience seems to have been waning over the past two decades.

Now, however, theory is resurfacing as it proves important for the new treatment-oriented direction of human neuropsychology (Diller & Gordon, 1981). Cognitive and learning theories are being adopted by those constructing cognitive rehabilitation programs (e.g., Szekeres et al., 1985), and such theories be used further in calculating why certain treatment techniques fail. Johnston and Diller's (1983) call for further research into clinically-relevant areas like the "dynamics of information utilization" may well become commonplace as more rigorous outcome studies of cognitive rehabilitation are conducted.

Cognitive scientists and others working on theory development in the area of information-processing may assist in providing explanations for unexpected clinical research findings. Cognitive theorists may provide explanations as to why error evaluation was unrelated to previous perceptual-cognitive retraining in brain-injured individuals (Johnston & Diller, 1983). Hypotheses may also be generated as to why no significant relationships were found between decreases in reaction time and error rate on a visual-perceptual computerized cognitive retraining task and increases in Performance IQ following a period of cognitive retraining in brain injured subjects (Stellner, Moehle, & Bracy, 1987).

Another area which has already benefited from use of theories of brain functioning is the investigation of nonspecific attentional deficits in all forms of brain injury, and the role that recovery of such a deficit area may play in cognitive rehabilitation (Gummow, Miller, & Dustman, 1983). The importance of attentional deficits was illustrated by: (1) reviewing the current concepts of recovery of neural function after brain injury, (2) defining attention, describing methods for measuring it, and discussing brain structures implicated in attentional processes, (3) relating definitions of attention to deficits that accompany adult brain injury, and (4) describing elements necessary for the development of successful remediation of attentional deficits (Gummow et al., 1983).

Pre-eminent Neuropsychological Theories

Although North American neuropsychology has been driven largely by "raw empiricism" (Russell, 1986), a number of theories do exist. Primary among the models or theories of brain function in the current literature are: (1) Luria's (1980) functional systems theory, (2) localizationism (the theories of Broca, Gall, and Bouillaud, see Head, 1926), (3) mass actionism or equipotentiality (Flourens, 1824; Leob, 1902; Lashley, 1929), (4) other hierarchical models (besides Luria's; e.g., MacLean, 1970), and (5) numerous lesser models, i.e., those dealing with a single brain system or process, e.g., Walley and Weiden's (1973) theory of attention.

Mass actionism will not be discussed further because there appears to be little current interest in this general theory, except for occasional discussions of how the brain functions as an integrated collection of separate processes and systems (e.g., Finset, 1984). Other hierarchical models, such as MacLean's (1970) Triune brain model of Pribram's (1974) quasi-hierarchical holographic theory, also will not be discussed further because our current literature search in the area of clinical neuropsychology did not indicate extensive clinical research involving them.

Early theories or models in clinical neuropsychology evolved from experimental neuropsychology and comparative research (e.g., Fritsch & Hitzig, 1960; Kluver, 1957). Such animal models may be questioned as to their appropriateness for humans, especially in consideration of higher mental processes such as language. Given the lack of language in animals, models from cognitive psychology (Gazzaniga, 1984; Goldstein & Oakley, 1985) seem more promising for the study of higher cortical functions than the biologically grounded but functionally limited animal models.

The embracing of cognitive models in clinical neuropsychology also encouraged an emphasis on the hierarchical, developmental nature of human cognitive abilities. This reflects cognitive psychology's investment in developmental studies (Kephart, 1968; Piaget, 1952). Rehabilitationists have applied the Piagetian developmental model to brain retraining, with the implication that one must complete one stage of "development" (retraining) before being ready for the next (Craine, 1982). This is much like moving through Piaget's stages of cognitive development as one matures. Such an approach has proven to have limitations when applied to the head-injured (Moehle, Rasmussen, & Fitzhugh-Bell, 1987a).

The Systems Approach has also recently influenced clinical neuropsychology (el.g., Piasetsky, 1982). According to this approach, complex behaviors derive from dynamic systems of "regional cooperation" in the brain. Different regions are devoted to certain complex processing activities, and complex behavior springs from the integration and coordination of these activities. This approach represents a melding of localizationism and mass actionism.

Cerebral specialization or lateralization of function, as mentioned above, is yet another time-honored framework for organizing brain function (Crockett, Clark, & Klonoff, 1981; Nebes, 1974; Woodruff & Baisden, 1986). Nebes, in summarizing the models of Bogan, Levy-Agresti, and Sperry, notes that the left hemisphere is analytical/propositional, and analyses sequentially; whereas the right hemisphere is synthetic/appositional, organizing and manipulating data in terms of organized wholes. Despite compelling evidence for lateralization of lower or more elemental functions, it is still unclear how well higher mental functions are lateralized (Russell, 1986; Woodruff & Baisden, 1986).

Since neuropsychologists have experienced the potential of drawing together two fields of study, neuropsychological theory and cognitive viewpoints are now being drawn together more frequently in an attempt to adequately explain human higher cognitive functions (Gazzaniga, 1984). Kaufman (1984), for example, has noted there is much in common between Luria's planning function and Piaget's formal operational thinking; both generally reflecting a more mature decision-making capacity.

This bond is further cemented by increasing awareness that an excellent way to study normal human cognition is to study humans with brain science techniques (including examination of disrupted neurological systems) in tandem with cognitive science methods (Gazzaniga, 1984). The goal is the generation of models of normal human cognition that have "biologic reality." It would appear such collaboration is going to continue for the foreseeable future.

A Systematic Computerized Search of the Literature.

To further examine extant neuropsychological models, we conducted a computer search of the literature. Use of the computer for this task saves time and also controls for personal bias on the part of the investigators because all articles matching the search terms are retrieved, not just the ones in the investigators' favorite journals.

For this search, the search terms "theory or model" were coupled with "neuropsychology." Four major computerized databases were searched, from the time period of their initial appearance "online" until the present (March-May of 1986). The four databases were *PsychINFO-Psychological Abstracts* (from 1967), *Medline*--includes *Index Medicus* (from 1981), *Educational Resources Information Center* (from 1966), and *National Rehabilitation Information Center* (from 1950). The complete results of this search are presented in the Appendix.

The articles retrieved were rationally grouped into eight major classes: (1) Metamodels or theories, (2) Clinical or treatment models, (3) Neuropsychological models. (4) Specific syndromes or behaviors, (5) Cognitive processes, (6) Statistical models, (7) Animal or neurophysiological models, and (8) Developmental or genetic models.

The search revealed that the primary theoretical approaches to brain functioning appear to be Luria's (1980) functional systems conceptualization and the general information-processing model (Atkinson & Shiffrin, 1968; Lachman, Lachman, and Butterfield, 1979). Luria's approach is tied to brain functioning through his neurological case-study investigations of individuals with disordered brain functioning (see, for example, Luria, 1972, *The man with a shattered world*). Cognitive viewpoints, conversely, have evolved largely from the impetus of Piaget's (1952, 1983) developmental studies with normal children.

The pre-eminence of these two theories has inevitably lead to comparisons being drawn between them (see Morgan, present volume). This has been heightened by methodological advances in which biological findings are being used increasingly in attempts to prove cognitively-oriented theories of brain functioning (e.g., Baddeley, 1982; cf. Gazzaniga, 1984). Fuller discussion of these types of theories can be obtained elsewhere (Lachman, Lachman, & Butterfield, 1979; Luria, 1980; Piaget, 1983). Having explored briefly the state of theory use in clinical neuropsychology, we now wish to turn our attention to the central theme of this chapter; confirming neuropsychological theory through psychometric methods.

Validation of Theory and Models in Clinical Neuropsychology

Numerous techniques and approaches have been utilized to validate neuropsychological theory. Included among these are statistical quasi-experimental group designs (see Knight & Wooles, 1980, for a review of research with organic amnesiacs), and case studies (e.g., Rao & Bieliauskas,

1983), which are usually lesion studies (e.g., Sperry, 1973). Each method has its difficulties (Heilman & Valenstein, 1985; Kolb & Whishaw, 1980).

As Tupper and Rosenblood (1984) recently noted, analysis of variance, matched group designs, and analysis of covariance may have their statistical assumptions violated by attribute variables, due to lack of theoretical and statistical independence. Lesion studies have been criticized because they are basing inference upon "deficit measurement" (McFarland, 1983). In such measurement a brain area's function is assumed from what the patient cannot do when that area is destroyed.

The connectionists (Geschwind, 1965) particularly object to such reasoning because there is no way to rule out connectionist hypotheses that the loss of a function from destruction of a brain area may be due to an interrupted connection from the area that organizes that function to the area that expresses it rather than due to destruction of the brain area actually subserving the function. Finally, the case study method has been criticized due to its heavy reliance on nonstandardized methods and clinical skill (Beaumont, 1983), and the limited generalizability and reliability of the findings obtained by such methods.

Given the difficulties inherent in these validation methods, alternatives, or at least supplemental modes of obtaining evidence, are in order. One such alternative is confirmatory factor analysis. Factor analysis is a psychometric method that has long been used to uncover "unseen" variables underlying measured variables. Kerlinger (1979) states that "Factor analysis is an analytic method for determining the number and nature of the variables that underlie larger numbers of variables or measures" (p. 180). The technique can be used as either a data reduction technique (mentioned above), or as a method to evaluate the structure of some set of variables. It has been used historically to test the validity of theories of human mental abilities (Guilford, 1954; Spearman, 1904; Thurstone & Thurstone, 1941). Theoretically, it could be used to isolate those "elemental functions" mentioned by Russell (1986) that should be measured by any good neuropsychological battery.

Confirmatory factor analysis (CFA) has only recently been applied to clinical neuropsychology. Attempts have been made by some to discover what factors underlay the mass of neuropsychological tests that have proliferated over the past several decades (Halstead, 1947; Swiercinsky, 1978, 1979). Secondarily, such research has also focused on identifying the "brain correlates" of these test factors by examining the effects of documented localized brain lesions on such factors (Royce, Yeudall, & Bock, 1976). This chapter promotes a third usage of factor analysis in clinical neuropsychology: psychometric evaluation of the validity of neuropsychological theories.

Confirmatory Factor Analysis

Confirmatory factor analysis is a subset of structural equation modeling (Bentler, 1980), and may be contrasted with exploratory factor analysis. Exploratory factor analysis (EFA) is illustrated by the studies mentioned above in which a mass of variables collected on the same sample is analyzed in such way that variables are correlated with each other in order to ascertain where clusters of highly interrelated variables exist (Kerlinger, 1979). No particular theory of brain functioning need be involved in exploratory analysis. Confirmatory factor analysis (CFA), however, involves the testing of a previously developed model which would allow one to specify how the data may order themselves in factors.

CFA requires: (1) the latent factors theorized to underlie the variables, (2) the variables that measure each factor, and (3) the structure of the relationship between factors (Newby, Hallenbeck, & Embretson, 1983). Through this method the adequacy of each model can be tested statistically, rather than rationally, judged against the criterion of how well the model fits actual clinical data.

Since the researcher establishes *a priori* the factor structure in terms of the number and nature of the factors and the nature of the loadings, CFA avoids the problem of obtaining a factor solution and then concocting a model to explain the results.

CFA, however, suffers specifically from three major flaws itself: (1) technical problems (e.g., cumbersome, specification of models in the LISREL software--Joreskog & Sorbom, 1984--used for most CFAs), (2) questioning of how "confirmatory" in nature CFA actually is (due to allowance of the use of modifications, which, if sufficient in number, actually amount to an EFA), and (3) difficulties with "goodness of fit" indices. Rigorous acceptable values for such indices have not been established. Furthermore, the effects of nonnormality, outliers, missing data, small case-to-variable ratios, etc., have not been adequately studied. Finally, as sample size decreases, the chances of the model achieving a good fit actually increase!

The above points represent the confusion that often surrounds a new but complicated technique. What is clear is that CFA is an experimental technique with great promise, but which must be used with appropriate caution until more is known.

Besides these statistical concerns, factor analytic studies of neuropsychological batteries are hampered by a shortage of clinical databases complete enough and with large enough samples to lend themselves to such analysis. Only a few major neuropsychological batteries have been in use long enough to produce the body of data needed for such analyses (Newby et al., 1983). The problem is compounded because such batteries, despite their great length, may still not have enough measures to assess all brain functions adequately (Newby et al., 1983; Swiercinsky, 1979).

Missing data provides a second problem. Methods of handling missing data are usually not addressed in clinical neuropsychological CFA studies. It is a difficult proposition to get a majority of patients with brain lesions to complete all the neuropsychological measures presented them when using a standard neuropsychological battery.

At best, one hopes to give most of the patients most of the tests most of the time. Patients will differ as to which tests they refused to do or did not have time to complete before discharge from hospital, etc. The clinician-researcher is left with a database with many patients, many neuropsychological variables, and many gaps, or missing data. They way in which these data are handled is an important detail in CFA that bears reporting, as confidence in one's conclusions is affected.

Another crucial factor is the question of, to what does one compare the models' fit: The null model? A random model? Another model? The null model would not seem a good idea, as we know from decades of factor analytic work in psychology that human abilities are positively correlated in most individuals (Galton, 1883; Thurstone & Thurstone, 1941). We would expect some relationship. The random model poses one alternative in that one could compare the theoretical model with a model with the same number of fixed and free parameters as the theoretical model, but which are placed in an arbitrary fashion.

These questions cannot be answered satisfactorily at this time. They are mentioned in order to raise awareness of these issues and to temper the interpretation of CFA results. With these caveats in mind, in order to briefly illustrate how CFA may be used to test the validity of neuropsychological theory, we will report an empirical study we conducted to test several neuropsychological models previously examined by Newby et al. (1983).

An Empirical Study

In the current study we attempted to replicate the findings of Newby et al. (1983) with regard to their CFA of four neuropsychological models. The models were: (1) Swiercinsky's (1979) orthogonally-rotated factor analysis model, (2) Royce's model from his theory of cognitive structure (1973) and factor analysis work (e.g., Royce et al., 1976), (3) Luria's (1980) theory and his 10 categories of higher cortical functions to be investigated, and (4) Lezak's (1976) rough scheme for outlining important neuropsychological functions, fleshed out by additions from the writings of others (e.g., Milner, 1970).

The disparity between sparse neuropsychological theory and increasingly abundant and popular clinical practice makes such a study important. This investigation and the one done by Newby et al. (1983) represent attempts to "promote theoretical integration" in the field of clinical and rehabilitation neuropsychology.

As mentioned, little research in the area of CFA has preceded us because techniques for latent structural equation quantitative methodology--of which CFA is a family member--are relatively new (Bentler & Bonnet, 1980), and their application to clinical neuropsychology has been limited (cf. Newby et al., 1983).

Based on the prior work of Newby et al., however, it is predicted that: (1) no models will fit the data well in an absolute sense, (2) models proposed will generally provide a better fit to the data than the null model of no relationship between or underlying the variables.

Further exploration will be done regarding comparative fit of the models and how their fit compares with a random model composed of numerous random samplings of the data, which are then combined or averaged.

Further predictions from Newby et al.'s findings, are: (1) Luria's model will not even converge to a solution and will be eliminated (this was due to the fact that there was not a wide enough selection of variables in the database to represent all the theory's areas of brain functioning, e.g., language functioning), (2) of the remaining three models, Lezak's modified schematization, with additional post-hoc modifications on our part, will result in the best fit to the data.

Method

Subjects

Subjects were 1376 patients seen in the Neuropsychology Laboratory, Neurology Department, Indiana University Medical Center, over the past 16 years for a variety of confirmed or suspected cerebral dysfunctions (see Table 1). The only selection criterion was that subjects had to be old enough to have taken the adult version of the Halstead-Reitan Neuropsychological Test Battery in use at the Neuropsychology Laboratory since Reitan developed the battery there some 30 years ago (Reitan, 1979; Reitan & Davison, 1974), and that they were old enough to have taken the adult version of the Wechsler intelligence scale (i.e., 16 years of age and older; Wechsler, 1955, 1981).

Subjects ranged in age from 16 to 91 years of age (mean = 42.81; standard deviation, SD = 17.80), and had an average of 11.49 years of education (SD = 3.57). Sixty-four percent of the sample was male and 82% were Caucasian, while race was not recorded in another 14% of the cases. Eighty percent of these patients were referred from other clinics and services within the Indiana University Medical Center, which means that most had a relatively thorough medical work-up before the decision was made to refer them for neuropsychological testing. Presumed etiology or type of disease, based on diagnosis by a neurologist or neurosurgeon, using all data except neuropsychological test results, is presented in Table 1.

Materials and Procedure.

All subjects were administered a comprehensive neuropsychological test battery, consisting of the Halstead-Reitan Neuropsychological Test Battery for Adults (Reitan & Davison, 1974), and some ancillary procedures that have been added in the Neuropsychological Laboratory over the years (e.g., Grooved Pegboard; Klove, 1963). Standard administration procedures were followed (Reitan, 1979), and all tests were given by carefully trained technicians (usually with degrees in psychology) under the supervision of an experienced clinical neuropsychologist (KBFB).

Table 1

Cerebral Disease Type of Etiology in Patient Sample

Disease type or Etiology	<u>N</u>	Percent
1. Vascular disease	420	30.5
2. Trauma	212	15.4
3. No statement as to etiology	201	14.6
4. No cerebral dysfunction in history	186	13.5
5. Neoplasm	123	8.9
6. Degenerative disease	88	6.4
7. Infection	57	4.1
8. Congenital disorder	41	3.0
9. Other	32	2.3
10. Metabolic disorder	16	1.2
Total	1376	100.0

Note. This same patient sample was used in the exploratory factor analysis of this database, reported elsewhere (Moehle et al., 1987b).

The variables selected for analysis (after Newby et al., 1983) were: Speech Sounds Perception Test, Seashore Rhythm Test, Tactual Performance Test (Total Time and Localization), Category Test, Finger Oscillation Test, Halstead-Wepman Aphasia Screening Test, Grip Strength, Reitan-Klove Tactile Form Recognition Test, Reitan-Klove Sensory Perceptual Exam, Tactile Finger Recognition, Finger Tip Number Writing, Trailmaking Test, Parts A and B, Grooved Pegboard Test, and subtests from the Wechsler Adult Intelligence Scale. Altogether, 33 variables were entered into the analysis. Variables were assigned *a priori* to specified factors within each of the four models tested (cf. Newby et al., 1983). The assignment of variables to factors for each model is presented Table 2.

Statistical Analyses

The two main analyses carried out were generation of an intercorrelation matrix and LISREL VI (Joreskog & Sorbom, 1984) analysis of the intercorrelation matrix.

Table 2
Factor Numerals Associated with the Four Models

	Model			
Variable	A	B	C	D
1. Aphasia-Listening	3	4	1,5	1
2. Aphasia-Reading	1,3	4	7	1
3. Speech Sounds Perception	3	4	5,7	1
4. WAIS-Information	1	4,5	10	2,3
5. WAIS-Vocabulary	1	4	6,10	2,3
6. Category Test	1,4	8	7,10	3
7. WAIS-Similarities	1	4	10	3
8. WAIS-Comprehension	1,2	4,5	10	3
9. WAIS-Arithmetic	1,4	4	8	3
10. Aphasia-Talking	3	4	6	4
11. Aphasia-Writing	3	4	7	4
12. Trail Making-A	6	1,5	4,7,8	4
13. Trail Making-B	6	1,6	4,7,8	4
14. Graphesthesia-Right Hand	8	5	3	5
15. Graphesthesia-Left Hand	8	5	3	5
16. Stereognosis-Right Hand	8	-	3	5
17. Stereognosis-Left Hand	8	-	3	5
18. Finger Gnosis-Right Hand	8	4,5	3	5
19. Finger Gnosis-Left Hand	8	6	3	5
20. Seashore Rhythm	4	3,4	2	5,6,7
21. Tactual Performance-Location	5,9	1	4,9	6
22. Tactual Performance-Time	5	1	1	7
23. WAIS-Picture Arrangement	4	1	10	7
24. WAIS-Block Design	4,5	1,7	4	7
25. WAIS-Object Assembly	5	1	4	7
26. WAIS-Digit Symbol	6	2	4	7
27. Spatial Relations	5	1	1,4	8
28. Grip Strength-Right Hand	7	-	1	8
29. Grip Strength-Left Hand	7	-	1	8
30. Finger Tapping-Right Hand	7	3	1,2	8
31. Finger Tapping-Left Hand	7	2,3	1,2	8
32. Grooved Pegboard-Right Hand	6,7	2	1,4	8
33. Grooved Pegboard-Left Hand	6,7	2	1,4	8

Note. Entries in table indicate which factor the variable was predicted to load on for the four models.

The data set contained a number of missing data points. The maximum percentage of missing data was 82.2% missing for the Grooved Pegboard Test, the minimum was 7.6% for Finger Oscillation. The median was 28.7% missing data. Due to the size and variability of percentages of missing data, the intercorrelation matrix was calculated using pairwise deletion along with eigenvalue smoothing using eigenvalues of 0.3 or greater. The analysis was carried out using the BMDPAM program from the BMDP-81, Biomedical Computer Programs package (Dixon, 1981). This procedure results in maximal use of the available data and a positive semidefinite intercorrelation matrix appropriate for factor analysis techniques. The confirmatory factor analysis was carried out by specification of the four models using LISREL VI.

Results and Discussion

The analyses for all models resulted in unreasonable values such as negative variances, correlations greater than unity, and matrices that were not positive definite. These are all indications that the models were fundamentally wrong and not suitable for the data (Joreskog & Sorbom, 1984).

The current results supported our hypotheses of no models fitting the data well in an absolute sense. Due to the failure of any of the models to converge to a solution, we were unable to test a second hypothesis that the models proposed will generally provide a better fit to the data than the null model. Nor were we able to carry out planned exploration of comparative fit of the models and how their fit compares with a random model.

As to why we received the results we did, we can echo many of the same reasons offered by Newby et al.(1983). First of all, we were tapping a very diverse theoretical gamut while using a fixed battery developed empirically. It could be that many of the latent constructs in the theories tested were not represented in the current battery of tests.

Statistical problems are another possibility. Missing data pose a problem. Although it was possible to analyze the data using exploratory factor analysis (Moehle, Rasmussen, & Fitzhugh-Bell, 1987b), the missing data may have presented a problem for the LISREL algorithms in the confirmatory factor analysis.

Another statistical problem that has plagued prior research (Newby et al., 1983), however, has been the possible violation of the multivariate normality assumptions in the data and the possibility that some relationships could have been nonlinear. It is not known how this will affect the CFA in general (Bentler, 1980), and the current study in particular.

Limitations of the current study include the lack of memory measures in the current edition of this database, the fact that the tests were not derived with theory in mind, and technical statistical problems which have no current answer. There was also not a wide enough selection of variables in the database to represent all theoretical areas of brain functioning, e.g., language functioning.

Conclusions regarding this particular study are certainly not clear at this point, except to say that none of the models fit well in an absolute sense, and that all failed to converge to a solution, precluding further comparisons and analysis.

Practical implications include the fact that this is an important new method of theory validation that needs to be considered. Batteries supposedly developed from theory (e.g., Luria Nebraska Neuropsychological Battery; LNNB) need to be examined. In addition, we echo the suggestions of Newby et al. (1983) that smaller batteries and more specific models may need to be tested in future studies in order to make the task more manageable statistically.

Conversely, the complexity of human brain functioning dictates that batteries be expanded to include more tests of language and memory and tests of general level of cortical arousal or tone. The latter may be accomplished through reaction time measures, physiological measures, or structured ratings of apparent alertness (cf. Newby et al., 1983).

Regarding the former point, Russell (1986) has given some guidelines as to what a good neuropsychological battery should encompass: (1) tests for the elemental functions of each brain lobe (e.g., basic sensory functions for parietal lobes), (2) more precise, extensive coverage of the better known functions (i.e., more language tests than drawing tests), (3) examination of the functions that exist but have not yet been clearly related to a brain area (e.g., long-term memory), and (4) measures of compound functions, or "fluid" measures to serve as general indices of the presence and severity of overall brain dysfunction (e.g., Category Test or Trailmaking Test, Part B).

Summary

In summary, we have outlined the predominant theories extant in clinical neuropsychology today (Luria's functional systems theory and information-processing approaches), have demonstrated a method for validating theory (confirmatory factor analysis), and have proposed greater reliance on theory in the continued development of clinical neuropsychology, especially as the field branches into the treatment or rehabilitation realm. Investigators and test developers in clinical neuropsychology are urged to: (1) conduct validation studies on old theories, (2) examine new theories from cognitive neuroscience, such as Pribram's (1974) quasi-hierarchical holographic theory, and (3) take Woodruff and Baisden's (1986) advice to "begin with a different point of view and to synthesize material of an amazingly diverse nature" (p. 53) in developing more adequate ways to conceptualize human brain function.

References

Armstrong, B. B., & Soelberg, P. (1968). On the interpretation of factor analysis. *Psychological Bulletin, 70*, 361-364.

Arnoult, M.D. (1972). *Fundamentals of scientific method in psychology.* Dubuque, Iowa: Brown.

Atkinson, R. C., & Shiffrin, R. M. (1968). Human memory: A proposed system and its control process. In K. W. Spence & J. T. Spence (Eds.), *The psychology of learning and motivation* (Vol. 2). New York: Pergamon Press.

Baddeley, A. D. (1982). Implications of neuropsychological evidence for theories of normal memory. *Philosophical Transactions of the Royal Society of London* (Biology), *298*, 59-72.

Beaumont, J. G. (1983). *Introduction to neuropsychology.* New York: The Guilford Press.

Bentler, P. M. (1980). Multivariate analysis with latent variables: Causal modeling. *Annual Review of Psychology, 31*, 419-456.

Bentler, P. M., & Bonnett, D. G. (1980). Significance tests and goodness of fit in the analysis of covariance structures. *Psychological Bulletin, 88*, 588-606.

Benton, A. L. (1965). *Sentence memory test.* Iowa City, IA: Author.

Boring, E. G. (1957). *A history of experimental psychology.* New York: Appleton Century Crafts.

Chaplin, J. P., & Kraviec, T. S. (1960). *Systems and theories of psychology.* New York: Holt, Rinehart, & Winston.

Craine, J. F. (1982). Principles of cognitive rehabilitation. In L. E. Trexler (Ed.), *Cognitive rehabilitation: Conceptualization and intervention.* New York: Plenum Press.

Crockett, D., Clark, C., & Klonoff, H. (1981). Introduction-an overview of neuropsychology. In S. B. Filskov & T. J. Bell (Eds.), *Handbook of neuropsychology.* New York: John Wiley & Sons.

Diller, L., & Gordon, W. A. (1981). Rehabilitation and clinical neuropsychology. In S. B. Filskov & T. J. Bell (Eds.), *Handbook of neuropsychology.* New York: John Wiley & Sons.

Diller, L., & Gordon , W. A. (1981). Interventions for cognitive deficits in brain-injured adults. *Clinical Psychologist, 49*, 822-834.

Dixon, W. J. (1981). *BMDP statistical software.* Berkeley, CA: University of California Press.

Finset, A. (1984). Re-integrating our regulerings funksjoner nevrosykologisk behandlings strategi. (Re-integration of regulatory functions as a neuropsychological treatment strategy.) *Fidskift For Norsk Psykologforening, 21*(3), 127-135.

Flourens, P. (1924). *Recherches experimentales sue les proprietes et les fouctious du systeme nerveux deus les animoux nertefres.* Paris: Cervot.

Fritsch, G., & Hitzig, E. (1960). On the electrical excitability of the cerebrum. In G. Van Boring (Ed.), *The cerebral cortex.* Springfield, IL: Charles C. Thomas.

Galton, F. (1883). *Inquiries into faculty and its development.* London: MacMillan.

Gazzaniga, M. (1984). *Handbook of cognitive neuroscience.* New York: Plenum Press.

Geschwind, N. (1965). Disconnexion syndromes in animals and man. *Brain, 88,* 237-294.

Goldstein, L. H., & Oakley, D. A. (1985). Expected and actual behavior capacity after diffuse reduction in cerebral cortex. A review and suggestions for rehabilitative techniques with the mentally handicapped and head-injured. *British Journal of Clinical Psychology, Feb. 24 (Pt. 1),* 13-24.

Guilford, J. P. (1954). A factor analytic study across the domains of reasoning, creativity, and evaluation: Hypotheses and descriptions of tests. *Reports from the psychological laboratory.* Los Angeles: University of Southern California Press.

Gummow, L., Miller, P. & Dustman, R. E. (1983). Attention and brain injury: A case for cognitive rehabilitation of attentional deficits. *Clinical Psychology Review, 3*(3), 255-274.

Halstead, W. C. (1947). *Brain and intelligence: A quantitative study of the frontal lobes.* Chicago: University of Chicago Press.

Heilman, K. M., & Valenstein, E. (Eds.) (1985). *Clinical neuropsychology* (2nd ed.). New York: Oxford University Press.

Howes, D. (1965, September 16-18). *Some experimental investigations in aphasia.* Paper presented at the Conference on Verbal Behavior, New York, NY.

Incagnoli, T., & Newman, B. (1985). Cognitive and behavioral rehabilitation interventions. *International Journal of Clinical Neuropsychology, 7*(4), 173-182.

Jackson, J. H. (1958). In J. Taylor (Ed.): *Selected writings of John Hughlings Jackson.* New York: Basic Books.

Johnston, C. W., & Diller, L. (1983). Error evaluation ability of right-hemisphere brain lesioned patients who has had perceptual-cognitive retraining. *Journal of Clinical Neuropsychology, 5*(4), 401-402.

Joreskog, K. G., & Sorbon, D. (1984). *LISREL VI analysis of linear structural relationships by the method of maximum likelihood.* Mooresville, IN: Scientific Software, Inc.

Kaufman, A. S. (1984). K-ABC and controversy. *Journal of Special Education, 18*(3), 409-444.

Kephart, N. C. (1968) *Learning disability: An educational adventure.* West Lafayette, IN: Kappa Delta Pi Press.

Kerlinger, F. N. (1979). *Behavioral research: A conceptual approach.* Chicago: Holt, Rinehart, and Winston.

Klove, H. (1963). Clinical neuropsychology. In F. M. Forster (Ed.), *Medical clinics of North America,* New York: Saunders.

Kluve, H. (1957). *Behavior mechanisms in monkeys.* Chicago: University of Chicago Press.

Knight, R., & Wooles, (1980). Experimental investigation of chronic organic amnesia: A review. *Psychological Bulletin, 88*(3), 753-771.

Kolb, B., & Whishaw, I. Q. (1980). *Fundamentals of Human Neuropsychology* (2nd ed.). New York: W. H. Freeman & Company.

Lachman, R., Lachman, J. L. & Butterfield, E. C. (1979). *Cognitive psychology information processing: An introduction.* Hillsdale, NJ: Erlbaum, West.

Lashley, K. (1929). *Brain mechanisms and intelligence.* Chicago: University of Chicago Press.

Lezak, M. D. (1976). *Neuropsychological assessment.* New York: Oxford University Press.

Leob, J. (1902). *Comparative physiology of the brain and comparative psychology.* New York: Putnam Press.

Luria, A. R. (1980). *Higher cortical functions in man.* (2nd ed., revised and expanded). New York: Basic Books.

Luria, A. R. (1972). *The man with the shattered world.* New York: Basic Books.

Luria, A. R., & Majovski, L. V. (1977). Basic approaches used in American and Soviet clinical neuropsychology. *American Psychologist, 32,* 959-968.

MacLean, P. D. (1970). The triune brain, emotion, and scientific bias. In F. O. Schmitt (Ed.), *The neurosciences: Second study program* (pp. 336-348). New York: Rockefeller University Press.

Marx, M. H., & Hillix, W. A. (1963). *Systems and theories in psychology.* New York: McGraw-Hill.

McFarland, K. (1983). Syndrome analysis in clinical neuropsychology. *British Journal of Clinical Psychology, 22,* 61-74.

Milner, B. (1970). Memory and medial temporal regions of the brain. In K. H. Pribram & D. E. Broadbent (Eds.), *International review of research in mental retardation.* New York: Academic Press.

Moehle, K. A., Rasmussen, J. L., & Fitzhugh-Bell, K. (1987a). Neuropsychological theories and cognitive rehabilitation. In J. M. Williams & C. J. Long (Eds.), *The rehabilitation of cognitive disabilities.* New York: Plenum Press.

Moehle, K. A., Rasmussen, J. L., & Fitzhugh-Bell, K. B. (1987b). *Factor analysis of neuropsychological tests with adults.* Manuscript submitted for publication.

Nebes, R. D. (1974). Hemispheric specialization in commissurotimized man. *Psychological Bulletin, 81,* 1-14.

Newby, R. F., Hallenbeck, C. E., Embretson, S. (1983). Confirmatory factory analysis of four general neuropsychological models with a modified Halstead-Reitan battery. *Journal of Clinical Neuropsychology, 5*(2), 115-133.

Oliver, J. III, Shaller, C. A., Majovski, L. V., & Jacques S. (1982). Stroke mechanisms: Neuropsychological implications. *Clinical Neuropsychology, 4*(2), 81-83.

Paneth, G. (1982). Rorschach B-Valaszok, A felettes-en es A mubrotalmi kus rendszer. Egy neuropzichologia teoria, vazlater. (M answers in Roscharch's test the Sugeryo and the Rubrothenlamic system: The network for neuropsychological theory). *Magyar Pszichologiai Szemle, 38*(6), 541-550.

Penfield, W., & Roberts, L. (1959). *Speech and brain mechanisms.* Princeton, NJ: Princeton University Press.

Piaget, J. (1952). *The origins of intelligence in children.* New York: International University Press.

Piaget, J. (1983). Piagetian theory. In W. Kene (Ed.), *Handbook of child psychology: Vol. 1 History, theory and methods* (pp. 103-128). New York: John Wiley & Sons.

Piasetsky, E. B. (1982). The relevance of brain-behavior relationships for relationships for rehabilitation. In L. E. Trexler (Ed.), *Cognitive rehabilitation: conceptualization and intervention*. New York: Plenum Press.

Pribram, K. H. (1974). How is it that sensing so much we can do so little? In F. O. Schmitt & F. G. Worden (Eds.), *The neurosciences: Third study program* (pp. 249-261). Cambridge, MA: The M.I.T. Press.

Rao, S. M., & Bieliauskas, L. (1983). Cognitive rehabilitation two and one-half years post right temporal lobectomy. *Journal of Clinical Neuropsychology, 5*(4), 313-320.

Reitan, R. (1979). *Manual for administration of neuropsychological test batteries for adults and children*. Tucson, AZ: Author.

Reitan, R. M., & Davison, L. A. (1974). *Clinical neuropsychology: Current status and applications*. New York: Winston/Wiley.

Rourke, B. P., & Brown, G. G. (1986). Clinical neuropsychology and behavioral neurology: Similarities and differences. In S. B. Filskov & T. J. Boll (Eds.), *Handbook of clinical neuropsychology* (Vol. 2). New York: John Wiley & Sons.

Royce, J. R. (1973). The conceptual framework for a multifactor theory of individuality. In J. R. Royce (Ed.), *Multivariate analysis and psychological theory*. London: Academic Press.

Royce, J. R., Yeudall, L. T., & Bock, C. (1976). Factor analytic studies of human brain damage: I. First and second order factors and their brain correlates. *Multivariate Behavioral Research, 11*, 381-418.

Russell, E. W. (1986). The psychometric foundation of clinical neuropsychology. In S. B. Filskov & T. J. Boll (Eds.), *Handbook of neuropsychology* (Vol. 2). New York: John Wiley & Sons.

Spearman, C. (1904). General intelligence, objectively determines and measured. *American Journal of Psychology, 15*, 201-293.

Sperry, R. W. (1973). Lateral specialization of cerebral function in the surgically separated hemisphere. In F. G. McGuigan & R. A. Schoonover (Eds.), *The psychophysiology of thinking*. New York: Academic Press.

Stellner, R. H., Moehle, K. A., & Bracy, O. (1987, October 28-30). *The relationship between change in reaction time and response errors on a computerized cognitive retraining task*. Paper presented at the meeting of The National Academy of Neuropsychologists, Chicago, IL.

Swiercinsky, D. (1978). *Manual for the adult neuropsychological evaluation*. Springfield, IL: Charles C. Thomas.

Swiercinsky, D. P. (1979). Factorial pattern description and comparison of functional abilities in neuropsychological assessment. *Perceptual Motor Skills, 48*, 231-241.

Szekeres, S. F., Ylvisaker, M., & Holland, A. L. (1985). Cognitive rehabilitation therapy: A framework for intervention. In M. Ylvisaker (Ed.), *Head injury rehabilitation*. San Diego: College Hill Press.

Tabachnick, B. G., & Fidell, L. S. (1978). *Using multivariate statistics*. New York: Harper Row.

Thurstone, L. L., & Thurstone, T. G. (1941). Factorial studies of intelligence. *Psychometric Monographs*. (No. 2), Chicago: University of Chicago Press.

Tupper, D. E., & Rosenblood, L. K. (1984). Methodological considerations in the use of attribute variables in neuropsychological research. *Journal of Clinical Neuropsychology, 6*(4), 441-453.

Wada, J. A., & Rasmussen, T. (1960). Intracarotid injection of sodium amytol for the lateralization of cerebral speech dominance: Experimental and clinical observations. *Journal of Neurosurgery, 17*, 266-282.

Walley, R. E., & Weiden, T. D. (1973). Lateral inhibition and cognitive masking: A neuropsychological theory of attention. *Psychological Review, 80*(4), 284-302.

Webster, W. G. (1985). Neuropsychological models of stuttering I. Representation of sequential response mechanisms. *Neuropsychologia, 23*(2), 263-267.

Wechsler, D. (1958). *Manual for the Wechsler adult intelligence scale.* New York: The Psychological Corporation.

Wechsler, D. (1981). *Wechsler adult intelligence scale-revised.* New York: The Psychological Corporation.

Wood, G. (1977). *Fundamentals of psychological research.* Boston: Little, Brown, & Company.

Woodruff, M. L., & Baisden, R. H. (1986). Theories of brain functioning: A brief introduction to the study of the brain and behavior. In D. Wedding, A. M. Horton, Jr., & J. Webster (Eds.), *The neuropsychology handbook.* New York: Springer Publishing Company.

Appendix

Neuropsychological Theory or Models: A Computerized Literature Search

Some non-English language journals were excluded if translations were not available. Also not included were a number of articles dealing with the Luria Nebraska Neuropsychological Battery, if it was judged that the primary thrust of the article was to defend the battery rather than seriously discuss theory or its application. "Metamodel" is our term for a complex model that attempts to account for more than one brain process, e.g., more than attentional processes alone, but which may not quite achieve theory status.

Theories or metamodels

Theory of integrated brain, Miran & Miran (1984), Both hemispheric and subcortical connectors are part of an organized information-processing system

Information-processing, Majovski (1984), Pros and cons of the information-processing approach as used in the K-ABC.

Luria's functional systems, Horoszowski (1983), Relationship between Luria's empirical foundation (science) and theoretical-philosophical construction (fiction) is discussed.

Luria's and Lezak's theories, Newby et al. (1983), Confirmatory factor analysis revealed that none of the models fit the data well in an absolute sense

Truine concept of brain and behavior, Chabliss (1982) Purposes theoretical model for therapy that incorporates MacLean's triune brain concept.

Luria's theory, Obrzut & Obrzut (1982), Recommends adoption of Luria's model of learning by educators because it describes functional systems interacting to produce behavior

Localizationism, Berndt & Caramazza (1980), Broca's aphasia seen as involving syntactic parsing component and articulatory deficit within localizationist framework.

Clinical or Treatment Models

Ecological syndromes, Pontius (1984), Certain cultural groups may have "delayed" cognitive functions secondary to underuse of those functions

Neuropsychological theory of Rorschach Response, Paneth (1981), Rubrothalamic system seen as responsible for ability to perceive reflex posture (movement) in the blot

Neuropsychological theories of psychopathology, Tress (1981), Mind and body connected by categories of rhythmic and figural patterns Self-consciousness originates from rhythmic-emotional and figural-cognitive systems.

Base rates and decision-making, Gordon (1977) The classification of greater incidence will be predicted more accurately than the one of lesser incidence.

Clinical quasi-experimental approach to retraining, Cooke (1973), Early cognitive rehabilitation attempt involving remediation in academic areas as well as individual and group counseling for emotional factors

Treatment approaches: 1) Medical/Neuropsychological; 2) Educational/perceptual-motor, Kershner & Bauer (1966), Derives treatment rationales for brain-injured children from wedding of two approaches.

Total Rehabilitation Model for Mild to Moderate Head Injury, Long et al.(1984) Outlines interdisciplinary model for total rehabilitation of individuals with mild to moderate head injury.

Sociopsychological, Neuropsychological, & Rehabilitation Planning Model, Sbordone (1985), Presents clinical model for rehabilitation planning that emphasizes socio-psychological interventions in addition to neuropsychological.

Neuropsychological Model of Behavior, Gaddes (1983), This model of behavior includes psychosocial knowledge and skills, a body of complex knowledge about the brain, and clinical skills.

The Neuropsychological Model, Goldstein (1976), Set apart from clinical psychology by empirical reality of the brain and replicable observational findings

Neuropsychology, Maruszewski (1973), Is linked with the structure and function sciences, social sciences, and clinical sciences.

Specific Syndromes or Behaviors

Functional State-Shift Hypothesis of Dreaming, Koukkou & Lehmann (1983), Different brain functional states during sleep and wakefulness are associated with differences in processing strategies, memory stores, and EEG patterns.

Interhemispheric-communication Theory of Automatic Verbal Behavior, Honegger (1980), Automatic phenomena are involuntary in the right hemisphere.

Developmental Dyslexia: 1) Brain-deficit model; 2) Maturational-lag model, Dalby (1979), Neither theory adequately accounts for the entire population of dyslexics. Must focus on theory articulation and reformulation in the future.

Dyslexia: 1) Dynamic Developmental Differences Model; 2) Developmental Maturational Lag Model, Usprich (1976), Dyslexics are different, rather than delayed.

Neuropsychological Model of Stuttering, Webster (1985), Normal lateralization of neural mechanisms associated with sequential processing found in stutters, contrary to hypothesis.

Cognitive Processes

Theories of Memory, Baddeley (1982), Neuropsychological evidence has clear implications for fractionation of (normal human) memory into subsystems

Walley & Weiden Theory of Attention, Walley & Weiden (1973),Proposes a neuro-psychological theory of attention compatible with current theories of information-processing.

Walley & Weiden Theory of Attention, Feeney et al. (1974), The theory cannot account for much current data.

Statistical Models

Polynomial Models, Adams & Grant (1984), Polynomial models can produce inflated correlation coefficients: Drinking history did not readily explain cognitive findings in sober alcoholics.

Factor Analytic Models, Warnock & Mintz (1979), Specificity and Semmes' L968 models were supported in lateralized brain-damaged patients.

Animal and Neuropsychological Models

Subhuman Animal Models, German (1971), Pros and cons of using animal models for agnosias, localization of brain functions, and species specific differences

Primate Models of Neuropsychiatric Disorders   Howard & Pollard (1983), Discusses appropriateness and cost-benefit of animal models for human nervous system disease and mental disorders.

Primate Models, Proceedings of International Primatology Society (1982), Discusses appropriateness of animal models for human mental disorders and diseases

Animal Models of Tourette's Syndrome, Shaywitz, et al., Discusses relevance of animal model, particularly with regard to Tourette's Syndrome

Neuropsychological Models, Bloom et al. (1972), (example) Purkinje cells of the rat cerebellum receive nonadrenergic inhibitory projections from the locus coeruleus, etc.

Developmental and Genetic Models

Goldberg-Costa Neuro-developmental Model, Rourke (1982), Model emphasizes differences between right and left hemisphere systems and appears to fit clinical observational data.

Eco-pharmaco-genetic Model, Radouco et al. (1980), Model based on combination of ecological and genetic factors proposed for alcoholism and pharmaco-dependence.

Doman-Delacato Theory of Physical and Cognitive Development, Kershner (1967), Physical activities derived from this theory improved creeping and crawling as well as IQ, but not perceptual-motor proficiency, in trainable Mentally Retarded children.

9

The Role of Motivation in Rehabilitation

Murry G. Mutchnick

The rehabilitation of cognitive disabilities involves active participation in what are often long, tedious and repetitive activities. Thus, it becomes very evident that a great deal of effort and cooperation is required of the patient. Motivation, therefore, is a very important factor in achieving successful rehabilitation (Anderson, Bourestom, & Greenberg, 1970; Fogel & Rosillo, 1969, 1971a, 1971b; Rabinowitz, 1961; Wepman, 1953). Unfortunately, this same population may also experience decreased motivation that is a direct and/or indirect consequence of their injury. (Brinkman, 1979). Wepman (1953) explains the necessity of a patient's motivation:

> ...mere stimulation of a neural system which is physiologically capable of functioning is not enough, for it is evident clinically that a psychological state of readiness must also exist before maximal learning of the formation of new, operative neural integrations are possible. (p. 10)

This paper will discuss some motivation theories, the effects of motivation on rehabilitation and address various motivation enhancing techniques. A primary focus of this paper, however, will be an examination of an attributional theory of motivation with a direct application of it to the rehabilitating brain damaged patient. This application model, which also incorporates other theoretical approaches, will attempt to explain the motivation of these patients as well as provide possibly unexplored solutions to the problem of how to motivate the low motivated patient.

Motivational Theories

This section will briefly discuss selected theories of motivation. Psychoanalytic, achievement, operant learning, social learning, and attributional theories will be addressed. This portion of the paper will outline principles which are the basis for the research and motivational model contained in following sections.

Mutchnick, M.G. (1988). The role of motivation in rehabilitation. In J. M. Williams & C. J. Long (Eds.), *Cognitive approaches to neuropsychology*, New York: Plenum.

Psychoanalytic Theory

The psychoanalytic approach to motivation can be considered as one precursor to the other approaches examined in this paper. On a fundamental level, psychoanalytic theory proposes that individuals must adapt to the limited resources of the environment, undertaking actions that lead to the goals of realistically satisfying personal needs, defined as the biological drives or instinctual wishes of the "Id," are the underlying motivators of behavior (Weiner, 1985). The drive reduction processes of the Id and the Ego result in direct or immediate expression of a drive or a mediating step, preventing immediate expression. Environmental mediation and delay of gratification are properties of the "Ego." Although itself powered by the energy of the Id, the Ego will postpone the expression of drives until the environment is amenable to their gratification. The model of drive reduction also results in mental events or cognitions as opposed to overt behaviors that can be considered wish fulfilling or satisfying in the absence of the drive object. These cognitions include the remembrance of past experiences and fantasies that these experiences are presently occurring. The most effective strategies adopted by the Ego result in overt behavior; the Id's energy is channeled by the Ego, delaying gratification, and resulting in satisfaction from some successful displaced activity. Realistic anticipation and planning by the Ego leads to satisfaction (Weiner, 1985). The foundation of psychoanalytic theories of motivation is drive reduction; people derive strategies and work to satisfy basic biological needs. As the person matures through the life span, these strategies become complex, socially integrated and sometimes so abstract that they lose their clear referents to biological drives.

Achievement Theory

John Atkinson's (1957, 1964) achievement theory states that all persons are driven by motive systems: the motive to achieve success and the motive to avoid failure. The motives can be described as emotional anticipations, such as hope and fear, derived in part from past experiences. These two opposing emotions are in conflict. The relative strengths of these emotions determines whether the individual will approach or avoid achievement-oriented activities. The individual with a greater level of motivation to achieve success relative to the level of motivation to avoid failure will choose tasks of moderate difficulty. This occurs because easy tasks are seen as unrewarding and difficult tasks are seen as out of the range of successful outcomes. The individual with a greater level of motivation to avoid failure relative to the level of motivation to achieve success will choose tasks that are either easy or hard. This occurs because easy tasks are seen as those that can be successfully completed and very difficult tasks for which the individual will be admired because he/she is seen as possessing high aspirations.

Operant Learning Theory

Unlike the previously mentioned theories of motivation, learning theory stresses the importance of environmental factors rather than intrapersonal ones. Operant conditioning (Skinner, 1938), in which an organism acquires habits through reinforcement, is dependent upon the strength of reinforcers as motivational factors. Motivation can be thought of as the energizing effect determined by this desire for a particular reinforcement. For example, the hungry animal is motivated to acquire food (Krech, Crutchfield, Livson, Wilson, & Parducci, 1982). Motivation can be measured, in this same example, as the hours of food deprivation. Levels of motivation have been shown to effect performance during testing rather than during training (Hillman, Hunter, & Kimble, 1953).

Premack (1959) provided evidence that a more probable response could be use to reinforce a less probable one; specifically, when two responses are to be made by an organism during an operant period, that which occurs most frequently can become a reinforcer. He also demonstrated that with proper experimental manipulations, the reinforcement relationship between the two responses can be reversed (Premack, 1962). He later found that these reinforcers are not trans-situational and that a response can be ranked in a hierarchy of frequency from least to most probable (Premack, 1963).

Social Learning Theory

Social learning theory elaborated traditional learning theory by asserting that mental processes and higher-order cognitions influence behavior (Weiner, 1985). Sherif (1936) and Lewin (1951) describe a "frame of reference" within which judgments and experiences of success and failure take place. They state that such a reference can be "...the interiorization of the norms and values of one's culture, the achievements of others, one's own level of aspiration (i.e., one's personal goals), or one's own past performance" (Higgins, Strauman, & Klein, 1986, p.24-25). Bandura (1982) differentiates such references as either being "personal standards," as exemplified by Freud's (1900) "superego," or "social referential comparison" standards which are interpersonal in nature. These self-evaluative judgments result in emotional responses. Desirable emotional responses serve to motivate the individual. Many models convey that each response is dependent on a judgment which involves a single standard (Higgins, Strauman, & Klein, 1986)). Recently, a self-evaluative model has been proposed where the judgment stage involves constructing specific causal attributions for performance that are each related to specific emotional responses (Weiner, 1982; Weiner, Russel, & Lerman, 1978). It is thought that self-assessment, or the attainment of self-image information may act as a primary goal of achievement behavior in addition to self-enhancement through positive affect (Trope, 1986).

Attributional Theory

Attributional theory asserts that a stimulus results in mediating cognitions which in turn determine the affective response of the individual as well as the "expectancy" of that individual. Finally, an instrumental response is made based on the preceding factors. More specifically, certain antecedent conditions, such as specific information, causal schemata, individual differences, and reinforcement schedules, are utilized by the individual to reach inferences about the causes of success and failure. The most important causal inferences are ability and effort. Other inferences include task difficulty, luck, mood, fatigue, illness, the actions of others, and motivation. The properties shared by all of these causes are stability, locus (internal versus external) and controllability. The "primary effect" of stability is expectancy change, that of locus is esteem-related affects, and the primary effect of control is interpersonal judgments and intrapersonal feeling states. Behavioral consequences include performance intensity, persistence, and choice. Thus, for example, the information of failure, a preceding factor, may be seen by the individual as being caused by a lack of ability (the casual inference) which is characterized by the properties of being uncontrollable and unchangeable. After primary affects and judgments occur, the individual may quit a task. Causal inferences of success related to external rather than internal factors may relate to avoidance of certain tasks. External causes for events may also be evidenced by the intensity of behavior. Individuals may, for example, be seen as performing with little vigor (Weiner, 1985). All behavioral consequences, such as those described above, can be used to describe the motivation level of an individual. The level of motivation observed can be said to be determined, perhaps indirectly, by the attributions of cause for certain antecedent conditions.

The Effects of Motivation on the Rehabilitation of Mental Disorders and Physical Disabilities

It seems appropriate that an examination be made of some of the research conducted on the motivation and rehabilitation of mental and general physically impaired patients. This will provide some insight into motivation in general as well as relate important information that is similar to that of neurological patients.

In a study concerned with the determinants of patient motivation for rehabilitation, Barry, Dunteman and Webb (1968) psychologically assessed physically impaired patients at a VA hospital with every effort to exclude any with psychiatric disabilities or brain damage. Test and interview data were obtained when the patients were beginning recovery. This was then compared to similar data obtained one year later. At the time of follow-up, patients having favorable attitudes toward self, a small discrepancy between ratings of real and ideal self, intelligence, attitudes of social restraint, and an interest in people and in getting along with them were the same patients who were described as having a strong motivation for recovery and return to work. In a study of physical disabilities, Equi (1973) found that highly motivated subjects were significantly more accepting of their disability and had a more favorable attitudes about themselves, the treatment staff and the treatment facility, than subjects rated low in motivation. This study provides an early picture of the motivated individual. However, it failed to determine whether motivation is related to rehabilitation goal attainment.

In a study which developed a prediction model for vocational rehabilitation, Kundu (1984) discovered that although internal locus of control was related to earlier employment in motivated subjects, there was not significantly higher employment in this group than in a low motivation group. He also found that demographics were significantly different in the employed versus the unemployed group. Miles (1968) proposed that achievement motivation might be a predictor of vocational success and failure. He found that achievement motivation was more useful in predicting workers prestige and job difficulty levels than it was in predicting employment. However, the subjects who participated in a failure-fearing workshop were more likely to enter employment at a higher prestige level than were non-participants. Viehman (1972) also examined the achievement motivation of male mental patients. He found that those patients low in need motivation and middle-class values failed in vocational training or on the job. They had fallen the farthest below their high achieving parents in social position. They felt bad about themselves and were more in tune with the reality of their chances of success. The group was the most flexible and realistic in terms of problem-solving. They performed well under the pressures of the rehabilitation program and their need achievement increased substantially under pressure, until the goal was in sight. At that point their basic low achievement motivation resurfaced and a realistic assessment was made of both their chances of success and the unbridgeable gap in social position between themselves and their parents. In a similar study, Salomone (1972) was also interested in whether clients who are judged to be motivated for a vocational rehabilitation program are likely to become successfully rehabilitated and employed. Salomone found conflicting results based on the agency outcome data examined. Patients were selected from closed cases of the Minneapolis Rehabilitation Center (MRC) who had been referred by a counselor at the Minnesota Division of Vocational Rehabilitation (DVR). Eighty-two percent of these subjects had physical and/or learning disorders, whereas the remaining eighteen percent had mental illness. Diagnostic conference reports were judged by three former MRC Vocational Service Department counselors with regard to the extent of each subject's motivation for rehabilitation services and for work. Five resulting categories, definitely motivated, probably motivated, unclassifiable, probably unmotivated and definitely unmotivated, were combined to form two groups, motivated and unmotivated. Subjects in the motivated group were described as "having good physical appearance and self-care, handling interviews well, being highly motivated to work, considering realistic kinds of work, and having average intelligence" (p.13). Subjects classified as not motivated were described as:

> ...unemployed because of a desire not to work, feeling ready to retire and to be content with puttering around the house, having no financial pressures at work, participating in the program so as not to jeopardize workman's compensation status, having many physical complaints involving headaches and irregular attendance at the MRC. (p. 13)

Using MRC outcome data, motivated clients did not differ from unmotivated clients in terms of proportion employed. However, using the DVR outcome data there was a significant difference between employed/unemployed proportions when comparing motivated and unmotivated clients. This could be explained by the criteria of each agency. The DVR counselors have a long term view of success or failure as opposed to a relatively short term view held by MRC counselors (usually three to four months). These MRC clients may have received additional rehabilitation services and achieved employment in a similar time span as DVR clients. Salomone also suggests that different administration pressures concerning case-closure as well as a possibly unreliable motivation rating system could account for the differences found.

In conclusion, it is apparent that there is some link between rehabilitation in general and motivation. Although methodologies and results vary, low motivation, as exemplified by Viehman (1972), does seem to impede the successful outcome of rehabilitation therapy.

Motivation and the Brain Damaged Patient

The mental patient as well as the general physically impaired patient parallel the neurological patient in terms of need for rehabilitation as well as in many of the psychological factors hampering the progress of such rehabilitation. Heaton, Baadi, & Johnson (1978) found that chronic schizophrenics are not discriminable from brain damaged patients using psychological tests. Beyond the controversial nature of schizophrenia, Golden (1981) explains that part of this differentiating problem is due to factors including lack of motivation, drug effects, length of hospitalization, and lack of response to normal reinforcers. Other, more situationally related, factors may relate to any type of rehabilitating patient. Consider the individual with minimal neuropsychological impairment and indicates no evidence of self-defeating attributions who will obtain a higher income from his "disability" than from the previous occupational position. This example represents one of the most frustrating obstacles for treatment staff members. The patient is actually motivated to maintain some level of functional deficits. The brain damaged individual does differ, however, from the mental patient in etiology of disorder, psychological status, as well as type of rehabilitation needed. Unfortunately, the research with the brain damaged population is much more limited. This section will examine the sources of motivational deficits in these patients.

Understanding the motivational problems of the neurological patient is often more complex than is the case with other patients. The reason for this involves differentiating primary and secondary effects of CNS damage. Traditionally, emotional and motivational problems were seen strictly as nonphysical in nature. Now it has become apparent that such problems may be a primary manifestation of some underlying CNS pathology (Benson & Blumer, 1975). Blumer and Benson's (1975) term for one of two clinical changes in frontal lobe patients is pseudodepression. These patients have such symptoms as outward apathy and indifference, reduced sexual interest, little overt emotion, little or no verbal output, and loss of initiative. They describe a forty-six year old salesman who sustained a compound depressed fracture of the left frontal lobe:

> Prior to the accident, the patient enjoyed people, had many friends and talked freely. He was active in community affairs, including Little League, church activities, men's club, and so forth.... Following the head injury, he was quiet and remote. He would speak when spoken to and made sensible replies but would then lapse into silence. He made no friends on the ward, [and] spent most of his time sitting alone smoking.... He could discuss many subjects intelligently, but was never known to initiate either a conversation or a request.... At no time did he request a discharge or weekend pass. He was totally unconcerned about his wife and children. Formerly a warm and loving father, he did not seem to care about his family. Eventually, the family ceased visiting because of his indifference and unconcern. (pp.156-157)

Patients with massive frontal lobe lesions (specifically to the basal and medial areas), according to Luria (1980), "...are as a rule in a state of reduced activity, that their attention is easily distracted by irrelevant stimuli, and that it is usually impossible to organize their attention and to keep it focused on a definite plan" (pp. 263-264). Luria continues that similar effects, involving these nonspecific forms of activation, are seen in lesions of the limbic system in the anterior part of the gyrus cingulus, hypothalamus, amygdala, and hippocampus. Interconnections of the limbic system and the frontal lobes may offer explanation to the similarity in symptomology from lesions to the two areas. Nauta (1971) suggests that the frontal cortex is, " the major -- although not the only -- neocortical representative of the limbic system" (p. 182). Numerous afferent and efferent connections of the frontal lobes is indicated by "the wide inflow of nonspecific and highly heterogeneous information into the cortex of the frontal lobes..." and by "...the possibility that the frontal cortex can influence nonspecific formations at different levels" (Luria, 1980, p. 264).

The possibility of the existence of primary and/or secondary symptomology makes accurate diagnosis and rehabilitation strategies much more confusing. Brinkman (1979) discusses such secondary effects and how they may interact with primary effects. He describes that "overlay phenomena," emotional reactions to primary cognitive changes, may occur as secondary effects. Secondary effects may, in turn, be the cognitive deficits that occur from depression and poor motivation. This interactive nature of primary and secondary effects makes understanding the patient's symptomology difficult and can lead to an overestimation or underestimation of the patient's primary deficits.

The complex cognitive processes involved in motivation depend upon more fundamental neuropsychological functions. Thus it follows that brain injury results in disruption of basic brain functioning which, in turn, alters more complex integrative cognitive processes. These altered cognitions relate directly to altered behavior with motivational deficiencies being a likely target.

Specifically, language and memory are necessary cognitive functions for the construction of predictions (stimulus-response-outcome predictions) which relate to self-reinforcement, rule development and reasoning and facilitate performance of behavior (Bandura, 1977). The reduction of self-reinforcement results in an increase in apathy and depression. The poor recall of behavioral rules can lead to withdrawal and isolation in brain injured clients if the resulting inappropriate behavior leads to severe or consistent punishment. Impaired reasoning, exemplified by arbitrary inference and overgeneralization also leads to depression (Malec, 1984).

Language's role in the self-motivating abilities is uncertain, however it may be involved in the coding of important stimulus-response-outcome events into verbal rules which can be stored into long term memory. In addition to this consolidation, memory is also needed for recalling stimulus-response, response-outcome, and stimulus-outcome relationships as well as personal performance abilities (Malec, 1984).

Bandura (1977) describes how prediction may function in the determination of faulty complex self-management skills of an individual. Accurate negative self-efficacy predictions, where the inability to produce a desired response is accurately assessed, may lead to maladaptive or distressed behavior. Fortunately, this distress is usually transient. The same behavior may result from inaccurate negative or positive self-efficacy predictions. Here, the overestimation or underestimation of personal competencies interfere with social adjustment and achievement.

Table 1 outlines the causes for motivational deficits incorporating both primary and secondary effects. The table only represents a guide of possible reasons for motivational problems. It is *not* a categorization/diagnostic chart where individual patients can be identified by one of the listed "sources". In-

Table 1

Causes of motivational deficits in brain damaged individuals

Source	Mediating Process	Resulting Behavior
frontal lobe/ midbrain injury	-	depression, hypo-/ hyper-emotionality
psychological adjustment to disability status:		
recognition of disability	uncertainty	acute distress
self-defeating cognitions	-	external, uncontrollable attributions
neuropsychological deficits (memory, learning, language)	faulty cognitive processing	inability to recognize important stimulus-response-outcome relationships, reasoning problems, prediction inabilities

stead, it represents sources and behaviors that are highly interactive in numerous combinations. The indicated "mediating processes" give explanatory power to observed behaviors offering the possible links of highly complex behaviors, such as motivation, with other neurological or psychological impairments. Primary and secondary effects could be accounted for by "source" and "resulting behavior" in this table.

The interactive nature of factors related to motivational deficits in brain impaired individuals cannot be stressed enough. Consider Table 1 when reading the following hypothetical case descriptions:

Case 1: This is a thirty-four year old single woman who lives with her mother. She was diagnosed as having a right frontal lobe tumor which was removed with no complications. She is moderately depressed as evidenced by psychological test data and clinical observations of low motivation to attempt or succeed at cognitive and physical tasks presented to her in the rehabilitation setting. The location of her brain injury suggests a probable source of her motivational deficiencies. However, the woman has discussed with the staff psychologist her disabilities including her present inability to succeed at the career as she had planned before the injury. This acute distress, from an uncertainty of future "caused" by her recognition of disabilities, only confounds the original symptomology. The woman's mother feels that her daughter will never "be the same because of the tumor." The mother's and the patient's external attributions represent an external, uncontrollable factor. The self-defeating nature of these attributions and the relegation of control to outside forces has precipitated and maintained a dependent and depressive life style.

It can be seen that the occurrence of a wide range of social/family problems, those relating to an individuals brain impairment and those separate from it, add to the conceptual complexity of cause for motivational deficits.

Case 2: This is a nineteen year old male who sustained a head injury from an automobile accident seven months prior. The patient shows low motivation for most rehabilitation activities. Upon neuropsychological assessment, he evidenced significantly impaired memory consolidation. Memory's inseparable association with learning is indicated by this patient's inability to remember reinforcement history regarding retraining tasks. Even though his previous attempts at the tasks were successful, each attempt is as if it were his first, with accompanying uncertainty. Explanations for this patients motivational problems can be expanded to include the possible effects of frontal lobe and limbic system damage, due to the diffuse nature of his trauma, indicating more direct cause for presenting depressive symptomology.

The two cases presented above allow for some insight into the extreme variability of cases evidencing motivational deficits that are seen in the clinical setting. These particular cases were invented to represent the wide range of important factors relevant to low motivation. Though the cases are very different in terms of etiology and extent of cerebral damage, these factors represent only two of many additional factors that must be understood. The nature of damage can provide the neuropsychologist with valuable information but may simply be only the foundation from which neuropsychological, cognitive, and family variables can be investigated. Case 1's tumor location would signal the clinician to causes for her depressive and low motivation symptomology. Though this localization information may be important, the multitude of more psychological and environmental factors seem to make the lesion site less important. Case 2 represents almost the reverse scenario as that of Case 1 in that limbic system involvement in his accident may be neglected by the neuropsychologist initially, but such damage could directly add to the observed motivational deficits. The possibility of damage to this brain area, resulting in depressive symptoms, becomes even more relevant when one considers the role of these brain areas in memory, which is the cognitive area most prominently weak in this individual.

To summarize, numerous factors in various combinations result in a multitude of possible explanations for the lack of motivation seen in some brain damaged patients. Each case, therefore, should be considered carefully with regard to neurological, psychological, neuropsychological, social/family and employment factors. It is the job of the neuropsychologist to determine the nature of motivational problems and incorporate some technique in the rehabilitation setting to alleviate them.

Attempts to Solve the Low Motivation Problem

Psychotherapy seems to be an essential component to rehabilitation from any traumatic event. In an investigation of the effects of group psychotherapy on recovering stroke patients, Oradei & Waite (1974) asserts that the response to disability may bring on feelings of anxiety, depression, hopelessness, and guilt. It was further expressed that such feelings could create a "stalemate" which may interfere with the progress of rehabilitation. A counselling group was created with the intention of alleviating some of these symptoms. These sessions provided a regular outlet for patients to express feelings and receive assistance from peers and the group leaders in understanding the nature of the social and psychological issues confronting them. According to the patients, these sessions helped them to cope with feelings of depression, understand their illness, and feel less alone because of the exchange of similar ideas and feelings with other patients. In another investigation by Crasilneck and Hall (1970), hypnotherapy was used for rehabilitation patients who had experienced complicated cerebrovascular or traumatic brain injury. Of the twenty-one out of twenty-five cases that were responsive to hypnotherapy the major change seen was an increase in motivation for recovery.

Wepman (1953), with an emphasis on aphasics, explains the need for therapists to "understand the patient's background, his interests and his capability of accepting...previously highly motivated areas of behavior in his post-traumatic state" (p. 11). He stresses that the therapist must be aware of a patient's readiness to act in a particular area. Unmotivated to succeed in language therapy, Wepman describes a case who had reached a plateau in his language rehabilitation. Upon reviewing the background information of the patient, it was discovered that the patient had a love of the outdoors. This information was used to incorporate sports into the vocabulary training and later into direct activities of the patient. He became so motivated that his "plateau was left behind and language therapy could be continued upon measurable and meaningful levels" (p. 10-11). Wepman also explains that the rehabilitation area of greatest concern to the therapist may not be that of the patient. Thus, it is not until therapy in the area of greatest concern to the patient (physical therapy, for example), has commenced that the patient is psychologically ready (motivated), to engage in other therapies. He also suggested that even the "pathways" of rehabilitating a certain function should be that of the patient. A particular patient may have a higher motivation for visual reception and graphic expression than for auditory reception and verbal expression. Wepman states that "at the very least, we must be prepared to accept as our goal what the patient feels to be his greatest need" (p. 12). Brinkman (1979) also stresses the importance of determining, through patient and family interviews, the concerns and expectations of the patient. In addition to patients that may want to deal with neurological problems with a priority that differs from that of the neuropsychologist, he also conveys that there may be psychological problems that have been exacerbated by the CNS damage (e.g. with career, children, marriage) that are of greater concern to the patient than any neurological or neuropsychological problems.

On a more behavioral level, Ince (1969) utilized Premack's (1959) reinforcement theory to increase patient's participation in multifaceted rehabilitation. Ince made attendance of therapy classes which were attended with high probability contingent upon attending classes of lower attendance probability. In one of the two successful cases described this reinforcement plan increased the patient's speech therapy attendance from zero to one hundred percent while keeping physical therapy at the same level.

Also behavioral in approach, Eames and Wood (1985a) discuss the use of a "special unit" for rehabilitating severe brain injury patients with behavioral problems, including low motivation. The unit incorporates behavior modification techniques in the setting of a Token Economy. Primarily, "positive" disorders, such as aggressiveness, impulsivity, disinhibited behavior and antisocial behavior, are diminished allowing for the enhancement and generalization of adaptive behavior. A two year follow-up to the program (Eames & Wood, 1985b) indicated lasting improvement for twenty-four patients who were unable to benefit from traditional rehabilitation settings due to behavior disorders. Specifically, however, drive and motivation data at follow-up did not reveal very promising results as there was a significant increase (a worsening) of behavioral ratings. The authors suggest, "Drive and motivation are clearly rather fragile aspects of behavior, and for many patients the stimulation of a busy structured program does seem to be missed" (p. 617).

Other, more task specific, strategies of increasing rehabilitation motivation are also being researched. At this more specific level, Carter and Miller (1971) significantly increased the perceptual-motor coordination of minimally brain-injured children by replacing the mechanical, repetitious, and discouraging activities such as drill with templates, tracing of forms and physical exercises with more creative activities. It was hypothesized that these rewarding and more pleasurable activities increased the motivation to learn in these children. Carter and Miller express that such motivation is of intangible quality, "Span of interest, attention span, and self-motivation do not completely express the development of a joy in learning, a desire to participate in learning activities" (p. 249).

An interesting frontier for research of enhancing motivation lies in Sperry's (1976) notion of mental events actually acting as *causal* agents for brain events. "Willing" to improve or having high levels of motivation may actually change physiological brain processes. A futuristic plan for cognitive retraining may include practiced motivation as a way to remediate motivation deficits.

A General Model of Motivation for Rehabilitation

This section will describe a model, designed by the author, for rehabilitation motivation that will encompass much of the theory and research findings described throughout this paper (Figure 1). The model will attempt to provide a process for providing and maintaining the most optimal level possible of motivation in brain damaged patients. The model is cyclic in nature and is therefore generated by a patient's motivation which should continually increase throughout the process. Because many patients will never be sufficiently motivated, the model also includes the processes of their rehabilitation.

The model consists of four major components: psychotherapy; the patient's free choice of rehabilitation tasks or therapy areas; attributional behavior of the patient; and a cycle for maintaining participation in *all* necessary therapy activities. Psychotherapy is necessary as an initial phase for alleviating any acute distress, anxiety, or depression. During therapy the therapist should encourage the patient to express major concerns which can be converted into goals for rehabilitation and, in turn, into specific therapy areas or tasks required to achieve such goals. If the patient does not generate any specific realistic goals through the above described psychotherapy then the patient engages in therapist selected tasks. If the patient does not participate sufficiently in such activities further psychotherapy is in order to assess and treat any persistent depression or anxiety and to determine if the patient's placement is appropriate. If the patient is participating in these rehabilitation activities sufficiently and does not have goals as described above then tangible rewards should be used as reinforcers (e.g. liberties, points, candy, etc.). If the patient does have goals for rehabilitation then he must determine or "choose" tasks or therapy areas for achieving such goals. Those goals of highest priority are assumed to have high achievement need associated with them; they are based on real concerns and desires of the patient. In order to insure that all necessary therapy areas are dealt with, the patient's participation in choice therapy is contingent upon participation in other needed therapy. This "therapy as a reinforcer for therapy" is described in the preceding section. The participation in the choice tasks or therapy areas should act a motivator for participation in this entire process. Starting with a high achievement need, attributional theory can explain the evolution of reinforcement. The patient works with high intensity and sees success as related to effort (controllable) and failure as related to lack of effort which leads to persistence at the task. These cognitions take the place of typical cognitions of, "the brain damage prevents success because it has reduced ability" (external and uncontrollable). When success is achieved it creates feelings of competence (based on a "frame of reference" as described in the first section). This competence acts a reinforcer for attempting the tasks associated with the goal of next priority. As each task results in success there is a greater level reinforcement and thus greater motivation.

Based on the various etiologies of the motivational deficits described above, each patient will proceed through this model in completely unique ways. It is therefore imperative that the proper aspects of this model only be applied when appropriate and that the aspects of the model that are applied be flexible to new discoveries about and changes in the patient's cognitive and neuropsychological functioning.

The patient suffering from deficits due to acute distress over the recognition of lasting disabilities or the other non-neurological/neuropsychological motivational problems are most suited for entire model utilizing the patients choice goals for more positive attributions. Based on their very nature, neurologically/neuropsychologically based motivation deficits would benefit minimally from this attributional change procedure.

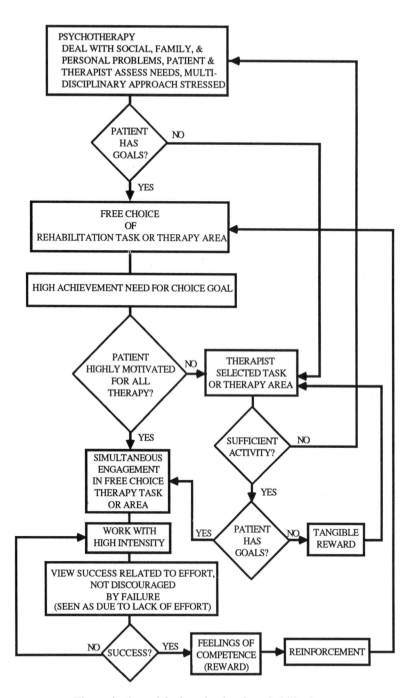

Figure 1. A model of motivation for rehabilitation.

Simple reinforcement of therapist selected tasks is the most appropriate program for patients described as having frontal lobe or midbrain emotional dysfunction as well as those patients with a disruption of reasoning, prediction or other cognitive functions rom impaired neuropsychological bases. Though this aspect of the model seems overly simple and "second nature" to most psychologists, the importance of consistent reinforcement must be stressed. As described above, patients with little or no *self*-reinforcement become very dependent on outside reinforcement and become significantly frustrated and hostile if external reinforcement is unreliable (Malec, 1984).

Summary

The success of rehabilitation of brain damaged patients is largely due to the psychological readiness and continued motivation of the patient. Other than deficits in motivation as a primary effect of damage, secondary effects also block productive therapy. This secondary symptomology can lead to attributions of the patient that can create a real "stalemate". Brain damage is often thought of by the patient as a detached, external phenomenon that is uncontrollable in nature. These cognitions result in little or no effort of the individual since ability (a result of brain damage) is thought to be causing poor performance rather than lack of effort. In order to reverse these attributions to more positive ones, the therapist must be sensitive to, and allow the incorporation of, patient selected therapy based on needs and goals *of the patient*. Sometimes determined with the aid of psychotherapy, these needs for achievement begin attributional cognitions that result in reinforcement rather than discouragement. This "choice" therapy also acts as a reinforcer for other needed therapy that may be recommended by the therapist.

Motivation, resulting from any of the methods described above, will hopefully provide the means for improved cognitive and behavioral functioning during rehabilitation as well as give the patient a sense of control that will enable them to try, grow, and feel a sense of competence and success throughout their lifetime.

References

Anderson, T. P., Bourestom, N., & Greenberg, F. R. (1970). *Rehabilitation predictors in completed stroke: Final report.* Minneapolis, American Rehabilitation Foundation.

Atkinson, J. W. (1957). Motivational determinants of risk-taking behavior. *Psychological Review, 64,* 359-372.

Atkinson, J. W. (1964). *An introduction to motivation.* Princeton, NJ: Van Nostrand.

Bandura, A. (1977). Self-efficacy: Toward a unifying theory of behavioral change. *Psychological Review, 84*, 191-215.

Bandura, A. (1982). The self and mechanisms of agency. In J. Suls (Ed.), *Psychological perspectives on the self* (Vol. 1, pp. 38-49). Hillsdale, NJ: Erlbaum.

Barry, J. R., Dunteman, G. H., & Webb, M. W. (1968). Personality and motivation in rehabilitation. *Journal of Counselling Psychology, 15*, 237-244.

Benson, D. F., & Blumer, D. (Eds.). (1975). *Psychiatric aspects of neurologic disease.* New York: Grune & Stratton.

Blumer, D., and Benson, D. F. (1975). Personality changes with frontal and temporal lobe lesions. In D. F. Benson and D. Blumer (Eds.), *Psychiatric aspects of neurologic disease* (pp. 156-157). New York: Grune & Stratton.

Brinkman, S. D. (1979). Rehabilitation of the neurologically impaired patient: The contribution of the neuropsychologist. *Clinical Neuropsychology*, 39-44.

Carter, J. L., & Miller, P. K. (1971). Creative art for minimally brain-injured children. *Academic Therapy, 6*, 245-252.

Crasilneck, H. B., & Hall, J. A. (1970). The use of hypnosis in the rehabilitation of complicated vascular and post-traumatic neurological patients. *International Journal of Clinical & Experimental Hypnosis, 18*, 145-159.

Eames, P. & Wood, R. (1985a). Rehabilitation after severe brain injury: a special-unit approach to behavior disorders. *International Rehabilitation Medicine, 7*, 130-133.

Eames, P. & Wood, R. (1985b). Rehabilitation after severe brain injury: a follow-up study of a behavior modification approach. *Journal of Neurology, Neurosurgery, and Psychiatry, 48*, 613-619.

Equi, P. J. (1974). The influence of psychological variables on motivation for physical rehabilitation. *Dissertation Abstracts International, 34*, 3493.

Fogel, M. L., & Rosillo, R. H. (1969). Correlation of psychological variables and progress in physical rehabilitation. *Disease of the Nervous System, 30*.

Fogel, M. L., & Rosillo, R. H. (1971a). Motor impersistence in physical rehabilitation. *Confina Neurologica, 33*.

Fogel, M. L., & Rosillo, R. H. (1971b). Correlation of psychological variables and progress in physical rehabilitation. II. Ego functions and defensive and adaptive mechanisms. *Archives of Physical Medicine and Rehabilitation, 52*.

Freud, S. (1923). The Ego and the Id. In *Standard edition of the complete psychological works of Sigmund Freud (Vol. 19)*. London: Hogarth Press, 1961.

Golden, C. J. (1981). *Diagnosis and rehabilitation in clinical neuropsychology.* Springfield, IL: Charles C. Thomas.

Heaton, R., Baadi, L., and Johnson, K. (1978). Neuropsychological test results associated with psychiatric disorders in adults. *Psychological Bulletin, 85*.

Higgins, E. T., Strauman, T., & Klein, R. (1986). Standards and the process of self-evaluation: Multiple affects from multiple stages. In R. M. Sorrentino & E. T. Higgins (Eds.), *Handbook of motivation and cognition: Foundations of social behavior* (pp. 23-63). New York: Guilford Press.

Hillman, B., Hunter, W., & Kimble, G. (1953). The effect of drive level on the maze performance of the white rat. *Journal of Comparative and Physiological Psychology, 46*, 87-89.

Ince, L. P. (1969). A behavioral approach to motivation in rehabilitation. *Psychological Record, 19*, 105-111.

Krech, D., Crutchfield, R. S., Livson, N., Wilson, W. A. Jr., & Parducci, A. (1982). *Elements of Psychology*. New York: Alfred A. Knopf.

Kundu, M. M. (1984). Developing a prediction model for vocational rehabilitation clients using demographic, locus of control, work motivation and work history variables: An exploratory study. *Dissertation Abstracts International, 45*, 1039-1040.

Lewin, K. (1951). *Field theory in social science*. New York: Harper.

Luria, A. R. (1980). *Higher Cortical Functions in Man*. New York: Basic Books.

Malec, J. (1984). Training the brain-injured client in behavioral self-management skills. In B. A. Edelstein & Eugene T.Couture (Eds.), *Behavioral assessment and rehabilitation of the traumatically brain-damaged* (pp. 121-149). New York: Plenum Press.

Miles, D. G. (1968). An evaluation of achievement motivation theory and work therapy participation as predictors in the vocational rehabilitation of psychiatric patients. *Dissertation Abstracts, 29*, 1107.

Nauta, W. J. H. (1971). The problem of the frontal lobes: A reinterpretation. *Journal of Psychiatric Research, 8*, 167-187.

Oradei, D. M. & Waite, N. S. (1974). Group psychotherapy with stroke patients during the immediate recovery phase. *American Journal of Orthopsychiatry, 44*, 386-395.

Premack, D. (1959). Toward empirical behavior laws: I. Positive reinforcement. *Psychological Review, 66*, 219-233.

Premack, D. (1962). Reversibility of the reinforcement relation. *Science, 136*, 255-257.

Premack, D. (1963). Rate differential of the reinforcement in monkey manipulation. *Journal of the Experimental Analysis of Behavior, 6*, 81-89.

Rabinowitz, H. S. (1961). Motivation for recovery: Four social psychologic aspects. *Archives of Physical Medicine and Rehabilitation, 42*.

Salomone, P. R. (1972). Client motivation and rehabilitation counselling outcome. *Rehabilitation Counselling Bulletin, 16*, 11-20.

Sherif, M. (1936). *The psychology of social norms*. New York: Harper & Brothers.

Skinner, B. F. (1938). *The behavior of organisms: An experimental analysis*. New York: Appleton.

Sperry, R. W. (1976). Mental phenomena as causal determinants in brain function. In B. Globus, G. Maxwell, & I. Savodnik (Eds.), *Consciousness and the Brain* (pp. 163-175). New York: Plenum.

Trope, Y. (1986). Self-Enhancement and Self-Assessment in Achievement Behavior. In R. M. Sorrentino & E. T. Higgins (Eds.), *Handbook of motivation and cognition: Foundations of social behavior* (pp. 350-378). New York: Guilford Press.

Viehman, E. H. (1972). Need achievement motivation in the rehabilitation of hospitalized mental patients. *Dissertation Abstracts International, 32*, 7089.

Weiner, B. (1982). The emotional consequences of causal attributions. In M. S. Clark & S. T. Fiske (Eds.), *Affect and cognition* (pp. 185-209). Hillsdale, NJ: Erlbaum.

Weiner, B. (1985). *Human motivation*. New York: Springer-Verlag.

Weiner, B., Russel, D., & Lerman, D. (1978). Affective consequences of causal ascriptions. In J. H. Harvey, W. Ickes, & R. F. Kidd (Eds.), *New directions in attribution research* (Vol. 2, pp. 59-90). Hillsdale, NJ: Erlbaum.

Wepman, J. M. (1953). A conceptual model for the processes involved in recovery from aphasia. *Journal of Speech and Hearing Disorders, 18*.

10

Brain Imaging: Positron Emission Tomography and Cognitive Functioning

Randolph W. Parks, David A. Loewenstein, and Jen Y. Chang

The application of positron emission tomography (PET) to the study of the functioning human brain provides researchers with a noninvasive procedure which allows in-vivo quantification of physiological and biochemical processes underlying cognition (Gur, 1985; Gur, 1987; Reivich, Alavi, Gur, & Greenberg, 1985). Techniques from a diverse set of fields must be effectively integrated for the application of PET technology. Organic chemistry and biochemistry make possible the synthesis of trace levels of the biological and physiological substrates which are used to examine biochemical pathways in the brain without perturbing the normal physiology. Physics and engineering are essential for the development of the equipment needed to measure the concentration of the radionuclides in tissue. Mathematics and physiology are used for the development of models to describe the behavior of those radioactive tracer agents. Medicine and neuropsychology pose the clinically relevant questions that can be answered by this technology (Mazziotta & Phelps, 1985a; Phelps, Mazziotta, & Huang, 1982; Phelps, Mazziotta, Schelbert, Hawkins, & Engel, 1985; Sokoloff, 1985). The role of the neuropsychologist is crucial in the assessment of baseline cognitive functioning, the development of experimental design and quantification of behavioral stimulation during scanning, and the evaluation of the effects of the imaging process, itself. In this chapter, we will describe the basic principles of PET and review current findings of PET applications to the study of cognitive functioning. In addition, we present data on new behavioral activation paradigms which have recently been developed to further elucidate the relationships between cognitive/neuropsychological functioning and metabolic activity within specific cerebral regions.

The Nuclear Theory of PET

The nuclear structure of an atom tends to consist of an equal mixture of two types of nucleons: neutrons and positively charged protons. As the atomic number increases, however, the balance of nucleons shifts to a slight excess of neutrons in order to counteract the repulsive forces between the positively charged protons. A plot of the number of neutrons versus the number of pro-

Parks, R. W., Loewenstein, D. A., & Chang, J. Y. (1988). Brain imaging: Positron emission tomography and cognitive function. In J. M. Williams & C. J. Long (Eds.), *Cognitive approaches to neuropsychology*, New York: Plenum.

tons for all stable nuclei can be approximated as a curve, sometimes referred to as a Segre plot. Isobars consisting of nuclides with the same number of nucleons will tend to undergo a transition in which the ratio of neutrons to protons will approach the line of stability for any given atomic number. This transition results in the emission of a charged particle. If the radioactive nuclide has an excess of protons, the emitted charged particle will be a positron. Once emitted by the nucleus, positrons follow a random path through the material which they traverse, continually losing energy through coulomb interactions. These are attractive and repulsive forces between the electrons and nuclei of the medium. Once reduced to the thermal energy of the medium, the positrons will combine with free electrons and form a hydrogen-like atom called positronium (Figure 1). The positronium has an extremely short lifetime (10^{-10} sec) and subsequently decays by the annihilation of the positron and electron and complete conversion of the positron and electron masses into energy in the form of gamma rays. In order to conserve the energy and momentum of the positronium the gamma rays will have equal energies (511 KeV) and will be emitted in directions nearly opposite one another (Ter-Pogossian, 1985). The colinear nature of gamma ray emission from positronium annihilation enables the quantitative imaging of positron emitting radionuclides within the brain.

PET Scanner Hardware and Limitations

PET scanners look similar to the widely used doughnut shaped CAT scanners. Inside the PET scanner, rings of detectors are used to measure the sum of radioactivity emitted by the gamma rays along straight lines adjoining

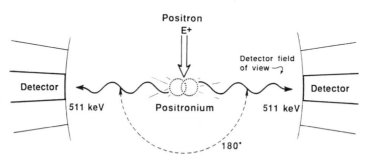

Figure 1. The detection of gamma rays from the breakdown of positronium

opposite detectors. The set of lines at all angles around the brain placed in the PET scanner (Figure 2) represent cumulative radioactivity counts of successive brain slices. Mathematical techniques then enable investigators to convert the radioactivity levels into computer generated pictorial representations of brain areas, or divert the numerical data to statistical programs for regional analysis of metabolism. The principles of the reconstruction process are beyond the scope of this chapter. Further details can be found in the excellent review by Brooks and Di Chiro (1976).

Many physical factors limit the spatial resolution and quantitative accuracy of the imaging approach (Kessler, Ellis, & Eden, 1984). The resolution limitation on multi-ring PET systems results from the total number of detectors which can actually be packed into the arrays. Directly opposite, photomultiplier tubes are then coupled for the detection of the two photons from the annihilation process. This limitation currently restricts the image resolution to approximately 4.0 - 6.0 mm.

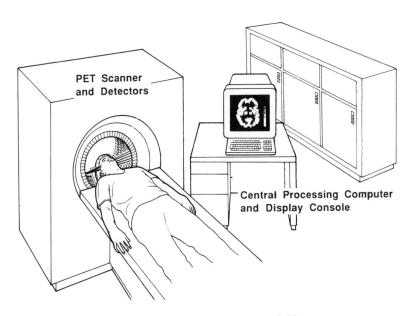

Figure 2. PET scanning equipment and layout.

The physical interaction of the gamma rays with the tissue mass of the object being imaged also limits the ability to quantify concentrations of radionuclides. The three primary forms of image degradation are attenuation, scatter, and random coincidence. Scatter and attenuation of gamma rays can be thought of as resulting from the collision of the gamma rays with electrons in the matter they are traversing. In this collision the electrons may either absorb all of the energy of the gamma ray or some fraction of the incident energy. This results in the scattering of gamma rays away from their original direction (Compton Scattering). The magnitude of these events in human tissue is a function of electron density. A detailed description of the effects and the procedures used to correct for their effects can be found in a review by Hoffman and Phelps (1986). Random coincidence occurs when unrelated gamma rays are detected within the time resolution for detection of true coincidence events. Random coincidence events become a serious concern in PET imaging studies when the total system count rate becomes high (i.e., the probability of detecting two unrelated photons in the detectors becomes non-negligible). Of course, the electronics incorporated in the instrumentation, as well as the power of the computing and analysis packages employed, serve as further possible limiters of image quality.

PET Measurements of Physiology

The intricate function of the human brain involves diverse and highly complex processes of physiology and biochemistry. In order to study this function with PET, radiopharmaceuticals can be designed to isolate important components of these biochemical pathways. In addition, the fate of the compound must involve a limited number of transformation steps so that simplified compartmental models can be employed for the functional evaluation of brain activity. One of the most commonly used radiopharmaceuticals is ^{18}F-2-Fluoro-2-deoxy-glucose (FDG). This analog competes with glucose for the carriers which transport glucose across the blood brain barrier. Once inside the tissue, the FDG enters the catabolic pathways for the breakdown of glucose and the production of ATP from ADP. Following this phosphorylation of FDG, the ^{18}F label becomes essentially "trapped" in the tissue. Since small amounts of phosphatase can be found in the brain, the phosphorylated analog is not irreversibly "trapped" in the tissue but is very slowly converted back into FDG. The set of processes which determine the fate of an FDG molecule can be described by a simple three compartmental model (blood compartment, tissue FDG compartment, tissue FDG-6P compartment) and a set of rate

Table 1

Common PET Studies

Physiology	Radiopharmaceutical
Cerebral Blood Flow	$H_2{}^{15}O$
Cerebral Blood Volume	$C^{15}O$
Oxygen Utilization	$O\text{-}^{15}O$
Glucose Utilization	$^{18}F\text{-}FDG$

constants describing the transport of ^{18}F between each compartment. Using mathematical techniques along with measurements of the tissue and blood ^{18}F concentrations, this simple model is fit to the data enabling the evaluation of glucose transport of reaction rates (Phelps et al., 1979; Reivich et al., 1979b; Sokoloff et al., 1977). Examples of other commonly employed radiopharmaceuticals and the physiological function which they measure are listed in Table 1.

The study of cognitive functioning with PET has been examined by stimulating various sensory modalities, e.g. visual, auditory, and somatosensory-motor systems. In order to focus our review, we examined data pertaining to healthy individuals during functional activation of these sensory systems. This was then contrasted with resting state scanning (i. e. minimal sensory input and motor output) in dementia and normal subjects.

Visual System

Studies investigating the human visual system based on lesions and vascular disorders have contributed to our understanding of neuroanatomical structures and the neuronal networks associated with precortical connections. Electrophysiological research using evoked potentials and scalp electrodes has been limited, however, by poor spatial resolution. Another brain imaging technique, regional cerebral blood flow, using the intracarotid or ^{133}Xenon inhalation method, has reliability problems in measuring inner cortical areas, as well as inadequate spatial resolution. PET, however, uses a non-invasive methodology with improved spatial resolution that allows examiners to investigate the proportional distribution of metabolic activity within the visual system that is not available with any other imaging technique (Heiss, Herholz, Pawlik, Wagner, & Wienhard, 1986; Reivich et al., 1979a). In the following sections we will review neuropsychological findings using only the most widely researched glucose radiopharmaceuticals.

Greenberg et al. (1981), Reivich & Gur (1985), and Reivich, Rosen, Kushner, Gur, & Alavi (1983) stimulated either the left or right visual hemifield with a small light that was dimmed at random. One half of a plexiglass hemisphere positioned in front of subjects was painted black to limit stimulation to a desired hemifield. The stimulus consisted of moving abstract color images and a black-and-white pattern of lines. They discovered increased metabolic activity in the calcarine area contralateral to the stimulated visual field. These results complemented existing knowledge of the visual pathways.

Kushner et al. (1982) investigated restricting the spatial extent of a visual stimulus to the central 20 degrees (macular region) of the left hemifield and the peripheral 60 degrees of the right hemifield. As predicted, right posterior striate cortex metabolism was higher than controls with macular stimulation and left anterior striate cortex was higher with peripheral stimulation. These findings suggested that mapping the representation of the retina upon the striate and extrastriate cortices was possible with PET.

Phelps et al. (1981) and Phelps, Kuhl, & Mazziotta (1981) found that when volunteers were stimulated with white light, the primary visual cortex (Brodmann area 17) exhibited bilaterally twice as much metabolic activation as did the associative visual cortex (Brodmann areas 18 and 19). When the researchers increased the complexity of the stimuli for some subjects by using a moving black and white checkerboard pattern, areas 17, 18, and 19 showed an increased metabolic response over the white light stimulation. In addition, for this more complex experiment, the associative visual cortex was substantially more activated than the primary visual cortex. When subjects received the checkerboard stimulation in just one eye, the primary visual cortex was activated 63 percent over that produced by binocular stimulation, with no differences noted in the visual association cortex. This visual experiment was made even more complex by requesting volunteers to view the park beside the laboratory. The primary areas demonstrated a 45 percent increase over the associative areas relative to baseline metabolic levels. These researchers concluded that local metabolic rates increased in areas 17,18, and 19 as the complexity of visual scenes increased, with the associative areas increasing more rapidly than primary areas. It was suggested that the associative areas are more involved in higher order complex visual interpretations.

The diversity of findings on the visual system, as well as in the succeeding auditory and somatosensory-motor system sections, and the significant promise of further exciting findings can be attributed to several factors. Dramatic improvements in spatial resolution have occurred since early PET studies and our increased understanding and diversified production of radiopharmaceuticals has also significantly improved the accuracy of regional cortical analysis. The majority of the initial studies used small numbers of subjects with a considerable amount of variability in health screening measures. Experimental design of behavioral tasks during scanning has become more sophisticated, with added control tasks. As indicated in the following section on the auditory system, cognitive strategies, in addition to stimulus demands, can dramatically influence regional cortical localization. Other factors such as motivation (e.g., paid vs. unpaid subjects), attention, anxiety, sex, handedness, and habituation to task demands will need to be explored in future neuropsychological paradigms.

Auditory System

The functional activation of the auditory system has been summarized in several studies (Mazziotta, Phelps, Carson, & Kuhl, 1982a; Reivich & Alavi, 1985; Reivich, Gur, & Alavi, 1983). Alavi et al. (1981) required subjects to listen to a tape-recorded factual story. Some subjects listened to the information via the right ear only, and others only with the left ear. In order to encourage attentiveness to the story, subjects were told they would be paid in proportion to the accuracy of their recall. In a second experiment using different subjects (Alavi et al., 1981), procedures were the same except that volunteers listened to a meaningless discourse in Hungarian and pushed buttons when they heard a predetermined stimulus word. Again, they were paid in relation to their accuracy. Interestingly, there was significantly increased metabolic activity in the right temporal lobe compared to other brain areas regardless of the stimulus used or the side of presentation. Although the results seemed inconsistent with most studies of lateralization of language perception, three hypotheses were proposed to explain the higher metabolic right hemisphere focus: (1) there is some evidence for right hemisphere involvement in the mediation of certain aspects of linguistic information (Searleman, 1977), (2) utilization of imagery and other visual strategies may have aided in encoding information (Berlin & McNeill, 1956; Broadbent, 1956), and (3) in both experiments, attentional factors may have been taxed more than the linguistic ones, resulting in significant right hemisphere involvement (Dimond & Beaumount, 1973; Dimond & Farrington, 1977).

Greenberg et al. (1981) found that when subjects heard monaurally presented factual stories, an increase in glucose metabolism occurred in the auditory cortex contralateral to the stimulated ear. These results were said to be consistent with data suggesting the predominance of crossed pathways in the human auditory system (Cullen, Berlin, Hughes, Thompson, & Samson, 1975).

As the complexity of the auditory stimulation increases, the pattern of cortical metabolic activity may extend beyond those areas associated with the primary auditory system. For example, when subjects received bilateral or unilateral stimulation from a taped radio mystery story, The Shadow, the frontal lobes were activated in addition to the auditory system (Phelps, 1981). The volunteers were paid in proportion to how much of the story they remembered. The experimenter suggested that the considerable amount of mentation and short-term memory recall required by the test probably increased frontal lobe activation. The specificity of this complex auditory system network has been extended to subcortical areas. The thalamus has been shown to be bilaterally activated in subjects hearing verbal stimuli for recall (Mazziotta, Phelps, & Carson, 1984).

In another series of experiments, when a Sherlock Holmes story was presented to either the left or right ear during scanning, multiple brain areas demonstrated a significant increase in metabolic activity from the resting state (Mazziotta, Phelps, Carson, & Kuhl, 1982). These areas included the left frontal cortex, left thalamus, and bilateral posterior and transverse temporal cortices. Overall, the left hemisphere showed a greater increase in metabolism than the right hemisphere whether the left or right ear was stimulated. As part of the same study, the researchers examined lateralization of two subtests of the Seashore Measures of Musical Talents (Seashore, Lewis, & Sactveit, 1960), known as the Timbre Test and Tonal Memory Test. Only the Timbre Test, which consists of identifying different complex harmonic cord pairs, had a significantly greater right hemisphere asymmetry in glucose metabolism. The results for the Tonal Memory Test, requiring discrimination between tone pairs, were more complicated and appeared to depend on the cognitive strategy (analytic vs. non-analytic) employed by the subject. The subjects using a non-analytic strategy exhibited increased right hemisphere metabolic and asymmetry in the frontal and parietotemporal regions. In contrast, subjects using an analytic strategy demonstrated greater left than right metabolism in the posterior superior temporal cortex with no right greater than left metabolic areas observed. In this last, more elaborate experimental paradigm, the researchers concluded that hemispheric specialization can be a function not only of stimulus demands but also of cognitive strategy of the subject.

Somatosensory-Motor System

Little research has been conducted on the somatosensory-motor system. Greenberg et al. (1981) used a tactile stimulus of rapid, light stroking of the volar and dorsal surface of the fingers of the left arm with a hand-held brush, which was just stiff enough to cause an appreciable stimulus without causing any discomfort. This procedure was repeated in a different set of subjects in which only the right hand received tactile stimuli. The results were in agreement with known studies of patients undergoing neurosurgical procedures in that the somatosensory input caused the postcentral gyrus contralateral to the stimulus to become metabolically more active than the homologous area in the ipsilateral cortex. Gur et al. (1983) demonstrated a cognitive-motor network by having volunteers solve Miller Analogies Test questions during scanning. A different set of subjects solved Benton's Line-Orientation Test questions also during scanning in the same experiment. The researchers found that the verbal task produced greater metabolism in Wernicke's area relative to the right hemispheric homotopic region, whereas the spatial task produced greater metabolic activity in the hemisphere homotopic region. The Broca's area and its right hemisphere counterpart showed symmetrical activity during the verbal task, but there was a significant asymmetry to the right during the spatial task. The authors additionally found lateralized task effects in the frontal eye fields. They concluded that this was the first experimental demonstration that lateralized metabolic activity, produced by different types of cognitive tasks, also produced similarly lateralized metabolic activity in a motor region.

Foster, Chase, Patronas, Gillespie, and Fedio (1986) have examined the relationship of Alzheimer patient's ability to mimic skilled movements or to pantomime them in response to spoken commands as compared with neuropsychological test performance and regional glucose metabolism. Imitation scores correlated best with visual-spatial ability and with right parietal lobe metabolism. Conversely, command scores related most closely with tests of verbal proficiency and with left inferior hemisphere metabolism. The authors concluded that apraxia to command and imitation may thus reflect neuronal dysfunction in distinct cerebral regions in patients with Alzheimer's disease.

Cognition and Resting State PET Scanning

PET scanning in the resting state refers to studies that are carried out under conditions which minimize sensory input and motor output (Mazziotta, Phelps, Carson, & Kuhl, 1982b; Mazziotta, Phelps, Miller, & Kuhl, 1981; Phelps & Mazziotta, 1985b). Typically, subjects are scanned in the supine position in a room with low ambient light with eyes covered and ears plugged. PET scanning and actual performance of the subject on neuropsychological tests are administered on different occasions. Hence, moment to moment changes in regional cerebral glucose metabolism are not reflected during specific cognitive tasks. This paradigm has been most useful to date in patients with impaired cognition and lower selective regional cerebral glucose metabolism, such as seen in Alzheimer's disease (Benson, 1982; Duara et al., 1986; Foster et al., 1983; Friedland et al., 1983; Haxby, 1984; Huff, 1984; McGeer et al., 1986).

A neurochemical abnormality, low somatostatin levels, is found in Alzheimer's disease. This degree of reduction has been significantly correlated with indices of intellectual impairment (Boston Naming Test, Mattis Dementia Scale, Rey-Osterreith Copy, and Wechsler Memory Scale) and decline in cortical glucose utilization as determined by PET (Tamminga, Foster, Bird, Fedio & Chase, 1987). Based on these findings, it was inferred that the loss of somatostatin-mediated synaptic function may have contributed to the cognitive decline in Alzheimer's disease. Foster et al. (1984) have found that cortical glucose metabolism was significantly correlated with WAIS Full Scale IQ, Wechsler Memory Quotient, and Mattis Dementia Scale in Alzheimer patients. Similarly, the degree of cognitive impairment in patients with Alzheimer's disease was significantly correlated with degree of diminution in regional metabolism (Farkas et al., 1982). Bilateral frontal grey and white matter glucose utilization was found to be significantly correlated with a global cognitive measure, the Mental Status Questionnaire, as well as Immediate and Delayed Paragraph recall, Paired Associates, and Design Recall from the Guild Memory Test (Ferris et al., 1980). Friedland et al. (1983) analyzed neuropsychological test correlates in Alzheimer patients by means of regional metabolism. They suggested that the Mattis Dementia Rating Scale and Verbal IQ test performance in Alzheimer's patients were sensitive to left frontal impairment, whereas Performance IQ was sensitive to right posterior hemisphere impairment.

Lateralization correlates of neuropsychological tests with PET has been investigated in several studies (Chase et al. 1983, Chase et al. 1984a, & Chase et al. 1985). In this research with Alzheimer's disease, WAIS Verbal IQ and Mattis Dementia Scale performance were significantly correlated with the metabolic activity in the left cerebral hemisphere. Conversely, WAIS Performance IQ and the copy score from the Rey-Osterrieth Complex Figure Test correlated largely with the metabolic activity in the right cerebral hemisphere. A closer examination of the relationship between WAIS test performance and metabolism in the same patient population (Chase et al. 1984b) demonstrated that most verbal subtests (Vocabulary, Information, Comprehension, and Similarities) correlated with the left temporoparietal areas. However, regional areas of correlation with the Arithmetic subtest extended to the left angular gyrus, and Digit Span was associated primarily with the bilateral anterior frontal lobe metabolism. WAIS Performance subtests (Picture Completion, Object Assembly, Digit Symbol, and Block Design) correlated primarily with right posterior lobe metabolism. Picture Arrangement correlated bilaterally with parietal metabolism. These researchers suggested that the bilateral component of the former test was probably due to one's ability to verbally organize visually presented material, whereas Digit Span's relationship with bilateral frontal areas was ascribed to the test's attentional and memory components.

Research on normal, healthy individuals in resting state PET scanning has revealed no correlations between indices of cerebral metabolism and performance on neuropsychological tests such as the Revised Visual Retention Test, WAIS, Syntax Comprehension Test and Extended Range Drawing Test (Birren, Butler, & Greenhouse, 1963; Duara et al., 1984; Grady, 1984; Haxby, Duara, Grady, Cutler, & Rapoport, 1985). Haxby et al. (1986) pointed out that their normal subjects were exceptionally screened for health and that by virtue of the subjects' optimal test performance and consequentially a smaller range of variability, it was more difficult to achieve statistical significance as a result of correlational analyses.

Of course, a significant correlation does not mean the relationship between two factors is causal in nature. Conversely, the fact that we cannot infer causation from correlation does not necessarily mean that a cause and effect relationship does not exist; it merely means that it is often difficult to obtain sufficient information as to determine the specific nature and direction of this causal relationship (Neale & Liebert, 1980).

Behavioral Activation and PET Using Cognitive Paradigms

Examination of brain-behavior relationships using PET has typically involved correlating neuropsychological test results with resting-state neuroimaging data obtained on a separate day. Although this paradigm has clearly enhanced our understanding of cerebral function, it does not provide an opportunity to observe simultaneous brain-behavior relationships. Fortunately, more recent advances have allowed us to directly assess cerebral metabolic activity as it relates to specific cognitive/neuropsychological task performance.

Earlier studies contrasted metabolic activity of subjects receiving an activation task versus those in the resting state. The obtained differences in cerebral metabolism presumably represented the effects of the behavioral activation produced by the neuropsychological task. The major limitation of this approach was its reliance on a between-groups design, which introduces more error variance than a more powerful within-subjects approach. An alternative method has been to administer PET scans to the same individual on two separate occasions to compare the effects of the resting state versus behavioral activation or to contrast different types of cognitive tasks. This method is also limited, particularly with regard to reliability. For example, Duara et al. (1987) have demonstrated a low correspondence between resting scans of normals taken two weeks apart. While there is less variability with regard to activation scans taken on separate occasions, this source of error variance, or "noise", complicates the interpretation of brain-behavior relationships.

Recent methodological advances have made it possible to obtain two separate PET scans for an individual during a single testing session. Fox et al. (1987) have utilized ^{15}O labeled water and PET to examine the effects of behavioral activation on cerebral blood flow. The advantage of this approach is that two PET studies can be conducted in close temporal sequence (10 minutes) because of the short half-life of ^{15}O (T/2 = 2 minutes). As a result, it is less likely that intervening variables may contribute to measurement error from one scan to another. However, assessment of cerebral blood flow is only an indirect measure of neuronal activity in the brain. A superior method of examining neuronal activity involves studying metabolic rates of glucose. Reivich et al. (1982) used [C-11]-deoxyglucose and PET to examine metabolic activity in the resting state. Because of the long half-life of ^{11}C (20 minutes), the separations between paired studies are much longer (100 minutes). In addition, an additional C-11-deoxyglucose sample, the cyclotron run, must be prepared for the second injection accompanying the second scan, which further introduces the possibility of technical error. Recently Chang et al. (1987) developed the double injection method using FDG which allows an initial resting or behavioral scan to be performed. Subsequently, another scan can be conducted utilizing a different type of behavioral activation. Because of the longer half-life of ^{18}F (T $1/2 = 109$ minutes), no additional cyclotron runs need to be conducted. An essential aspect of this procedure is to calculate and to partial out the residual isotope from the first scan so that images from the second scan can be accurately reconstructed. Using this double activation method, Chang and his associates have demonstrated that subjects given an identical activation task on two sequential scanning occasions exhibit less than a 5% difference in metabolic rates between the two scanning conditions. This method reduces error variance by conducting PET scans in close temporal sequence (50 minutes) and by allowing the subject to serve as his or her own control.

Procedures Involved in Conducting a Behavioral Activation Scan

Examination of the in vivo relationship between cognitive/neuro-psychological performance and cerebral metabolic activation is typically examined by comparing a subject's resting or control task scan to his/her behavioral activation scan. For descriptive purposes the procedures involved in a single-study verbal fluency paradigm will be presented.

Before scanning commences, {F 18} fluorodeoxyglucose (FDG) is prepared by the cyclotron staff. Subjects are asked to arrive one hour prior to the commencement of PET scanning. Subjects must fast for a minimum period of three hours prior to the study and can not take any medication, coffee, tea, or alcohol on the day of the study. When the study begins, subjects lie supine and two intravenous catheters are introduced into the dorsal vein of each hand into which normal saline is infused. FDG is also administered at this time. One hand is heated in a chamber to approximately 45 degrees Celsius and arterialized venous blood samples are drawn at predetermined intervals during the PET study so that the plasma concentration of radioactivity and glucose can be measured. For thirty minutes after the injection of FDG, the subject is administered a verbal fluency task modified for PET scan use (Chang et al., 1987) based on widely used forms of the test (Parks et al., in press). Subjects remain supine with their eyes closed and blindfolded. They are subsequently given different letters of the alphabet for which they have to generate words beginning with that letter. One minute is allowed for each letter. Following thirty minutes of behavioral activation (verbal fluency), scanning is conducted for approximately 20 minutes with a PETT V, seven slice camera.

In analyzing the obtained PET data, correction for attenuation is necessary since each pair of photons emitted from different regions of the brain will travel different distances inside the brain before being detected by the crystals within the scanner. In addition, each of the seven brain slices are assigned a level using a standard brain atlas. Cerebral regions of interest are obtained by a computer program which places 8 mm by 8 mm boxes over the entire cortex and peak subcortical gray matter structures. An experienced operator can adjust these boxes and select 1-4 boxes to correspond to each of the 67 regions of the brain as specified in a standard brain atlas. Regional cerebral metabolic rates (rCMRglc) are calculated using operational equations (Chang et al., 1987). Metabolic values for supertentorial brain regions such as hemispheres, lobes, and lobules can be calculated by examining the mean metabolic rates for all of the boxes that are contained in a specific region of interest. While absolute metabolic rates can be examined, there is often considerable variability among normal subjects on these measures. A well-established method of reducing variability involves normalizing the metabolic rate for a region of interest to the whole brain or a specific reference region such as the occipital lobe.

Recent Investigations of Cerebral Metabolic Activity Using Different Behavioral Activation Paradigms

We now report on the results of several recent investigations which have been conducted in collaboration with Dr. Ranjan Duara. A primary focus has been on the effects of a verbal fluency task on metabolic activity within the brain.

Using a word fluency paradigm, Parks et al. (in press) demonstrated that normals receiving a verbal fluency task exhibited 23% more activation over the entire cortex relative to controls who had received resting PET scans. Moreover, the greatest amount of activation was in the bilateral temporal (27%) and frontal (25%) regions. In another study, Duara et al. (1986) utilized the double injection method so that subjects received the verbal fluency test and then an automatic verbalization task, which required the subject to count slowly up to a target number, one target per minute. This latter task served as a control procedure so that the effects of verbalization could be partialed out. Results indicated that the verbal fluency test resulted in greater metabolic activation in the left orbitofrontal, basal ganglia and both cerebellar hemispheres relative to the automatic verbalization task. It should be noted that the number of subjects in this study was small so it is unclear to what extent these results can be generalized. A replication study is currently under way.

Another aspect of the verbal fluency paradigm has been to correlate the actual performance on the word fluency task with the degree of metabolic activation. Parks et al. (in press) found an inverse relationship between proficiency on a verbal fluency task and metabolic activity in the frontal, temporal, and parietal regions. In contrast, Duara et al. (1986) found no correlation between performance on a memory for passages test (MP) and metabolic activation. The differential effects of verbal fluency and MP tasks on metabolic activation may be explained by the different components inherent to each neuropsychological measure. Verbal fluency has been construed as "effortless" responding so that those patients with greater fluency likely have more efficient cognitive strategies which resulted in a minimal expenditure of effort. On the other hand, given the sizeable number of elements to recall on the MP test, it is likely that performance was more related to more complex effortful processes than required for verbal fluency.

Another interesting line of investigation is based on the work of Ginsberg et al. (1987) who have examined task-specific somatosensory activation on PET. Using a sequential rest-activation double-injection paradigm, normal subjects were assigned to different activation conditions. The first condition involved having subjects palpate mah-jong tiles and sort them according to specific characteristics of the tile identified by touch. This somatosensory procedure was relatively specific to increased metabolic activation (18%) in the somatosensory cortex. Similar results were obtained in a graphesthesia condition in which the examiner traced one-digit numbers on the subject's palm which the subject had to identify using a nonverbal response modality. A condition in which subjects were given continuous vibrotactile stimulation showed a minimal amount of activation, perhaps because of habituation to the stimuli. Taken together, these results indicate that somatosensory tasks which involve active participation and conscious effort tend to activate somatosensory regions.

There are a number of other behavioral activation tasks which have provided considerable information about both normal subjects and those with different neurological disorders such as Alzheimer's Disease or Dyslexia. These include picture preference tests which activate the primary visual and associative visual cortex as well as sections of the temporal and parietal lobes in normal young subjects. However, elderly subjects were found to have more restricted activation limited to the visual cortex. Patients with Alzheimer's disease demonstrated no activation at all (Yoshii et al., 1986). Reading tasks in which real and nonsense syllables have also been utilized have been used to study patients diagnosed with dyslexia.

The immediate challenge for the psychologist or behavioral neurologist is to contend with the considerable amount of activation that occurs as a result of any test which has a verbal or a visual component. The problem of nonspecific arousal is being approached by using more sophisticated control tasks. For example, an examination of the differences between the verbal fluency task and control tasks that are comparable with regard to attention, effort, and the amount of vocalization can provide meaningful data as to which areas of the brain are associated with verbal fluency per se. Another method of dealing with the issue of nonspecific activation has been the development of sophisticated multivariate techniques which are designed to partition out the effects of general arousal from activation of a particular cerebral region of interest.

The Utility of Behavioral Activation Paradigms

Resting state PET scan studies often show dramatic and sometimes unexpected alterations in physiology when little or no structural abnormality is present (Duara et al., 1986). However, in conditions such as Huntington's

Disease, expected cortical abnormalities in resting state scans have not been found (Young et al., 1986). In such cases, it is conceivable that the activation of the brain may result in an abnormality of cortical activation patterns. This is consistent with recent findings by Gross-Glenn et al. (1986) who have demonstrated that dyslexic subjects are unable to activate specific brain regions relative to normals when performing reading tasks during PET studies.

The application of the double injection/double activation method and the use of sophisticated behavioral activation paradigms with appropriate control tasks hold considerable promise in elucidating the interaction among different brain regions in the execution of specific neuropsychological functions. Such data will provide valuable information about the normal functioning of the brain. More importantly, application of this paradigm to abnormal populations can ultimately assist us in better understanding the pathogenesis and physiology of neurological diseases such as those associated with dementing disorders.

Conclusions

Positron emission tomography represents an exciting new technology which has greatly elucidated brain-behavior relationships in both normal and abnormal populations. The present challenge to neuropsychology and behavioral neurology is to develop sophisticated behavioral activation tasks in which the effects of general arousal, habituation and/or anxiety is minimized so that the specific areas of the brain associated with a particular behavior/neuropsychological task can be examined. Determination as to networks of brain regions which work together in the execution of a cognitive/neuropsychological function will greatly enhance our understanding of physiological substrates of such complex processes as memory and learning.

References

Alavi, A., Reivich, M., Greenberg, J. H., Hand, P., Rosenquist, A., Rintelmann, W., Christman, D., Fowler, J., Goldman, A., MacGregor, R., & Wolf, A. (1981). Mapping of functional activity in brain with ^{18}F-fluro-deoxyglucose. *Seminars in Nuclear Medicine, 11*, 24-31.

Benson, F. D. (1982). The use of positron emission tomography scanning techniques in the diagnosis of Alzheimer's disease. In S. Corkin (Ed.), *Alzheimer's disease: A report of progress [Vol. 19]* (pp. 79-82). New York: Raven Press.

Berlin, C. J., & McNeill, M. (1956). Dichotic listening. In N. Nass (Ed.), *Contemporary issues in experimental Phonetics*. New York: Academic Press.

Birren, J. E., Butler, R. N., & Greenhouse (1963). Interdisciplinary relationships: Inter-relations of physiological, psychological and psychiatric findings in healthy elderly men. In J.E. Birren & R.N. Butler (Eds.), *Human aging I. A biological and behavioral study* (PHS Publication No. 986, 283-305). Washington, DC: U.S. Government Printing Office.

Broadbent, D. (1956). Growing points in multichannel communication. *Journal of the Acoustical Society of America, 28*, 533-535.

Brooks, R. A., & Di Chiro, G. (1976) Principles of computer assisted tomography (CAT) in radiographic and radioisotopic imaging. *Physics in Medicine and Biology, 21*, 689-732.

Chang, J.Y., Duara, R., Barker, W., et al. (1987). Two behavioral states studied in a single PET/FDG procedure: theory, method and preliminary results. *Journal of Nuclear Medicine, 28*, 852-860.

Chase, T. N., Foster, N. L., Fedio, P., Di Chiro, G., Brooks, R., & Patronas, N. J. (1983). Alzheimer's disease: Local cerebral metabolism studies using ^{18}F-Fluorodeoxyglucose-positron emission tomography technique. In D. Samuel (Ed.), *Aging of the brain* (pp.143-154). New York: Raven Press.

Chase, T. N., Foster, N. L., Fedio, P., Brooks, R., Mansi, L., & Di Chiro, G. (1984a). Regional cortical dysfunction in Alzheimer's disease as determined by positron emission tomography. *Annals of Neurology, 15(Suppl.)*, 170-174.

Chase, T. N., Fedio, P., Foster, N. L., Brooks, R., Di Chiro, G., & Mansi, L. (1984b). Wechsler Adult Intelligence Scale performance: Cortical localization by fluorodeoxyglucose F 18-positron emission tomography. *Archives of Neurology, 41*, 1244-1247.

Chase, T. N., Brooks, R. A., Di Chiro, G., Fedio, P., Foster, N. L., Kessler, R. A., Mansi, L., Manning, R. G., & Patronas, N. J. (1985). Focal cortical abnormalities in Alzheimer's disease.In T. Greitz, D. H. Ingvar, & L. W. Widen (Eds.), *The metabolism of the human brain studied with positron emission tomography* (pp. 433-440). New York: Raven Press.

Cullen, J. K., Berlin, C. I., Hughes, L. F., Thompson, C. L., & Samson, D. S. (1975). *Proceedings of a Symposium on Central Auditory Processing Disorders* (pp.108-127). Omaha, Nebraska: University of Nebraska Press.

Dimond, S., & Beaumont, G. (1973). Difference in the vigilance performance of the right or left hemispheres. *Cortex, 9*, 259-265.

Dimond, S., & Farrington, L. Emotional response to films shown to the right or left hemispheres of the brain measured by heart rate. *Acta Psychologica, 41*, 255-260.

Duara, R., Chang, J.Y., Barker, W.W., Yoshii, F., & Apicella, A. (1986). Correlation of regional cerebral metabolic activation to performance in activating tasks. *Neurology, 36 (Supplement 1)*, 349.

Duara, R., Grady, C., Haxby, J., Ingrav, D., Sokoloff, L., Margolin, R.A., Manning, R. G., Cutler, N. R., & Rapoport, S.I. (1984). Human brain glucose utilization and cognitive function in relation to age. *Annals of Neurology, 16*, 702-713.

Duara, R., Grady, C., Haxby, J., Sundaram, M., Cutler, N. R., Heston, L., Moore, A., Schlageter, N., Larson, S., & Rapoport, S. I. (1986). Positron emission tomography in Alzheimer's disease. *Neurology, 36*, 879-887.

Duara, R., Gross-Glenn, K., Barker, W.W., Chang, J.Y., Apicella, A., Loewenstein, D. A., & Boothe, T. (1987). Behavioral activation and the variability of cerebral glucose metabolic measurements. *Journal of Cerebral Blood Flow and Metabolism, 7*, 266-271.

Duara, R., Sheremata, W.A., Parks, R.W., Barker, W.W., Chang, J.Y., Yoshii, F., & Apicella, A. (Unpublished manuscript). Regional cerebral glucose metabolism (rCMRglc) activation by the Word Fluency Test (WFT). Mount Sinai Medical Center.

Farkas, T., Ferris, S. H., Wolf, A. P., De Leon, M. J., Christman, D. R., Reisberg, B., Abass, A., Fowler, J. S., George, A. E., & Reivich, M. (1982). ^{18}F -2-Deoxy-2-fluoro-D-glucose as a tracer in the positron emission tomographic study of senile dementia. *American Journal of Psychiatry, 139*, 352-353.

Ferris, S. H., De Leon, M. J., Wolf, A. P., Farkas, T., Christman, D. R., Reisberg, B., Fowler, J. S., MacGregor, R., Goldman, A., George, A. E., & Rampal, S. (1980). Positron emission tomography in the study of aging and senile dementia. *Neurobiology of Aging, 1*, 127-131.

Foster, N. L., Chase, T. N., Fedio, P., Patronas, N. J., Brooks, R. A., & Di Chiro, G. (1983). Alzheimer's disease: Focal cortical changes shown by positron emission tomography. *Neurology, 33*, 961-965.

Foster, N. L., Chase, T. N., Mansi, L., Brooks, R., Fedio, P., Patronas, N. J., & Di Chiro, G. (1984). Cortical abnormalities in Alzheimer's disease. *Annals of Neurology, 16*, 649-654.

Foster, N. L., Chase, T. N., Patronas, N. J., Gillespie, M. M., & Fedio, P. (1986). Cerebral Mapping of apraxia in Alzheimer's disease by positron emission tomography. *Annals of Neurology, 19*, 139-143.

Fox, P.T., Petersen, S.E., Posner, M.I., & Raichle, M.E. (1987). Language-related brain activation measured with PET: Comparison of auditory and visual word presentations. *Journal of Cerebral Blood Flow and Metabolism, 7, (Supplement 1)*, S294.

Friedland, R. P., Budinger, T. F., Ganz, E., Yano, Y., Mathis, C. A., Koss, B., Ober, B. A., Huesman, R. H., & Derenzo, S. E. (1983). Regional cerebral metabolic alterations in dementia of the Alzheimer type: Positron emission tomography with [^{18}F] Fluorodeoxyglucose. *Journal of Computer Assisted Tomography 7*, 590-598.

Ginsberg, M.D., Yoshii, F., Vibulsresth, S., Chang, J.Y., Duara, R., Barker, W.W., & Boothe, T.E. (1987). Human task-specific somatosensory activation in man. *Neurology, 37*, 1301-1308.

Grady, C. L. (1984) Neuropsychology and Cerebral Metabolism in Normal Aging. In N. R. Cutler (moderator), Brain imaging: Aging and Dementia. *Annals of Internal Medicine, 101*, 358-360.

Greenberg, J. H., Reivich, M., Alavi, A., Hand, P., Rosenquist, A., Rintelmann, W., Stein, A., Tusa, R., Dann, R., Christman, D., Fowler, J., MacGregor, B., & Wolf, A. (1981) Metabolic mapping of functional activity in human subjects with the [^{18}F]Fluorodeoxyglucose technique. *Science, 212*, 678-680.

Gross-Glenn, K., Duara, R., Yoshii, F., Barker, W.W., Chang, J.Y., Apicella, A., Boothe, T., & Lubs, H.A. (1986). PET scan studies during reading in dyslexic and non-dyslexic adults. *Society of Neuroscience Abstracts, 12*, 1364.

Gur, R. C. (1985). Imaging regional brain physiology in behavioral neurology. In M-M. Mesulam (Ed.), *Principles of behavioral neurology* (pp. 347-362). Philadelphia: F. A. Davis.

Gur, R. C. (1987). Imaging the activity of the human brain. *National Forum, 67,* 13-16.

Gur, R. C., Gur, R. E., Rosen, A. D., Warach, S., Alavi, A., Greenberg, J., & Reivich, M. (1983). A cognitive-motor network demonstrated by positron emission tomography. *Neuropsychologia, 21,* 601-606.

Haxby, J. V. (1984). Neuropsychology and cerebral metabolism in dementia. In N. R. Cutler (moderator), Brain imaging: Aging and Dementia. *Annals of Internal Medicine, 101,* 362-364.

Haxby, J. V., Duara, R., Grady, C. L., Cutler, N. R., & Rapoport, S. I. (1985). Relations between neuropsycholoical and cerebral metabolic asymmetries in early Alzheimer's disease. *Journal of Cerebral Blood Flow and Metabolism, 5,* 193-200.

Haxby, J. V., Grady, C.L., Duara, R., Robertson-Tchabo, E., Koziarz, B., Cutler, N. R., & Rapoport, S. I. (1986). Relations among age, visual memory, and resting cerebral metabolism in 40 healthy men. *Brain and Cognition, 5,* 412-427.

Heiss, W. D., Herholz, K., Pawlik, G., Wagner, R., & Wienhard, K. (1986).Positron emission tomography in neuropsychology. *Neuropsychologia, 24,* 141-149.

Hoffman, E. J., & Phelps M. E. (1986). Positron emission tomography: Principles and quantitation. In M. E. Phelps, J. C. Mazziotta, & H. R. Schelbert (Eds.), *Positron emission tomography and autoradiography: Principles and applications for the brain and heart* (pp 237-286). New York: Raven Press.

Huff, F. J. (1984). Alzheimer's disease: Advances in basic research and therapies. *Neurobiology of Aging, 5,* 157-179.

Kessler, R. M., Ellis, J. R., & Eden, M. (1984). Analysis of emission tomographic scan to date: Limitations imposed by resolution and background. *Journal of Computer Assisted Tomography, 8,* 514-522.

Kushner, M., Rosenquist, A., Alavi, A., Reivich, M., Greenberg, J., & Cobbs, W. (1982). Macular and peripheral visual field representation in striate cortex demonstrated by positron emission tomography. *Annals of Neurology, 12,* 89.

Mazziotta, J. C., & Phelps, M. E. (1985a). Human neuropsychological imaging studies of local brain metabolism: Strategies and results. In L. Sokoloff (Ed.), *Brain imaging and brain function,* (pp. 121-137). New York: Raven.

Mazziotta, J. C., & Phelps, M. E. (1985b). Results and strategies in studies of human sensory stimulation and deprivation with positron emission tomography. In T. Greitz, D. H. Ingvar, & L. W. Widen (Eds.), *The metabolism of the human brain studied with positron emission tomography* (pp. 315-334). New York: Raven Press.

Mazziotta, J. C., Phelps, M. E., & Carson, R. E. (1984). Tomographic mapping of human cerebral metabolism: Subcortical responses to auditory and visual stimulation. *Neurology, 34,* 825-928.

Mazziotta, J. C., Phelps, M. E., Carson, R. E., & Kuhl, D. E. (1982a) Tomographic mapping of human cerebral metabolism: Auditory stimulation. *Neurology, 32,* 921-937.

Mazziotta, J. C., Phelps, M. E., Carson, R. E. & Kuhl, D. E. (1982b). Tomographic mapping of human cerebral metabolism: Sensory deprivation. *Annals of Neurology, 12,* 435-444.

Mazziotta, J. C., Phelps, M. E., Miller J., & Kuhl, D. E. (1981) Tomographic mapping of human cerebral metabolism: Normal unstimulated state. *Neurology, 31*, 503-516.

McGeer, P. L., Kamo, H., Harrop, R., Li, D. K. B., Tuokko, H., McGeer, E. G., Adam, M. J., Ammann, W., Beattie, B. L., Calne, D. B., Martin, W. R. W., Pate, B. D., Rogers, J. G., Ruth, T. J., Sayre, C. I., & Stoessel, A. J. (1986). Positron emission tomography in patients with clinically diagnosed Alzheimer's disease. *Canadian Medical Association Journal, 134*, 597-607.

Neale, J. M. & Leibert, R. M. (1980). *Science and behavior.* Englewood Cliffs, N.J.: Prentice-Hall.

Parks, R., Loewenstein, D.A., Dodrill, K.L., Barker, W.W., Yoshii, F., Chang, J.Y., Emran, A., Apicella, A., Sheremata, W.A., & Duara, R. (In press). Cerebral metabolic effects of a verbal fluency test: A PET scan study. *Journal of Clinical and Experimental Neuropsychology.*

Phelps, M. E., Huang, S. C., Hoffman, E. J., Selin, C., Sokoloff, L., & Kuhl, D. E. (1979). Tomographic measurement of local cerebral glucose metabolic rate in humans (F-18) 2-fluoro-2-deoxy-D-glucose: Validation of method. *Annals of Neurology, 6*, 371-388.

Phelps, M. E., Mazziotta, J. C., Kuhl, D. E., Nuwer, M., Packwood, J., Metter, & Engel, J. (1981). Tomographic mapping of human cerebral metabolism: Visual stimulation and deprivation. *Neurology, 31*, 517-529.

Phelps, M. E. (1981). Positron computed tomography studies of cerebral glucose metabolism in man: Theory and application in nuclear medicine. *Seminars in Nuclear Medicine, 11*, 32-49.

Phelps, M. E., Kuhl, D. E., & Mazziotta, J. C. (1981) Metabolic mapping of the brain's response to visual stimulation: Studies in humans. *Science, 211*, 1445-1448.

Phelps, M. E., Mazziotta, J. C., Huang, S. C. (1982). Review: Study of cerebral function with positron emission tomography. *Journal of Cerebral Blood Flow and Metabolism, 2*, 113-162.

Phelps, M. E., & Mazziotta, J. C. (1983). Human sensory stimulation and deprivation as demonstrated by positron emission tomography. In W. D. Heiss & M. E. Phelps (Eds.), *Positron emission tomography of the brain* (pp. 139-152). Berlin: Springer-Verlag.

Phelps, M. E., Mazziotta, J. C., Schelbert, H. R., Hawkins, R. A., & Engel, J. (1985). Clinical PET: What are the issues? *The Journal of Nuclear Medicine, 26*, 1353-1358.

Reivich, M., Alavi, A., Greenberg, J.H., Fowler, J., Christman, D., MacGregor, R., Jones, S.C., London, J., Shiue, C., & Yonekura, Y. (1982). Use of 2-deoxy-D-[1-^{11}C] glucose for the determination of local glucose metabolism in humans: Variation within and between subjects. *Journal of Cerebral Blood Flow and Metabolism, 2*, 307-319.

Reivich, M., Greenberg, J., Alavi, A., Christman, J. Fowler, P., Hand A., Rosenquist, W., Rintelmann, W., & Wolf, A. (1979a). The use of the F-fluorodeoxyglucose technique for mapping functional neural pathways in man. *Acta Neurologica Scandinavica, 60*(Suppl. 72), 198-199.

Reivich, M., Kuhl, D., Wolf, A., Greenberg, J., Phelps, M., Ido, T., Casella, V., Fowler, J., Hoffman, E., Alavi, A., Som, P., & Sokoloff, L. (1979b). The [^{18}F] fluorodeoxyglucose method for the measurement of local cerebral glucose utilization in man. *Circulation Research, 44*, 127-137.

Reivich, M., Alavi, A., Gur, R. C., & Greenberg, J. (1985). Determination of local cerebral glucose metabolism in Humans: Methodology and applications to the study of sensory and cognitive stimuli. In L. Sokoloff (Ed.), *Brain imaging and brain function* (pp. 105-119). New York: Raven.

Reivich, M., & Alavi. (1985) Effect of psychophysiological stimuli on local cerebral glucose consumption in humans. In T. Greitz, D. H. Ingvar, & L. W. Widen (Eds.), *The metabolism of the human brain studied with positron emission tomography* (pp. 305-313). New York: Raven Press.

Reivich, M., Gur, R. & Alavi, A. (1983). Positron emission tomographic studies of sensory stimuli, cognitive processes and anxiety. *Human Neurobiology 2*, 25-33.

Reivich, M., & Gur, R. (1985) Cerebral metabolic effects of sensory and cognitive stimuli in normal subjects. In M. Reivich & A. Alavi (Eds.), *Positron emission tomography* (pp. 329-344). New York: Alan R. Liss.

Reivich, M., Rosen, A. D., Kushner, R. C., Gur, R. C., & Alavi, A. (1983). Local cerebral glucose consumption in man in health and disease. In P. L. Magistretti (Ed.), *Functional Radionuclide Imaging of the Brain* (pp. 311-318). New York: Raven Press.

Searleman, A. (1977). A review of right hemisphere linguistic capabilities. *Psychological Bulletin, 84*, 503-528.

Seashore, C. E., Lewis, D., & Sactveit, J. G. (1960). *Seashore measures of musical talents, Series B*. New York: Psychological Corporation.

Sokoloff, L., Reivich, M., Kennedy, C., DesRosiers, M. H., Patlak, C. S., Pettigrew, K. D., Sakurado, O., & Shinohara, M. (1977). The [^{14}C] deoxyglucose method for the measurement of local cerebral glucose utilization; theory, procedure, and normal values in the conscious and anesthetized albino rat. *Journal of Neurochemistry, 28*, 897-916.

Sokoloff, L. (1985). Basic principles in imaging of regional cerebral metabolic rates. In L. Sokoloff (Ed.), *Brain imaging and brain function* (pp. 21-49). New York: Raven.

Tamminga, C. A., Foster, N. L., Fedio, E. D., Bird, E. D., & Chase, T. N. (1987). Alzheimer's disease: Low cerebral somatostatin levels correlate with impaired function and cortical metabolism. *Neurology, 37*, 161-165.

Ter-Pogossian, M. M. (1985). Positron emission tomography instrumentation. In M. Reivich & A. Alavi (Eds.), *Positron emission tomography* (pp. 43-61). New York: Alan R. Liss.

Yoshii, F., Barker, W.W., Chang, J.Y., Apicella, A., Ginsberg, M., Emran, A., & Duara, R. (1986). Effect of age and gender on resting and visually activated cerebral glucose metabolism. *Society of Neuroscience, 12* (2), 1509.

Young, A.B., Penney, J.B., Starosta-Rubenstein, S., Markel, D.S., Berent, S., Giordani, B., Ehrenkaufer, R., Jewett, D., & Hichwa, R. (1986). PET scan investigations of Huntington's disease: Cerebral metabolic correlates of neurological features and functional decline. *Annals of Neurology, 20*, 296-303.

11

Child Neuropsychology and Cognitive Developmental Theory

Sam B. Morgan

Child neuropsychology is typically defined as the study of brain-behavior re-lationships in the developing child (Rourke, Bakker, Fisk, & Strang, 1983; Obrzut & Hynd, 1986). As a specific field of study, it is itself in its early childhood and undergoing a period of rapid growth, especially in applied as opposed to theoretical areas. This growth is evidenced by the widening accep-tance and use of child neuropsychological techniques in diverse settings and the spate of recent publications on the clinical and educational application of these techniques (e. g. Rourke, Fisk, & Strang, 1986; Hartlage & Telzrow, 1986). The applied orientation is also strongly reflected in child neuropsy-chological research, a large portion of which has addressed immediate practi-cal problems, such as assessment of impairment and dysfunction presumed to have a neurological basis. While such research is worthwhile, relatively few studies have been based on theoretical constructs and few attempts have been made to formulate any comprehensive, integrative theories of neuropsycho-logical development in children (Fletcher & Taylor, 1984).

The lack of theoretically based research in child neuropsychology be-comes readily apparent when we compare the area with cognitive-develop-mental psychology, where most of the research is derived from theory. Until the relatively recent development of neuropsychological scales based on Luria's (1973) theory, clinical neuropsychology has been generally atheoreti-cal and radically empirical. While Luria's theory has been interpreted within a developmental context (Golden, 1981; Hooper & Boyd, 1986), child neu-ropsychology still does not have a theory that approaches the breadth and heuristic value of developmental theories of cognition, such as Piaget's theory of cognitive development.

In this chapter, I first discuss the benefits that theory could provide to child neuropsychology and the need to incorporate concepts from develop-mental psychology into child neuropsychological theory, research, and prac-tice. I then review and evaluate certain aspects of Piaget's theory of cognitive development, and attempt to relate his theory in a preliminary way to concepts of developmental neuropsychology based on Luria's general theory. Through

Morgan, S. B. (1988). Child neuropsychology and cognitive developmental theory. In J. M. Williams & C. J. Long (Eds.), *Cognitive approaches to neuropsychology*, New York: Plenum.

this analysis I attempt to show some underlying conceptual compatibilities that may provide a basis for productive research. In the final section I offer some research questions oriented toward integrating the two areas of study.

Benefits of Theory to Child Clinical Neuropsychology

As a rapidly growing area of study and practice, child neuropsychology would certainly benefit from the theory development and theory-based research that has traditionally characterized developmental psychology. Some might contend that we do not need elaborate theorizing, only a knowledge of consistent empirical relations that allow us to make predictions. Indeed, adult clinical neuropsychology in this country has made significant progress in expanding our knowledge of empirical brain-behavior relationships in the mature human; much of this progress was made without strong theoretical underpinnings. Nevertheless, I maintain, as others have (e. g., Fletcher & Taylor, 1984), that more attention to theory could result in significant contributions to child neuropsychology, especially at this stage in its development.

A theory, in its ideal form, can be defined as a set of assumptions systematically related to each other and to empirical data (Hall & Lindzey, 1957). Of course, many theories only approach this ideal, but still may serve useful functions. In a given research area, a theory serves as a conceptual basis for organizing and expanding knowledge in a systematic way. It helps us to summarize, integrate, and interpret diverse, complex empirical findings within a logically consistent framework. All other things being equal (and they rarely, if ever, are), the most parsimonious theory is the better one. In child neuropsychology, research results are accumulating at such a rapid rate that they may sometimes appear fragmented and incomprehensible without a unifying model of development to organize them. In contrast, findings regarding cognitive development are probably easier to assimilate (to use a Piagetian term) because we can interpret them within the framework of Piaget's comprehensive developmental model.

A theory not only serves to organize and interpret existing empirical relations but also provides, through the predictions and hypotheses that we derive from its assumptions, a guiding format and motivating force for systematic expansion of knowledge in a given area. Piaget's theory has generated myriad hypotheses and stimulated intensive research over many years. Although certain specific aspects of his theory have been revised in light of new research findings, the overall result is that we now have a much more comprehensive and more unified body of knowledge about cognitive development in children because of the theory.

A theory can also serve useful functions in the practical sphere. It can provide a conceptual basis for organizing and interpreting complicated clinical data that otherwise may appear incoherent and confusing. When interpreting psychological data on children with suspected learning disability, for example, I often find it helpful to use a neuropsychological construct of learning disability based on subtypes proposed by various researchers (e. g., Rourke, 1985). While this is neither a comprehensive model nor one that is as yet empirically valid in all details, it provides at least a preliminary interpretive scheme as long as I apply it cautiously and consider alternative explanations. Moreover, the model is helpful in translating clinical findings into provisional predictions concerning the learning disabled child's response to remedial programs--programs based on the child's pattern of neuropsychological strengths and weaknesses within the context of other relevant variables. The eventual utility of this theory for remediation would depend on whether its predictions regarding the response of children to such programs prove to be valid.

The Need to Relate Child Neuropsychology to Developmental Psychology

In their zeal to apply techniques to pressing clinical problems, practitioners of child neuropsychology may overlook critical information from developmental psychology. Two-day workshops on child neuropsychological techniques are becoming more prevalent and popular. Techniques are disseminated at a rapid rate to practitioners, who may not have any background in developmental psychology, or appreciation of developmental issues. To a great extent, practitioners want to jump on the child neuropsychology bandwagon and immediately apply an impressive array of tests, and corresponding neuropsychological explanations, to a multitude of diverse clinical and educational problems. Child neuropsychology will suffer as a science if the assessment techniques and explanations are applied simplistically and accepted without skepticism. Moreover, as one who is more closely identified with developmental than neuropsychology, I naturally think that child neuropsychology must consider, in its research and practice, existing theory, methodology, and knowledge from developmental psychology.

There is, of course, another side to the coin. Traditional developmental psychologists often fail to give much attention to neurological factors in cognitive development and might consider neurological views as irrelevant or even antithetical to their own. Rather than necessarily being in conflict, however, cognitive-developmental and neuropsychological approaches are attempting to describe and explain cognition at different levels. Both approaches rely on behavioral observations from which inferences are drawn about internal processes. The cognitive psychologist's inferences typically focus on the psychological or phenomenological level of cognition, whereas the neuropsychologist's extend to the neurological substrate. The two levels, of course, are interrelated and study of their interaction is certainly warranted. However, when conflict emerges between the two levels of explanation, I agree with Howard Gardner's (1983) contention that findings from the nervous system represent the more basic level and should serve as the final arbiter or "court of last resort." Furthermore, I subscribe to Gardner's view that the most valuable and least misleading information about cognition "is likely to come from a deep knowledge of the nervous system; how it is organized, how it develops, how it breaks down" (p. 30).

Although cognitive neuropsychology is still a long way from achieving this "deep knowledge" of the nervous system, it seems worthwhile to to try to relate, if only in a preliminary way, child neuropsychology to cognitive-developmental theory and research. A major reason for doing this is that the most complicating variable in the study of child neuropsychology is the developmental variable. The growing child has a rapidly changing nervous system that confounds the study of neuropsychological functions. The starting point, then, in the interpretation of neuropsychological performance in children would be a consideration of the child's developmental level and expectations for that level. As Fletcher and Taylor (1984) point out, developmental concepts allow us to consider the sequence in which skills are acquired as well as their rate of development.

A second reason for relating the two areas is that a major portion of child neuropsychological assessment involves evaluation of cognitive abilities. Although neuropsychologists try to determine brain-behavior relationships, they also draw inferences about intervening cognitive skills and try to relate these skills to the end variables of brain and behavior. In fact, some of the most substantial inferences made from neuropsychological testing come from tests of intellectual and cognitive functioning (Rattan & Dean, 1987).

A third reason for relating the areas is that we already have a well-established, widely accepted theory of cognitive development that has been responsible for greatly enhancing our knowledge of how thinking develops in children. Despite some of the weaknesses of Piaget's theory, there are no other cognitive theories that can be viewed yet as serious competitors; his theory is the only comprehensive, integrated model of intellectual development. For this reason, Piaget's theory, and the knowledge it has generated, certainly appears to have relevance to the study of neuropsychological development and could provide a framework for a better understanding of the interrelationships between cognitive and neuropsychological development. Furthermore, the application of Piaget's theory to neuropsychological development, both normal and abnormal, should also serve to test the generality of the theory and its validity at the neurological level.

The Assumptions of Piaget's Theory and their Relationship to Developmental Neuropsychology

Although Piaget's theory approaches cognition at a psychological level, the assumptions of the theory have clear biological underpinnings, which is not surprising in view of the fact that Piaget received his doctorate in biology. First is the assumption that children, from the moment of birth, actively use their brains to impose order on and make sense of the world (McGraw, 1987). A second related assumption is that children, in order to make sense of the world, must fit experience into the expanding cognitive structures that they develop to represent the world. These assumptions contrast with the traditional behavioristic assumption that children are the passive recipients of conditioning experiences that shape how they view and respond to the world. From the Piagetian view, the child's brain is an active processor and categorizer of experience. This ability to process and categorize at higher and higher levels, however, depends not only on the maturational readiness of the child's nervous system but also on the opportunity that the child has to interact with the world.

A third assumption of Piagetian theory, one quite consistent with developmental neuropsychology, is that intelligence functions like a biological system that can be compared to other systems such as the digestive system (Piaget, 1967/1971). In fact, terms like "assimilation" were borrowed directly from the digestive process. The overriding goal of these systems is to promote adaptation of individuals to their environment.

A fourth assumption is that cognition is accomplished through holistic mental structures which provide a general framework for more specific aspects of thought (McGraw, 1987). The holistic structure was termed a *structure d'ensemble* which is translated as "structure of the whole". Piaget used the structure d'ensemble as a unifying concept to tie together particular modes of thinking at a given developmental stage. For example, formal operational thought, which emerges in Piaget's last stage and represents the highest form of cognition, is viewed as a structure d' ensemble that governs the various aspects of thinking at this level. McGraw (1987) compares this concept to the global concept of personality, which, in a sense, is a holistic structure used by personality theorists to explain particular attitudes and behavioral tendencies of individuals. The concept of holistic structures is also somewhat analogous to Luria's (1973) concept of functional systems, although Luria related his systems to brain anatomy and function much more directly than did Piaget.

A fifth assumption of Piaget's theory is that children have an intrinsic biological proclivity to resolve cognitive disequilibrium with adaptation. This propensity to achieve equilibration provides the drive for children to become more and more advanced in their thinking ability.

A final assumption of Piagetian theory is that cognitive development proceeds through distinct, discrete stages, with each stage being defined by a particular cognitive structure (McGraw, 1987). The assumption of stage-wise cognitive development that is largely determined by maturational change is highly consistent with the developmental neuropsychological proposition that different systems emerge with maturation of different areas of the brain.

Piaget's Stages of Cognitive Development

Piaget (1936/1952; 1962) proposed four sequential stages of cognitive development beginning with the *sensorimotor period* from birth to approximately two years. During this stage, for which Piaget delineated six substages, the child understands the world only through concrete actions and without symbolic representations. The child starts with basic reflexive activity and proceeds through increasingly refined sensorimotor activity, which provides the substrate for the higher level thinking that develops later. This period is culminated in the child's development of symbolic representations of the world, which allow the child's thinking to transcend physical actions.

With the appearance of representations the child enters the *preoperational period*, which extends from about two to seven years of age. The child's thinking during this period is intuitive and based more on perception of superficial characteristics of phenomena than on understanding underlying concepts. In attempting to solve problems involving the concept of conservation, for example, the child cannot consider multiple dimensions (e. g., length and width) of a stimulus at the same time. Especially during the early stages of this period, the child's thinking is egocentric; that is, the child shows difficulty in seeing things (literally) from another's point of view. During this period, then, the child's thinking is still somewhat inflexible and bound by his or her own immediate perception.

In the *concrete operational period*, from about seven to eleven or twelve years of age, the child develops operational thinking that allows systematic, although concrete, manipulation of symbols, such as that required in reasoning and simple arithmetic operations. The child understands the concept of conservation--which Piaget considered a critical hallmark in cognitive development--and can consider simultaneously more than one dimension of a stimulus. The child can also classify objects on the basis of a common concept (e. g., color, form, function) and can reason about quantitative relations among classes of objects. Further, the child can arrange objects in a series along a quantitative dimension (e. g., number, size) and recognize that there is an underlying logic to the arrangement (e. g., if A is bigger than B, and B is bigger than C, then A is bigger than C.). However, despite the child's facility for logical thought, he or she still cannot reason in a purely abstract way.

At about eleven or twelve years, the child enters the *period of formal operations*, which represents the highest level of human thought. During this period the child develops the ability to engage in abstract reasoning, that is, to logically relate concepts that have no concrete representations. With such thinking the child can go beyond concrete reality ("what is") and contemplate what is possible ("what if") (McGraw, 1987). One of the highest forms of such reasoning is hypothetico-deductive thinking, which consists of deriving principles to explain phenomena in the world. Great scientific thinkers such as Darwin and Einstein exemplified to an exceptional degree this level of reasoning in the formulation of their theories.

Piaget proposed that all children follow a similar sequence in progressing through these stages. This "similar sequence" hypothesis, which appears to have implications for developmental neuropsychology, states that normal children, as well as retarded children, go through the same cognitive stages in precisely the same order; retarded children, however, are slower in rate of development and lower in eventual ceiling reached (Zigler, 1969; Weiss & Zigler, 1979). Disagreement has arisen over whether the hypothesis applies to all retarded individuals. Theorists advocating the developmental position (e. g., Zigler, 1969) proposed that the hypothesis applies to cultural-familial retardation but not to retardation caused by demonstrable organic variables. Those espousing the cognitive-developmental position (e. g., Piaget, 1956; Kohlberg, 1969) argued that the hypothesis holds for all retarded individuals regardless of etiology.

In a critical review of research on this issue, Weiss and Zigler (1979) concluded that the similar sequence hypothesis applies to all retarded individuals with the possible exception of those with clear EEG anomalies. This raises the question of whether the hypothesis holds for children who show atypical development due to selective brain damage or dysfunction of one type or another. Do children with severe learning disabilities, developmental language disorders, or pervasive developmental disorders follow the same sequence of cognitive development as normal children and most retarded children? Autistic children, for example, show an inconsistent pattern of intellectual strengths and weaknesses that cannot be readily accounted for with a purely unidimensional sequence of cognitive development. For this reason, some writers (Cowan, 1978; Morgan, 1984, 1986) have proposed that Piaget's similar sequence hypothesis may have to be modified to explain adequately the atypical cognitive development of children with such disorders. Morgan (1984; 1986) has suggested that autistic children have a brain dysfunction that results in an imbalance in the development of figurative (representational) versus operative (conceptual) functions, with the latter functions being impaired in most of these children. A related explanation has been applied to children with learning disabilities (Klees & Lebrune, 1972).

Evaluation and Current Status of Piaget's Theory

Although Piaget's theory has been subjected to extensive and stringent scientific scrutiny, it has survived in fairly intact form as a useful model of cognitive development. Piaget's views have not only provoked substantial research but have also precipitated a radical revision in our thinking about how intelligence develops in children. It is now acceptable for psychologists to view intellectual development as a process of biological adaptation that follows a predictable sequence according to age. Moreover, research has verified that most children follow this sequence and generally show at each stage the cognitive abilities proposed by Piaget.

While the theory has received general verification through extensive research, some specific aspects have been seriously challenged. One assumption that has failed to receive support is related to Piaget's concept of sensorimotor intelligence, which he contended was an absolute prerequisite for later cognitive development. The child, according to this assumption, must first progress through elementary sensorimotor activities characteristic of infancy in order to engage in the later operations of reflective thought. Some research findings have cast strong doubt on this assumption. Children, for example, who suffered from Thalidomide deformities that precluded normal sensorimotor interaction with the environment have nonetheless shown normal cognitive development in most cases (Kopp & Shaperman, 1973). Jordan (1972) reported the fascinating case of a girl whose brain developed normally but whose body remained as a neonate. Although she was incapable of purposeful sensorimotor acts, she showed normal cognitive development. Such findings render untenable the assumption that early sensorimotor activity is a *sine qua non* for later cognitive development. As McGraw (1987) has suggested, in order to account for this inconsistency, revisions of Piaget's theory will have to give more weight to sheer brain maturation as an explanation for cognitive development or to perceptual learning as an alternative to learning through sensorimotor action. These findings also relate to the developmental neuropsychological concept of brain plasticity, which is discussed later in this chapter.

Piaget's assumption of holistic structures underlying cognitive development has also failed to receive experimental support. If a single structure d'ensemble defined a child's thinking at a given stage of development, we would find consistency in the child's ability across various cognitive tasks at this stage. This is not the case. In fact, children show a great deal of inconsistency in dealing with cognitive tasks within a given stage. With conservation tasks, for example, the child does not solve all tasks equally well but rather can solve certain problems (e. g., conservation of amount) before others (e. g., conservation of weight) (Piaget, 1964/1968). These findings suggest that there is not a unitary structure underlying conservation but instead specific structures, at least in the beginning phases of this period. Furthermore, as noted earlier, children who show atypical development, as in autism and other pervasive developmental disorders, exhibit isolated compartments of ability that cannot be readily explained with the holistic structure concept. As Gardner (1983) has noted, Piaget himself concocted a "fudge factor", termed *decalage*, to account for what he viewed as exceptions to the rule. However, it now appears that the exceptions are the rule as far as holistic structures are concerned.

A final criticism of the theory is that the stages do not appear to be as well-defined and discrete as Piaget proposed. Rather than progressing in sharp, qualitative leaps from stage to stage, the child's cognitive development proceeds in a more continuous and gradual manner. In addition, there appears to be more variability in the ages at which normal children achieve stages than would be predicted by Piaget's theory. Although most children appear to go through the same sequence, some children reach certain stages either earlier or later than the ages specified by Piaget. Finally, as discussed previously, there is still the unresolved question of whether children with certain types of brain dysfunction follow the same sequence as normal children.

Luria's Model of Functional Systems and Its Relationship to Piaget's Theory

The most comprehensive theory that deals with relationships between cognitive functions and brain areas is that proposed by Luria (1973), who approached mental functions from a different perspective than Piaget. While Piaget's theory is based on the study of normal children with intact cognitive functions, Luria's theory is based primarily on the study of brain-damaged adults whose cognitive functions were impaired. Moreover, Luria's theory, unlike Piaget's, was not presented explicitly as a developmental theory, although developmental assumptions are implicit in his concepts.

Luria viewed higher mental processes as involving the integrated activity of "functional systems" with various neuroanatomical substrates. Instead of a single area of the brain being responsible for a given mental function or behavior, a restricted number of brain areas are involved, with each area participating in a specific manner within the functional system. A functional system may be viewed as a chain, with a particular area of the brain representing a necessary link (Golden, 1981). Further, a particular area of the brain is not restricted to a particular functional system but can contribute to many systems. Moreover, more than one functional system may be involved in a given mental activity or behavior. For example, learning to read involves the coordinated effort of several functional systems.

Three Basic Functional Units

Luria proposed that all functional systems involve three basic units of the brain: the arousal unit, sensory input unit, and output/planning unit. The *arousal unit* is present at birth and is based primarily in the reticular activating system (RAS). The RAS, which modulates arousal and filters sensory input, plays an essential role in wakefulness and attention as well as arousal from sleep (Chusid, 1982). Damage to the RAS is especially likely to occur during the prenatal period; such damage may be a cause of hyperkinesis and attention deficit disorders (Satterfield & Dawson, 1971; Douglas, 1983; Rutter, 1983) and also has been related to autism (Rimland, 1964; Ornitz, 1985).

The *sensory input unit* can be divided into primary, secondary, and tertiary levels which correspond to certain brain areas. The primary areas, which are highly localized in the brain, serve as reception centers for visual, auditory, and somesthetic (tactile/kinesthetic) senses. The occipital lobe is the primary area for vision; the temporal lobe for audition; and the parietal lobe for somesthetic senses. Each primary area has a corresponding secondary area, which organizes sensations at a higher perceptual level; it analyzes and synthesizes the information from the primary area and processes information sequentially. At the secondary level the hemispheres become more specialized, with the left hemisphere predominantly processing verbal information and the right hemisphere nonverbal information. The tertiary level, located in the parietal lobe and surrounding areas, is involved in cross-modality integration, that is, the combining and simultaneous analysis of auditory, visual, and tactile information. The hemispheres become even more specialized at the tertiary level, with the left hemisphere assuming primary responsibility for language and symbolic abilities (such as reading) and the right hemisphere assuming primary responsibility for nonverbal, visual-spatial skills (such as pattern recognition).

The *output/planning unit* also consists of three levels. The primary level involves the motor output area of the brain, which controls specific muscles needed for given motor activities, including speech. The secondary level is responsible for organizing and sequencing the temporal pattern of movement. The tertiary level, primarily seated in the prefrontal lobes, is the last to develop and does not fully mature until puberty. Among the psychological functions controlled at this level are planning and decision-making, evaluation of one's activity, impulse and emotional control, focusing of attention, and creativity. This level might be viewed as providing the control mechanisms for "mature" psychological activity and behavior because it mediates such functions as long-range adaptive planning as well as "meta-analysis" and evaluation of behavior. As the prefrontal lobes develop, they take over control of the arousal unit and eventually regulate attention and level of arousal.

Development of Functional Units: Relationship to Piaget's Theory

Luria's theory, like Piaget's, proposes a sequence of development of psychological functions. However, it specifies the neurological substrate upon which the functional units and their levels are based (Luria, 1973; Golden,

1981; Hooper & Boyd, 1986). It should be stressed that Luria's theory, as interpreted within a developmental context, has not been studied nearly so intensively and systematically as Piaget's theory. The five major stages in this neurodevelopmental sequence involve development of: (a) the arousal unit, (b) primary motor and sensory cortical areas, (c) secondary motor and cortical sensory areas, (d) tertiary areas of the sensory input unit, and (e) tertiary areas of the output/planning unit. Unlike Piaget's periods, which appear sequentially with age, these stages overlap substantially in their emergence.

Stage 1: Arousal Unit

This unit, which develops primarily during the the prenatal period, is functional at birth and fully operative by one year after conception. As noted earlier, it is anatomically based in the RAS and related structures and is essential for such functions as arousal, wakefulness, and attention, which are basic to higher cognitive activity. Massive damage to this system while it is being formed could result in death or severe mental retardation. Rutter (1983) has noted that injuries to the RAS occurring within the 12-month period after conception are more likely to cause attention deficit/hyperactive disorders than are later injuries.

Piaget's theory appears to be based on the implicit assumption that functions associated with this unit must be intact in order for normal cognitive development to take place. Indeed, this unit provides the substrate for all cognitive activity from sensorimotor to concrete operations because it plays a critical role in maintaining an optimal level of arousal for modulation of sensory input. Dysfunctional arousal and inadequate modulation of stimuli appear to be characteristic not only of children with hyperactive/attention deficit disorder but also of children with severe developmental disorders such as autism (Golden, 1981; Rimland, 1984; Ornitz, 1985). In the case of autism, some of the more plausible theories postulate a defect in functioning of the reticular formation--a defect that typically exerts it influence early in the child's life and undermines subsequent cognitive development in certain areas (Ornitz, 1985).

Stage 2: Primary Motor and Sensory Cortical Areas

Cognitive development during this stage, which proceeds concurrently with Stage 1, involves the four primary areas of the brain: visual, auditory, somesthetic, and motor. These areas, like those of the arousal unit, are operative at birth and fully functional within 12 months after conception. Most reflexes, which require sensory as well as motor areas, develop well before the child is born and are present in the neurologically intact child at birth. The effects of damage to the primary areas would depend on the child's age and the extent of the injury. With damage that occurs before birth or shortly thereafter, total destruction of a primary area in one hemisphere can be compensated for by the corresponding area in the opposite hemisphere. Later injuries in childhood usually exert more serious effects, but the intact areas of the brain may still show considerable compensation (Golden, 1981).

This stage of neuropsychological development bears an obvious relationship to Piaget's early sensorimotor period, during which the child's activity is dominated by the primary sensory and motor areas of the brain. Piaget (1936/1952) himself stated that sensorimotor intelligence presupposes a "system of reflexes whose connection with the organism's anatomical and morphological structure is apparent" (p. 1). During the first substage of this period, the infant practices reflexes; the ability to perform these reflexes serves as a reflection of the basic intactness of the nervous system. Throughout the the first two years there is a gradual refinement of this sensorimotor intelligence, which requires an increasing degree of coordination between sensory and motor areas of the brain at first the primary and then the secondary cortical levels.

As noted previously, some research findings have cast doubt on Piaget's assumption that early sensorimotor activities are essential to later intellectual development. These findings appear to be consistent with neuropsychological research results that show the young human brain to have remarkable compensatory powers in certain ability areas (e. g., Byrne & Gates, 1987). Nevertheless, early disruption or impairment of sensorimotor functioning may be related in some cases to later learning problems. Rourke (1982) has proposed that a neuropsychological subtype of learning disability, characterized by problems in dealing with nonverbal concepts such as mathematics, may have its roots in the sensorimotor period when cause-and-effect relationships are being learned through basic sensorimotor activities.

Stage 3: Secondary Motor and Sensory Cortical Areas

This stage begins concurrently with the first two stages, but continues through the child's fifth year (Golden, 1981). During this stage the secondary cortical areas corresponding to each of the primary areas mature and become functional. The more primitive sensorimotor behaviors are superceded by higher level perceptions and more complex coordination of sensory input and motor output. The child, at about two years of age, begins to develop consistent verbal skills; this marks the early phase of progressive lateralization of hemispheric function (Golden, 1981). During the first five years, the secondary cortical areas are the primary sites for learning, which occurs mainly within single sensory modalities rather than between modalities. Crossmodality learning does not emerge until the next stage.

As to the relationship between Stage 3 and Piaget's theory, it is during the early part of this stage (at about two years) that the child passes from the sensorimotor period to the preoperational period; this transition is defined by the child's development of representation, which allows thinking independent of sensorimotor activity. The emergence of spoken language early in Stage 3 greatly facilitates the ability to represent and cognitively process experience at the preoperational level. Further, the development of the higher level perceptual skills in the secondary cortical areas appears to coincide with the perceptually-based, intuitive thinking of the young preoperational child.

Stage 4: Tertiary Cortical Areas of Sensory Input Unit

According to Golden (1981), this unit, located primarily in the parietal lobes, is not psychologically active until the child is five to eight years of age, which coincides with the beginning school years. The area is responsible for the cross-modality processing that is so critical to the mastery of educational skills such as reading, spelling, and arithmetic. Major injuries to this area may cause mental retardation, whereas smaller injuries may result in specific learning disabilities involving problems with cross-modality integration (Golden, 1981).

This stage overlaps developmentally with Piaget's period of concrete operations (seven to eleven years of age). Cross-modality integration associated with this tertiary sensory unit appears to be related to certain concrete operations, such as those involved in reading and simple arithmetic, which entail the combining of stimuli across modalities. The relationship between development of this unit and emergence of the concrete operational skills of classification, seriation, and conservation represents an interesting research question.

Stage 5: Tertiary Areas of Output/Planning Unit

During this final stage the tertiary level of the the output/planning unit, located in the prefrontal areas, develops. Luria (1973) thought that this region served as the main integrative and regulatory unit of the brain; he felt that it did not become operative until the child is four to seven years of age and then it continues to develop through early adulthood. Golden (1981) proposed that this area did not make a functional difference until adolescence. Based on some recent evidence (Passler, Isaac, & Boyd, 1985), however, Hooper and Boyd (1986) suggest that development of frontal lobe functions occurs in several stages; the greatest period of development extends from six to eight years of age, with development being largely complete by twelve years of age.

Prefrontal injuries may result in impairment of attention, abstraction, planning, self-evaluation of performance, and mental and behavioral flexibility (Stuss & Benson, 1984). The effects of such injuries may not be apparent until the child reaches the age when skills associated with this area are expected to emerge; that is, the child "grows into the injury" (Golden, 1981).

The abstract reasoning and meta-analytic abilities that emerge in Stage 5 with development of the frontal lobes correspond closely to Piaget's formal operational thinking, which begins to appear at eleven or twelve years of age. Kohlberg's (1963) theory of moral development, which is derived from Piagetian concepts, proposes that an individual cannot achieve the highest level of ethical thinking--that is, principled moral reasoning--without having achieved formal operations. Some evidence supporting the relationship between the frontal lobes and formal operations has come from studies indicating an impaired ability for abstract thought as well as impaired moral judgement and self-monitoring as sequelae of frontal lobe damage (Freedman, Kaplan, & Sadock, 1975; Stuss & Benson, 1984).

Implications for Research

This preliminary discussion of relations between cognitive-developmental and neuropsychological concepts raises many more questions than it answers. One fundamental question concerns the relationship between general physical development of the brain and cognitive development. In order to answer this question, studies will have to employ the cross-sectional and longitudinal designs traditionally used in developmental psychology. A recent study by Thatcher, Walker, and Giudie (1987) illustrates the use of the cross-sectional design to obtain information that relates certain physical indices of brain development to stages of cognitive development as outlined by Piaget. These researchers used EEG measures of brain growth in 577 subjects ranging in age from two months to early adulthood. Their results revealed a continuous growth curve that followed an exponential function with discrete growth spurts in specific anatomical locations at specific postnatal periods. Moreover, the timing of these spurts was generally consistent with Piagetian periods of cognitive growth, a finding that represents a preliminary confirmation of Piaget's stage theory at the physical level of brain development.

A number of other research questions arise as we consider neurological development and its cognitive concomitants. One set of questions pertains to the relationships between particular brain areas and cognitive functions in developing children. What systems and components of the brain underlie the different cognitive operations proposed by Piaget? For example, what areas or functional units of the brain subserve the ability to do conservation tasks? Do the frontal lobes have to be at a certain level of developmental maturity before the child can engage in formal operational thought? A related set of questions, of particular interest to clinical child neuropsychology, concerns the issue of how brain damage or dysfunction disrupts the development of functional units and sequence of cognitive development that we expect in children with intact, normally functioning brains. As noted earlier, an unresolved issue is whether children with severely dysfunctional brains show the same sequence of cognitive development as other children.

Another set of questions concerns the measures we use in assessing cognitive functions vis-a-vis neuropsychological functions. What are the relationships between performance on Piagetian tasks and performance on neuropsychological tests? How much can neuropsychological tests, including psychometric tests of intelligence, tell us about Piagetian level of cognitive development, and vice-versa? How sensitive are Piagetian tasks in detecting brain damage and dysfunction in children?

These questions, which represent only a sample of the research issues that emerge when we attempt to relate child neuropsychology and cognitive developmental theory, underscore the need to integrate the two areas of study. They also point to the challenges that lie ahead in developing a systematic body of knowledge in the young and promising field of child neuropsychology.

References

Byrne, J. M., & Gates, R. D. (1987). Single-case study of left cerebral hemispherectomy: Development in the first five years of life. *Journal of Clinical and Experimental Neuropsychology, 9,* 423-434.

Chusid, J. G. (1982). *Correlative neuroanatomy and functional neurology.* Los Angeles: Lange Medical Publications.

Cowan, P. A. (1978). *Piaget: With feeling*. New York: Holt, Rinehart, & Winston.

Douglas, V. (1983). Attentional and cognitive problems. In M. Rutter (Ed.) *Developmental neuropsychiatry*. New York: Guilford Press.

Fletcher, J. M., & Taylor, H. G. (1984). Neuropsychological approaches to children: Towards a developmental neuropsychology. *Journal of Clinical Neuropsychology, 6,* 39-56.

Freedman, A. M., Kaplan, H. I., & Sadock, B. J. (Eds.)(1975). *Comprehensive textbook of psychiatry* (Vol. 1). Baltimore: Williams & Wilkins.

Gardner, H. (1983). *Frames of mind: The theory of multiple intelligences*. New York: Basic Books.

Golden, C. J. (1981). The Luria-Nebraska Children's Battery: Theory and formulation. In G. W. Hynd & J. E. Obrzut (Eds.), *Neuropsychological assessment and the school-age child: Issues and procedures* (pp. 227-302). New York: Grune & Stratton.

Hall, C. S., & Lindzey, G. (1957). *Theories of personality*. New York: John Wiley & Sons.

Hartlage, L. C., & Telzrow, C. F. (1986). *Neuropsychological assessment and intervention with children and adolescents*. Sarasota, FL: Professional Resources Exchange.

Hooper, S. R., & Boyd, T. A. (1986). Neurodevelopmental disorders. In J. E. Obrzut & G. W. Hynd (Eds.), *Child neuropsychology, volume 2: Clinical practice* (pp. 15-58). Orlando: Academic Press.

Jordan, N. (1972). Is there an Achilles' heel in Piaget's theorizing? *Human Development, 15,* 379-382.

Klees, M. & Lebrun, A. (1972). Analysis of figurative and operative processes of thought of 40 dyslexic children. *Journal of Learning Disabilities, 5,* 389-396.

Kohlberg, L. (1963). The development of children's orientations toward a moral order: I. Sequence in the development of moral thought. *Vita Humana, 6,* 11-33.

Kohlberg, L. (1969). Stage and sequence: The cognitive-developmental approach to socialization. In D. Goslin (Ed.), *Handbook of socialization theory and research* (pp. 347-480). Chicago: Rand McNally.

Kopp, C. B., & Shaperman, J. (1973). Cognitive development in the absence of object manipulation during infancy. *Developmental Psychology, 9,* 430.

Luria, A. R. (1973). *The working brain: An introduction to neuropsychology*. (B. Haigh, Trans.). New York: Basic Books, Inc.

McGraw, K. O. (1987). *Developmental psychology*. New York: Harcourt Brace Jovanovich.

Morgan, S. B. (1984). Early childhood autism: Cognitive-developmental perspectives. In B. Gholson & T. L. Rosenthal (Eds.), *Applications of cognitive-developmental theory* (pp. 215-241.). Orlando: Academic Press.

Morgan, S. B. (1986). Autism and Piaget's theory: Are the two compatible? *Journal of Autism and Developmental Disorders, 16,* 441-457.

Obrzut, J. E., & Hynd, G. W. (1986). Child neuropsychology: An introduction to theory and research. In J. E. Obrzut & G. W. Hynd (Eds.) *Child neuropsychology, volume 1: Theory and research* (pp. 1-12). Orlando: Academic Press.

Ornitz, E. M. (1985). Neurophysiology of infantile autism. *Journal of the American Academy of Child Psychiatry, 24,* 251-262.

Passler, M. A., Isaac, W., & Hynd, G. W. (1985). Neuropsychological development of behavior attributed to frontal lobe functioning in children. *Developmental Neuropsychology, 1*, 17-37.

Piaget, J. (1952). *The origins of intelligence in children.* (M. Cook, Trans.), New York: International Universities Press. (Original work published 1936).

Piaget, J. (1956). The general problem of psychobiological development of the child. *Discussions of Child Development, 4*, 3-27.

Piaget, J. (1962). The stages of intellectual development of the child, *Bulletin of the Menninger Clinic, 26*, 120-145.

Piaget, J. (1968). *Six psychological studies.* New York: Vintage Books. (Original work published 1964).

Piaget, J. (1971). *Biology and knowledge.* (B. Walsh, Trans.). Chicago: University of Chicago Press. (Original work published 1967).

Rattan, G., & Dean, R. S. (1987). The neuropsychology of children's learning disorders. In J. M. Williams & C. J. Long (Eds.), *The rehabilitation of cognitive disabilities* (pp. 173-196). New York: Plenum Press.

Rimland, B. (1964). *Infantile autism.* New York: Appleton-Century-Crofts.

Rourke, B. (1982). Central processing deficiencies in children: Toward a developmental neuropsychological model. *Journal of Clinical Neuropsychology, 4*, 1-18.

Rourke, B. (Ed.). (1985). *Neuropsychology of learning disabilities: Essentials of subtype analysis.* New York: Guilford Press.

Rourke, B. P., Bakker, D. J., Fisk, J. L., & Strang, J. D. (1983). *Child neuropsychology.* New York: Guilford Press.

Rourke, B. P., Fisk, J. L., & Strang, J. D. (1986). *Neuropsychological assessment of children: A treatment-oriented approach.* New York: Guilford Press.

Rutter, M. (1983). Behavior studies: Questions and findings on the concept of a distinctive syndrome. In M. Rutter (Ed.), *Developmental neuropsychiatry.* New York: Guilford Press.

Satterfield, J. & Dawson, M. (1971). Electrodermal concepts of hyperactivity in children. *Psychophysiology, 8*, 191-197.

Stuss, D. T., & Benson, D. F. (1984). Neurophysiological studies of the frontal lobes. *Psychological Bulletin, 95*, 3-28.

Thatcher, R. W., Walker, R. A., & Giudice, S. (1987). Human cerebral hemispheres develop at different rates and ages. *Science, 236*, 1110-1113.

Weiss, J. R., & Zigler, E. (1979). Cognitive development in retarded and nonretarded persons: Piagetian tests of the similar sequence hypothesis. *Psychological Bulletin, 86*, 831-851.

Zigler, E. (1969). Developmental versus difference theories of mental retardation and the problem of motivation. *American Journal of Mental Deficiency, 73*, 536-556.

12

Neuropsychological Aspects of Simultaneous and Successive Cognitive Processes

Seija Äystö

Information processing models have been a widely used approach in cognitive psychology for the last three decades (e.g., Miller, Galanter & Pribram, 1960; Neisser, 1967; Lindsey & Norman, 1972; Newell & Simon, 1972). In recent years, intelligence, memory and associated abilities have been approached from the perspective of information processing (e.g., Das, Kirby & Jarman, 1975, 1979; Hunt, 1980; Kail & Pellegrino, 1985; Klatzky, 1984; Sternberg, 1985). The static and fixed nature of abilities is challenged by a more flexible and dynamic approach which attempts to study shared qualities in human intellectual functioning and to measure individual cognitive differences.

In the present article, the issue of information processing is viewed from the aspects of cognitive and clinical neuropsychology. The modes of information processing are seen as if as a set of latent variables or underlying properties defining the basic operations of cognitions. These main principles are simultaneous and successive synthesis - proposed by Luria (1966a, b) and Das et al. (1975, 1979) - which organize and further encode information from the environment or from the mental systems. The focus in the definition and identification of the modes of processing is based on a careful analysis of the stimulus material and its supposed interaction with the central nervous system.

The information processing perspective taken here considers the brain as a flexible and dynamic processor of information in interaction with the stimulus environment. The dynamic nature of information processing suits well the idea of dynamic localization in neuropsychology (Luria, 1973) where the mental and functional systems are seen as dynamic and changing due to environmental influences. In explicit theories of intelligence the ability factors are described as verbal comprehension, fluency, spatial visualization, numerical, reasoning, perceptual speed, etc. and these are claimed to comprise a fixed and static structure of different hierarchical organizations, levels or other dimensions (e.g., Cattell, 1963; Guilford, 1967; Horn & Cattell, 1967; Jensen, 1973; Spearman, 1927; Thurstone, 1938). The study of individual differences in cognition is especially emphasized in educational psychology

Äystö, S. (1988). Neuropsychological aspects of simultaneous and successive cognitive processes. In J. M. Williams & C. J. Long (Eds.), *Cognitive approaches to neuropsychology*, New York: Plenum.

where the content- or structure- and process-oriented approaches would suggest different applications to the learning process.

Therefore, the integration of neuropsychology and information processing theory is considered to provide invaluable insights into the nature of cognition. One such model which combines the clinical neuropsychological findings of Luria (1966a, 1966b, 1973) with information processing has been presented in educational psychology by Das, Kirby and Jarman (1975, 1979).

Modes of Processing

In cognitive psychology and in theories of information processing dichotomized modes of thought have fundamentally been presented by labelling them differently (Blumenthal, 1977). The content of pairs of concepts like parallel-serial (Neisser, 1967; Cohen, 1973), appositional-propositional (Bogen, 1977), simultaneous-successive (Luria, 1966a, 1966b, 1973; Das et al., 1975, 1979), holistic-synthetic and analytic (Levy-Agresti & Sperry, 1968; Nebes, 1974; Bever, 1975; Bradshaw & Nettleton, 1981), primary process versus secondary process (Martindale, 1981), perceptual-associative (DeRenzi et al., 1969), and controlled versus automatic processing (Shiffrin & Schneider, 1977) all refer to the polar types of cognition but obviously do not include the same core matter of information processing. The existence of the two hemispheres in the brain has provided a useful basis for testing hypotheses about different dichotomies of thought and cognition, although the research on hemispheric specialization has been limited (Davidoff, 1982). Based mainly on empirical evidence from experimental psychology, it has been asserted that serial processing is typical of the left hemisphere, which deals with temporal ordering, sequencing, and rhythm. In contrast, the right hemisphere processes information in parallel, with spatial ordering (Cohen, 1973; Nebes, 1974; Bradshaw & Nettleton, 1981; Martindale, 1981; Davidoff, 1982; Hammond, 1982). Also, it has been cautiously stated by Madden and Nebes (1980) that it is difficult to draw any firm conclusions about the relationship of serial processing to the cerebral hemispheres until more is known about hemispheric interaction as a function of stimulus material, practice effects and short- and long-term memory.

Defining the above mentioned concept pairs is a fundamental in constructing a paradigm of information processing and the mere labelling of the processes as belonging to either category of the modes of processing is unjustified without carefully specifying the task demands. Without considering here all the above mentioned concept pairs, only those having most similarity with the simultaneous and successive processing (parallel and serial) are dealt with.

Bradshaw and Nettleton (1981) consider serial and parallel processing as special cases of analytic and holistic dichotomy. The primacy of this distinction is questioned by Cohen (1981) and it seems to be the case that the exact content of the concept pairs described above is poorly understood (i.e., Nottebohm, 1979, for commentaries see Bradshaw & Nettleton, 1981).

The distinction between serial and parallel processing is theoretically quite clear according to Palmer and Kimchi (1984) but empirically in experimental settings both modes of processing can make predictions which are indistinguishable from each other. Theoretically, a lot of controversy about the nature of serial and parallel processing has appeared. Anderson (1976) thinks the issue to be empirically unresolvable.

Townsend (1972) has given a theoretical description of serial and parallel systems by relating the stimulus to the "black box" assumptions so that in a serial processor only one element is focused upon any given time and the output appears in the same order as the processing. In parallel systems, the elements to be processed are operate simultaneously so that the processing begins and proceeds simultaneously although it may terminate at a different time. Interaction or correlation between the elements is possible in the parallel processor contrary to the operating of the serial processor where interaction is not assumed. Townsend (1972) is not interested in defining the serial or parallel nature of certain psychological processes but is interested in the systems of serial and parallel processes. The need for constructing hybrid models for serial and parallel processing systems is expressed by Townsend (1972), Luria and Simernitskaja (1977), Gazzaniga and LeDoux (1978), Ben-Dov and Carmon (1976) and Moscovitch (1979) although not specified. The general trend in published literature on information processing up to recent times has been to look at the extreme ends of the processing dichotomy without emphasizing the possible interactive nature of the modes of processing.

Concepts of serial and parallel processing are closely related to attention and to the notions of controlled vs. automatic processing. There is evidence in the psychophysiological literature (e.g., Näätänen, 1982, 1985, 1986) that at the level of sensory processing serial and parallel processing are differentially related to attention. If selective attention is not required in task-unrelated processing, the processing occurs in parallel, preconsciously and automatically. If the processing is related to the task at hand and thus requires task-related attention, it becomes selective, serial, controlled and conscious. With practice, task-related processing may become automatic, but then it is acquired through controlled processing and is different from the basic-level automatic processing. Thus, there is differentiation between automatic processing which is conscious (acquired through practice) and unconscious (the basic-level processing).

Operationalization of Modes of Processing

In experimental literature, the serial and parallel processes have been identified on the basis of reaction time measures. In a visual search task the time required for decision making (same/different) in response production is considered unchanged in parallel processing regardless of the number of items in the set whereas in serial processing the reaction time increases as a function of the number of items in the set. A different way of defining and operationalizing the two modes of processing, i.e. simultaneous (parallel) and successive (serial) processing is presented by Das et al. (1975, 1979).

As was mentioned earlier, simultaneous and successive processing are the principles by which the central nervous system organizes and integrates input into the system. The outcome of these two modes of processing is cognition (Das et al., 1979), or, they are seen as processing abilities which determine the success of performance in certain tasks (Biggs & Kirby, 1984). Simultaneous processing means the integration of information into quasi-spatial groups where the elements of information are relatable each other and surveyable at any one time. Successive processing refers to the integration of information into temporal sequences. The elements in the temporal series are not surveyable at any one time but only at the end of the sequence. The elements also are separate from each other. Both forms of information integration - simultaneous and successive - can according to Das et al. (1979) appear in verbal and nonverbal tasks.

The modes of processing in Das et al. are operationalized by the help of a number of psychometric marker tests (i.e., Raven's (1947) Coloured Progressive Matrices, Graham and Kendall's (1960) Memory-for-Designs, Figure Copying Test (Ilg & Ames, 1964), Digit Span, Visual Short-Term Memory, Serial and Free Recall) using factor-analysis. The differences in definitions of successive (serial) and simultaneous (parallel) modes of processing in the model of Das et al. compared to the reaction-time definitions operationalized in experimental literature lie in the different emphases of theoretically based stimulus analysis and its empirical verification. The main dimensions obtained in factor-analysis are thought to describe the underlying common properties of cognition which are the simultaneous or successive syntheses made on task material.

The Das, Kirby and Jarman Model of Information Integration

A very comprehensive theory which integrates the theoretical concepts associated with information processing and neuropsychology has been presented by Das, Kirby and Jarman (1975, 1979). The model is sympathetic to the systemic approach to human cognitions as an interrelated set of capacities. Innate capacities and learning experiences are included in the model. As an information processing model it covers many more human behavioral aspects than the general information processing models (e.g., Lachman, Lachman & Butterfield, 1978) which often are more oriented toward processing from the perspective of a computer. Because the neuropsychological aspects of this model are the main theme of the present article, the model and supporting research deserves a detailed presentation.

The Das, Kirby and Jarman (1975, 1979) model of information integration is based on Luria's (1966a, 1966b, 1973) theory of clinical neuropsychological functioning where the three basic functional units (arousal, coding and storing of information, and planning) interact with three anatomically different divisions of the brain. The associated processes can take the form of simultaneous or successive synthesis. Planning utilizes the coded information for purposeful and organized action (Das, 1980; Das & Jarman, 1981) and becomes identifiable from the coding factors when competence in these has been increased (Molloy & Das, 1980a).

Das et al. distinguish four basic components in information processing, namely the input, sensory registration, central, and output units. The input may arrive at the senses according to Das et al. (1979) in simultaneous or successive order and both modes of processing operate on verbal as well on nonverbal information although here Luria (1966a, 1966b) makes a modality distinction in the processing modes by emphasizing the role of motor and acoustic stimuli in successive synthesis and visual and tactile stimuli in simultaneous synthesis. The same task (test) may be approached either simultaneously or successively (and within each mode of encoding, there may be variations in solution strategies). The approach would be determined by the interaction of the subject's degree of (1) competence in the dominant mode of encoding; (2) habitual mode of encoding when competent in both modes; and (3) task demands that can be modified by instructions. From sense receptors the input proceeds, if attended to, through the sensory register to the central processing unit.

In the central unit the simultaneous and successive cognitive processes as well as planning may take place in three varieties of cognition, namely perceptual, conceptual and mnestic. In the central unit the planning and executive programming function uses simultaneously or successively coded information. In the output unit, the response may be organized either simultaneously or successively.

According to Das et al. simultaneous and successive processes are not hierarchical. Neither one is dependent upon the other. Simultaneous and successive processes are seen as operating upon cognitive structures which can be hierarchical and thus the two modes of coding can be involved to different degrees in the levels of abstraction within the hierarchy of cognitive structures. This point distinguishes this model of information processing from those emphasizing the level of processing, e.g. Jensen (1970, 1973) who considers level I (rote learning) to be hierarchically dependent on level II (reasoning and abstraction). However, on the basis of research evidence (e.g., Das et al., 1979; Kaufman et al., 1982; Biggs & Kirby, 1984) it seems likely that simultaneous and successive processing are not equal to level I and level II abilities.

The Das et al. model also deals more with the neuropsychological realities by assuming that the coding of information in the central nervous system is done differently and in different loci depending on task demands. Simultaneous processing is linked with the functioning of the posterior (parieto-occipital) regions and successive processing with the functioning of the anterior (frontal or fronto-temporal) regions of the brain (Luria, 1966a, p. 125). Planning is mainly the function of the third unit (the frontal lobe) of Luria's theory and uses information obtained through simultaneous and successive processes. However, the neuropsychological nature of simultaneous and successive processing remains further unspecified. The unit of information processing is considered more from the functional neuropsychological than from the neurophysiological level. Thus, the gross division of the brain according to its anterior and posterior parts is taken to represent the anatomical basis of information processing. This is in opposition to those supporters of the theory of hemispheric asymmetry.

The basic foundations of the model are discussed in more detail in Das et al. (1975, 1979; Das, 1984a). A slightly modified version of this model is presented in Figure 1 by emphasizing the relationship between the stimulus input and its encoding in the central nervous system in the way specified in the section on classification of the tests. The response modality is not particularly specified in the model although it is indicated that planning plays an important role in output performance due to the result of simultaneous and successive processes. The elements of information to be processed can be ordered in presentation either simultaneously or successively, and the synthesis formed at the level of the central processor can also be of both types depending on the location of synthesis formation. The notions of hemispheric asymmetry have been included in the model by acknowledging that the verbal and nonverbal stimulus material have different functional localizations. In Das et al. (1979) there appears a lack of attention to the content being processed and the issue of content is regarded as irrelevant.

The concept of 'schema' or cognitive structure which is central in other theories of information processing (e.g., Anderson, 1977) does not appear in the Das et al. model. The conventional theories of human information processing (e.g., Broadbent, 1958, 1963; Atkinson & Shiffrin, 1968) also emphasize the role of short- and long-term memory which is not dealt separately in the Das et al. model. Memory is treated as one of the other cognitive functions and working in co-operation with these. Kirby (1980) has elaborated the coding unit (the second unit in Luria' theory) by separating the short- and long-term memory which both are controlled by the planning unit (the third unit in Luria's theory) through the intermediate-term (contextual) memory.

The Das et al. model is a flow chart model of information which emphasizes the role of the modes of processing (simultaneous and successive synthesis) and these concepts have been adopted from the philosophical writings of Sechenov and Kant (cf. Das et al, 1979), not from communications-channel or engineering terminology. The identification of simultaneous and successive modes of processing lies not in distinguishing between processes that are simultaneous or successive, but between processing that treats information as a simultaneous event and processing that treats information as a series of events. Thus, basically every task is analyzable in terms of successive and simultaneous properties included in the process starting with information from the external environment (i. e., the initial encounter with the stimulus) and its flow through the senses into the central nervous system where either kind of synthesis is made on the task material. This interactional definition of simultaneous and successive cognitive processes with the external environment represents a slight extension to the definitions given by Das et al. (1979) and Luria (1966a, b). The emphasis in the present article is on the inferred relationship between the stimulus input and its encoding at the central nervous system and not so much on specifying the response modality.

The Das et al. model takes account of individual differences and has remedial suggestions built-in to it — unlike in most conventional models of information processing. Both approaches to information processing are interested in studying the underlying mechanisms behind cognitive functioning and what happens between input and output, but using different techniques. According to Zaidel (1978) the evaluation of brain function (and hemispheric differences) with the use of factor analytical theories of human intelligence might be a more fruitful approach than just labelling different styles of brain functioning. One of the objectives of the present article is to apply this approach to analyzing the relationship between the modes of processing and brain functioning.

Supporting Empirical Evidence

Empirical research on simultaneous and successive processing has focused on the validation of processing factors in different ability (e.g., Das, 1972; Kirby & Das, 1977, 1978; Jarman & Das, 1977; Ryckman, 1981), age (e.g., Das & Molloy, 1975; Das et al., 1979; Merritt & McCallum, 1984; Cowart & McCallum, 1984; Molloy & Das, 1980a; Vernon, Ryba & Lang, 1978; Naglieri et al., 1981), socioeconomic (e.g., Das, Cummins, Kirby & Jarman, 1979; Molloy & Das, 1979), cultural (Das et al., 1975, 1979; Klich & Davidson, 1984), and diagnostic (e.g., Das & Cummins, 1978) groups as well as on studying the relationship between cognitive processes (e.g., Das, Cummins, Kirby & Jarman, 1979; Cummins & Das, 1978; Kirby & Das, 1978; Mwamwenda et al., 1984; Dash & Das, 1984), learning difficulties (e.g., Das et al., 1982; Hooper & Hynd, 1985), school achievement (e.g., Das et al., 1979; Das, 1973; Hunt & Randhawa, 1983), hyperactivity (Das, Leong & Williams, 1978; Molloy & Das, 1980b), and intervention (Krywaniuk cited from Das et al., 1975; Kaufman & Kaufman, 1979; Lesak et al., 1982; Brailsford et al., 1983) etc. Also, developmental changes in simultaneous and successive modes of processing have been studied across the preschool and elementary school age range (2 1/2 - 12 1/2 years old children) by using the K-ABC test battery (Kaufman et al., 1982; Kaufman & Kaufman, 1983). No sex-related mode of processing differences have been found in studies on children (Randhawa & Hunt, 1979) or on adults (Merritt & McCallum, 1983).

The samples studied have varied among child populations with only a relatively few on adult populations and only one on an elderly sample (Cowart

& McCallum, 1984). It is also important to notice from the point of view of cross-validation that basically the same results have been obtained by using different sets of tasks. No general factor has been found empirically in the studies of Das et al. (e.g., 1975, 1979), and the best g-factor measure has been a mixture of simultaneous and successive tests (Kaufman et al., 1982). The independence of the factors of simultaneous and successive processing has been demonstrated most often among non-retarded, retarded, and learning-disabled children. Factors of simultaneous and successive processing have emerged orthogonally to the factor of planning in studies on gifted, mentally retarded and normal 14-year-olds (Das, 1980; Ashman & Das, 1980; Ashman et al., 1981; Karnes & McCallum, 1983). Speed of processing is generally emphasized in cognitive theories, but in the Das et al. model it is not considered theoretically, although empirically speed has also appeared as a third factor in addition to simultaneous and successive processing. Das (1984b) mentions that the factor of speed has appeared as separate from the factor of planning, too, which has been reported to include different clusters (e.g., search, rehearsal, clustering, and metacognition) and to be teachable (Kirby, 1984b).

Neuropsychological Aspects of Simultaneous and Successive Cognitive Processes

The need for a more detailed picture of the complex relationship between different cognitions and simultaneous-successive processing is recognized by Das et al. (1979). The applicability and usefulness of the model in the treatment of learning disabilities has been acknowledged as one of the possible approaches particularly in cases of neurological etiologies (e.g., Hartlage & Telzrow, 1983). Although the model of information integration is based on Luria's clinical neuropsychological findings no research on the neuropsychological correlates of the model has appeared. The extension of research from child samples to adult and elderly samples would demonstrate the appropriateness of the model as a general human information processing model.

Theoretically, a description of the modes of processing is not enough if one cannot at the same time specify the conditions under which a change in the modes of processing brings about change in behavior. Therefore, if the foundations of information processing are neuropsychological, it should be possible to point to different neurobehavioral outcomes as a result of variously applying the modes of processing. The reverse situation also holds true; the neuropsychological factors should be able to predict differentially the status of the modes of processing. The value of the information processing perspective in describing and interpreting neuropsychological dysfunctioning might offer new scope for neuropsychological rehabilitation if applied more frequently than has been done in the area of clinical neuropsychology. The problems in the present writer's study (1987) were defined in the following way.

1) Whether it is possible to integrate information processing perspective into standardized measures of intelligence and, thus, validate simultaneous and successive modes of processing by using novel tasks.

2) Whether it is possible to extend the model of information integration (Das et al., 1979) on the part of coding (simultaneous-successive processing) to include adult samples and the extent to which the model of information integration of Das, Kirby and Jarman (1975, 1979) can be cross-validated in different adult samples such as neurological patient groups and elderly people. Included here is the problem of how background variables like sex, education, occupation, socioeconomic level, and age relate to the modes of processing, whether simultaneous and successive processing cluster meaningfully around the neurobehavioral measures and identifying and accounting for those neurological variables which are associated with the modes of processing.

3) Whether it is possible to validate the model of Das et al. according to the neuropsychological characteristics (the theory of three functional units claimed by Luria) and whether there is any hemispheric superiority for preferring a certain kind of mode of processing over the other. This involves identifying the neuropsychological variables which have the closest relationship with the modes of processing and which of them predict the level of simultaneous and successive processing. If there were a close relation between brain and cognitive functions at the behavioral and psychological levels this would suggest the importance of studying the role of neuropsychological variables in the relationship between brain and cognition.

The present research (Äystö, 1987) was an attempt to combine some key aspects of Lurian neuropsychology (simultaneous and successive processing and three functional units of the brain) with the measurement of intelligence when interpreting these measurements in terms of information processing. Three consecutive studies on neurological patients, brain- injured adults and normal elderly persons were conducted in order to study the cross-validation, construct, and concurrent predictive validation of the model of information integration presented by Das et al. (1975, 1979) and as was specified neuropsychologically in Figure 1.

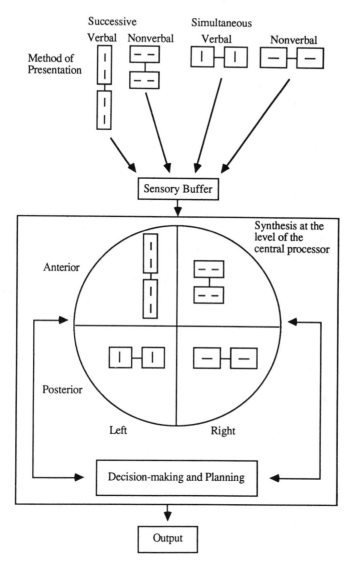

Figure 1. The nature of simultaneous and successive processing modified according to the Das model and hemispheric asymmetry (Äystö, 1987).

Factor Structure of the Simultaneous and Successive Tasks

Classification of the Tests

For the purposes of the present research certain conventional and traditional intelligence and memory tasks (subscales of the Wechsler Adult Intelligence Scale, 1955, the Wechsler Memory Scale, 1945, and the Benton Visual Retention Test, 1963) were redefined as specified below. Goetz and Hall (1984) mention that there have been no attempts to integrate an information processing perspective into standardized measures of intelligence. Quite recently, Naglieri et al. (1983) have applied this perspective to intelligence by classifying some subscales of the WISC-R according to simultaneous and successive modes of processing and have found empirical support so that different diagnostic groups (e.g., mentally retarded, learning-disabled) employ simultaneous and successive modes of processing differently from normals.

It is certainly a controversial challenge to put new interpretations on hitherto "static" mental abilities and certain conventional psychometric tests from a more dynamic point of view such as information processing, especially if these tests happen to lack a consistently clear theory of their own. Finding the most appropriate tasks to describe the modes of processing is, of course, always problematic due to the simple fact that complex cognitive tasks are seldom entirely unidimensional. The factor structure of these tasks was explored in order to identify underlying constructs and to test hypotheses about the structure of task variables.

Tests of simultaneous synthesis

The criteria for the tests of simultaneous synthesis were defined *a priori* according to Luria (1966a,1966b), Das, Kirby and Jarman (1975, 1979) and Townsend (1972). The task was considered to require more of the simultaneous than the successive mode of processing where the elements of information were surveyable at once and relatable to each other (Luria, 1966a, 1966b; Das, Kirby & Jarman, 1975, 1979) or were equally present at the time of processing and proceeding simultaneously, or were correlatable at the level of the central processor (Townsend, 1972) (see Figure 1). The following tasks were considered to meet these criteria.

WAIS - Similarities (S). Adequate performance in the task of Similarities requires the successful integration of two components of verbal input. In other words, the correlation or integration of the input at the level of central nervous processor is necessary for the production of correct response. Tasks which require an understanding of the relations between concepts and subconcepts are considered by Cummins and Das (1978) to be examples of simultaneous verbal processing. Das, Kirby and Jarman (1975) used the task of Similarities as a marker test of simultaneous synthesis.

WAIS - Information (I). Luria (1966a, p. 74) states that the recall of earlier experiences or their organization demands the integration of separate elements into simultaneous groups. The task of WAIS Information is an example of recalled memorized knowledge as a reaction to the criteria (or question) specified by the experimenter. The question asked by the investigator requires the re-integration or organization of already experienced or acquired knowledge. This condition elicits the correlation of stimuli at the level of the central processor.

WAIS - Block Design (BD). The task of Block Design is a typical test of simultaneous synthesis (Luria, 1966a, 1966b) which demands the production of complex spatial relations. The task corresponds closely to the simultaneous task of Spatial Manipulation used by Vernon, Ryba and Lang (1978).

The Benton Visual Retention Test (BVRT). The Benton Visual Retention Test (series C; Benton, 1963) requires that simple geometric figures are drawn immediately from memory after a 10 seconds' presentation. All the figures in a display card are presented at the same time. This condition meets the criteria of parallel processing in Townsend (1972). Although drawing calls for successive pencil movements the fundamental demand of this task is, however, the ability to draw the elements in their relative positions. The test items also have a resemblance to Graham-Kendall's (1960) Memory-for-Designs Test which has been used as a marker test of simultaneous synthesis in studies by Das, Kirby and Jarman (1975). The test also shares certain common features with the Figure Copying Test, although it is more complex due to immediate memory performance. Figure Copying has been classified as a test of simultaneous synthesis (Luria, 1966a, 1966b; Das, Kirby & Jarman, 1975; Vernon, Ryba & Lang, 1978).

WMS : the subscale of Visual Reproduction (VR). The test items in the Visual Reproduction subscale of the WMS and the method of presentation are similar to the above-described Benton Visual Retention Test. The test requires short-term nonverbal memory and its correct reproduction by drawing. The task demands retention and recall of geometric figures and their relations and thus has characteristics of simultaneous synthesis. Possibly the test of Visual Reproduction of WMS is somewhat more difficult to perform than the Benton Visual Retention Test because of the more complex nature of the visual items in the WMS.

Tests of successive synthesis

In the temporal order of processing the elements to be processed are presented one by one and the whole sequence is not surveyable at any one time (Luria, 1966a, 1966b; Das et al., 1975, 1979) (see Figure 1). The information components are not necessarily related to each other in any systematic way, but may acquire meaning as the result of the whole sequence. A correlation (or a direct association) between stimuli is not required at the level of the central processor (Townsend, 1972), although this may well happen in some cases. The issue is then no longer one of successive synthesis but a reflection of the appearance of strategic differences in the actual performance (e.g. chunking, memorizing). The interpretation of successive processing in a case of serially organized and presented material is obscured because the subject may use strategic approaches in resolving the tasks of successive synthesis and in this way the processing might acquire the characteristics of simultaneous synthesis. The following tasks were employed as tests of successive synthesis.

WMS: the subscale of Digit Span (DSp). The subject is asked to reproduce immediately an aurally presented series of numbers. The forward and reverse series were both presented in two trials if the subject failed on the first one. Digit span or serial recall is a typical example of successive synthesis (Luria, 1966a; Das, Kirby & Jarman, 1975; Vernon, Ryba & Lang, 1978).

WMS: the subscale of Associate Learning (AL). A list of ten pairs of words is presented to the subject aurally in three trials. After each presentation the recall of pairs of words is requested. Every presentation of the list follows a different order and the recall of pairs of words is also varied. Six pairs of words are easy associates and four pairs difficult or hard associates. Generally, paired-association learning is thought to be an example of successive synthesis (Luria, 1966a; Das, Kirby & Jarman, 1975, 1979; Vernon, Ryba & Lang, 1978).

WMS: the subscale of Logical Memory (LM). Two short stories are read aloud by the experimenter. After the first reading is over the subject is asked to tell as much as s/he can recall from the story. The number of ideas as marked off in the memory passage are coded as record of verbatim. After the first story is read and recalled the investigator reads the second story and proceeds as before. The order of recalled ideas is not important, only the amount of correctly produced ideas matters.

The mode of presentation is organized serially, but at the stage of recall simultaneous synthesis is quite likely to happen. Luria (1966a, p. 76) states that the remembering of any logical text requires simultaneous synthesis. However, Vernon, Ryba and Lang (1978) have used the task of Logical Memory as a marker test of successive synthesis. If one follows the criteria described by Townsend (1972), it is clear that the story repetition does not require the combination of the story with the substance learned earlier and so the correlation at the level of the central processor is not necessarily assumed.

WAIS - Digit Symbol (DSy). Nine visual symbols are simultaneously presented on paper in numerical organization so that each number and symbol correspond to each other. The symbols must be copied on the paper as fast as possible according to the numbers randomly presented. Although in principle the symbols are surveyable at any time it is unlikely that the symbols and their corresponding numbers are mastered completely even after a brief training period. Rather, it is probable that the subject proceeds serially and sequentially checks the display symbols and their corresponding numbers when performing the task (the so called "multiplexing-phenomenon"). The task demands of Digit Symbol include the successive synthesis of kinesthetic-motor and visual functions associated with speed and accuracy of the performance.

The cross-validation of the model of information integration (Das et al., 1975, 1979) was studied in three different Finnish samples where factor analyses by the principal axial method were performed separately for two-, three-, and four-factor Varimax-solutions (Äystö, 1987). The four-factor Varimax-rotated solution was selected for interpretation in the neurological (Table 1) and elderly samples (Table 3) because this solution clearly separated the simultaneous and successive components and gave interpretatively the simplest factor structure. In the case of the brain-damaged sample (Table 2), the three-factor Varimax-solution gave the best description of the factor structure. The four-factor Varimax-solution accounted for 55 % of the total variance in the neurological sample, and 78 % in the elderly sample. In the brain-damaged sample the three-factor solution accounted for 52 % of the total variance.

In all the samples, some tests seem to have more a consistent structure in respect of the underlying processing modes. Four simultaneous tasks (VR,

BVRT, I, S) loaded highly on simultaneous factors (with nonverbal, verbal or mnestic content) in all samples and without profound covariation on other factors. Also, three successive tasks (LM, ALe, ALh) loaded on successive factors without notable covariation on other factors except the subscale of Logical Memory which had a high loading on the simultaneous memory factor (Table 1). This finding is understandable because remembering a logical text requires simultaneous synthesis (Luria, 1966a, p. 76) although, alternatively, the factor may reflect holistically the underlying organizational components of cognition or planning.

The Block Design loaded on the simultaneous (nonverbal) factor in two neurological patient groups (Tables 1 and 2) but on the successive nonverbal factor in the elderly sample (Table 3). Nevertheless, the Block Design also loaded quite highly (over .30) on both simultaneous factors (Table 3) although not as clearly as in the other samples (Tables 1 and 2).

The differential loading of the Block Design in the elderly sample suggests that some of the elderly people may use more successive strategies in re-

Table 1

Varimax-rotated factor matrix for the neurological patients (N = 121).

| Test | Factors | | | | Communality |
	I Sim.n-v.	II Succ.	III Sim V	IV Sim mem	h^2
BVRT	.320	.039	.024	.597	.461
I	.059	.167	.653	.156	.482
S	.218	.173	.641	-.050	.490
DSy	.707	.290	.035	.254	.649
BD	.752	.116	.168	.174	.638
LM	.111	.573	.221	.496	.635
DSp	.596	.153	.269	.165	.421
VR	.471	.203	.089	.477	.498
ALe	.208	.691	.230	-.082	.581
ALh	.224	.722	.159	.255	.662

% of total variance = 55.1

Table 2

Varimax rotated principal factors for brain-damaged and a control group
(N=106)

| Test | Factors | | | |
	I Sim. n-v.	II Sim.v.	III Succ.	h^2
BVRT	.491	.110	.069	.258
I	.085	.798	.151	.667
S	.203	.748	.233	.655
DSy	.725	.179	.236	.613
BD	.733	.231	.052	.593
LM	.250	.298	.531	.433
DSp	.413	.529	.075	.456
VR	.637	.050	.211	.453
ALe	.057	.149	.663	.465
ALh	.183	.057	.731	.571

% of total variance = 51.6

solving the task and that the manipulospatial skills play an important role in Block Design performance. The Digit Symbol loaded on the simultaneous nonverbal factors in both neurological samples but on the successive factor, as hypothesized, only in the elderly sample. The result in the neurological samples may be due to the fact that processing emphasizing content is more determining when it is likely that patients with clearly lateralized injuries are included in the sample.

The most inconsistent behavior was shown in the Digit Span which had unexpected covariation on two simultaneous factors (Tables 2 and 3). The overlapping of the Digit Span between the two simultaneous (verbal and nonverbal) factors (Tables 2 and 3) might be explained by individual differences in the strategies used in resolving the problem (e.g., different memorizing aids, chunking etc.) or by the fact that the scaled score of the sum of the Digit Span Forward and Backward reflects more simultaneous than successive synthesis. It has been suggested (e.g., Naglieri et al., 1981) that the Digit Span Backwards requires the memory of the Digit Span Forward and so the demand for simultaneous synthesis is greater in the task of the Digit Span as a whole.

Table 3

Varimax-rotated factor structure in the age group 75 - 85-years old (N=58).

Test	I Succ.v.	II Sim.v.	III Sim. n-v.	IV Succ. n-v.	h^2
BVRT	.366	.169	.716	.344	.794
I	.433	.634	.320	.217	.739
S	.177	.731	.062	.240	.627
DSy	.306	.197	.293	.776	.821
BD	.197	.376	.320	.489	.521
LM	.578	.250	.242	.093	.464
DSp	.152	.494	.402	.031	.430
VR	.147	.208	.531	.360	.477
ALe	.758	.313	.181	.132	.723
ALh	.787	.064	.129	.366	.774

% of total variance = 78.0

The dissociation of simultaneous verbal synthesis from simultaneous nonverbal synthesis in every adult sample studied and the dissociation of the successive processing factors according to code content in the elderly sample have not been demonstrated in earlier studies on child samples. It is to be assumed that sample characteristics are responsible for the result obtained. The factors described above each have a special nature and in principle they reflect the same properties as have been found in earlier studies by Das and his colleagues.

In summary, support for the Das et al. model was generally found. The three or four factors obtained in three samples, however, included simultaneous and successive factors so that simultaneous processing could be interpreted either with or without code content. The interpretation of the processing factors was not restricted by code content, because all simultaneous factors cut across different varieties of cognition (e.g., mnestic, conceptual, perceptual). Thus, the interpretation of simultaneous and successive factors containing various codes is consistent and well in accordance with the theoretical constructs of the model of Das et al. (1979). It can be stated on the basis of the data presented in Tables 1 - 3 that no substantial overlapping (except Digit Span) occurred between the tasks selected to measure simultaneous and successive processing. In every study, no g-factor was found. The refinements made in the interpretation of factors in the present study can be explained adequately by the information integration model of Das, Kirby and Jarman (1975, 1979) and were specified in Figure 1. Whether the use of content-based interpretations of the simultaneous-successive dimension is needed or not depends on the actual problem under study and on the interpretative specification thus suggested. If the objective is to study the relationship between modes of processing and brain function, content-based interpretations might be appropriate. The verbal and nonverbal functions are found to be dissociated in cases of aphasias or other differently localized brain injuries (e.g. Luria, 1966a, 1966b, 1973) and so it is hypothesized that simultaneous and successive processing might further be specified according to the characteristics of the neurological patient sample.

The two contradictory propositions (i.e. the Luria-Das and hemispheric asymmetry positions) concerning the gross level systems of brain organization responsible for preferring a certain mode of processing need to be tested in the light of simultaneous and successive processing in future studies.

Processing Modes in Relation to Background Variables

The aim of Study 1 (neurological patients, Äystö, 1987) was to examine more thoroughly the relationship between the modes of processing and certain background variables such as sex, age, education, socioeconomic status, handedness, place of habitation and some factors associated with the neurological disease itself (i.e. the length of the time since the onset of injury, the number of clinical syndromes, the length of unconsciousness following trauma or injury, the evaluated need for neuropsychological rehabilitation and the degree of organic alteration).

It was found that education was the only background variable correlating positively and significantly ($p < .05 - .001$) with all the processing factors. The more education the individual had the more higher the factor scores in all modes of processing tended to be. If the two modes of processing are assumed to form the basis for cognition, then these correlations suggest the importance of the role of education (or intervention, rehabilitation) in improving the basic processes of cognition (and consequently cognition itself). In Study 2 (brain-damaged sample, Äystö, 1987) education correlated significantly with all three processing factors mentioned in Table 2.

Age correlated negatively and in a predictable way with three of the factor scores for processing but not with the factor for simultaneous verbal processing (Study 1). The verbal functions or "crystallized intelligence" have been found to be most resistant to the effects of aging in studies concerning the ability structure of intelligence (Cattell, 1964). In the neurological sample the correlation between age and verbal simultaneous synthesis remained non-significant as well as in Study 2 (brain-damaged), where the correlation of age with the modes of processing was nonsignificant in the case of simultaneous verbal processing, but reached .01 level in factor of successive processing and .001 level in the factor of simultaneous nonverbal processing. The correlations were consistent and in the same direction as the earlier findings published on the differential decline of verbal and visuospatial functions with aging (e.g. Schludermann et al., 1983).

Socioeconomic status correlated only with the factor of simultaneous verbal synthesis indicating that the higher the socioeconomic level the higher the scores for simultaneous verbal factor. The relationship between the modes of processing and socioeconomic status (SES) did not reach statistical significance in the cases of successive and simultaneous nonverbal and memory factors. One explanation for the lack of correlations in these cases might be that the mean of the socioeconomic level in the neurological sample (Study 1) was quite low and the distribution of the values of the SES variable was skewed at the lower end. However, despite the skewedness of the distribution, socioeconomic status was powerful enough to influence significantly factor scores for simultaneous verbal processing. The role of high socioeconomic status has been found (e.g. Mussen, Conger & Kagan, 1974, pp. 261-267) to associate with higher language ability in children. The weak correlation between simultaneous verbal processing and the SES variable points to a possible existence of one potential external mediator (SES) in the simultaneous mode of processing, but not in the case of successive processing. In the brain damaged sample (Study 2), SES correlated only with the simultaneous verbal factor so that the higher the socioeconomic status, the better the performance in simultaneous verbal factor.

The degree of occupational incapacity and inefficiency following trauma or disease - which was evaluated on the basis of clinical psychological assessment - correlated negatively with all the processing factors, although not significantly in the case of the simultaneous verbal factor (Study 1). There were more defects in successive and simultaneous (with nonverbal and memory content) processing the greater was the involvement of occupational incapacity.

One of the striking findings in the neurological sample (Study 1) was that the external variables associated with the disease itself did not seem to correlate with the processing factors at all. The length of time since the onset of injury, the number of different clinical symptoms or the dysfunction of the nervous system, the presence and the length of unconsciousness following trauma or injury and the evaluated need for neuropsychological rehabilitation did not correlate significantly with the modes of processing. The degree of psychologically evaluated organic alteration or deterioration correlated negatively and significantly with simultaneous nonverbal factor and recall processes (factor IV in Table 1), but not with successive or simultaneous verbal processing. This observation might indicate that one of the most profound changes after the occurrence of brain dysfunction is to be seen first in the impairment of simultaneous nonverbal and recall processes. This finding in adults is in reverse pattern to the observations found by Das et al. (1979) according to which the role of simultaneous processing is emphasized in the process of cognitive skill acquisition. Simultaneous synthesis also seems to play an important role in the breakdown of cognitive systems as a result of brain dysfunction.

There was an interesting finding between sex and the modes of processing in neurological patient group (Study 1) so that males seemed to perform better than females in the tasks of simultaneous synthesis, but less well in successive synthesis. However, sex-related differences became significant (p < .05) only in simultaneous verbal and memory factors and this was probably partly due to functions at occupational level which were significantly higher in males than females (p < .05). The other background variables were not represented significantly differently in the groups of males and females. No sex-related mode of processing differences have been found in studies on adults elsewhere (Merritt & McCallum, 1983). The elderly sample of the present research (study 3, Äystö, 1987) also showed no sex differences in the processing modes.

There were no differences between males and females on any of the factors of simultaneous and successive processing in the localized brain-damaged group (N = 67) as a whole or in their control group (N = 32). However, there was a statistically significant difference between the sexes (Study 2) in the case of the left hemisphere so that the females did better than the males in successive factor (t =2.56, df =31, p < .02). This finding partially supports the conclusions of Kimura (1983) that there are sex differences in the organization of speech and praxis within the left hemisphere, and supports indirectly the existence of a differential sex effect according to anterior or posterior involvement. As Kimura (1983) states, the role of the left anterior region is important in females for the control of speech and praxic function, and so the female superiority in successive processing in the present study might indirectly reflect this assumption. In the case of right hemisphere dysfunction the males and females did not differ. In the groups of anterior or posterior dysfunction the sex differences were also nonsignificant. Further, it should be noted that there were no differences between males and females in background variables such as age, occupation, education, intelligence (WAIS IQ) or memory (MQ of the WMS) in the brain-damaged group.

Hemispheric and Anterior-Posterior Effects

The second study (Äystö, 1987) aimed at testing the two major neuropsychological hypotheses viz. the Luria-Das position and hemispheric asymmetry concerning the relationship between the modes of processing and their neuro-anatomical structure in brain-damaged people.

The study consisted of 106 adult neurological patients (73 men and 33 women) where focal lesions were found in 67 cases and these distributed as follows: left anterior damage (N =12), right anterior damage (N =17), left posterior damage (N =17) and right posterior damage (N =21). The mean age of the patients was 35.8 years ranging from 16 years to 67 years of age and the mean ages for the groups were respectively 33.5 (LA), 31.6 (LP), 39.3 (RA) and 32.7 (RP) years with no differences between the groups. Also, there were no differences between the lesion groups in level of education and occupation. The mean verbal, performance and full scale IQ scores (the WAIS) for the sample were respectively 102.5 (SD =16.9), 94.8 (SD =21.1) and 99.7 (SD = 17.3).

The factor scores for three factors (see Table 2) were calculated by the regression method and the means of factor scores were compared in groups of patients with left anterior (LA), left posterior (LP), right anterior (RA) and right posterior (RP) lesions. The results of the two-way variance analysis (ANOVA) showed some slight differences ($p < .07$ to $p < .09$) among the four groups in factor scores for simultaneous and successive processing. There were no interactions between laterality and anterior - posterior division in any of the processing factors. The main effects of laterality were significant in factors of simultaneous verbal processing ($p < .01$) and successive processing ($p < .05$). The main effects of the anterior - posterior division of the brain was only significant at the level of $p < .10$ in the factor of simultaneous nonverbal processing.

It can be concluded that both main hypotheses i.e., the hypothesis emphasizing the importance of the anterior/posterior division of the brain and that of hemispheric asymmetry were partially supported but not exclusively.

The hypothesis concerning the existence of different modes of information processing in both hemispheres was also only partially supported. In case of the left hemisphere dysfunction the successive processing was impaired as compared to the right hemisphere dysfunction and so the hypothesis of hemispheric differences became supported. However, a right hemisphere dysfunction did not significantly impair simultaneous nonverbal processing. On the contrary, the results tentatively suggested that there is an anterior/posterior division effect on the factor of simultaneous nonverbal processing. Contrary to the hypothesis of the existence of hemispheric differences in the modes of information processing it was found that simultaneous (parallel) verbal processing was impaired after left rather than right hemispheric dysfunction. The above finding is more acceptable when one considers the explanations combining code content and mode of processing which are obviously needed when interpreting results observed in brain damaged samples. In the neuropsychological literature, left hemisphere damage is known to have a deteriorative influence on verbal rather than nonverbal functions, and vice versa in right hemisphere lesions.

The proposed distinction between successive and simultaneous processing according to anterior (fronto-temporal) and posterior (parieto- occipital) locations of cerebral dysfunction was weakly supported only in case of simultaneous nonverbal processing ($p < .10$), but not so clearly in case of successive synthesis. The results showed that the means of the factor of simultaneous nonverbal processing tended to be lower when there was posterior rather than anterior damage. The result is consistent with the neuropsychological findings often observed in clinical settings that impaired performance at the level of visuospatial functions is associated with temporo-parietal or parieto-occipital lesions (e.g., Christensen, 1974; Lezak, 1976). In case of successive processing, only the left anterior group was more deficient ($p < .10$) than the right posterior group. However, the overall main effect of the anterior/posterior dimension did not reach statistical significance in successive processing.

It is, perhaps, premature to think that processing systems divide themselves in an arbitrary manner according to hemispheres or anterior/ posterior division of the brain. The complexity of the interpretative issues and the interdependence of hemispheres or anterior/posterior regions from each other make strong statements about the direct relationship between the modes of processing and the brain premature. The interactive and complementary role of the modes of processing in cases of disturbed brain functions needs further to be explained. It may well be the case that both hemispheres share properties of simultaneous and successive processing which are represented differently in the anterior and posterior parts of the brain. Also, the dual nature of brain functioning (e.g., verbal - nonverbal) and the modes of processing in a brain-damaged population points to the need for developing a more complex model of information integration if the structural base (neuroanatomy) is to be taken into account. The issue concerning the code or quality of information (e.g., auditory, visual) mediated in its processing is controversial, because the functional and processing theories of hemispheric specialization often tend to ignore each other's contributions.

There are, of course, many difficulties in doing research on brain-dam-aged people due to the difficulty of getting comparable and well-matched sub-samples, especially in regard to central nervous system variables. With regard to matching external factors such as age, education and socioeconomic level the brain-injured sample was remarkably homogeneous in the present study.

Neuropsychological Variables and the Modes of Processing

A more thorough study on the relationship between neuropsychological variables and simultaneous and successive cognitive processes was performed on a representative sample of elderly persons between 75 - 84 years of age (N = 58) who underwent extensive neuropsychological testing and interviews. Factor analysis (Table 3) yielded empirically those factors which were specified in Figure 1 and thus the sample offered a good opportunity for investigating the neuropsychological assumptions of the model. If the assumptions concerning the neuropsychological domain of simultaneous (posterior divisions of the brain or alternatively the right hemisphere) and successive (fronto-temporal and anterior divisions of the brain or alternatively the left hemisphere) processing hold any truth then the neuropsychological functions aimed at measuring different sides and lobes of the brain should according to theoretical assumptions correlate and predict differently the modes of processing. Compared to the second study in brain-damaged people the present study represents a more functional and neurobehavioral approach to the modes of processing and deals with a relatively healthy, normal elderly population.

The battery of neuropsychological variables was created to reflect a wide range of perceptual, motor, sensory, memory and cognitive functions on the basis of Luria's (Christensen, 1974, 1975) or of the Lurian type of neuropsychological battery (the Finnish version of Maruszewski's battery, 1972). A short form of the Facial Recognition Test (Benton et al., 1975) was also used. The neuropsychological tasks were selected to measure different levels of difficulty in a given function, to reflect any neuro-behavioral characteristics of brain dysfunction and to be sensitive to the functioning of different brain areas (e.g., lobes and sides). One of the assumptions underlying Luria's qualitative neuropsychological battery is the notion that performance disturbances in a task indicate brain dysfunction at some level compared to undisturbed performance in respect to the same task.

Lurian-type Qualitative Neuropsychological Factors and the Modes of Processing

In order to get an economic description of the large number of neuropsychological variables and to identify the underlying dimensions behind an eclectically combined test battery a factor analysis was performed separately for Lurian-type "qualitative" tasks and for a set of "left" and "right" hemisphere tasks. The six Lurian-type qualitative factors (Varimax-rotated) which were labelled as the 1) speech regulation of the motor act, 2) visuospatial, 3) tactile perception and recognition, 4) spatial praxis, 5) hand praxis and 6) dynamic praxis, explained about 74 % of the total variance. Considering the nature of the six factors from the view point of Luria's theory about three functional units of the brain it can be approximately stated that the first, fifth and sixth factor characterize more the workings of the third unit (the frontal lobes or the anterior division of the brain) and the second, third and fourth factors mainly feature the workings of the second unit (temporo-parieto-occipital lobes or the posterior division of the brain). In the case of the fourth factor which was the disturbance of spatial praxis the distinction of its belonging to the workings of the second or third unit is unclear because if motor regulation and performance is emphasized it would describe more the workings of the third (anterior) unit and if the visuospatial and organizational aspects of the performance are emphasized more then the fourth factor would mainly characterize the workings of the second (posterior) unit. In the present study, the speech regulation of the motor act was moderately (.42 and .43) loaded on the fourth factor of spatial praxis disturbance and so the fourth factor might reflect the functioning of the anterior as well as the parietal lobes. However, disturbed spatial praxis has typically been associated with parietal lobe damage (Luria, 1973; Christensen, 1974).

The neuropsychological tasks selected for the present study mainly included qualitative tasks of the kind commonly used in investigations of brain-damaged and aphasic samples. Although the elderly sample in the present study was rather healthy and without known brain damage or dysfunction, the factor structure of the neuropsychological tasks constituted the composition of the test battery such that factor content resembled quite consistently and systematically the main characteristics and dimensions observed in locations of various brain dysfunctions. The result of the factor analysis of neuropsychological qualitative tasks was as if a syndrome analysis of a whole sample of elderly people and thus comparable to the Luria's clinical-anatomical method of performing a syndrome analysis inside a brain injured individual. An important aspect of syndrome analysis is the qualitative and multidimensional evaluation of the performance (i.e., how the task was resolved), especially in cases of focal brain damages. However, its use in investigating normal samples is much more questionable. Therefore, only the degree of severity in neuropsychological functioning (undisturbed - strongly disturbed) was scored and the qualitative type of error neglected as a nonrelevant dimension in the relatively healthy elderly sample. Scoring the severity of the performance made the neuropsychological variables unidimensional and, thus, better suitable for factor-analytical treatments. The clear neuropsychological implications of the factor structure contributes to testing the neurobehavioral properties of simultaneous and successive processing. If simultaneous and successive processing systematically correlate and predict the hypothesized relationship between the modes of processing and qualitative neuropsychological functions, a more confident statement about the differential nature of normal aging is possible. At the same time, at the neurobehavioral level it is also possible to study both hypotheses concerning the relationship between the modes of processing and their corresponding neuropsychological domains (anterior/posterior and the left/right hemisphere).

A multiple stepwise and a fixed (all factors included) regression analysis was calculated for neuropsychological factor scores as independent variables and the modes of processing as dependent variables. Due to the orthogonal factor structures the intercorrelations between neuropsychological factor scores were almost zero as was the case between the factor scores of the modes of processing. Thus, there was no multicollinearity among predictors. The significant results of multiple stepwise regression analyses are summarized in Figure 2 and the order of the variables entered in the model is numbered. The inclusion of predictors in the multiple stepwise procedure was continued until the significance limit reached the .05.

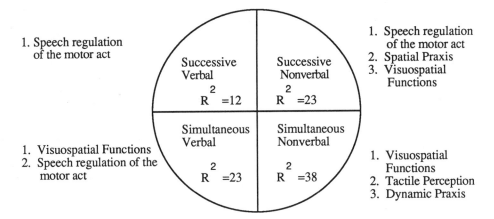

1. Speech regulation
   of the motor act

1. Visuospatial Functions
2. Speech regulation of the
   motor act

1. Speech regulation
   of the motor act
2. Spatial Praxis
3. Visuospatial
   Functions

1. Visuospatial
   Functions
2. Tactile Perception
3. Dynamic Praxis

Figure 2. Neuropsychological factors as predictors of the modes of processing. Summary of the multiple stepwise regression analyses (Äystö, 1987).

Figure 2 points out that simultaneous processing (with either verbal or nonverbal content) was best predicted by the visuospatial functions which alone could explain 17 % of the total variance of verbal and 23 % of nonverbal simultaneous processing. The visuospatial functions are generally considered to reflect more the functioning of the posterior than anterior division of the brain and so the empirical results here demonstrating the linkage between simultaneous processing and Luria's second unit are well in accordance with the assumptions presented in the Das et al. model. The speech regulation of the motor act was also a significant predictor of the simultaneous verbal factor, although not of the nonverbal simultaneous factor where the absence of any disturbance in dynamic praxis was more emphasized. It can be inferred that underlying the simultaneous mode of processing is a motor component of performance which by its nature in either the verbal or nonverbal content of simultaneous processing is dynamic movement. This dynamic property of movement is seen basically to be the function of Luria's third unit having at least two possible alternative interpretations one reflecting the motor executive component and the other exhibiting the emergent property of planning.

Successive processing (either verbal or nonverbal content) was best predicted by the speech regulation of the motor act which characterizes the functioning of the frontal lobe. Spatial praxis and the visuospatial factor also emerged as significant predictors of successive nonverbal processing. Spatial praxis and the visuospatial functions are typically considered to express the workings of Luria's second unit but here in the multiple regression analysis their order of appearance was after the task characterizing Luria's third unit. It can be stated that simultaneous processing underlies successive processing in contrast to the situation mentioned in the above paragraph. The interdependence of the workings of Luria's second and third unit is thus conceptually reflected in the results of the regression analyses.

The Left and Right Hemisphere Tasks and the Modes of Processing

One means of internal validation is to classify the tasks according to theoretical statements and to compare the consistency of results. Here the neuropsychological and those psychometric tasks not used for the operationalization of the modes of processing were reclassified according to their assumed indications of measuring, more or less, either left (mainly verbal) or right (visuospatial, nonverbal) hemisphere functioning. The LH and RH tasks were factor-analyzed by the principal axis method with Varimax rotations and the rotated factor matrices used for factor score calculations.

The "LH and RH factors" (conceptually latent factors by definition) seemed to be relatively pure (simple) as far as the factor loadings (over .40) of the tasks were concerned. The factor analyses of LH tasks yielded three factors which were interpreted as speech regulation of the motor act, verbal reasoning and memory, and disturbed praxis. The RH factors included factors of memory for personal facts and motor fluency, successful praxis, visuospatial functions, tactile perception and recognition and memory for objects. The LH factor explained about 54 % of the total variance and the RH factors 67 % respectively.

The claims of the theory of hemispheric asymmetry concerning the relationship between successive (serial) processing and left hemisphere functioning and between the simultaneous (parallel) processing and right hemisphere functioning suggest that there should be a stronger relationship between simultaneous and successive verbal processing with left hemisphere factors than between simultaneous and successive non-verbal processing. A contrary relation should hold true for behaviors associated with right hemisphere processes where simultaneous and successive nonverbal processing should have a stronger relationship with that hemisphere. If this turns out to be the case it would suggest that there are both simultaneous and successive units inside each hemisphere and these are separable in terms of code content.

The "left hemisphere"
factors as predictors
of simultaneous and
successive processing.

The "right hemisphere"
factors as predictictors
of simultaneous and
successive processing

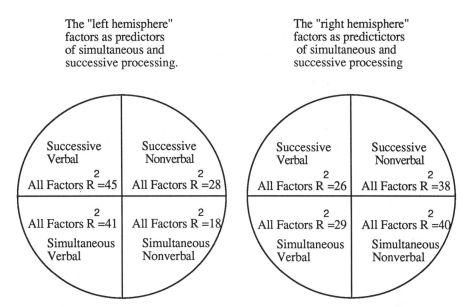

Figure 3. The conceptual hemispheric factors as predictors of the modes of processing. Summary of the results in the elderly sample (Äystö, 1987).

The Figure 3 gives the summary of the results of the fixed regression models, the R^2 -values and the relative contribution of the left and right hemisphere factors as predictors of simultaneous and successive processing. It can be seen that the left hemisphere factors were better able to predict those modes of processing which included a verbal code content whether simultaneous or successive. Respectively, the right hemisphere factors predicted more exactly the nonverbally accentuated modes of processing than the processing modes with verbal content. These results suggest conceptually that there are inside each hemisphere the units for successive and simultaneous processing which are differentiated from each other according to their code content.

The results in the elderly people are well in accordance with the neuropsychological definitions and assumptions of simultaneous and successive processing. Although the results of the regression analyses are meaningful and in accordance with theoretical notions, it should be remembered that there still remains considerably more unexplained variance. Also, this study was conducted with a small number of subjects so these conclusions should be interpreted with caution.

General Discussion

Integrating the approach of information processing and intelligence

The present article has presented an attempt to integrate the perspective of information processing into standardized measures of intelligence by giving a new interpretation to some traditional intelligence and memory measures. This interpretation was based on a careful analysis of stimulus characteristics according to the neuropsychological theory of Luria (1966a, 1966b, 1973), the model of information integration of Das et al. (1975, 1979) and according to statements expressed by Townsend (1972) concerning the identification of serial and parallel systems. The aspect of the manner of information presentation and its assumed interaction at the level of the central processor (the brain) was especially attended to in definitions of the nature of stimulus encoding. Kaufman et al. (1982) state that it is the type of mental processing rather than the nature of stimulus or response which determines whether a test is simultaneous or successive. However, on a theoretical basis Townsend (1972) also considers the mode of presentation important when identifying parallel and serial systems. Thus, in the present study, the modes of processing were considered as a way of structuring input and so attention was paid to the manner of stimulus presentation and its assumed way of organizing information at the level of the central processor (the brain). Based on definitions by Das et al. (1975, 1979), Luria (1966a, 1966b) and Townsend (1972) one can propose definitions of simultaneous and successive processing by taking account not only of the stimulus task, but also of the component processes within the task and their supposed (either direct or indirect) correlation at the level of the central processor.

Sternberg (1984) has doubted the applicability of Luria's theory as a basis for theories of intelligence or information processing due to the lack of empirical support. Goetz and Hall (1984), too, conclude that at present there is no theoretical basis in information processing theory for the Kaufman type simultaneous-sequential analysis of intellectual ability. In fact, in evaluating the K-ABC battery (which aims to measure sequential and simultaneous processing in children) Sternberg (1984) considers that the theory developed by Wechsler (1958) or Binet is far more superior to the Lurian theory on which the K-ABC test (Kaufman et al., 1983) of simultaneous and sequential processing is based. Further, Sternberg (1984) carefully hints that such a theory might be forthcoming although he suspects, for several reasons, that this is unlikely to happen. On the other hand, Goldberg (1976) sees the Lurian "nonfactorial" and multi-dimensional ("qualitative") approach as an interesting research issue for the "factorial" approach. In the present study, a number of psychometric tests of intelligence and memory (the WAIS and the WMS of Wechsler, 1958, 1945) were selected for the purposes of studying their ability to measure simultaneous and successive processing in normal elderly and adult brain-damaged samples. Certain subscales of traditional and widely used psychometric tests were given a new interpretation in the light of Lurian neuropsychological theory and this operationalization was used to study primarily the cross-validation of the model of information processing presented by Das et al. (1975, 1979). The approach here differs from that of Kaufman's (1983) who created new scales for measuring simultaneous and sequential processes instead of giving a new interpretation to old tasks. Also, the neuropsychological Lurian-type tasks were given a psychometric "quantitative" interpretation, thus, providing them with a unidimensional nature better suitable for factor-analytical calculations. These measures were thought to describe the graded differences in the functioning of the hemispheres and different areas of the brain. In the present study, it was found that the specificity offered by process-based interpretations compared to content-based interpretations gave rise to more detailed predictions and hypothesis testing than would have been the case with traditional verbal/nonverbal dichotomy approach.

The approach selected here was a molar, top-down analysis of cognitive processes and so here the presentation of the results describes global level events. The operationalization of the modes of processing was performed factor-analytically as has been done by Das et al. (1975, 1979). The empirical verification focused on adult samples (neurological patients, elderly healthy people) and, thus, it was possible to extend the cross-validation of the model of information integration into adult samples and more closely to study the neuropsychological properties of the modes of processing. There has been a marked lack of research especially on the factors to do with neuropsychological side of the Das model (1984a). The model of simultaneous and successive cognitive processing combined with reinterpreted intelligence measures and applied to studying brain-damaged populations may offer one way out of the multiple controversies prevalent in the literature at the present time. The applicability of any memory or ability test to reinterpretation in the light of the model of information integration (Das et al., 1979) is promising because mnestic, perceptual and conceptual functions are included in the model so that they appear as some of the many varieties of cognitions which are formed on the basis of differentially employing the simultaneous and successive modes of processing.

Methodological considerations

In intelligence models the choice of factor analytical method has influenced the method of data handling. Typically, in ability measurements, there has not often been sufficient consideration of the underlying theoretical method. In the present study of information processing and as assumed by Das et al. (1975, 1979) the modes of processing were considered to be independent of each other and in equal relationship to each other. The emphasis on orthogonal factor structure accords with the theory formulated by Das et al. (1975, 1979). The results of factor analysis (and regression analyses, too) are here, of course, explorative and thus preliminary. In further studies, it might be fruitful to study the relationship between the oblique rotated factor scores with the help of the LISREL-model (e.g., Jöreskog & Sörbom, 1981) and how the both factor structures (namely processing factors and neuropsychological factors) explain simultaneously each other.

The factors in the present study were formed from the combination of such tasks (e.g., Block Design, Visual Retention Test, Digit Span and Digit Symbol) which have been found to discriminate quite satisfactorily in cases of brain pathology. The combination of single tests by means of their content analysis to measure the modes of processing can be seen as clustering the internal structure of cognition into some meaningful unit. In the present study, equivalent tasks employing a variety of stimulus material including perceptual (e.g., Block Design), memory (e.g., Logical Memory) and conceptual (e.g., Similarities) tasks were used for definitions of simultaneous and successive processing. However, by the factor-analytical method one is able to deal with the global structure of the processing, but not to separate different subcomponents or stages of the processing. The factors provide one way of organizing information and including underlying properties common to the test items included in analyses but they are less useful for specifications of the subcomponents of processing.

Cross-validation

Here the cross-validation of the Das model was extended to an adult population and completed with novel tasks compared to the measures used in previous child samples. It was thus considered to achieve a better generalization and validation of the modes of processing in adult samples and to extend the research results on children to a broader age span. The results in three different samples (adult neurological patients, brain-damaged adults and healthy elderly people) demonstrated that the factors of simultaneous and successive processing appeared as having similar characteristics as observed in child studies. The slight loading disparities in the three samples here might represent strategic differences rather than age differences or they could be due to the variability in sample sizes. The successful cross-validation of simultaneous and successive processing in adult samples and by using traditional psychometric tasks also showed the applicability of Lurian theory as a basis for understanding certain intelligence and memory tasks. This conclusion was further confirmed in the study on the elderly (75-84-year old) sample when Lurian type neuropsychological variables predicted meaningfully simultaneous and successive processing and vice versa.

In regression analyses the independent variables as predictors are considered to be causal antecedents of dependent variables. Although in the Das et al. model it is assumed that the modes of processing form the basis for cognition, nothing, however, is stated about the causal direction of the relationship between the neuropsychological variables and the modes of processing. It might be implicitly assumed that the modes of processing also form the basis for the neuropsychological functions. The identity issue cannot be studied here, but instead it is possible to change the direction of prediction so that neuropsychological variables are used as criteria or dependent variables and the modes of processing as predictors or independent variables. The results in positing the opposite direction of prediction (where the modes of processing were used as predictors and neuropsychological variables as dependent variables) were unambiguous and consistent with the earlier findings. Successive processing was closely related to those neuropsychological factors featuring the functioning of the anterior region of the brain whereas simultaneous processing associated more closely with the neuropsychological factors characterizing the functioning of the posterior division of the brain.

Simultaneous and successive processing were found to be relatively independent of such background variables as sex, dominant handedness, place of habitation and certain disease variables (i.e., length of time since injury, amount of clinical symptoms, length of unconsciousness following injury or trauma, evaluated need for neuropsychological rehabilitation). Socioeconomic level correlated in the neurological patients (Study 1) only with simultaneous verbal processing and education with all the modes of processing as expected on the basis of the literature. Age correlated significantly with simultaneous nonverbal, memory and successive processing but not with simultaneous verbal memory (Study 1). This finding corresponds to similar observations in other studies.

Brain functions appear to be hierarchically organized from lower level functions to higher level functions (Luria, 1973). Complex psychological functions can be viewed from the level of constructions rather than from their localization. The hierarchical organization of brain functions also means that the lower levels are controlled by higher level functions but that they are also capable of functioning independently. The controversial issue concerning the hierarchical organization of the modes of processing has been much debated (e.g., Vernon et al., 1978; Das et al., 1979). In the present research, no g-factor was found and so the results are in accordance with the statements expressed by Das et al. (1975, 1979) and with their empirical findings demonstrating no hierarchical structure between the modes of processing.

Construct and predictive concurrent validity

The results of studies 1, and 2 also demonstrated that the simultaneous and successive modes of processing were clearly differentiated according to code content. In study 3 (elderly sample) this was particularly noticeable where the verbal and nonverbal content of the modes of processing were also closely and differentially related to the neuropsychological variables. Therefore, it was concluded that the need for content-based specifications of simultaneous and successive processing would be important in remedial training where the process and content areas are practised conjointly.

The results demonstrated clearly, especially in the elderly sample that simultaneous processing cannot be equated solely with nonverbal coding and successive processing with verbal coding. On the contrary, both verbal and nonverbal content in simultaneous processing as well as verbal and nonverbal content in successive processing were observed in factor analyses. This finding supports one of the basic statements of the model of information integration (Das et al., 1975, 1979) about the independence of material specificity in the modes of processing but it also points to the need for separating the modes of processing according to their content (Figure 1). Also Willis and Hynd (1987) have observed that simultaneous and successive processing style interact with modality (i.e., auditory/vocal or visual/motor). In their opinion, particularly with regard to studies in which children or developmental populations are examined, a serious problem is related to variability in cross-task difficulty both in simultaneous and successive domains. Thus, in experimental studies, modality x task difficulty interactions are difficult to explain let alone control for (Willis & Hynd, 1987).

Two hypotheses concerning the neuropsychological domain of successive (serial) and simultaneous (parallel) processing differ in their basic assumptions.   Researchers in experimental psychology (e.g., Cohen, 1973; Bradshaw & Nettleton, 1981) have associated serial processing with left hemisphere functioning, and parallel processing with right hemisphere functioning. The theory of hemispheric specialization treats hemispheres as separate processors of information. Based on Luria's neuropsychological findings on clinical subpopulations, Das et al. (1975, 1979) have proposed that neuroanatomically the posterior unit (either in the left or right hemisphere) is more responsible for making syntheses on simultaneously processed material whereas the anterior unit (the fronto-temporal areas, frontal lobe) is specialized for handling successively presented material. The direct mapping of psychological functions onto the cerebral cortex is successful only in cases where the model and the neural system are believed to be isomorphic. Luria (1973) characterizes the cerebral cortex as a network of dynamic interactions between disparate regions and zones of the brain with each having a special role in contributing to the complex functional system. Thus, the cerebral cortex is not organizationally fixed and does not necessarily map structure isomorphically to function.

The results in the brain-damaged sample (Study 2), however, did not resolve the issue in favor of either hypotheses although both approaches were weakly supported. Due to many internal factors (like the difficulty of establishing and matching exactly the neuropathological factors in the lesion groups, the possibility of the complementary and interactive functioning of brain areas etc.) it was felt that experimental designs where the subject acts as own control might be more profitable. In study 3 (normally-aged elderly sample), it was possible to study the relationship between the modes of processing and the neuropsychological variables from the perspective of syndrome analysis inside the group (as compared to the Lurian-type syndrome analysis performed inside an individual). Actually, the results in the elderly demonstrated that the neuropsychological variables characterizing more the workings of the posterior divisions of the brain correlated and predicted more accurately simultaneous processing, whereas neuropsychological variables typical of the functioning of the anterior lobe predicted more closely successive processing (Figure 2). The results also tentatively suggested that within each hemispheres there are separate units for simultaneous and successive processing which can be distinguished according to their code content (as described in Figure 1). Verbal processing content would seem to be mediated through the left hemisphere and nonverbal content through the right hemisphere. Thus, successive verbal and successive nonverbal processing would be performed in different hemispheres as would simultaneous verbal and nonverbal processing (Figure 3). This tentative model needs further testing in respect of the simultaneous equation but the claim is well in accordance with the principle expressed by Das et al. (1979) concerning the orthogonality of the two modes of processing and code content.

The evidence in the present research suggests that the rigorous position of hypothesizing a different mode of processing for each cerebral hemisphere seems to be overstated. There seems to be some little evidence that hemispheres as such process information according to successive (serial) or simultaneous (parallel) modes of processing. Rather, there units exist inside each hemisphere capable of both types of processing (Figures 2 and 3). One can argue that this position also represents a continued search for dichotomized models. However, the purpose of the present study is not in reclassification but rather in providing predictive neuropsychological confirmation of simultaneous and successive processing. It is another issue as to whether there are any additional and smaller processing units inside the brain and what is their likely nature.

The results of study 3 demonstrated that the theory of information integration had predictive value. Neuropsychological variables aimed at measuring the functioning of different brain areas and sides were meaningfully associated with the claimed characteristics of simultaneous and successive processing and predicted quite accurately and consistently the modes of processing in the elderly sample (Figure 2). The predictive value of the model of information integration presented by Das et al. (1975, 1979) is important and worthy of consideration when it comes to the applicability of any ability or processing theory to explain the basis of human cognitive functioning.

Implications for Remediation and Future Studies

The present study dealt only with cognitive processing. For human behavior as a whole it is also important to understand affective processing. Whether cognitive and affective processing are separate, or work in a parallel or interactive fashion is a fundamental issue to the theory of information processing, but little dealt with.

The recovery of functioning as a result of brain damage is of particular interest and if the concepts of simultaneous and successive processing can be applied to the recovery process, then these observations have important applications in the area of rehabilitation and special education. Aside from the focus of the present article, it can be mentioned that it was possible to explain a sudden and complete recovery from a profound aphemia with the aid of the theory of simultaneous and successive modes of processing which momentarily converged so that it was possible to observe the transition from an aphemic state into a normal speaking state. Although the generalizability of a single case study is usually limited, here its significance can be seen as providing one possible piece of evidence about the nature of the functional interaction of simultaneous and successive processing. At any rate, the case demonstrates the usefulness of the concepts of the modes of processing in understanding (one) cognitive dysfunction and recovery from it. Simultaneous and successive processing probably have other applications, too. The author's own experiences are that child dysphasics from 7 to 10 years old seem to have either association or dissociation between simultaneously performed verbal and motor tasks; in some cases the simultaneously performed motor act facilitates speech output whereas in other cases it clearly inhibits verbal utterances. The issue what are these individual characteristics in each case is yet to be resolved.

In the neurolinguistic literature (Jakobson & Halle, 1971) similarity and contiguity disturbances have been separated and, because essentially they resemble the concepts of simultaneous and successive processing, it would be interesting to study the predictions they give rise to. Syntactic disorders in language are stated as reflecting disorders of the anterior lobe of the brain and paradigmatic disorders dysfunction of the posterior lobe (Luria, 1976; Caramazza & Berndt, 1978; Jarman, 1980). One possible future research topic in the light of the present study would be to study these linguistic properties in relation to information processing in an elderly sample (e.g., the analysis of narrative speech). In this respect a start has already been made (Äystö in press). Studying the linguistic properties of the neuropsychological model (Figure 1) is thought to be profitable for example for the reasons given by Arbib and Caplan (1979; Arbib, 1982) for using Lurian neuropsychological theory as one of their approaches in constructing their computational model of neurolinguistics.

If processing components are considered as underlying cognition or intelligence, then this point of view changes the emphasis from static task-oriented abilities to a dynamic, process-oriented perspective in educational psychology and in the clinical therapy of learning disorders. What then matters, is the processing components of the task performance, not the type of task. But these aspects, again, are an extreme point; the interaction of processing components with task type has not been emphasized or studied adequately. The emphasis on processing over ability factors has been put forth by

Das et al. (1979) and Sternberg (1985) whereas the contrary view is advanced by Paivio (1971, 1978) and supporters of the classical theories of intelligence or ability structure (e.g., Cattell, 1963; Thurstone, 1938). It has been pointed out by Sternberg (1985) that the information processing approach to intelligence is not a replacement for the "old" psychometric theories of intelligence but only a contribution to a finer and more analytical identification of tasks. The neuropsychological knowledge applied to information processing could be one possible approach in clarifying the internal structure of cognitive functions.

Future studies should address the question whether one of the organizing principles of the brain is simultaneous and successive synthesis and to what extent cognitive tasks are reducible into these two forms of syntheses. Some tentative suggestions in this direction have been presented in the present article.

References

Anderson, J. R. (1976). *Language, memory and thought*. Hillsdale, N. J.: Lawrence Erlbaum.

Anderson, R. (1977). *The notion of schemata and the educational enterprise: acquisition of knowledge*. Hillsdale, N. J.: Lawrence Erlbaum.

Arbib, M. A. (1982). Perceptual-motor processes and the neural basis of language. In Arbib, M. A., Caplan, D. & Marshall, J. C. (Eds.), *Neural models of language processes*. New York: Academic Press.

Arbib, M. A. & Caplan, D. (1979). Neurolinguistics must be computational. *The Behavioral and Brain Sciences, 2,* 449-483.

Ashman, F. & Das, J. P. (1980). Relation between planning and simultaneous successive processing. Perceptual and Motor Skills, 51, 371-382. Ashman, A. F., Molloy, G. N. & Das, J. P. (1981). Coding, planning and mental retardation. Theory, evidence and implications. Part II. *Australian Journal of Developmental Disabilities, 7,* 57-63.

Atkinson, R. C. & Shiffrin, R. M. (1968). Human memory: A proposed system and its control processes. In Spence, K. W. & Spence, J. T. (Eds.) *The psychology of learning and motivation*. Vol. 2. New York : Academic Press.

Äystö, S. (1987). Neuropsychological aspects of simultaneous and successive cognitive processes. *Jyväskylä Studies in Education, Psychology and Social Research, 59.* (Dissertation).

Äystö, S. (in press). Language of the elderly: Can information processing perspective be integrated with linguistic and neuropsychological functions? *Joensuu Papers in Neurolinguistics and Neuropsychology*.

Ben-Dov, G. & Carmon, A. (1976). On time, space and the cerebral hemispheres: A theoretical note. *International Journal of Neuroscience, 7,* 29-33.

Benton, A. L. (1963). *The Revised Visual Retention Test*. New York: Psychological Corporation.

Benton, A. L., van Allen, M. W., Hamsher, K. de S. & Levin, H. S. (1975). *Test of facial recognition.* University of Iowa Hospitals and Clinics.

Bever, T. (1975). Cerebral asymmetries in humans are due to the differentiation of two incompatible processes: Holistic and analytic. In Aaronson, D. & Rieber, R. W. (Eds.) *Developmental psycholinguistics and communication disorders.* New York: New York Academy of Sciences.

Biggs, J. B. & Kirby, J. R. (1984). Differentiation of learning processes within ability groups. *Educational Psychology, 4,* 21-39.

Blumenthal, A. L. (1977). *The process of cognition.* Englewood Cliffs: Prentice-Hall.

Bogen, J. E. (1977). Some educational implications of hemispheric specialization. In Wittrock, M. C. (Ed.) *The human brain.* EnglewoodCliffs: Prentice-Hall.

Bradshaw, J. L. & Nettleton, N. C. (1981). The nature of hemispheric specialization in man. *The Behavioral and Brain Sciences, 4,* 51-91.

Brailsford, A., Snart, F: & Das, J. P. (1983). Strategy training and reading comprehension. *Journal of Learning Disabilities, 17,* 287-290.

Broadbent, D. E. (1958). *Perception and communication.* London: PergamonPress.

Broadbent, D. E. (1963). Flow of information within the organism. *Journal of Verbal Learning and Verbal Behavior, 4,* 34-39.

Caramazza, A. & Berndt, R. S. (1978). Semantic and syntactic processes in aphasia: A review of the literature. *Psychological Bulletin, 85,*888-918.

Cattell, R. B. (1963). Theory of fluid and crystallized intelligence: A critical experiment. *Journal of Educational Psychology, 54,* 1-22.

Cattell, R. B. (1964). *Personality and Social Psychology.* San Diego: Knapp.

Christensen, A-L. (1974). *Luria's neuropsychological investigation.* Text. Copenhagen: Munksgaard.

Christensen, A-L. (1975). *Luria's neuropsychological investigation.* Manual and cards. Copenhagen: Munksgaard.

Cohen, G. (1973). Hemispheric differences in serial versus parallel processing. *Journal of Experimental Psychology, 97,* 349-356.

Cohen, G. (1981). Explaining hemispheric asymmetry: New dichotomies for old ? *The Behavioral and Brain Sciences, 4,* 67.

Cowart, C. A. & McCallum, R. S. (1984). Simultaneous-successive processing across the life-span: A cross-sectional examination of stability and proficiency. *Experimental Aging Research, 10,* 225-229.

Cummins, J. & Das, J. P. (1978). Simultaneous and successive syntheses and linguistic processes. *International Journal of Psychology, 13,* 129-138.

Das, J. P. (1972). Patterns of cognitive ability in nonretarded and retarded children. *American Journal of Mental Deficiency, 77,* 6-12.

Das, J. P. (1973). Structure of cognitive abilities: Evidence for simultaneous and successive processing. *Journal of Educational Psychology, 65,* 103-108.

Das, J. P (1980). Planning: Theoretical considerations and empirical evidence. *Psychological Research, 41,*141-151.

Das, J. P. (1984a). Intelligence and information integration. In Kirby, J. R. (Ed.) *Cognitive strategies and educational performance.* San Francisco: Academic Press.

Das, J. P. (1984b). Aspects of planning. In Kirby, J. R. (Ed.) *Cognitive strategies and educational performance.* San Francisco: Academic Press.

Das, J. P. & Cummins, J. (1978). Academic performance and cognitive processes in EMR children. *American Journal of Mental Deficiency, 89,* 197-199.

Das, J. P., Cummins, J., Kirby, J. R. & Jarman, R. F. (1979). Simultaneous and successive processes, language and mental abilities. *Canadian Psychological Review, 21,* 1-11.

Das, J. P. & Jarman, R. F. (1981). Coding and planning processes. In Friedman, M. P., Das, J. P. & O'Connor, N. (Eds.) *Intelligence and learning.* New York: Plenum Press.

Das, J. P., Kirby, J. R. & Jarman, R. F. (1975). Simultaneous and successive syntheses: An alternative model for cognitive abilities. *Psychological Bulletin, 82,* 87-103.

Das, J. P., Kirby, J. R. & Jarman, R. F. (1979). *Simultaneous and successive cognitive processes.* New York: Academic Press.

Das, J. P., Leong, C. K. & Williams, N. H. (1978). The relationship between learning disability and simultaneous-successive processing. *Journal of Learning Disabilities, 11,* 618-625.

Das, J. P. & Molloy, G. N. (1975). Varieties of simultaneous and successive processing in children. *Journal of Educational Psychology, 67,* 213-220.

Das, J. P., Snart, F. & Mulcahy, R. F. (1982). Information integration and its relationship to reading disability. In Das, J. P., Mulcahy, R. F. & Wall, A. E. (Eds.) *Theory and research in learning disabilities.* New York: Plenum Press.

Dash, U. N. & Das, J. P. (1984). Development of concrete operational thought and information coding in schooled and unschooled children. *British Journal of Developmental Psychology, 2,* 63-72.

Davidoff, J. (1982). Information processing and hemispheric function. In Burton, A. (Ed.) *The pathology and psychology of cognition.* London: Methuen.

DeRenzi, E., Scotti, G. & Spinnler, H. (1969). Perceptual and associative disorders of visual recognition. *Neurology, 19,* 634-642.

Gazzaniga, M. S. & LeDoux, J. E. (1978). *The integrated mind.* New York: Plenum Press.

Goetz, E. T. & Hall, R. J. (1984). Evaluation of the Kaufman Assessment Battery for Children from an information-processing perspective. *The Journal of Special Education, 18,* 281-296.

Goldberg, E. A. (1976). The Luria battery of tests: Techniques and philosophy. In Corson, S. S. & O'Leary Corson, E. (Eds.) *Psychiatry and psychology in the USSR.* New York: Plenum Press.

Graham, F. K. & Kendall, B. S. (1960). Memory-for-Designs Test: Revised General Manual. *Perceptual and Motor Skills, 11,* 147-188.

Guilford, J. P. (1967). *The nature of human intelligence.* New York: McGraw-Hill.

Hammond, G. R. (1982). Hemispheric differences in temporal resolution. *Brain and Cognition, 1,* 95-118.

Hartlage, L. C. & Telzrow, C. F. (1983). The neuropsychological basis of educational intervention. *Journal of Learning Disabilities, 16,* 521-528.

Hooper, S. R. & Hynd, G. W. (1985). Differential diagnosis of subtypes of developmental dyslexia with the Kaufman Assessment Battery for Children (K-ABC). *Journal of Clinical Child Psychology, 14,* 145-152.

Horn, J. L. & Cattell, R. B. (1967). Age differences in fluid and crystallized intelligence. *Acta Psychologica, 26,* 107-129.

Hunt, E. (1980). Intelligence as an information processing concept. *British Journal of Psychology, 71*, 449-474.

Hunt, D. & Randhawa, B. S. (1983). Cognitive processes and achievement. *The Alberta Journal of Educational Research, 29*, 206-215.

Ilg, F. L. & Ames, L. B. (1964). *School readiness: Behavior tests used at the Gesell Institute.* New York: Harper & Row.

Jacobson, R. & Halle, M. (1971). *Fundamentals of language.* The Hague: Mouton.

Jarman, R. F. (1980). Cognitive processes and syntactical structure: Analyses of paradigmatic and syntagmatic association. *Psychological Research, 41*, 153-167.

Jarman, R. F. & Das, J. P. (1977). Simultaneous and successive syntheses and intelligence. *Intelligence, 1*, 151-169.

Jensen, A. R. (1970). Hierarchical theories of mental ability. In Dockrell, W. B. (Ed.) *On intelligence.* Toronto: Methuen.

Jensen, A. R. (1973). *Educational differences.* London: Methuen.

Jöreskog, K. & Sörbom, D. (1981). LISREL V. *Analysis of linear structural relationship by maximum likelihood and least squares method.* Research Report 81 - 8. University of Uppsala, Department of Statistics.

Kail, R. & Pellegrino, J. W. (1985). *Human intelligence perspectives and prospects.* New York: Freeman.

Karnes, F. A. & McCallum, R. S. (1983). Evidence for the Luria-Das model of information processing for gifted students: a preliminary investigation. *Educational and Psychological Research, 3*, 133-137.

Kaufman, A. S. & Kaufman, N. L. (1983). *K-ABC. Kaufman Assessment Battery for Children. Interpretive manual.* Circle Pines, MN.: American Guidance Service.

Kaufman, A. S., Kaufman, N. L., Kamphaus, R. W. & Naglieri, J. A. (1982). Sequential and simultaneous factors at ages 3 - 12 1/2: Developmental changes in neuropsychological dimensions. *Clinical Neuropsychology, 4*, 74-80.

Kaufman, D. & Kaufman, P. (1979). Strategy training and remedial techniques. *Journal of Learning Disabilities, 12*, 416-419.

Kimura, D. (1983). Sex differences in cerebral organization for speech and praxic functions. *Canadian Journal of Psychology, 37*, 19-35.

Kirby, J. R. (1980). Individual differences and cognitive processes: Instructional application and methodological difficulties. In Kirby, J. R. & Biggs, J. B. (Eds.), *Cognition, development, and instruction.* New York: Academic Press.

Kirby, J. R. (1984). Educational roles of cognitive plans and strategies. In Kirby, J. R. (Ed.) *Cognitive strategies and educational performance.* San Francisco: Academic Press.

Kirby, J. R. & Das, J. P. (1977). Reading achievement, IQ and simultaneous-successive processing. *Journal of Educational Psychology, 69*, 564-570.

Kirby, J. R. & Das, J. P. (1978). Information processing and human abilities. *Journal of Educational Psychology, 70*, 58-66.

Klatzky, R. L. (1984). *Memory and awareness. An information-processing perspective.* New York: Freeman.

Klich, L. Z. & Davidson, G. R. (1984). Toward a recognition of Australian aboriginal competence in cognitive functions. In Kirby, J. R. (Ed.) *Cognitive Strategies and Educational Performance.* San Francisco: Academic Press.

Krywaniuk, L. W. (1974). Patterns of cognitive abilities of high and low achieving school children. Unpublished Ph.D. Thesis. Department of Educational Psychology, University of Alberta, Edmonton. Canada. Cited from Das, J.P., Kirby, J. R. & Jarman, R. F. (1979). *Simultaneous and Successive Cognitive Processes*. New York: Academic Press.

Lachman, R., Lachman, J. L. & Butterfield, E. C. (1979). *Cognitive psychology and information processing: An introduction*. Hillsdale: Lawrence Erlbaum Associates.

Leasak, J., Hunt, D. & Randhawa, B. S. (1982). Cognitive processing, intervention, and achievement. *The Alberta Journal of Educational Psychology, 28*, 257-266.

Levy-Agresti, J. & Sperry, R. (1968). Differential perceptual capacities in major and minor hemispheres. *Proceedings of the National Academy of Sciences, 61*, 1151-1159.

Lezak, M. D. (1976). *Neuropsychological assessment*. New York: Oxford University Press.

Lindsey, P. H. & Norman, D. A. (1972). *Human information processing. An introduction to psychology*. New York: Academic Press.

Luria, A.R. (1966a). *Human brain and psychological processes*. New York: Harper & Row.

Luria, A. R. (1966b). *Higher cortical functions in man*. New York: Basic Books.

Luria, A. R. (1973). *The working brain. An introduction to neuropsychology*. Harmondsworth: Penguin Books.

Luria, A. R. (1976). *Basic problems of neurolinguistics*. The Hague: Mouton.

Luria, A. R. & Simernitskaja, E. G. (1977). Interhemispheric relations and the functions of the minor hemisphere. *Neuropsychologia, 15*, 175- 178.

Madden, D. J. & Nebes, R. D. (1980). Visual perception and memory. In Wittrock, M. C. (Ed.) *The brain and psychology*. New York: Academic Press.

Martindale, C. (1981). *Cognition and consciousness*. Homewood, Ill.: The Dorsey Press.

Maruszewski, M. (1972). *Maruszewskin neuropsykologinen testipatteristo. Kokeiluversio*. Helsinki: HYKS. (In Finnish).

Merritt, F. M. & McCallum, R. S. (1983). Sex-related differences in simultaneous-successive information processing. *Clinical Neuropsychology, 5,* 117-119.

Merritt, F. M. & McCallum, R. S. (1984). The relationship between simultaneous-successive processing and academic achievement. *The Alberta Journal of Educational Research, 30*, 126-132.

Miller, G. A., Galanter, E. & Pribram, K. H. (1960). *Plans and the structure of behavior*. New York: Holt.

Molloy, G. N. & Das, J. P. (1979). Intellectual abilities and processes: An exploratory study with implications for person-teaching method interactions. *The Australian Journal of Education, 23,* 83-92.

Molloy, G. N. & Das, J. P. (1980a). Simultaneous-successive syntheses, planning strategies and education: A process approach toward an integrated theory. *Australian Journal of Education, 24*, 289-301.

Molloy, G. N. & Das, J. P. (1980b). Coding, planning and mental retardation: theory, evidence and implications. *Australian Journal of Developmental Disabilities, 6*, 111-117.

Moscovitch, M. (1979). Information processing and the cerebral hemispheres. In Gazzaniga, M. (Ed.) *Handbook of behavioral neurobiology. Vol. 2. Neuropsychology*. New York: Plenum Press.

Mussen, P. H., Conger, J. J. & Kagan, J. (1974). *Child development and personality*. Fourth edition. New York: Harper & Row.

Mwamwenda, T., Dash, U. N. & Das, J. P. (1984). A relationship between simultaneous-successive synthesis and concrete operational thought. *International Journal of Psychology, 19*, 547-563.

Näätänen, R. (1982). Processing negativity: An evoked-potential reflection of selective attention. *Psychological Bulletin, 92*, 605-640.

Näätänen, R. (1985). Selective attention and stimulus processing: Reflections in event-related potentials, magnetoencephalogram, and regional cerebral blood flow. In Posner, M. I. & Marin, O. S. (Eds.) *Attention and performance XI*. Hillsdale, N. J.: Lawrence Erlbaum.

Näätänen, R. (1986). Neurophysiological basis of the echoic memory as suggested by event-related potentials and magnetoencephalogram. In Klix, F. & Hagendorf, H. (Eds.) *Ebbinghaus Symposium*. Amsterdam, North-Holland.

Naglieri, J. A., Kamphaus, R. W. & Kaufman, A. S. (1983). The Luria-Das simultaneous-successive model applied to the WISC-R. *Journal of Psychoeducational Assessment, 1*, 22-34.

Naglieri, J. A., Kaufman, A. S., Kaufman, N. L. & Kamphaus, R. W. (1981). Cross-validation of Das' simultaneous and successive processes with novel tasks. *The Alberta Journal of Educational Psychology, 27*, 264-271.

Nebes, R. D. (1974). Hemispheric specialization in commisurotomized man. *Psychological Bulletin, 81*, 1-14.

Neisser, U. (1967). *Cognitive psychology*. New York: Academic Press.

Newell, A. & Simon, H. A. (1972). *Human problem solving*. Englewood Cliffs, N. J.: Prentice-Hall.

Nottebohm, F. (1979). Origins and mechanisms in the establishment of cerebral dominance. In Gazzaniga, M. S. (Ed.), *Handbook of Behavioral Neurobiology. Vol. 2. Neuropsychology*. New York: Plenum Press.

Paivio, A. (1971). *Imagery and verbal processes*. New York: Holt, Rinehart and Winston.

Paivio, A. (1978). A dual-coding approach to perception and cognition. In Pick, H. L. & Saltzman, E. (Eds.) *Modes of perceiving and processing information*. Hillsdale, N. J.: Lawrence Erlbaum.

Palmer, S. E. & Kimchi, R. (1984). The information processing approach to cognition. Berkeley Cognitive Science Report No. 28. November 1984.

Randhawa, B. S. & Hunt, D. (1979). Some further evidence on successive and simultaneous integration and individual differences. *Canadian Journal of Behavioral Sciences, 11*, 340-355.

Raven, J. C. (1947). *Coloured progressive matrices*. London: Lewis & Co. Ltd.

Ryckman, D. B. (1981). Reading achievement, IQ, and simultaneous-successive processing among normal and learning-disabled children. *The Alberta Journal of Educational Research, 27*, 74-83.

Schludermann, E. H., Schludermann, S. M., Merryman, P. W. & Brown, B. W. (1983). Halstead's studies in the neuropsychology of aging. *Archives of Gerontology and Geriatry, 2*, 49-172.

Shiffrin, R. M. & Schneider, W. (1977). Controlled and automatic processing: II. Perceptual learning, automatic attending, and a general theory. *Psychological Review, 84*, 127-190.

Spearman, C. (1927). *The abilities of man*. New York: Macmillan.

Sternberg, R. J. (1984). The Kaufman Assessment Battery for Children: An information-processing analysis and critique. *Journal of Special Education, 18,* 269-279.

Sternberg, R. J. (1985). *Beyond IQ. A triarchic theory of human intelligence.* Cambridge: Cambridge University Press.

Thurstone, L. L. (1938). *Primary mental abilities.* Chicago: University of Chicago Press.

Townsend, J. T. (1972). Some results concerning the identifiability of parallel and serial processes. *British Journal of Mathematical and Statistical Psychology, 25,* 168-199.

Vernon, P. E., Ryba, K. A. & Lang, R. J. (1978). Simultaneous and successive processing: An attempt at replication. *Canadian Journal of Behavioral Science, 10,* 1-15.

Wechsler, D. (1945). A standardized memory scale for clinical use. *Journal of Psychology, 19,* 87-95.

Wechsler, D. (1955). *Manual for the Wechsler Adult Intelligence Scale.* New York: Psychological Corporation.

Wechsler, D. (1958). *The measurement and appraisal of adult intelligence.* Baltimore: Williams & Wilkins.

Willis, W. G. & Hynd, G. W. (1987). Lateralized interference effects: Evidence for a processing style by modality interaction. *Brain and Cognition, 6,* 112-126.

Zaidel, E. (1978). The split and half brains as models of congenital language disability. In NINCDS Monograph No. 22: *The neurological bases of language disorders in children: Methods and directions for research.* U.S. Department of Health, Education and Welfare Bethesda.

13

Familial Sinistrality and Syntactic Processing

Wayne Cowart

This paper reviews recent indications that subjects with no left-handed relatives (FS- subjects) differ from FS+ subjects in syntactic processing. An experiment contrasting the performance of these two subject types on subordinate and coordinate clause sentences appears to support indications that FS- subjects have more ready access to some specifically syntactic representation of incoming sentences.

Familial Sinistrality and Language Function

There have been several studies over the last two decades that associate some difference in language performance with familial sinistrality. Until quite recently, however, the effects reported involved only relatively simple linguistic stimuli, such as single words or syllables. Taylor and Heilman (1982), using dichotic and visual half-field procedures, were able to demonstrate a right-ear advantage only for FS- males. McKeever, et al. (1983), McKeever & VanDeventer (1977) and Andrews (1977) (and others) have demonstrated various interactions between visual processing and familial sinistrality that are relevant to object naming. Hecaen & Sauget (1971) reviewed several hundred case reports and found some evidence that the frequency of disturbances of oral language and reading accompanying unilateral cerebral lesions in left-handers was sensitive to familial sinistrality. Several other studies have considered familial sinistrality but failed to find any effects or interactions attributable to it.

Bever, et al. (1987) report on a number of experiments bearing on variation in syntactic processing that seem to be linked to familial sinistrality. One of these is a study in which subjects heard sentence fragments such as (1):

(1) If John was careful to call <up> everybody in the class <up> yesterday...

Each fragment contained a particle that could appear in one of two locations (see the two sites with <up> in this phrase.). Shortly after hearing one of these fragments the subject would hear a probe word in isolation. The subject had to indicate rapidly whether the probe word was or was not one of the words in

Cowart, W. (1988). Familial sinistrality and syntactic processing. In J. M. Williams and C. J. Long (Eds.), *Cognitive approaches to neuropsychology*, New York: Plenum.

the fragment. For this and some other experiments, two groups of subjects differing in familial sinistrality were formed. The groups were balanced for sex, handedness (all were strongly right-handed), and verbal SAT score. Subjects were categorized as FS+ if they reported at least one left-hander among their biological relatives (i.e., parents, siblings, grandparents, aunts and uncles).

Considering only the cases where the subject correctly responded 'yes', the results for the two groups differed markedly. FS- subjects, those with no left-handers in their families, showed a clear serial order effect; they responded more slowly to probes occurring late in the sentence than to those occurring early. By contrast, the FS+ subjects showed no linear order effect at all. Apparently, the FS- subjects were searching some linear representation of the fragment; when they got to the relevant item, they responded. FS+ subjects seemed able to access the early and late parts of the fragment at the same time, suggesting that they rely on some non-linear representation of the utterance. Further results suggest that whatever distinguishes FS- and FS+ subjects is of special relevance to the syntactic system.

Some recent experiments conducted in the author's lab have also shown differences between the performance of FS- and FS+ subjects. One experiment used simple two clause sentences in which the second clause contains a pronoun subject. The first clause sometimes contains an antecedent for this pronoun and sometimes does not. The relation between the two clauses also varies; half the cases are subordinate clause/main clause structures and half are coordinate main clauses. The experiments use a version of the word-by-word reading task in which subjects must press a key to see each new word in the sentence.

Preliminary results (Cowart, 1987, Bever, et al., 1987) suggest that FS- subjects are more sensitive to syntactic structure in certain respects. There is a general tendency for subjects to read a little faster in the second clause when the pronoun subject of that clause has an antecedent in the first clause. This tendency seems to be more or less uniform for FS+ subjects. For FS- subjects, however, the effect seems to arise only in the syntactically more integrated subordinate/main structures, but not in coordinate structures.

Further analyses and some additional data suggest, however, that these patterns may be sensitive to the particular subordinating conjunction used and perhaps to other factors.

Another experiment related to FS-/+ differences was conducted re-cently by D. Smetters. This involved classroom presentation of printed lists of sentences about which subjects were asked to make acceptability judgments. The materials were modeled on those used in some experiments reported by Freedman and Forster (1985). They were primarily targeted on what have sometimes been called specified subject violations in the linguistic literature, as in (2d) below. In (2b-d) the critical fact is that the wh- item ("what") is taken to be related to the missing noun phrase position inside the prepositional phrase (indicated here with an underscore) at the end of the sentence. The lin-guistic and psycholinguistic issue is what kinds of factors can interfere with the establishment of this relation. In the present experiment a condition was added to help assess the role that the definiteness of the noun phrase that includes the prepositional phrase might play in these cases; that is, a contrast was estab-lished between three kinds of cases, ones where the determiner of the critical noun phrase was indefinite, definite or a proper name (Conditions b, c and d, respectively). An example item appears in (2).

(2)   (a) Why did the scientist criticize Max's proof of the theorem? (control)

        (b) What did the scientist criticize a proof of_?

        (c) What did the scientist criticize the proof of_?

        (d) What did the scientist criticize Max's proof of_?

On a straightforward reading of another proposed grammatical principle (subjacency; see Chomsky, 1981, Riemsdijk & Williams, 1986), cases (2b,c,d) also involved subjacency violations. Thus, one of the questions addressed was whether cases (2b,c) showed any evidence of being unacceptable, contrary to the assumptions of Freedman and Forster.

The results showed a grading off of acceptability judgments from the cases with indefinite noun phrases to those with proper names as determiners. That is, cases (2b,c,d) were significantly less acceptable than cases like (2a), $p<.001$.

More importantly, there is a rather neat contrast between the perfor-mance of FS- and FS+ subjects. The broad pattern of effects across the three degrees of definiteness is identical in the two kinds of subject. But, in condi-tion (2d), taken to be uncontroversially unacceptable, and in conditions (2b,c), suspected of being unacceptable, the responses of the FS- subjects were a little more negative than those of the FS+ subjects. This pattern appeared with 19 of 24 sentences, p<.001. Somehow, the FS- subjects were more disturbed by the doubtful or unacceptable sentences than were the FS+ subjects. Or to put it another way, the FS+ subjects may have found it easier to see past the eccentric forms to some plausible analysis of the writer's intention.

Candidate explanations of these results might be developed in at least two ways: 1) by proposing a general cognitive mechanism that is sensitive to handedness background and that differentially modifies the manifestations of syntactic processing in FS- and FS+ subjects (while the syntactic system is assumed to show no systematic differences between these groups); or 2) by proposing that there are systematic differences in the syntactic processing systems of FS- and FS+ subjects.

See Cowart (1987) for discussion of the relation between this line of investigation and the proposals of Geschwind and Galaburda (1987).

Sinistrality and Subordinate and Coordinate Clauses

Linguistic Rationale

The aim of the work reported here was to compare FS- and FS+ subjects on two basic but quite different syntactic structures. In two clause sentences, English provides means by which a) the second clause may be subordinated to the first, or b) made coordinate with it. Superficially, sentences exemplifying these relations may seem virtually identical, as in (3).

(3)   (a) The man liked the book, *though* he didn't buy it.

        (b) The man liked the book, *but* he didn't buy it.

In many pairs with structures parallel to those in (3) any differences in sense associated with the contrast between "though" and "but" are subtle. However, simple observations readily support the traditional view that surface similarity here obscures an important difference in structure. Note, for example, that the subordinate clause of (3a) can be repositioned ahead of the main clause in exactly the form in which it is shown here (and indeed is commonly preferred in this position). But with (3b) the same alteration yields a clearly unacceptable result. By contrast, in (3b) it is possible to delete "he"; the resulting sentence has the same sense as the reading of (3b) in which "he" is coreferential with "the man" (the reading in which it is not coreferential is no longer available). But, in (3a) deleting "he" yields a flatly unacceptable sentence for most speakers.

Perhaps the most important observation for present purposes is that conjunctions that behave similarly to "though" in the two respects enumerated above (e.g., "since", "because", "while", "if") impose markedly different constraints on reference relations linking the subjects of the two clauses. In (4a), for example, "the man" generally cannot be taken to refer to the same individual as does "he".

(4)   (a) He liked the book, since the man didn't buy it.

        (b) He liked the book, but the man didn't buy it.

In (4b), however, this pattern of interpretation seems to be accessible for most speakers. Judgments in these matters are sensitive to various other features of the sentences and their contexts. Nevertheless, as a class, subordinating conjunctions that behave similarly to "though" strongly resist coreference between (non-pronoun) definite noun phrase subjects in the second clause of structures like (3) and (4) and pronoun subjects in the first clause.

A more detailed account of these phenomena is beyond the scope of this paper. For present purposes, it must suffice to note that the second clause in (3a) and (4a) is evidently (as traditional analyses suggest) a subsidiary member of a larger sentence based on the first clause. In these structures, certain elements of the main clause seem to 'command' (in a specific technical sense) the material in the subordinate clause (see discussions of c-command, pronominal anaphora, binding theory and related matters in, for example, Reinhart, 1983, and Chomsky, 1981). By contrast, coordinate clauses, as in (4b), stand more nearly as autonomous structures having a much looser connection to the first clause. Note for example, that if the conjunction is left in place but the content of the two clauses is exchanged, the effect on the sense of (4b) is much less dramatic than if the same rearrangement is attempted with (4a).

One central assumption that underlies the experiment to be reported below is that subordinate clauses such as in (3) and (4) are, at least to some degree, syntactically integrated with the main clauses they are associated with. Each clause in the coordinate structures in these same examples, by contrast, functions as an essentially autonomous domain coequal with the other. The claim that this is a syntactic (as opposed to semantic) difference can be read for these purposes as a claim about the character of the processing system(s) involved. It asserts that there is some system that treats the subordinate clauses as subdomains within their main clauses solely on the grounds that the conjunction is identified as of the subordinating type. This is done, by hypothesis, regardless of any idiosyncratic semantic or pragmatic features that might weigh against this analysis in the particular case.

These claims in no way deny that any such syntactic mechanism operates in close association with semantic and pragmatic mechanisms. It seems clear that any syntactic differences between the two kinds of clause relation are correlated with important semantic and pragmatic differences. What it does claim is only that, even if semantic and pragmatic considerations might ultimately override analyses suggested by the syntactic system, they cannot be used to prevent the syntactic system from executing whatever analysis is indicated by the structural properties of the elements that make up the utterance. The "modularity" theory on which these suggestions draw is discussed in Fodor (1983). Structural properties are taken to include essentially those that are expressible in terms of grammatical (roughly, part-of-speech) categories. Thus each word characteristically has some category identity, can occur only in certain contexts defined in terms of such categories and may impose certain well-defined types of features on other elements of the structures (as in number agreement in English) in which it participates.

Note that the contrast between "though" and "but" in (3) tends to place special emphasis on the claim that there are important syntactic differences between subordinate and coordinate clauses quite independently of any semantic or pragmatic difference. As noted earlier, "though" and "but" are quite similar from a semantic point of view. Indeed, the semantic contrast between these conjunctions seems to be as small as can be obtained for English subordinate/coordinate pairs.

It should also be noted that while the syntactic contrast between "though" and "but" seems less attenuated than the semantic contrast, "though" does not seem to invoke the characteristic properties of subordinate clauses as clearly as do other subordinating conjunctions. For example, if the "the man" and "he" are exchanged in (3a), the bar against "the man" being coreferential with "he" is much more clearly in force with almost any subordinating conjunction other than "though". Thus, syntactic effects found with "though" ought to be more clearly revealed with other subordinating conjunctions.

Processing Implications

The basic processing implication of this analysis of the "though/but" contrast is that subordinate clauses ought to be generally harder to process than coordinate clauses because each must be treated as a subdomain within a larger complex structure, while a coordinate clause can be treated more nearly as an isolated unit. The earlier results relevant to familial sinistrality and syntactic processing (Bever, et al., 1987, in preparation, Cowart, 1987) suggest, however, that any such difficulty will operate differently on FS+ and FS- subjects. Since FS- subjects have, by hypothesis, ready access to a specifically syntactic representation of the utterance, they have more ready access to a representational system well-suited to dealing with the relation between a subordinate clause and its associated main clause. Access to this resource should be expressed as greater facility in dealing with these structures; that is these subjects might a) experience less difficulty than FS+ subjects, b) resolve that difficulty more quickly, c) detect the challenge associated with subordinate structures sooner, or some combination of these effects. Furthermore, any familial sinistrality contrasts should be most evident on subordinate clauses rather than coordinate clauses since the hypothesized characteristic resources of FS- subjects should be more relevant to the subordinate cases.

Experimental Evidence

An experimental approach to the issues raised above has been mounted by way of a variant of the word-by-word reading procedure. Kennedy and Murray, 1984, compared three forms of the word-by-word task and found that the cumulative form was sensitive to syntactic effects in ways that other variants are not. In this variant, as in others, the subject must press a key when he/she finishes reading the most recently displayed word. This brings up the next word and the interval between key presses provides an approximation to a reading time measure per word across the sentence. This task differs from earlier word-by-word procedures in that each word appears on the screen to the right of the preceding word (apart from line breaks, which here never fell in experimentally critical regions of the sentence); it then stays on the screen until the subject reaches the end of the sentence. Thus, at the end of a sentence presentation something like a normal text display of the material is on the screen. A yes/no question was presented after each item and the subject's answer and response time were recorded. A feedback message reported on the correctness of the subject's reply and the reaction time for that reply. When a subject's average reading time fell below 550 msec. per word, an additional message reported the average reading time to the subject and encouraged them to try to go somewhat faster.

The experimental materials presented via this task were modeled on the pair in (3),[2]. The materials also implemented a contrast between cases where the first clause did and did not contain an antecedent for the pronoun in the second clause. This contrast will be ignored here. The materials were presented in the same randomly-determined order to all subjects.

The experimental design crossed Position with Clause Relation (Subordinate, Coordinate) and Familial Sinistrality. The hypotheses discussed above are not refined enough to predict the exact word or zone within which a given effect might appear. Thus, the implementation of the Position factor in this exploratory analysis was determined post hoc and varied across analyses, including from one to three words in a single zone. It is left to the reader to decide whether the choices made reasonably reflect the hypotheses. All analyses involve only two contiguous zones.

Subjects were recruited from undergraduate courses at Ohio State University. A brief questionnaire was distributed to several hundred students. The questionnaire requested information on familial sinistrality and a very few potentially related phenomena (e.g., personal and familial allergies and other immune system disorders). It also included a slightly modified form of Geschwind's variant of the Oldfield handedness inventory. About a quarter of the students who filled out this form indicated that they were willing to participate in an experiment. Returns from this survey were entered into a database system which computed a laterality score, The laterality measure used was Geschwind's LS, ranging from -100 for strongly left-handed subjects to 100 for strong right-handers., and an index of familial sinistrality. Following Bever's lead, respondents were counted as FS+ if they had one or more left-handed or ambidextrous relatives in either the primary or secondary family.

Experimental subjects were recruited from among those respondents who showed laterality scores of 70 or more. Subjects filled out a much more extensive questionnaire when they came to the laboratory. The data from the two forms overlapped and did not always agree. The 58 subjects who had been run as of the date of the preliminary analysis described here were predominantly women. The sample was too small to permit any meaningful attempt to balance sex and laterality across sinistrality groups.

Prior to analysis based on the experimental questions described above the subjects were evaluated for overall average per word reading time and the standard deviation of this mean. This analysis showed that three subjects were clear high outliers. When these subjects were removed from the pool, the distribution of average reading times closely approximated a normal distribution.

Previous work with the word-by-word reading procedure had shown that a substantial fraction of all subjects essentially cannot or will not do the task on a genuinely word-by-word basis. Results obtained by these subjects are characterized by substantially attenuated local effects (as around the clause boundary), a lack of substantial hesitation on the last word (which is easily recognized, being marked by a period), and average response times well below those that appear in the balance of the sample. To correct for this phenomenon, a further preliminary analysis calculated a measure of the subject's tendency to hesitate on the last word of each sentence. This was simply the mean RT on all final words divided by the mean RT on all non-final words. Subjects were then ranked according to the size of this effect. In order not to bias the results should sinistrality groups differ in this regard, approximately one third of the subjects showing the least hesitation in each sinistrality category was excluded from the main analysis. (Due to a clerical error, one subject too many was recategorized for the FS+ subjects.) Thus the analyses discussed below cover 18 FS- subjects and 19 FS+ subjects, all of whom show roughly an 8% or greater hesitation effect on last words.

Results: FS Effects in Processing Subordinate Clauses

It must be emphasized that this is a preliminary analysis of a continuing study. As noted earlier there are indications that any effects attributable to familial sinistrality are sensitive to sex. Thus the definitive analysis of this experiment will be based on a much larger sample that provides better balance for sex and laterality and provides for more refined assessment of familial sinistrality (i.e., distinguishes primary and secondary relatives).

The results for the present analysis are summarized in Figure 1. The figure displays mean reading time per word over a span that begins on the last word of the first clause and ends on the fifth word of the verb phrase of the second clause. Inspection of Figure 1 suggests several potentially important features of these results: a) responses in subordinate clauses are generally slower than those in coordinate clauses, b) this difference is more evident in the FS+ subjects, c) the subordinate/ coordinate difference seems to be distributed differently over the clause for the two kinds of subject, with FS- subjects showing the effect at the clause boundary while FS+ subjects show the effect over the whole of the clause, d) the general pattern of word position effects is similar for the two kinds of subject (slowest responses at the clause boundary and toward the end of the second clause, fastest on Word 1 at the beginning of the verb phrase), but the amplitude of these effects seems to be a little greater for FS- subjects.

The principal statistical analysis focused on the question whether there was a robust Clause Relation effect and whether this effect was distributed differently for FS- and FS+ subjects. Figure 1 reveals that the clearest contrast between subject types seems to lie in a comparison between responses at the subject position of the second clause (marked 'Pron') and the average over the following three word positions. Thus, in this analysis, the Position factor had two levels; the first being a one-word zone including just 'Pron', and the second being the average reading time over the next three words (Figure 2).

The most important result of this analysis is that there was a significant interaction among the Position, Clause Relation and Familial Sinistrality factors, $F(1,35)=4.82$, $MS_e=465.4$, $p<.05$. This indicates that the subject types do indeed differ in the way the difficulty associated with subordinate structures is distributed over the clause. That is, it seems that FS- subjects experience the extra difficulty associated with a subordinate clause at or very near the clause boundary; by contrast, FS+ subjects experience a more sustained difficulty that seems to first appear at the clause boundary, but which is then sustained for several words into the clause.

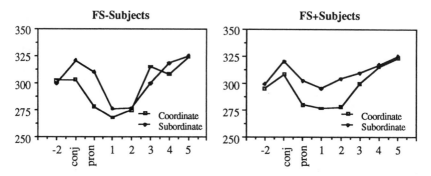

Figure 1. Reading time per word (msec) at the clause boundary and in the second clause as a function of word position, clause type and familial sinistrality.

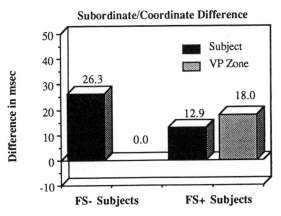

Figure 2. Difference between reading time in the two clause type conditions as a function of zone and familial sinistrality. ('Subject' zone covers just the word at the position marked 'Pron' in Figure 1, while 'VP Zone' data is averaged over the positions marked 1 - 3.)

In addition, there was a significant interaction between Clause Relation and Zone, $F(1,35)=6.55$, $MS_e=465.4$, $p<.02$. This reflected the fact that responses in subordinate clauses accelerated from the first to the second zone (304 vs. 296 msec.) while those in coordinate clauses were approximately stable (285 vs. 286 msec.). There was also a significant main effect for Clause Relation, reflecting the generally faster responses in Coordinate cases, $F(1,35)=8.58$, $MS_e=372.7$, $p<.01$.

A further analysis used a six-level Position factor ('Conj' through Word 4), Clause Relation and Familial Sinistrality. This analysis detected only a main effect for word position, $F(5,175)=9.42$, $MS_e=986.3$, $p<.001$.

As suggested above, any contrast between subject types ought to be most apparent with subordinate clauses. Thus, Figure 3 juxtaposes the subordinate clause data from Figure 1. While the close similarity between the subject types over the first three words in the graph may be partly fortuitous, clearly there is no hint here that the pattern of response differs at the clause boundary. Rather, the patterns diverge sharply at the onset of the verb phrase, with FS- subjects showing a marked advantage. To test these differences an analysis was done on this data using averages over two zones; the first was essentially the clause boundary ('Conj' and 'Pron') and the second the beginning of the verb phrase (Words 1 and 2).

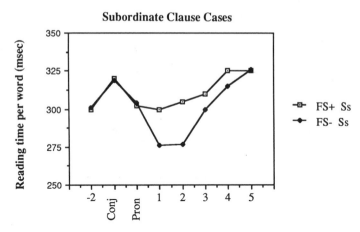

Figure 3. Reading time per word at the clause boundary and in the second clause in subordinate clause sentences as a function of word position and familial sinistrality. (Subset of the data from Figure 1.)

The interaction between Zone and Familial Sinistrality was significant, $F(1,35)=4.92$, $MS_e=564.0$, $p<.05$, suggesting that there is a reliable difference between subject types in the way the difficulty associated with these clauses is handled. There was also a significant main effect for Zone, $F(1,35)=16.2$, $MS_e=564.0$, $p<.001$.

Conclusions

Though these results reflect a preliminary analysis, there is some encouragement here for the theoretical proposals discussed above. There is evidence that subordinate clauses are indeed harder to process, but that this added difficulty does not affect FS- and FS+ subjects in the same way. FS- subjects seem to cope with these structures more easily in the sense that evidence of special difficulty associated with such clauses appears only at the beginning of the clause, and only briefly. Where it arises, the magnitude of the effect seems larger than that experienced by FS+ subjects. The latter, however, seem to experience most of the extra difficulty about two words further into the clause, and they may feel the effects for longer. There is no support here for the suggestion that FS+ subjects might detect the problems associated with the subordinate clause more slowly than FS- subjects.

More generally, these results lend some support to the suggestion that FS- and FS+ subjects bring somewhat different resources to bear on the task of syntactic analysis. In particular, they lend some indirect support to the proposal that FS- subjects exploit some representation of the utterance that is specially suited to syntactic analysis.

These results have important implications for experimental studies of language processing and research on the relation between language and the brain. Where they have been sought, syntactic effects on processing have often been hard to identify. The present results suggest that a part of the problem may be that results have been clouded by the unsystematic mixing of subjects taking systematically different approaches to comprehension. To put it another way, we might consider whether, if there is such a thing as a specific subsystem of the brain/mind that is dedicated to some aspect of language processing, this subsystem might be more accessible for study in certain definable subsets of the general population. These results also present a challenge to neuropsychology, which is to determine how the resources deployed by FS- and FS+ subjects differ and how those differences might arise. Somewhat different research methodologies seem necessary for this task.

The work reported in this paper has been supported in part by a grant from the National Institutes of Health (1 R01 NS22606-01) and a Seed Grant provided by the Office of Graduate Studies and Research at OSU. Some of the material in this paper is derived from a presentation to the Eastern States Conference on Linguistics, October 1987. The work has benefited from discussions with Tom Bever (whose own work provided the original impetus for this line of inquiry), Helen Cairns, David Michaels, Michael Studdert-Kennedy, and Michael Torello, though these colleagues bear no responsibility for any deficiencies that may be found here. I am grateful to Heidi Carman, John Dai, Maureen Harbaugh, Carol McEwen, Miles Russell, and several other graduate and undergraduate associates for their enthusiasm and diligence in the conduct of the experimental work reported here.

References

Andrews, R. J. (1977) Aspects of language lateralization correlated with familial handedness. *Neuropsychologia, 15*, 769-778.

Bever, T.G., Carrithers, C. & Townsend, D. (1987) In *Proceedings: Ninth Annual Conference of the Cognitive Science Society,* Hillsdale, NJ: L. Erlbaum Assoc. Pp 764-773.

286   Chapter Thirteen

Bever, T.G., Carrithers, C., Cowart, W. & Townsend, D. (in preparation) Right-handers with no left-handed relatives are more sensitive to syntactic structures than right-handers with left-handed relatives.

Chomsky, N. (1981) *Lectures on Government and Binding.* Amsterdam: Foris.

Cowart, W. (1987) Syntax and the accessibility of antecedents in relation to neurophysiological variation. In *Proceedings: Ninth Annual Conference of the Cognitive Science Society*, Hillsdale, NJ: L. Erlbaum Assoc. Pp 811-823.

Fodor, J.A. (1983) *The modularity of mind.* Cambridge: MIT Press.

Freedman & Forster, K.I. (1985) The psychological status of overgenerated sentences. *Cognition, 19*, 101-131.

Geschwind, N. & Galaburda, A. (1987) *Cerebral lateralization.* Cambridge, MA: MIT Press.

Hecaen, H. & Sauguet, J. (1971) Cerebral dominance in left-handed subjects. *Cortex, 7*, 19-48.

Kennedy, A. & Murray, W.S. (1984) Inspections times for words in syntactically ambiguous sentences under three presentation conditions. *Journal of Experimental Psychology: Human Perception and Performance, 10,* 833-849.

McKeever, W. F. et al (1983) Interacting sex and familial sinistrality characteristics influence both language lateralization and spatial ability in right handers. *Neuropsychologia, 21*, 661-668.

McKeever, W. F. & VanDeventer, A. D. (1977) Visual and auditory language processing asymmetries: Influences of handedness, familial sinistrality, and sex. *Cortex, 13*, 225-241.

Reinhart, T. (1983). *Anaphora and semantic interpretation.* Chicago, IL: Univ. of Chicago Press.

Riemsdijk, H. & Williams, E. (1986) *Introduction to the theory of grammar.* Cambridge, MA: MIT Press.

Taylor, H. G. & Heilman, K. M. (1982) Monaural recall and the right-ear advantage. *Brain & Language, 15*, 334-339.

14

Adult Cognition: Neuropsychological Evidence and Developmental Models

Susan Kotler-Cope, Fredda Blanchard-Fields, and Wm. Drew Gouvier

Neurologists and neuropsychologists have long been aware that cognitive functions change as a consequence of brain injury. Indeed, this assumption forms the basis of the diagnosis and treatment of brain-injured patients. Recently, cognitive psychologists have rediscovered the important role such deficits can play in elucidating aspects of normal cognitive functioning (Jacoby & Witherspoon, 1982; Schacter, 1988). Developmental theorists seeking to establish models of cognitive development have also begun to acknowledge the relevance of neuropsychological research to their theories (Labouvie-Vief, 1985). Neurologists and neuropsychologists also acknowledge that cognitive functioning changes as a consequence of aging. Recent arguments concerning the nature and the significance of these changes, however, have generated considerable controversy. A coherent and comprehensive developmental framework which accounts for age-related cognitive changes would be of great practical and theoretical benefit to neuropsychologists. To facilitate continued progress in neuropsychology, it is desirable to give consideration to the current theories and research in cognitive developmental psychology. Of particular significance for neuropsychology is the recent emphasis on developing models of adult cognition and detailing the effects of the normal aging processes on a variety of cognitive functions.

Why should aging be such an important consideration; Indeed, what is aging? Biologically-based models of aging have tended to emphasize in decrements in cognitive functioning, downplaying the possibility of enhancement or at least maintenance of cognitive abilities in older adults. However, there is a growing trend in the literature which suggests that the interactions between biological aging, biological growth in adulthood, pathology, and level of cognitive functioning are quite complex (Birren, 1970). Models which describe a decline in cognitive functioning dependent upon biological aging may no longer be entirely accurate and may therefore need to be revised. The whole concept of aging is in a process of redefinition, a process which is being pursued vigorously in developmental psychology.

Kotler-Cope, S., Blanchard-Fields, F., & Gouvier, Wm. D. (1988). Adult cognition: Neuropsychological evidence and developmental models. In J. M. Williams and C. J. Long (Eds.), *Cognitive approaches to neuropsychology*, New York: Plenum.

Many theories of cognitive development seem to imply that the final stage of cognitive development occurs at a relatively early point in life - for example, with the attainment of formal operations around the onset of adolescence, according to the Piagetian system. It is obvious from everyday experience, however, that adult cognitive processes are qualitatively different from those of adolescents. Some developmental theorists, therefore, have proposed various models of post-formal cognitive development which extend cognitive development well into adulthood (Commons, Richards, & Armon, 1984). Because clinical neuropsychologists treat many adult clients, and the number of older clients will increase over the next few decades, such models are timely. If a sixty-five year old stroke patient scores significantly lower on the Performance measures relative to the Verbal measures of the WAIS, how can one determine if this deficiency is caused by the type of brain injury sustained or due to the normal aging process? What are our expectations for aged adults? What level of functioning should we consider normal? Recent research in adult cognition is challenging traditional concepts of what constitutes normal neuropsychological functioning in the aging adult.

The purpose of this chapter is not to resolve the controversies arising from the research and theories from adult cognitive development, aging, and neuropsychology. We do not intend to present an exhaustive review of all the pertinent issues. We plan to highlight these controversies by examining the neurological and neuropsychological changes associated with aging, particularly with reference to cognitive processes and current models of adult cognitive development. It is hoped that with this approach, we can help foster the creation of a more complete, coherent picture of neuropsychological functioning, promote the development of more effective methods of assessment and treatment of neuropsychological patients, and better guide further neuropsychological research.

The Aging Brain

Several changes can be observed at the microscopic and gross levels in the aging brain. Granulovacuolar changes in the neuronal cytoplasm (Ball, 1978) and neurofibrillary tangles (Terry & Davies, 1980) are found in the brains, particularly in the hippocampal areas, of normal adults and can be observed to a greater degree in demented individuals. Senile plaques, which may contribute to the degeneration of neuronal processes in cortical tissue, increase in number with age and are found in even larger numbers in demented patients (Roth, Tomlinson, & Blessed, 1966). Cell loss is particularly noticeable in the hippocampus, neocortex, and cerebellum of elderly patients, although demented patients do not show a greater degree of overall cell loss than normals (Tomlinson & Henderson, 1976). Dendritic atrophy is one of the most obvious, widespread, and apparently inevitable effects of aging and dementia. Yet, Coleman and Buell (1983; Buell & Coleman, 1979) have found evidence for an age-related increase in dendritic growth which they interpret as representing a "compensatory response to loss of neurons" (p.5). Although the net effect of this death and growth process is unclear, it probably represents a balance of regressive and regenerative forces - a process where by adequate functioning is maintained. Finally, as the brain ages there is a considerable loss of neural tissue, particularly in the cortex (Petit, 1982). However, there is only an imperfect correlation between brain tissue loss and deterioration of function, which again implies some type of ongoing compensatory process.

Recovery of Function, Plasticity, and Aging

The notion of compensation for losses sustained at the neuronal level is most familiar in the context of recovery of function. One of the difficulties in evaluating the neurological evidence for compensation is the level of analysis, which bears directly on the issues of recovery of function, plasticity, and aging. Where is it most appropriate to search for the material correlates of cognition and behavior - at the neurochemical, neuronal, structural, regional or hemispheric level? What degree of change at a given level is necessary for the effects of that change to become manifest in behavior? Regardless of which approach one adopts to explain recovery of function - whether structural, general and reorganizational processes, physiological processes (Laurence & Stein, 1978), or behavioral strategy approaches (Johnson & Almli, 1978; Gazzaniga, 1978) - many neuropsychologists would argue that "functional deficit and structural deficit are not necessarily coextensive" (Goldstein & Shelly, 1981, p.68).

Based on this argument, functional recovery does not necessarily mean structural recovery has taken place. Improvement in function may not necessarily reflect neurological recovery but the "ingenious ability of the organism to maintain a behavioral status quo by using other mental and behavioral resources" (Gazzaniga, 1978, p.413). Laurence and Stein (1978) propose that "function" should be conceived in terms of goal attainment and its return examined using means-ends analysis. "Recovery," then, refers to the acquisition or re-institution of a "behavior or set of behaviors which allow an organism to attain a goal" provided that the organism was capable of performing them prior to neural injury (p.37). One might wonder how dendritic growth alone could compensate for the cortical cell loss observed in the adult brain. A structural explanation might be that as the size of dendritic fields grow, surviving neurons can take over the functions of neighboring neurons which have fallen victim to trauma or degeneration. But it seems likely that other factors must be involved in order to maintain behavioral and cognitive competence. For example, a person's ability to "recover" may change with age. This may depend on the changes in plasticity that occur with aging.

The plasticity of the adult brain is of critical importance to the concepts of recovery of function, compensation and adaptation and understanding adult cognitive development. The majority of research on recovery of function and neurological aging indicates that the flexibility of the brain to compensate for damage depends in part on the location, degree, and nature of injury, and the condition of the brain as a whole. For example, more "loosely coupled" areas which are non-topographically arranged, such as the association cortex, may be less vulnerable to insult, leading us to expect an easier recovery from damage than "tightly coupled" areas which are topographically arranged, such as primary motor cortex (Johnson & Almli, 1978). According to this argument, if functions become more specialized and more localized within areas of the adult brain and thus more tightly coupled, older adults may experience more difficulty in recovering from certain types of injuries. However, if in adults the "specific interconnections between neurons are highly variable and virtually unlimited" (Labouvie-Vief, 1985, p.514), and areas such as the association cortex are more extensive in the adult brain, the structural basis for plasticity may be considerable. Factors affecting the general condition of the brain, such as cardiovascular status, exposure to toxic substances, or disease, also affect the degree of plasticity at a given age.

Premorbid developmental level and age are additional factors affecting plasticity. Russell and Smith (1961) have found that the age of a person at the time of injury was the single most important factor in estimating degree of recovery from head trauma. Brain damage sustained early in life is associated with less deleterious effects than brain damage later in life. This suggests that overall, the adult brain has less plasticity than a younger brain. This generality is subject to several important qualifications.

First, localization schemas change with our conceptions of which structures a given function, particularly a cognitive function involves. In addition, the locus of a function may migrate in the natural course of development as well as because of injury (Luria, 1980). This process makes it difficult to localize cognitive functions at various stages in development and to assess adult plasticity.

Second, the ontogenetic pattern of brain tissue growth and differentiation of regions, is not homologous across time. Levels of neural maturity
within a single brain and within a given age cohort will not be equivalent
(Johnson & Almli, 1978). For example, during development, there is a continuous and fluctuating interplay of the influence of one part of the nervous
system on another. "Specific modes of function and realized circuitry are
highly influenced by experience" (Labouvie-Vief, 1985, p.514). We would
therefore expect to find great individual differences and variability at all levels of neural functioning (Whitaker, 1987).

Third, behavior is not homologous across a lifespan. Although an infant and adult may share the same neural destruction, the effect on behavior
will be different for each. For example, if a neural area has not yet become
"functionally committed to a specific behavior" at the time it sustains damage,
behavioral deficits may not be immediately apparent. As the individual matures and as that "brain region would normally become committed to the behavior in question, deficits in behavior . . . become manifest" (Johnson &
Almli, 1978, p.122). This suggest that some behaviors are more vulnerable
than others to the consequences of injury, and that this vulnerability changes
with age. Also, the importance of a given structure for a given function
changes with age and covaries with the dependence of a given behavior on the
intactness of the structure. Disruption of structures involved in the acquisition, but not the maintenance of a learned behavior may not affect the behavior
in a mature individual but may preclude its acquisition in a person who had
never learned the behavior.

Fourth, Gould (1977) has also proposed that certain aspects of the nervous system remain immature until late in human life when certain functions
become necessary. For example, the process of socialization and transmission
of cultural information takes place over an extended period of time and requires that the brain remain plastic well into adulthood. The chronological
upper limits of neurological development have not been well established but
clearly extend into the second decade (Luria, 1980).

Fifth, the behavioral capacity of the individual at the time of injury must
also be taken into consideration when evaluating plasticity. If recovery of
function refers to those behaviors used to achieve a goal, plasticity could be
conceived of in terms of the capacity to devise adaptive strategies as well as
neurological restitution. Because the behavioral repertoire of older persons is

generally greater than younger persons, this capacity for adaptation and compensation would be more powerful for adults.

In one sense, then, plasticity refers to a biologically-determined capacity to recover from traumatic brain damage. This represents the perspective most often adopted by neuropsychologists. In another sense - that used most often by cognitive developmentalists - plasticity is viewed more as an environmentally-influenced capacity for behavior which, as normal aging occurs, develops in response to a naturally-occurring, gradual deterioration of certain brain structures. How an individual deals with sudden damage depends not only on the age of that individual but a host of complex, interwoven variables which determine "plasticity." Plasticity, in turn, is a meta-factor affecting adult cognitive development. Determining the characteristics of adult cognitive processes has been the focus of a great deal of research. Examination of those findings will help delineate the neuropsychological changes which accompany aging.

Research on Adult Cognition

One of the most dominant concerns in adult cognitive research has centered around determining which cognitive functions, if any, deteriorate more than others as a consequence of aging, and, by implication, which neural structures might be involved. Generally, research on adult cognitive functions has shown that not only do individual differences in performance on cognitive measures increase with age but that a pattern of differential decline in certain cognitive abilities emerges with age. Several broad-based studies examining many different indices of cognitive abilities of elderly subjects have found "no necessary association between age and general decline in all individuals" (Benton, Eslinger, & Damasio, 1981; Rabbitt, 1983, p.15; Schaie & Labouvie-Vief, 1974). We will now examine some of the specific findings from research on adult cognition.

Sensation and Perception

Studies in perception and sensation have revealed several decrements associated with aging. The "stimulus persistence" model describes a situation in which the effects of stimulation persist longer in the aged nervous system making it refractory to subsequent stimulation. This has been demonstrated with fusion and afterimage effects using visual, auditory, and tactile stimuli (See Botwinick, 1981, for a summary). Additional research has shown that it takes longer for external physical stimuli to be transformed into nervous energy and processed by elderly people. For example, Walsh (1982) demonstrated that older adults are slower than young adults in processing visual information at all stages of the process. Griew and Davies (1962) found that older subjects performed comparably to younger subjects on a simple auditory vigilance task, but they exhibited increasing decrements in auditory vigilance performance as increasingly complex information processing and motor output demands were required of them. The authors attributed this to an increased load on short-term memory, increased levels of sensory stimulation, and the interaction of the two. The integration of sensory and perceptual information is apparently slower and more difficult for older people.

Memory, Learning, and Problem-solving

Similar decrements can be observed in the performance of older subjects on memory, learning, and problem-solving tasks. Craik and Byrd (1982) attribute memory difficulties in the elderly to a decrease in the attentional resources available caused by vascular or structural changes in the aging brain and the overall decline in somatic energy level. The reduction in attentional resources leads to a decrease in the "depth of processing operations at both encoding and retrieval" (p.208). Consequently, older people encode material based on more general and salient features (Rabinowitz & Ackerman, 1982, p.152). Reduced depth of processing produces encodings that contain less elaborated, associative, inferential, context-specific, and unique information about an event. Thus, older people appear to experience difficulty integrating novel relations with old information and retrieving newly-learned information. Deficits can also be observed in the formation of concepts and the organization of information for long-term memory storage. Mack and Carlson (1978) found that elderly subjects experienced difficulty attaining the concepts on the Halstead Category Test because they were unable to simultaneously attend to several aspects of the stimuli and to alternate between taking in information for retention and responding. Arenberg (1965) has also shown that the performance of elderly people on a verbal learning task is impaired if information is presented rapidly and if the time to respond is limited. Older people do not or can not spontaneously make use of memory formation strategies such as elaboration, rehearsal, or mnemonic aids, as effectively as younger adults (Botwinick, 1981; Jolles & Hijman, 1983). Winocur (1982) demonstrated that institutionalized elderly people exhibited an exaggerated vulnerability to interference from "extraneous" information. They failed to derive enough information from task-inherent cues and required more "discrimination information . . . to dissociate conflicting experiences and suppress competing responses" (p.176). The elderly subjects tended to search beyond the context of the task for additional information that "could be used to compensate for their deficiency" (p.177), although this strategy proved effective only when extraneous cues were sufficiently salient. Since the use of contextual cues to facilitate learning and memory is governed by the hippocampus (Loftus, 1980), impaired performance on high interference tasks implies a loss of hippocampal function, perhaps accelerated or exacerbated by the less stimulating institutional environment.

Elderly people exhibit deficits in problem-solving behavior as well. Old people are slower to recognize and learn regularities in the environment which could optimize their search for solutions to problems (Rabbitt, 1982). They select information which is redundant, their information-seeking strategies seem to be random (Denney & Denney, 1974), and they are less able to discern relevant from irrelevant information (Arenberg, 1965). They often fail to consider alternative strategies, often experience difficulty in switching strategies fast enough to meet task demands, and lose track of the steps they have already performed in a search sequence (Rabbitt, 1982). These difficulties indicate a primary deficit in the planning, control, and evaluation of behavior. The frontal cortex which assists in integrating environmental information with memory, making plans, and evaluating outcomes (Luria, 1973), may therefore be implication in this malfunction.

Thus, there seem to be specific cognitive and neuropsychological deficits associated with normal aging. These deficits are characterized mainly by difficulties in processing and integrating information, particularly if the stimuli are novel, ambiguous, complex, manifold, presented rapidly or require the simultaneous use of a variety of sensory modalities. These changes might be associated with compromised functioning of certain brain structures. In interpreting these findings, however, there are several considerations that need to be made. These issues are crucial in evaluating the research on adult cognitive development.

Considerations for Interpretation

One consideration involves the ability to locate neural correlates of cognitive functions. If levels of competence at different skills are uncorrelated, does this necessarily imply that they are carried out by different mechanisms or different structures? Perhaps not. The mechanisms or structures may simply be more adept at one task than another. For example, the same skeletal and neural mechanisms move the bodies of a gymnast and a Sumo wrestler. While the gymnast might wrestle and the wrestler might swing, their bodies are better adapted for one task than the other. Similarly, if skill level and mechanisms or structures are correlated, does this imply that they depend on the same neurological system (Rabbitt, 1983)? Obviously this need not be the case either.

Another consideration centers on which type of model of aging is most appropriate in describing trends in aging. One interpretation of the findings provides little support for the universal application of the "continuous decline" model where cognitive abilities peak when young, then undergo a continuously accelerating decline. Instead, it would appear to support the "terminal drop" model, where cognitive abilities rise to a plateau early in life and stay at that optimal level with little or no change until there is a sudden decline which accompanies a physiological catastrophe in old age. The continuous decline model seems to represent the group data of a specific cohort and may be an inappropriate model, given the increases in interindividual variability with age. Improvements in the health status of more recent cohorts may decrease the incidence of chronic illness which had previously contributed to the impression of a continuous decline (Birren, 1970).

If individual differences in performance increase dramatically with age, such that a minority of elderly perform at a highly efficient level while the majority perform with some decrement, it would seem more appropriate to analyze individuals' performances on certain tasks, rather than examine group means based on a limited number of subjects (Rabbitt, 1982; Arenberg, 1982). There are also methodological problems in the aging research which have important theoretical implications. One major difficulty involves the type of study used to reveal differences among groups. Longitudinal studies minimize age trends because of subject attrition, and confound "pure" age changes with the effect of intervening environmental influences (Botwinick, 1981). Cross-sectional studies exaggerate age trends because they confound maturational change with the different cultural experiences of young and old cohorts. The resulting age performance functions "can rarely be taken as indicators of ontogenetic patterns" (Schaie & Labouvie-Vief, 1974, p.35). This is especially crucial in interpreting the apparent general decrement in intellectual functioning demonstrated in many studies of adult cognition in which cultural-historical ("generational") rather than ontogenetic factors may be mainly responsible for same-age different-cohort differences. For example, cohorts of various ages may differ greatly in their educational backgrounds. The deficits in intelligence demonstrated by elderly cohorts examined today may not be found in same-age cohorts examined 20 years from now because they will have been better educated.

Much of the research on adult cognition may therefore be criticized on theoretical and methodological grounds. Further complicating the situation is the lack of an adequate framework which can integrate the findings and provide a much-needed context for their interpretation. Many researchers have relied on the construct of intelligence to fill this role. The wholesale and often uncritical adoption of this frame of reference is, as we will show, not without problems.

Adult Intelligence

Cattell and Horn's theory of fluid and crystallized intelligences has been a dominant influence in adult and elderly cognition research. This model seems to provide the most comprehensive structure for describing adult intelligence and, until recently, has been accepted almost without question. Fluid intelligence (Gf) is predominantly biologically-based, dependent on neurophysiological structures and status, and involves mainly sensory and perceptual processes. Its development is determined largely by ontogenetic factors. Fluid abilities are dedicated to performance in novel contexts and acquisition and use of new information. Crystallized intelligence (Gc) is not biologically-based, but is shaped by formal education and social-cultural experiences. Its development is influenced by generational factors. Crystallized intelligence operates in familiar contexts and pertains to the manipulation of familiar or overlearned materials. Fluid intelligence developmentally precedes crystallized intelligence. These types of intelligence pertain to a wide variety of cognitive behaviors such as memory, learning, problem-solving, and attention. The model also accounts for biological and environmental influences on intelligence which has made it particularly appealing for neuropsychology. Employing a multitude of measures designed to identify components of these hypothetical constructs of intelligence, researchers have found that fluid intelligence (Gf) decreases with age while crystallized intelligence (Gc) increases with age (Horn, 1982). For example, Horn (1982) suggests that "losses in capacities for maintaining spontaneous alertness, focused intensive concentration, awareness of possible organization for otherwise unorganized information are largely responsible for aging decline of these features of short-term memory and performance speediness that are involved in the aging decline of fluid intelligence during the middle years of adulthood" (p.274). These findings have been corroborated by the research on perception and cognition in aging adults presented earlier in this chapter.

If the deficits in adult cognitive functioning seem to be more representative of fluid than crystallized abilities, why do fluid abilities decline and crystallized abilities remain relatively preserved as aging takes place? To answer this, we might speculate on the localization of Gf and Gc.

The Localization of Intelligence

One approach attempts to localize the greater proportion of the deficits into one hemisphere. There is evidence to suggest that right hemisphere functions deteriorate more with age than left hemisphere functions (Klisz, 1978; Goldstein & Shelly, 1981; Stern & Baldinger, 1983). Although age-related neuroanatomical changes are not localized to the right hemisphere, it may be that this hemisphere is more vulnerable to damage or that damage to other critical structures affects right hemisphere functioning. If abilities are less specifically localized in the right hemisphere (Semmes, Weinstein, Ghent, & Teuber, 1960), or if the neural organization of the left hemisphere is based on processing within regions and the right hemisphere involves transfer of information across regions (Gur, Packer, Hungerbuhler, Reivich, Obrist, Amarnek, & Sackheim, 1980) we might expect the right hemisphere to suffer disorganization more easily than the left hemisphere. It is a matter of some controversy how the arguments presented earlier regarding tightly and loosely organized areas may be applied in discussing the effects of aging or damage on the hemispheres. In any case, if right hemisphere tasks are considered measures of fluid abilities, then there is further support for a relative decline of Gf.

Horn (1982), however, has noted that damage to either hemisphere produces "irreversible" decrements in fluid intelligence but reversible decrements in crystallized intelligence. Thus, fluid and crystallized intelligence should not be localized to one hemisphere or the other. If fluid abilities are biologically-based, then where in the brain do they reside? Horn has suggested that limbic system processes are "the central features of fluid intelligence" (p.272). The vascular anatomy of the hippocampus is particularly vulnerable to injury from changes in blood pressure (Hachinski, 1980). Therefore, the cumulative effects of alterations in blood pressure incurred throughout a lifetime as part of normal development should be eventually detectable initially in measures of fluid intelligence - specifically, decrements in encoding organization ability, concentration, and spontaneous alertness.

Improvements in crystallized intelligence, according to Horn (1982), "probably reflect individuals' restructurings of their knowledge systems to make the knowledge increasingly more cohesive, correct, and accessible" (p.266). Because development of Gc is shaped by educational and cultural experiences, older people would be expected to be higher in Gc than younger people. Adults have not only had more time to overlearn the information they have acquired, but the have also amassed a considerably larger body of information which facilitates the access to even more information. If the white fibers of the brain represent the "location" of the essential organization of knowledge systems (Dimond, 1980), Gc could be represented diffusely throughout the cortex. This suggests that Gc abilities are "overdetermined" in that they have "neurological supports . . . in excess of what is minimally required" (p.273) and can compensate when Gf, apparently lacking in this overdetermination, is "knocked out." Diffuse organization has been hypothesized to be advantageous for the relative preservation of function. The rise in Gc could then be due to the relative resistance of information to loss once it has been stored and the "complex interlaced firing patterns" would "promote more of the same" with "patterns for neural firing . . . built from already established patterns" (Horn, 1982, p.274). It is difficult to reconcile this apparent entrenchment of information with the simultaneous process of restructuring referred to above. One might wonder how older people can learn from educational and cultural experiences if they can not attend, concentrate, or remember very well. The mechanisms involved in the apparent decline of fluid intelligence, if indeed they are accurate, are better articulated than those responsible for the improvement in crystallized intelligence.

Intelligence and Normal vs. "Abnormal" Aging

Normal cognitive aging from this perspective is characterized by an increase in crystallized intelligence over the vital years of adulthood (from early 20s to mid-50s and early 60s) and a simultaneous decrease in fluid intelligence. This pattern of cognitive abilities associated with deteriorating efficiency in the functioning of limbic and frontal neocortical structures. The decrease in fluency and speed of information processing observed in elderly subjects, then, represents the first manifestation of the normal aging process. A decline in verbal functioning, a crystallized ability, represents the first stage of "abnormal" aging due to dementia or pathology (Jarvik & Falek, 1963; Rosen, 1980). In the context of Luria's three types of frontal syndromes which are characterized by different frontal localizations (Luria, 1980), the "temporal sequence of development of cognitive deficits in senile dementia . . . suggests that there is a gradual increase in the number of neocortical areas involved, the tertiary areas degenerating before the secondary areas and the primary areas staying relatively intact until very late in the disease process (Jolles & Hijman, 1983, p.247). If we accept the argument that senile dementia can be characterized as "exaggerated aging" (Jolles & Hijman, 1983, p.244), then we would expect the normal aging process to follow the same course of degeneration described above, only more slowly. The order of this regression is the opposite of that in ontogenetic development. This suggests that the processes underlying dementia, and by analogy, aging, reverse those of ontogenesis.

Criticisms of the Model

It would appear from the perspective of this decline model, that deterioration in cognitive functioning is inevitable, inextricably bound to an ontogenetic process which paradoxically results in an apparent reversal or regression of cognitive development. However, extreme caution must be exercised in interpreting the findings from research plagued by the theoretical and methodological problems referred to earlier. For example, the effect of structural changes in the brain on cognitive functioning, whether due to injury or aging, is not always predictable. The multiple factors affecting plasticity, such as the individual variability which increases with age, limit generalizations about observed changes in adult cognition.

In addition, it seems clear that there are differences in performance between younger and older subjects on a variety of cognitive tasks. Apparent decrements in the performance of older subjects may be attributable to several factors which are not biological in origin. One criticism is that cognitive function has been conceptualized using "youth-centered" definitions, standards of evaluation, and assessment instruments which may not be appropriate for use with older people (Labouvie-Vief, 1985, p.505). This controversy is particularly pertinent to intelligence. Some researchers question relying on the use of age-adjusted IQ scores to compare the performances of old and young subjects, for these scores are adjusted based on the prejudicial assumption of intellectual decline with age (Rabbitt, 1983). Others question the validity of inferences about adult cognitive abilities based on test scores from instruments containing items unrepresentative of situations important to older people. Tasks which favor the qualities of youth, such as speed of response, may not be relevant or appropriate measures of adult intelligence. The adaptive significance of various cognitive abilities changes for different age levels. Intelligence defined by "adult" criteria may be qualitatively different from intelligence defined by "youth" criteria. Just as a clinical neuropsychologist makes decisions about elderly individuals based on the clinical meaningfulness of a given finding, the significance of "decrements" revealed in adult cognitive functioning merits careful consideration as well. Thus, although Horn's model appears comprehensive and integrative, it does not present the complete picture. The view of aging as a pathological process which reverses development is too rigid, narrow, and partial to be of much practical value in clinical neuropsychology. Furthermore, there is a growing body of evidence in support of the idea that intellectual growth continues and that some aspects of cognitive functioning can improve with age.

Toward a New Model of Adult Cognitive Functioning

A study performed by Labouvie-Vief and Gonda (1976) demonstrated that elderly people can not only benefit from specific training in problem-solving but "can develop skills in solving unfamiliar problems without intervention when given opportunity to become experienced with the tasks" (Arenberg, 1982, p.233). Both self-developed and instructed strategies were equally effective in helping the subjects solve problems and were equally likely to be retrained over time. If the problem-solving performance of the elderly can be improved by such interventions, can the age-related changes in such performance still be attributed largely to biological factors? In an earlier study, Arenberg (1968) found that older subjects presented with a concept formation task using concrete and meaningful items, such as foods, performed better than those presented with abstract stimuli, such as colors and shapes. This does not appear to be a simple matter of realistic material enhancing logical performance (Wason, 1983), but may represent qualitative changes in adult cognition.

Baltes and Willis (1982) investigated the modifiability of intellectual functioning in later adulthood and old age. They emphasized the negative effect of a "disadvantaged" living environment on the intellectual functioning of elderly people and proposed that the large discrepancy between actual performance (active reserve) and potential performance (latent reserve) levels could be attributed to the absence of "performance enhancing conditions" (p.359). They contended that cultural and ecological conditions tend to support optimization of intellectual performance in childhood and young adulthood, but not in later adulthood. Arguing that fluid abilities, because they involve the processing of new information, would be more easily influenced by interventions, the authors provided elderly subjects with training on three tasks representing fluid intelligence factors. They found evidence for substantial "intellectual plasticity" at the individual level and suggested that "intellectual decline during the sixties and seventies (if it occurs) can be slowed down, halted, or even reversed if proper education interventions are designed and implemented" and as long as no other countervailing forces, such as illness, intervene (p.380). This study contradicts Horn's model in which fluid abilities must suffer an "irreversible" decline with age.

Schaie and Labouvie-Vief (1974) found that certain cohorts did not show decrements in fluid intelligence measures when their scores were projected 7 years in the future. This implies that "biologically-based slowing might, at least in part, be linked to specific cultural historical contingencies" (p.318) and that the "rate and direction of intellectual ontogeny are continually monitored by more pervasive changes in environmental systems" (p.319). It is possible that the pattern of developmental decline observed in most of the studies on adult cognition may not be observed in future research on elderly populations as the quality of life for these cohorts changes - for example, if social institutions become more supportive of a competent, active elderly population. Perhaps overall health status, particularly cardiovascular fitness, will become the best predictor of both recovery from neurological damage and an extended lifespan with limited neurological pathology or compromises in neuropsychological functioning. The detrimental effects of decreased circulatory efficiency on structures essential particularly for the maintenance of fluid abilities has been well-documented.

What begins to emerge is not an image of universal and wholesale deterioration dictated by biological processes but a picture of differential decline and simultaneous adaptation determined by the interaction of ontogenetic and generational factors. In recalling the earlier discussion of plasticity, we remember that the best way to conceive of plasticity is not as a biologically-determined process but as a capacity for behavioral compensation. There is evidence to support the idea that as adults age, they develop more extensive adaptive cognitive and behavioral strategies to compensate for the varying degrees of ongoing neurological deterioration.

As an example, the practice of two eye surgeons known to one of the authors comes to mind. The younger surgeon, who trained in part with the elder, used a continuous running suture to attach a transplanted cornea. When finished, the ends of the sutures were tied together and clipped. The older surgeon, no longer possessing the intensity of concentration and steadiness of hand to match the technical precision of the younger surgeon, used a different strategy. He would initially re-attach the cornea using eight single stitches, which were individually placed, tied, and clipped, then reinforced with a series of pairs of diagonal stitches. While this approach required more frequent tying and clipping, it could also be completed segmentally, allowing him frequent opportunities to put down his operating instruments and rest his hands and eyes.

Although ability to compensate in terms of cognitive functioning may decrease with age, the capacity for behavioral compensation increases. Specifically, it appears that as individuals age, personality and social factors become more important than intellectual factors in maintaining environmental adaptability and that these factors come to dominate adult cognitive functioning.

Adult cognition is therefore qualitatively different from youthful cognition in many ways. Labouvie-Vief (1984) has argued that the attainment of formal logical thought is not the "crowning achievement of human ontogeny" and that Piaget's model "fail[s] to provide a comprehensive model of mature adult adaptation" (p.160). She has identified additional levels beyond the formal operations stage which are pertinent to adult life - the intersystemic level where there is a "movement away from logical absolutism to logical relativism" and the autonomous level, "characterized by a shift in focus from the logic of formal systems to the logic of self-regulating systems" (p.176). During this latter stage, "truths" are defined in terms of pragmatic, social, cultural, moral, and personal values. The maturing adult uses these truths to develop moral integrity, constructive generativity, social responsibility, and individual autonomy. The qualitative changes observed in adult cognition reflect this process and therefore, may not represent a mere compensatory response to biological decline.

Because older adults are responsible for the maintenance and stability of the social system, they tend to be pragmatic, cautious, and conservative in their problem-solving behavior (Labouvie-Vief, 1985). They isolate dimensions which decrease the ambiguity of information presented in a situation and work with ambiguous information creatively (Labouvie-Vief & Blanchard-Fields, 1982). Older adults question the premises of arguments, going beyond the information given in a task, letting their "real-world" knowledge "interfere" as they solve problems. Older adults tend to evaluate problems in terms of personal goals and other relativistic criteria rather than absolute correctness. Their modes of thinking integrate personal experience and knowledge, affective components, information from multiple and conflicting sources, and social considerations. Use of more "socially-centered reasoning allows older adults to make use of the complex social matrix to optimize their decisions" (Labouvie-Vief, 1985, p.523) about delegation of responsibility, intercoordination of resources, and the investment value of an undertaking. Many of these qualities have been judged as deficits in performance on cognitive tasks. All of these qualities are characteristic of adult cognition and argue in favor of a model of adaptive intelligence. Indeed, "intellectual competence will need to be redefined within the criteria of successful cultural adaptation: those of responsibility and generativity" (Labouvie-Vief, 1985, p.526).

How can we reconcile these assertions with the findings from neurological, cognitive, and neuropsychological research presented here? It should be clear that the Piagetian model of cognitive development is limited and inadequate for explaining changes in adult cognition. It should also be evident that the model of decline proposed by Horn is at best incomplete. We have pointed out the gaps in the model and have proposed how they might be filled. We see adult cognitive development not as a series of eventual and complete compromises in overall functioning, but as a continuous series of constructive compensations, where what is no longer functional or adaptive is de-emphasized, replaced, or transcended, and what provides maintenance of competence and growth is retained and nurtured by the individual, and it is hoped by society as well.

References

Arenberg, D. (1965). Anticipation interval and age differences in verbal learning. *Journal of Abnormal Psychology, 10,* 419-425.

Arenberg, D. (1968). Concept problem solving in young and old adults. *Journal of Gerontology, 23,* 279-282.

Arenberg, D. (1982). Changes with age in problem-solving. In F. I. M. Craik & S. Trehub (Eds.), *Aging and cognitive processes* (pp. 221-235). New York: Plenum Press.

Ball, M. J. (1978). Topographic distribution of neurofibrillary tangles and granulovacuolar degeneration in hippocampal cortex of aging and demented patients. A quantitative study. *Acta Neurologica, 42,* 73-80.

Baltes, P. B., & Willis, S. L. (1982). Plasticity and enhancement of intellectual functioning in old age: Penn State's Adult Development and Enrichment Project (ADEPT). In F. I. M. Craik & S. Trehub (Eds.), *Aging and cognitive processes* (pp. 353-389). New York: Plenum Press.

Benton, A. L., Eslinger, P. J., Damasio, A. R. (1981). Normative observations on neuropsychological test performances in old age. *Journal of Clinical Neuropsychology, 3,* 33-42.

Birren, J. E. (1970). Toward an experimental psychology of aging. *American Psychologist, 25,* 124-135.

Botwinick, J. (1981). Neuropsychology of Aging. In S. B. Filskov & T. J. Boll (Eds.), *Handbook of clinical neuropsychology: (I)* (pp. 135-171). New York: John Wiley & Sons.

Buell, S. J., & Coleman, P. D. (1979). Dendritic growth in the aged human brain and failure of growth in senile dementia. *Science, 206,* 854-856.

Coleman, P. D., & Buell, S. J. (1983). Dendritic growth in the aging brain? In W. H. Gispen & J. Traber (Eds.), *Aging of the brain*. Proceedings of the First International Tropon Symposium on Brain Aging held in Cologne, Federal Republic of Germany on November 15-16, 1982 (pp. 3-8). New York: Elsevier Science Publishers.

Commons, M. L., Richards, F. A., & Armon, C. (Eds.). (1984). *Beyond formal operations: Late adolescent and adult cognitive development*. New York: Praeger Publishers.

Craik, F. I. M., & Byrd, M. (1982). Aging and cognitive deficits: The role of attentional resources. In F. I. M. Craik & S. Trehub (Eds.), *Aging and cognitive processes* (pp. 191-211). New York: Plenum Press.

Denney, W. W., & Denney, D. R. (1974). Modeling effects in questioning strategies of the elderly. *Developmental Psychology, 10*, 458.

Dimond, S. (1980). Memory. In S. J. Dimond, *Neuropsychology* (pp. 257-286). Boston: Butterworth.

Gazzaniga, M. (1978). Is seeing believing: Notes on clinical recovery. In S. Finger (Ed.), *Recovery from brain damage: Research and theory* (pp. 410-414). New York: Plenum Press.

Goldstein, G., & Shelly, C. (1981). Does the right hemisphere age more rapidly than the left? *Journal of Clinical Neuropsychology, 3*, 65-78.

Gould, S. J. (1977). *Ontogeny and phylogeny*. Cambridge, MA: Harvard University Press.

Griew, S., & Davies, D. R. (1962). The effect of aging on auditory vigilance performance. *Journal of Gerontology, 17*, 88-90.

Gur, R., Packer, I., Hungerbuhler, J., Reivich, M., Obrist, W., Amarnek, K. W., & Sackheim, H. (1980). Differences in the distribution of grey and white matter in human cerebral hemispheres. *Science, 207*, 1226-1228.

Hachinski, V. (1980). Relevance of cerebrovascular changes to mental function. *Mechanisms of Aging and Development, 10*, 1-11.

Horn, J. L. (1982). The theory of fluid and crystallized intelligence in relation to concepts of cognitive psychology and aging in adulthood. In F. I. M. Craik & S. Trehub (Eds.), *Aging and cognitive processes* (pp. 237-278). New York: Plenum Press.

Jacoby, L. L., & Witherspoon, D. (1982). Remembering without awareness. *Canadian Journal of Psychology, 36(2)*, 300-324.

Jarvik, L. F., & Falek, A. (1963). Intellectual stability and survival in the aged. *Journal of Gerontology, 18*, 173-176.

Johnson, D., & Almli, C. R. (1978). Age, brain damage, and performance. In S. Finger (Ed.), *Recovery from brain damage: Research and theory* (pp. 115-134). New York: Plenum Press.

Jolles, J., & Hijman, R. (1983). The neuropsychology of aging and dementia. In W. H. Gispen & J. Traber (Eds.), *Aging of the brain: Proceedings of the First International Tropon Symposium on Brain Aging* held in Cologne, Federal Republic of Germany on November 16-18, 1982 (pp. 227-250). New York: Elsevier Science Publishers.

Klisz, D. (1978). Neuropsychological evaluation in older persons. In M. Storandt, I. C. Siegler, & M. Elias (Eds.), *The clinical psychology of aging* (pp. 71-95). New York: Plenum Press.

Labouvie-Vief, G. (1984). Logic and self-regulation from youth to maturity: A model. In M. L. Commons, F. A. Richards, & C. Armon (Eds.), *Beyond formal operations: Late adolescent and adult cognitive development* (pp. 158-179). New York: Praeger.

Labouvie-Vief, G. (1985). Intelligence and cognition. In J. E. Birren & K. W. Schaie (Eds.), *Handbook of the psychology of aging* (pp.500-530). New York: Van Nostrand Reinhold Company, Inc.

Labouvie-Vief, G., & Blanchard-Fields, F. (1982). Cognitive aging and psychological growth. *Ageing and society, 2*, 183-209.

Labouvie-Vief, G., & Gonda, J. N. (1976). Cognitive strategy training and intellectual performance in the elderly. *Journal of Gerontology, 31*, 327-332.

Laurence, S., & Stein, D. G. (1978). Recovery after brain damage and the concept of localization of function. In S. Finger (Ed.), *Recovery from brain damage: Research and theory* (pp. 369-407). New York: Plenum Press.

Loftus, E. (1980). *Memory*. Reading, MA: Addison-Wesley.

Luria, A. R. (1973). *The working brain*. Harmondsworth, U.K.: Penguin Books.

Luria, A. R. (1980). *Higher cortical functions in man*. (2nd ed.). New York: Basic Books.

Mack, J. L., & Carlson, N. J. (1978). Conceptual deficits and aging: The Category Test. *Perceptual and Motor Skills, 46*, 123-128.

Petit, T.L. (1982). Neuroanatomical and clinical neuropsychological changes in aging and senile dementia. In F. I. M. Craik & S. Trehub (Eds.), *Aging and cognitive processes* (pp. 1-31). New York: Plenum Press.

Rabbitt, P. M. A. (1982). How do old people know what to do next? In F. I. M. Craik & S. Trehub (Eds.), *Aging and cognitive processes* (pp. 79-98). New York: Plenum Press.

Rabbitt, P. M. A. (1983). How can we tell whether human performance is related to chronological age? In D. Samuel, S. Algeri, S. Gershon, V. E. Grimm, & G. Toffano (Eds.). *Aging of the brain* (pp. 9-18). New York: Raven Press.

Rabinowitz, J. C., & Ackerman, B. P. (1982). General encoding of episodic events by elderly adults. In F. I. M. Craik & S. Trehub (Eds.), *Aging and cognitive processes* (pp. 145-154). New York: Plenum Press.

Rosen, W. (1980). Verbal fluency in aging and dementia. *Journal of Clinical Neuropsychology, 2*, 135-146.

Roth, M., Tomlinson, B. E., & Blessed, G. (1966). Correlation between score for dementia and counts in senile plaques in cerebral gray matter of elderly subjects. *Nature, 209*, 106.

Russell, W. R., & Smith, A. (1961). Post-traumatic amnesia in closed head injury. *Archives of Neurology, 5*, 16-29.

Schacter, D. (1988). Toward a cognitive neuropsychology of complex learning. In J. M. Williams and C. J. Long (Eds.), *Cognitive approaches to neuropsychology*, New York: Plenum.

Schaie, K. W., & Labouvie-Vief, G. (1974). Generational versus ontogenetic components of change in adult cognitive behavior: A fourteen-year cross-sequential study. *Developmental Psychology, 10*, 305-320.

Semmes, J., Weinstein, S., Ghent, L., & Teuber, H-L. (1960). *Somatosensory changes after penetrating brain wounds in man*. Cambridge, MA: Harvard University Press.

Stern, J. A., & Baldinger, A. C. (1983). Hemispheric difference in preferred modes of information processing and the aging process. *International Journal of Neuroscience,*

18, 97-106.

Terry, R. D., & Davies, P. (1980). Dementia of the Alzheimer type. *Annual Review of Neuroscience, 3*, 77-95.

Tomlinson, B. E., & Henderson, G. (1976). Some quantitative cerebral findings in normal and demented old people. In R. D. Terry & S. Gershon (Eds.), Neurobiology of aging (pp. 183-204). New York: Raven Press.

Walsh, D. A. (1982). The development of visual information processes in adulthood and old age. In F. I. M. Craik & S. Trehub (Eds.), Aging and cognitive processes (pp. 99-125). New York: Plenum Press.

Wason, P. C. (1983). Realism and rationality in the selection task. In J. St B. T. Evans (Ed.), *Thinking and reasoning - Psychological approaches* (pp. 44-75). London: Routledge & Kegan Paul.

Whitaker, H. A. (1987). Changing concepts of the neurological bases of language. Paper presented at the Fifth Mid-South Conference on Human Neuropsychology in Memphis, Tennessee, May 15-16, 1987.

Winocur, G. (1982). Learning and memory deficits in institutionalized old people: An analysis of interference effects. In F. I. M. Craik & S. Trehub (Eds.), *Aging and cognitive processes* (pp. 155-181). New York: Plenum Press.

15

Preserved Cognitive Functions in Dementia

William W. Beatty

Recent neuropsychological studies have established that there are marked differences in the pattern of loss and preservation of cognitive function among patients with dementias of differing etiologies. These distinctions are most clear early in the course of the patients' illnesses, when the patients would be considered mildly or moderately demented on the basis of their scores on standard mental status examinations. As the dementias progress, their distinctive cognitive features tend to blur, yet some patients who have suffered severe losses in most areas of mental functioning retain the capacity to perform some skilled activities remarkably well. The major purpose of this chapter is to describe several of these cases, attempting to identify common features of these preserved cognitive capacities. To provide a background from which to consider the severely demented patients' performances, I will first review recent findings concerning cognitive functions that are relatively well preserved in less seriously demented patients.

Preservation in Mildly and Moderately Demented Patients

Several workers (Albert, Feldman & Willis, 1974; Cummings & Benson, 1984; Huber & Paulson, 1985; McHugh & Folstein, 1975) have argued for a distinction between cortical (e.g., Alzheimer's Disease (AD), Pick's Disease) and subcortical (e.g., Huntington's Disease (HD), Parkinson's Disease (PD) dementias. Patients with subcortical dementias are said to have marked difficulties on tasks that require rapid processing of information, but generally do not exhibit the aphasic and apraxic disturbances commonly observed in patients with cortical dementias. Amnestic disturbances accompany all forms of dementia, but the memory deficits in subcortical and cortical dementias are thought to involve different cognitive processes. Retrieval failure appears to be responsible for much of the memory difficulties of patients with subcortical dementias while encoding and storage failures are prominent sources of amnesia in patients with cortical dementias. Although the validity of the cortical - subcortical distinction has been questioned (Mayeaux, Stern, Rosen, & Benson, 1983) the results of a number of recent investigations support the utility of this concept.

Beatty, W. W. (1988). Preserved cognitive functions in dementia. In J. M. Williams & C. J. Long (Eds.), *Cognitive approaches to neuropsychology*, New York: Plenum.

Tests of confrontation naming such as the Boston Naming Test (Kaplan, Goodglass & Weintraub, 1983) reveal a clear distinction between the cortical and subcortical dementias. Early in the course of their disease most patients with subcortical dementia perform almost normally, but most patients with cortical dementia are impaired (Bayless & Tomoeda, 1983; Butters, Sax, Montgomery, & Tarlow, 1978; El-Awar, Becker, Hammond, Nebes, & Boller, 1987). As their disease progresses, the cortically demented patients' anomia worsens and comprehension deficits appear, but the ability to repeat remains fairly well preserved until the late stage of the disease (Cummings, Benson, Hill & Read 1985). In the later stages of subcortical dementia, speech becomes dysarthric and naming deficits develop, but the degree of anomia remains mild compared to that observed in cortically demented patients (Butters et al., 1978).

Memory disturbances are, of course, ubiquitous in dementia, but recent studies suggest that the pattern of memory failure in cortical and subcortical dementia differs, even when the patient groups are equated in terms of their overall level of cognitive functioning, as indexed by their performance on standard mental status examinations. Further, the performance of demented patients on certain memory tasks can be distinguished from that of amnesic patients even when no differences exist on standard clinical measures such as the Wechsler Memory Scale. Based on direct comparisons of HD and AD patients the following differences emerged: 1) HD patients, but not AD patients, showed improved recall of pictorial material when provided with verbal mediators (Butters, Albert, Sax, Miliotis & Sterste, 1983). 2) HD patients were superior to AD patients on verbal recognition even when their impairments on verbal recall are equally severe (Butters, Wolfe, Martone, Granholm, & Cermak, 1985). 3) AD patients were highly susceptible to proactive interference while HD patients were not. This difference was observed on short-term memory tests (Beatty, Butters, & Janowsky, 1986), on the recall of prose passages (Butters, Granholm, Salmon, Grant & Wolfe, 1987) and on verbal fluency tasks, which require retrieval of information from semantic memory (Butters et al., 1987). On all of these tasks, the AD patients commit a much higher proportion of perseverative errors than do HD patients, whose performance on this measure usually does not differ from that of controls. In this respect the performance of AD patients resembles that of amnesic patients with alcoholic Korsakoff's syndrome (AK). Although HD patients usually make relatively few perseverative errors on fluency tests, their output is markedly depressed. In fact, HD patients usually produce fewer responses, both correct and incorrect, than do AD patients of comparable overall mental status (Butters et al., 1987).

Patients with cortical and subcortical dementias also differed in their performance on tests of remote memory (RM) such as the Famous Faces and Public Events Questionnaire (Albert, Butters & Levin, 1979). Both HD and PD patients exhibited deficits which were equally severe for information from the recent and more distant past (Albert, Butters, & Brandt, 1981a; 1981b; Freedman, Rivoira, Butters, Sax, & Feldman, 1984; Huber, Shuttleworth & Paulson, 1986). That is, the temporal gradient of retrograde amnesia (RA) in these patients was "flat". The RM deficits of patients with AD on tests such as the Albert et al. (1979) battery were quite severe (Wilson, Kaszniak, & Fox, 1981), affecting memories for the distant as well as the more recent past. The overall severity of the RM deficit can easily mask the slight temporal gradient of RA which was apparent in the performance of AD patients. When special precautions were taken to avoid floor effects, it is clear that AD patients re-called relatively more information from the distant past (i.e., the 40s and 50s) than from the more recent past (i.e., the 60s, 70s and 80s). (Beatty, Salmon, Butters, Heindel, & Granholm, in press). This temporally graded pattern of RA is also seen in the remote memory performance of AK patients (e.g., Albert et al., 1979).

Procedural learning refers to a heterogeneous group of tasks that am-nesic patients perform at near normal levels. Examples include motor skills, such as the pursuit motor task, perceptual skills, such as identifying frag-mented line drawings and learning to read mirror-reversed or inverted text, and classically conditioned responses (e.g., Cohen & Squire, 1980; Milner, Corkin, & Teuber, 1968). Amnesics also evidenced the ability to unintention-ally recall words that they can neither recall nor recognize intentionally (e.g., Graf, Squire, & Mandler, 1984; Jacoby & Witherspoon, 1982). Examples of this phenomenon include various forms of priming in which prior exposure to verbal stimuli that cannot be overtly remembered influences subsequent be-havior in a way that indicates that some trace of the experience must have been recorded. Squire (1986) has suggested that all forms of procedural learning demand acquiring general rules as opposed to specific facts, but a clear defini-tion that distinguishes rule from fact-based tasks has remained elusive. At present, it appears that amnesics perform normally when learning is measured implicitly, but not when explicit recall or recognition is required. However, the processes that distinguish implicit from explicit memory are presently unclear.

Recent studies of mildly and moderately demented HD and AD patients revealed marked differences in the pattern of preservation and loss on various measures of procedural learning. Patients with HD were impaired in pursuit rotor learning (Heindel, Butters & Salmon, in press) and in learning to read mirror-reversed text (Martone, Butters, Payne, Becker & Sax, 1984), but they exhibited normal performance on a word stem-completion priming task, a measure of implicit learning on which amnesics perform normally (Shimamura, Salmon, Squire, & Butters, 1987). AD patients on the other hand, show impaired priming (Shimamura et al., 1987) but normal acquisition on the pursuit rotor task (Eslinger & Damasio, 1986; Heindel et al., in press). Other work has shown that many AD patients show evidence of learning repeating sequences on a serial visual reaction time task (Knopman & Nissen, 1987) and improvement with practice in recognizing incomplete figures (Vollmecke & Schwartz, 1986).

Recent studies reviewed above support the distinction between subcortical and cortical dementia by indicating that the pattern of preserved and disturbed memory functions in HD and AD is quite different. HD patients have difficulty retrieving information regardless of whether it is recently acquired or well established, but their capacity to encode and store new verbal information seems relatively intact. In these patients motor learning is impaired, but stem-completion priming, which is thought to depend upon activation of semantic memory, is intact. This is consistent with their normal performance on confrontation naming tasks and suggests that the HD patients' marked deficiencies on verbal fluency tasks arises either from a general slowing in processing information or a more specific retrieval deficit.

AD patients, on the other hand, present a very different pattern. While they can acquire some motor and perceptual skills fairly normally, their semantic memory functions are clearly compromised. Whether this represents a loss of semantic knowledge from storage or a profound disruption of access, perhaps because of their progressive aphasia, is not yet clear. What is certain is that the deficit is pervasive, contributing to these patients' difficulties in naming, fluency, priming and remote memory. The degraded semantic memory system may also be responsible for some of the anterograde memory deficits in AD by limiting the possibility of efficient processing. Finally, heightened sensitivity to proactive interference compromises recall of both newly acquired and previously established memories by these patients.

Preserved Functions in Severely Demented Patients

Case reports (e.g. Anastasi & Levee, 1960; Rife & Snyder, 1931; Shuter-Dyson, 1982) indicate that certain children and young adults sometimes exhibit exceptional artistic talent despite much lower than normal general intelligence. More limited evidence indicates that some demented patients may remain proficient at their artistic specialties long after other cognitive functions have seriously deteriorated. For example, Sacks (1985) described a patient, suspected of having Alzheimer's disease, who continued to sing proficiently and to give voice lessons despite severe visual agnosia and anterograde memory problems. Unfortunately, no formal neuropsychological test results are presented so it is impossible to judge the patient's level of functioning in other areas.

Cummings and Zarit (1987) recently studied a semi-professional painter with probable Alzheimer's disease as determined by extensive neurologic and neuropsychological testing. The patient continued to paint spontaneously for about seven years after the onset of his disease. Compared to his earlier works, his later paintings were simpler and lacked shading and perspective. Eventually he gave up original productions entirely, but would sometimes copy his earlier works.

Serial neuropsychological testing documented the progressive decline in the patient's overall mental status, naming, verbal fluency and anterograde memory, but his constructional skills deteriorated more slowly. In fact, he did not cease producing original paintings until about the time that his score on the copy of the Rey-Osterrieth complex figure declined below the normal range.

As Cummings and Zarit point out the relative preservation of copying ability could be interpreted to mean that in this patient neuropathologic changes affected the left hemisphere much more than the right. However, his verbal and performance IQ scores were equally low, a finding which suggests involvement of both hemispheres by the disease process. Instead they favor the view that the patient's inherent ability for and extensive practice in the visuomotor skills essential for painting rendered these abilities less vulnerable to decline.

Beatty, Zavadil, Bailly, Rixen, Zavadil, Farnham and Fisher (in press) studied an 81-year old musician who suffered from dementia of the Alzheimer type for 11 years. The patient completed 19 years of formal education and holds a masters degree in music with a major in piano. She had taught music at the college level and also worked as a writer. In addition to her dementia, the patient also exhibited a resting tremor in the fingers of both hands and cogwheel rigidity in both elbows, but she was not bradykinetic.

Extensive testing in 1986-87 revealed severe and global cognitive deficits (Mini-mental status exam = 10 in October, 1986, 8 in February, 1987) with marked anomia (28 on the Boston Naming test without cues, 33 with stimulus and phonemic cues), severely depressed verbal fluency (0 words on the FAS test), constructional apraxia (0/13 to command and 5/13 to copy on the Parietal Lobe Drawings from the Boston Diagnostic Aphasia Examination) and impaired abstract reasoning (0 on WAIS Similarities). Performance on WAIS Information, Vocabulary and Picture Completion was approximately normal, but she scored well below the level of age and education - matched controls on these tests.

Formal measures of remote memory revealed severe deficits. On the Famous Faces Test she recalled only 1/30 persons who were well known in the 40s, 50s, 60s and 0/25 persons famous during the 20s and 30s. Her performance did not improve with recognition or cueing. Geographical knowledge was also deficient and she was badly impaired at identifying the titles of common Christmas songs or well known pieces of classical music.

Despite these global deficits, the patient retained considerable skill at playing the piano and some knowledge of music theory. To estimate the quality of her playing, we made tape recordings of the patient and four other pianists who varied in age and training. Blind ratings of these recordings by skilled musicians indicated that the overall quality of the patient's playing approximated that of a formerly proficient, mentally intact 81 year-old pianist whose finger mobility was compromised by arthritis. These findings indicate that our patient can still play familiar tunes fairly well. We do not know how much of her former skill she has lost, but she has certainly lost some skill since she can no longer transpose keys, which she could do as recently as two years ago.

The patient easily played scales to command and could recognize scales when they were played by another pianist. She correctly identified both bass and treble chief, major and minor keys, and diatonic scales. She sight read unfamiliar music accurately, at least for brief passages and could transpose an unfamiliar melody from a right handed to a left handed version. She could not identify time signatures, key signatures, chromatic scales or the difference between waltz and march tempo.

At this point, it seemed likely that the patients preserved piano playing simply reflected retention of highly overlearned motor responses. This hypothesis seemed reasonable since less seriously demented AD patients learn some perceptual and motor skills normally as described above. However, our patient showed no improvement over trials on the pursuit rotor task, even at the slowest possible turntable speed (15 RPM). She also failed to show improvement in recognizing the Gollin incomplete figures. Furthermore, our patient showed clear evidence of ideomotor apraxia. She correctly performed only 4/14 simple motor acts to pantomime, improving to 12/14 when allowed to imitate or use real objects.

Additional evidence against the idea that our patients' piano playing is simply an overlearned motor skill came from a successful demonstration that she could transfer her piano playing skill to another output mode. First, we demonstrated the use of a xylophone, an instrument that she had not seen or played for at least 11 years. Then we asked her to play a simple song on the piano from memory, which she did without error. She also sang the song spontaneously with accurate pitch and tempo. After a single demonstration of the song on the xylophone, she played it accurately. Because the spatial arrangement of keys on a xylophone and a piano are similar but the motor acts required to play the two instruments are different, the patient apparently retains the "concept" of how to play the piano.

Taken together, these observations argue for a relatively selective preservation of skills related to musical performance and against a more general retention of highly overlearned motor acts or the capacity for procedural learning as a description of our patients' preserved piano playing. Reasoning along the same lines as Cummings and Zarit (1987) it might be proposed that in this patient the neurological substrate supporting musical performance was inherently superior and highly developed and thus less vulnerable to impairment.

If this concept has merit for predicting the fate of artistic skills in dementia, does it also apply to other cognitive domains? For example, would chess or bridge playing skill deteriorate more slowly than other aspects of cognition in demented patients who were once accomplished at these games? Alternatively, the range of abilities that remain relatively intact in dementia may be restricted to a more circumscribed set of artistic skills. Additional studies of patients with exceptional premorbid talents who develop dementia or other neurological conditions can clarify these issues.

I thank Jeffrey Cummings who allowed me to describe material from his unpublished study, and Gloria Rixen and Pat Beatty who made helpful suggestions concerning the manuscript.

References

Albert, M.L., Feldman, R.G., & Willis, A.L. (1974). The subcortical dementia of progressive supranuclear palsy. *Journal of Neurology, Neurosurgery and Psychiatry, 37*, 121-130.

Albert, M.S., Butters, N., & Brandt, J. (1981b). Development of remote memory in amnesic and demented patients. *Archives of Neurology, 38*, 495-500.

Albert, M.S., Butters, N., & Brandt, J. (1981b). Development of remote memory loss in patients with Huntington's disease. *Journal of Clinical Neuropsychology, 3*, 1-12.

Albert, M.S., Butters, N., & Levin, J. (1979). Temporal gradients in the retrograde amnesia of patients with Korsakoff's disease. *Archives of Neurology, 36*, 211-216.

Anastasi, A., & Levee, R.F. (1960). Intellectual deficit and musical talent: A case report. *American Journal of Mental Deficiency, 64*, 695-703.

Bayless, K.A., & Tomoeda, C.K. (1983). Confrontation naming impairment in dementia. *Brain and Language, 19*, 98-114.

Beatty, W.W., Butters, N., & Janowsky, D.S. (1986). Patterns of memory failure after scopolamine treatment: Implications for cholinergic hypotheses of dementia. *Behavioral and Neural Biology, 45*, 196-211.

Beatty, W.W., Salmon, D.P., Butters, N., Heindel, W.C., & Granholm, E.L. (in press). Retrograde amnesia in patients with Alzheimer's disease or Huntington's disease. *Neurobiology of aging.*

Beatty, W.W., Zavadil, K.D., Bailly, R.C., Rixen, G.J., Zavadil, L.E., Farnham, N., & Fisher, L. (in press). Preserved musical skill in a severely demented patient. *International Journal of Clinical Neuropsychology.*

Butters, N., Albert, M.S., Sax, D.S., Miliotis, P., & Sterste, A. (1983). The effect of verbal elaborators on the pictorial memory of brain damaged patients. *Neuropsychologia, 21*, 307-323.

Butters, N., Granholm, E., Salmon, D.P., Grant, I., & Wolfe, J. (1987). Episodic and semantic memory: A comparison of amnesic and demented patients. *Journal of Clinical and Experimental Neuropsychology, 9*, 479-497.

Butters, N., Wolfe, J., Martone, M., Granholm, E., & Cermak, L.S. (1985). Memory disorders associated with Huntington's disease: Verbal recall, verbal recognition and procedural memory. *Neuropsychologia, 23*, 729-743.

Butters, N., Sax, D., Montgomery, K., & Tarlow, S. (1978). Comparison of neuropsychological deficits associated with early and advanced Huntington's disease. *Archives of Neurology, 35*, 585-589.

Cohen, N.J., & Squire, L.R. (1980). Preserved learning and retention of pattern analyzing skills in amnesia: Dissociation of knowing how and knowing that. *Science, 210*, 207-210.

Cummings, J.L., & Benson, D.F. (1984). Subcortical dementia: Review of an emerging concept. *Archives of Neurology, 41*, 874-879.

Cummings, J.L., Benson, D.F., Hill, M.A., & Read, S. (1985). Aphasia in dementia of the Alzheimer type. *Neurology, 35*, 394-397.

Cummings, J.L., & Zarit, J.M. (1987). Probable Alzheimer's disease in an artist. *Journal of the American Medical Association, 258*, 2731-2734.

El-Awar, M., Becker, J.T., Hammond, K.M., Nebes, R.D., & Boller, F. (1987). Learning deficit in Parkinson's disease: Comparison with Alzheimer's disease and normal aging. *Archives of Neurology, 44*, 180-184.

Eslinger, P.J., & Damasio, A.R. (1986). Preserved motor learning in Alzheimer's disease: Implications for anatomy and behavior. *Journal of Neuroscience, 6*, 3006-3009.

Freedman, M., Rivoira, P., Butters, N., Sax, D.S., & Feldman, R.S. (1984). Retrograde amnesia in Parkinson's disease. *Canadian Journal of Neurological Sciences, 11,* 297-301.

Graf, P., Squire, L.R., & Mandler, G. (1984). The information that amnesic patients do not forget. *Journal of Experimental Psychology: Learning, Memory and Cognition, 10,* 164-178.

Heindel, W.C., Butters, N., & Salmon, D.S. (in press). Impaired learning of a motor skill in patients with Huntington's disease. *Behavioral Neuroscience.*

Huber, S.J. & Paulson, G.W. (1985). The concept of subcortical dementia. *American Journal of Psychiatry, 142,* 1312-1317.

Huber, S.J., Shuttleworth, E.C., & Paulson, G.W. (1986). Dementia in Parkinson's disease. *Archives of Neurology, 43,* 987-990.

Jacoby, L.L., & Witherspoon, D. (1982). Remembering without awareness. *Canadian Journal of Psychology, 32,* 300-324.

Kaplan, E., Goodglass, H., & Weintraub, S. (1983). *Boston naming test.* Philadelphia: Lea & Febiger.

Knopman, D.S., & Nissen, M.J. (1987). Implicit learning in patients with probable Alzheimer's disease. *Neurology, 37,* 784-788.

Martone, M., Butters, N., Payne, M., Becker, J., & Sax, D.S. (1984). Dissociations between skill learning and verbal recognition in amnesia and dementia. *Archives of Neurology, 41,* 965-970.

Mayeaux, R., Stern, Y., Rosen, J., & Benson, D.F. (1983). Is "subcortical dementia" a recognizable clinical entity? *Annals of Neurology, 10,* 278-284.

McHugh, P.R., & Folstein, M.F. (1975). Psychiatric syndromes of Huntington's chorea: A clinical and phenomenological study. In D.F. Benson & D. Blumer (Eds.) *Psychiatric aspects of neurological disease.* (pp. 267-295). New York: Grune & Stratton.

Milner, B., Corkin, S., & Teuber, H.L. (1968). Further analysis of the hippocampal amnesic syndrome: 14-year follow-up study of H.M. *Neuropsychologia, 6,* 215-234.

Rife, D.C., & Snyder, L.H. (1931). Studies in human inheritance VI. A genetic refutation of the principle of "behavioristic" psychology. *Human Biology, 3,* 547-559.

Sacks, O. (1985). *The man who mistook his wife for a hat and other clinical tales.* New York: Summit Books.

Shimamura, A.P., Salmon, D.P., Squire, L.R., & Butters, N. (1987). Memory dysfunction and word priming in dementia and amnesia. *Behavioral Neuroscience, 101,* 347-351.

Shuter-Dyson. (1982). Musical ability. In D. Deusch (Ed.) *The psychology of music.* (pp. 391-412). New York: Academic Press.

Squire, L.R. (1986). Mechanisms of memory. *Science, 232,* 1612-1619.

Vollmecke, T.A., & Schwartz, M.F. (1986). Preserved learning in memory-impaired DAT patients' performance on a degraded figures task. Paper presented at the 14th Annual Meeting of the International Neuropsychological Association, Denver CO.

Wilson, R., Kaszniak, A.W., & Fox, J.H. (1981). Remote memory in senile dementia. *Cortex, 17,* 41-48.

16

A Preliminary Neuro-cognitive Model of Tactuo-spatial Motor Learning

Robert L. Pusakulich, Geri R. Alvis and Jeannette P. Ward

The present authors recently examined the motor and cognitive functions in a right-handed male patient (J.S.) with transection of the anterior two-thirds of the cerebral corpus callosum. Among the functions examined was the patient's ability to acquire and retain the tactuo-spatial motor learning required for mastery of finger maze tasks (Figure 1). It was observed that even though J.S. demonstrated better acquisition performance with his nondominant left hand, transfer of learning to an identical maze from that hand to his dominant right was less efficient than transfer in the opposite direction (Table 1). Patient J.S.'s findings, in conjunction with results from a study investigating finger maze acquisition and transfer in intact subjects (Ward et. al., 1987), served as the basis for a preliminary functional model for cerebral cortical areas and information pathways that might be involved in tactuo-spatial finger maze learning and performance.

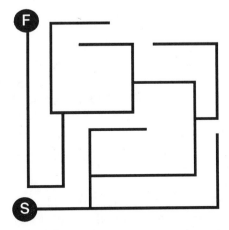

Figure 1. This five choice point finger maze could be turned over to provide either an alternate acquisition and identical maze transfer task, for anterior callosotomy patients, or a mirror-image maze transfer task for intact subjects.

Pusakulich, R. L., Alvis, G. R., & Ward, J. P. (1988). A preliminary neuro-cognitive model of tactuospatial motor learning. In J. M. Williams & C. J. Long (Eds.), *Cognitive Approaches to Neuropsychology*, New York: Plenum.

Table 1

Acquisition and transfer performance results on a finger maze task for an anterior callosotomy patient.

	Errors	Trials	Latencies
Acquisition (right hand)	84	7	10 min 57 sec
Transfer (left hand)	8	5	1 min 7 sec
Acquisition (left hand)	22	1	3 min 42 sec
Transfer (right hand)	26	10	5 min 25 sec

In the above cited study with intact dextral and sinistral subjects, it was noted that left-handed learning facilitated the initial acquisition performance of all subjects, regardless of handedness, just as had been observed in J.S.. This was especially true for sinistrals learning with the left hand, who demonstrated significantly better acquisition performance regardless of whether the dependent measure was trials to criterion, errors, or total lapsed maze time. Together these data suggest that finger maze learning may inherently involve nondominant right hemisphere activity. However, unlike the anterior callosotomy patient's diminished left-to-right hand transfer performance, intact dextral subjects demonstrated equally proficient transfer to an identical maze with either hand. In J.S., the absence of transcallosal communication between the two frontal lobes may have been responsible for his deviation from the transfer performances of intact dextrals. This implies that frontal lobe activity plays an essential role in tactuo-spatial finger maze learning and performance. Furthermore, J.S.'s asymmetrical transfer performance obviously suggests unequal contributions of the left and right frontal lobes in this process. These points together with the evidence of a general right hemisphere advantage in tactuo-spatial finger maze learning and performance distinctly implicate the right frontal lobe as a critical component in tactuo-spatial motor learning.

Specifically, it is postulated that when the anterior callosal pathways are not available, as in J.S., the observed transfer of learning from the left to the right hand is diminished because of the following situation. In the case of right hand maze acquisition and left hand transfer, even though the postulated inter-hemispheric, right frontal control over the contralateral left frontal motor area is attenuated, the information eventually "learned" by the right hand in its maneuvers through the maze can be transferred via non-frontal, sensory-per-ceptual areas across the intact posterior corpus callosum. That information is then available to the right frontal area and can be directly called into play when the left hand is tested in transfer, resulting in the observed, relatively good transfer of maze learning from the right to the left hand. With left hand acquisition, the maze information "learned" by the left hand can also be di-rectly mediated by the right frontal lobe. But transfer demands right hand ex-pression of that learning. Normally during such a test the right frontal motor area could exert its control across the anterior callosal areas to assist the less able left motor area in manifesting the transfer of learning. However, if the anterior corpus callosum is absent, then the left motor area lacks its interhemispheric assistance. Thus the observed transfer of learning to the right hand is proportionally diminished relative to transfer in the reverse di-rection because left to right hand transfer then must rely on less efficient, residual callosal pathways.

Moreover, this account assumes that a transfer of learning indeed oc-curs when the finger maze task is performed with the opposite hand after ini-tial acquisition by its counterpart. It could be argued that better left hand per-formance after right hand acquisition can be solely accounted for by inherent left hand superiority in maze performance, or conversely, that right hand performance following left hand acquisition would naturally be worse given this inherent left hand superiority. However, given the extensive literature on transfer of training, it seems likely that some transfer of learning occurs be-tween the two hands. Furthermore, if that were not the case, then one would expect similar magnitudes of the differences between the two hands' perfor-mances on the two tasks. Even granting some effects of practice during the second maze task, the two transfer performances should be more symmetrical than the dramatically unequal, asymmetrical differences that J.S. demon-strated. In view of these considerations, unequal transfer of learning due to impaired right frontal cortical control of tactuo-spatial performance via the corpus callosum, as outlined above, appears to be a more feasible way to ac-count for this observed asymmetry.

Further support for the proposal that tactuo-spatial maze learning and performance involve a right anterior cortical locus of control is provided by findings of Corkin (1965). She discovered that the right-handed stylus maze learning of blindfolded dextral subjects was rendered much more difficult when lesions of the right prefrontal lobe were present. Maze learning was also impaired by right posterior lesions, but to a lesser extent, and left prefrontal lesions had still less detrimental effect on the right-handed stylus maze learning. The magnitude of the right prefrontal lesions' effect in Corkin's study is impressive: the right prefrontally lesioned subjects made more than twice as many errors as left prefrontally lesioned subjects, and three times more errors than intact subjects. Requirements for efficient performance on a stylus maze thus appear to be similar to those of a finger maze. Performance on both tasks seems to involve a similar form of tactuo-spatial motor learning which necessarily engages the right hemisphere, and particularly the right prefrontal area, regardless of handedness. Such a right anterior locus would fit the general "spatial-gestalt" specialization of the right hemisphere which might in turn mediate tactuo-spatial motor learning superiority, perhaps in a manner analogous to the putatively superior left hemisphere mediation of sequential manual motor acts (Kimura & Archibald, 1974).

Thus the previous proposal, that learning and performance on tactuo-spatial maze tasks has an intrinsic right frontal-motor component, and that the contribution of the right hemisphere motor and motor associational areas is essential to mastery of the finger maze task, is substantiated by and consistent with the cited findings in brain-lesioned subjects. Yet the right anterior locus of control model proposed here is obviously sketchy and simplified. The complete and final model of cortical mediation of tactuo-spatial learning under consideration must await much more theoretical and empirical investigation. Also, the presented model pertains mainly to the motor component involved in this learning, even though there has been an earlier allusion to the fact that sensory areas are involved. Additionally, certain information obtained from the transfer findings of the previously discussed normal subjects suggests considerable non-visual sensory-perceptual cue encoding by the posterior cerebral cortex, and that also should be considered in more detail.

In the study of intact subjects, it was noted that there were some remarkable differences between the transfer performances of right- and left handed subjects to an identical finger maze, and to a mirror-reversed version of the maze. When identical maze transfer was tested, sinistrals who had learned the finger maze with their nondominant right hand and transferred to the left hand performed much like dextrals who had learned with either hand. But sinistrals who had learned with the dominant left hand showed striking difficulty when they transferred to the identical maze with the right hand. Yet these same sinistrals were surprisingly superior to all other groups when a mirror-reversed configuration of the original acquisition maze was used for that left to right hand transfer. Such pronounced differences require an explanation. Why should the sinistrals' left-handed learning lead to superior transfer to a mirror maze but not to the more straightforward identical maze?

In answer to this question, it is suggested that these left-handed subjects had encoded the cues provided in the initial maze experience quite differently than other subjects. The present authors suppose that both left and right hemisphere encoding strategies may be employed in manipulospatial, nonvisual finger maze learning, but that the left hemisphere strategy is qualitatively different from that of the nondominant (right) hemisphere. An explanation as to how that might occur requires a closer examination of differences in the kind of learned information necessary for successful intermanual transfer to either an identical or a mirror version of the finger maze. Again, both dextrals' and sinistrals' transfer to the identical maze pattern was good when the maze had been learned first with the right hand and then the left hand was used in transfer. There is considerable clinical support for the mediation of L-R orientation by the left inferior parietal lobule and the angular gyrus in particular (Benton, 1959, 1968). A left-right oriented strategy would certainly be consistent with the verbal-abstract capacities commonly associated with the speech dominant left hemisphere. Since right hand maze acquisition involves direct activation of the left hemisphere, then even though right frontal mediation remains essential the left frontal activation may foster the overlay of a more sequential, abstract-conceptual (possibly verbal) left-hemispheric strategy. And in this case the spatial configuration of the maze may be encoded primarily as a series of left and right turns.

Although such an approach could certainly be considered a verbal mediation strategy, it also might be more broadly characterized as a strategy that encodes movements through space in an abstract, left-right framework in which the subject's body is the neutral reference point in an external space possessing equal and symmetrical, left and right halves. After learning the maze configuration using such a L-R spatial strategy, intermanual transfer to the identical pattern would be straightforward and relatively easy with the same learning cues fully applicable. In a mirror version of the maze, however, the task would be quite different and probably more difficult, requiring a left-to-right directional transposition. Because all the observed right-handed learning as well as the left-handed learning of dextrals easily transferred to the identical and not the mirror-reversed maze task, such an abstract, left hemisphere mediated, L-R strategy might have been used by all dextrals and by those sinistral subjects learning with the right hand.

However, a quite different encoding strategy seems to have been employed in the case of left-handed acquisition by sinistrals. These subjects' demonstrated superiority in intermanual transfer to the mirror-image maze pattern suggests that they used an approach which allowed facile transfer to a maze environment that required a directional reversal of originally encoded cues. A spatial strategy meeting the requirements of that approach would be one which uses a frame of reference that treats space external to the body as an extension of the body: limb movement might be proprioceptively encoded as being either toward or away from the body rather than more "abstractly" left or right. In such a reference system movements toward the body could be considered "medial" and would be adductions of limbs toward the body midline; movements away from the body could be considered "lateral" and would include abductions of limbs away from the body midline.

Thus one could learn a finger maze as a series of medially and laterally directed movements proprioceptively sensed as either "adductive" or "abductive" movements of the upper extremities. This would be in contrast to learning that involves conceptual division of space into left and right halves. Learning a maze in such a lateral-medial code would facilitate intermanual transfer to a mirror version because the spatial framework would remain unaltered in this mirror configuration; i.e., a movement that was laterally cued during acquisition would remain a lateral movement during transfer, and the same for medially cued movements. However, in transfer to the identical maze this would not be the case, as the movement cues would be reversed; i.e., lateral=medial and medial=lateral, or, e.g. what was an "abductive" movement of a limb joint during acquisition would become an "adduction" during transfer testing with the contralateral limb. This would be obviously more difficult than learning the mirrored configuration using cues not requiring such a transposition.

The authors further suggest that spatial encoding based upon proprioceptive feedback rather than a more verbal and abstract left-right orientation might be the product of a more concrete and nonverbal mediation of behavior and thus compatible with right (nondominant) hemisphere activity, especially right posterior cortex and perhaps even right parietal lobe in particular. Parietal lobe function in nonhuman primates has long been associated with the mediation of accurate limb movement in space (Mountcastle et. al., 1975). Perhaps the human nonverbal hemisphere retains a more "primitive" parietal capacity that allows limb movements in space to be encoded as movements relative to an axis vertical to the midline of the body; this capacity may have been lessened in the left (dominant) parietal lobe because of its evolved mediation of language and perhaps a more abstract L-R analysis of space. If the right hemisphere were specialized relative to the left for a concrete, body-oriented, or lateral-medial encoding strategy, then one could expect the most robust manifestation of this influence during maze acquisition in the limb contralateral to that right hemisphere, namely the left arm and hand.

The additional possibility of an important role for left and right posterior cortical involvement in finger maze learning is not meant to exclude the right anterior control of tactuo-spatial activity outlined earlier. However, a more comprehensive model is needed to account for and incorporate the various separate but interacting and interdependent sensory and motor processes that appear to be involved in the mastery of a finger maze task. In some ways it is probably gratuitous to attempt to separate and differentiate between motor and sensory-perceptual contributions to a learning process. Nevertheless, it may be conceptually advantageous to consider such contributions individually, in order to delineate the neuropsychological basis of tactuo-spatial maze learning. Therefore, an attempt has been made to construct an expanded model of cortical functioning that incorporates both these components, and that can account for data from the intact subjects as well as the findings obtained from the anterior callosotomy patient.

First, the sensory-perceptual information that is used in learning the task is held to be processed by either left or right posterior cortex, from where the information can be transmitted to the active hand either intrahemispherically or via posterior corpus callosum communication between those areas. But the manifestation of that information in motor behavior, regardless of its type, is hypothesized to occur most efficiently under the control of the right anterior frontal lobe working directly through its contralateral left hand, and less efficiently across the anterior corpus callosum through the left hemisphere and right hand. Under that assumption frontal and posterior cortical inputs to the maze task must be coordinated, and consideration must be given to the likelihood that processing of these inputs in a majority of cases is interhemispheric and transcallosal in nature. In considering the data for intact subjects, eight possible conditions of acquisition and transfer are present. Each of these can be accommodated by an expanded version of the previously discussed right frontal locus model. The coordination of cortical areas and processes hypothesized to be involved in both initial maze learning and its intermanual transfer are depicted in Figure 2.

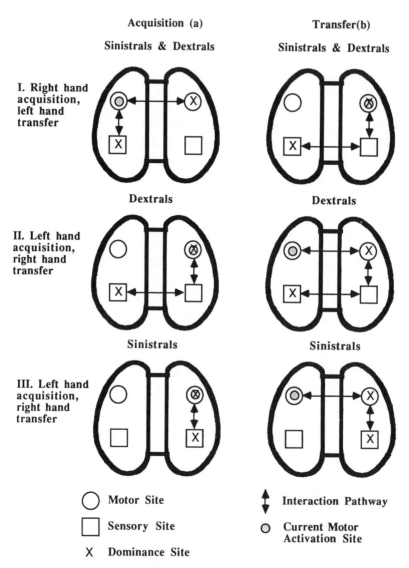

Figure 2. Cortical activity patterns of sinistrals and dextrals are depicted for possible conditions of acquisition and transfer on a finger maze task.

Figure 2 presents schematic pathways of interaction and informational flow for gross cerebral cortical regions such as right or left hemisphere and anterior or posterior areas, and transcallosal pathways. Postulated intra- and inter-hemispheric interactions are given for normal subjects under two learning conditions: a) acquisition of learning, and b) intermanual transfer of learning. Figure 2 depicts the two preceding conditions for dextral subjects: dextrals who learn with the dominant right hand (Ia) and transfer to the left hand (Ib); dextrals who learn with the nondominant left hand (IIa) and transfer to the right hand (IIb). This figure illustrates the same two conditions applied to sinistral subjects: sinistrals who learn with the nondominant right hand (Ia) and transfer to the left hand Ib); and finally sinistrals who learn with the dominant left hand (IIIa) and transfer to the right hand (IIIb). In viewing Figure 2, it becomes apparent that for all learning conditions the right frontal area plays a crucial role; also the left parietal lobe is involved in all conditions except that of sinistrals learning with their dominant left hand. These commonalities, as well as the differences that occur in the proposed cortical interactions for each of the eight conditions, are explained in detail in the following discussion.

First, it is held that dextrals, regardless of the hand used in finger maze acquisition, will use a left posterior cortex mediated, L-R cue encoding strategy, due to their greater language lateralization and accompanying left hemisphere dominance (Hecaen & deAjuriaguerra, 1964). Sinistrals' hemispheric dominance, however, is postulated to be governed more by the hand that is active during acquisition. In effect, the hemisphere contralateral to the hand employed assumes a sensory dominance in the task. Therefore, sinistrals learning with the right hand will employ left hemisphere L-R strategy, in contrast to sinistrals learning with the left hand who will use right hemisphere L-M strategy. Secondly, it is proposed that the hand of acquisition in any of the eight learning conditions determines the state of routing and flow of information within and between the two cerebral hemispheres for both acquisition and later transfer. In effect, it is stipulated that the cortical processing patterns established during acquisition also persist during transfer. This is held to occur because transfer performances utilize and express mostly retrieval of already learned information, thus making the retrieval process dependent on cortical areas and pathways previously used during acquisition learning.

Based on these assumptions, the proposed cortical interactions occuring in each of the conditions of learning and transfer for dextral and sinistral subjects will now be described in detail; the reader is urged to refer to the accompanying figures during this discussion. Beginning with dextrals who learn with the dominant right hand and transfer to the left (Ia), one finds direct motoric involvement of the left frontal area. But this area is only indirectly or passively involved in the tactuo-spatial motor learning per se, since it is postulated that such learning even by the right hand is mediated in the right frontal area via the anterior corpus callosum. However, the use of an abstract, left-right cue strategy is hypothesized as governed by the left posterior cortex. Therefore, during the acquisition of maze learning the information gained through the experience of the right hand in the maze diverges into two pathways, one intra-hemispherically to the left posterior cortex for sensory-perceptual mediation, the other to the right anterior cortex for the tactuo-spatial motor mediation, as shown in Figure 2. The left hand transfer test for this group (Ib) results in the direct and contralateral control of movement by the right anterior frontal area during expression of the acquired tactuo-spatial learning. Furthermore, that expression also depends upon sensory-perceptual information in the form of left-right cueing from the left posterior cortex, which is suggested to be transmitted transcallosally, via the right posterior cortex to the right anterior cortex.

As also shown in Figure 2, in the case of dextrals learning with the left hand (IIa), direct control of tactuo-spatial motor learning by the right anterior cortex now combines with a left-right sensory-perceptual strategy still mediated by the left posterior cortex. However, the contralateral right posterior parietal area is now also directly involved, and must transmit this information to the left posterior areas via the posterior corpus callosum for processing. When the test for transfer of learning occurs (IIb), the right anterior cortex transcallosally guides the activities of the left frontal area during right-handed expression of the previously acquired tactuo-spatial motor learning. However, the left-right spatial cues employed in transfer movements must still be communicated inter-hemispherically to the right frontal area from the left posterior hemisphere via right posterior cortex.

In all the dextral conditions then there will always be a left posterior cortical contribution to the sensory-perceptual processing, and either direct, contralateral, or indirect, transcallosal control of motor expression by the right anterior area; thus there is a interhemispheric partitioning of sensory-perceptual and motor information. But that is not the case for sinistrals. Because cue use apparently differs remarkably in sinistrals, depending upon whether they use the dominant left or nondominant right hand in acquisition of learning, it has been proposed that posterior parietal mediation of sensory-perceptual information is not the same in the two instances. As shown in Figure 2, the case of sinistrals learning with the nondominant right hand (Ia) is modeled as being the same as for dextrals learning with their dominant hand, i.e. intra-hemispheric mediation of left-right encoded sensory-perceptual information by the left posterior cortex and transcallosal control of motor learning by the right anterior area. Transfer of learning to the left hand (Ib) is also much the same as for dextrals transferring to the left hand: again there is direct control of motor expression by the right anterior cortex, and abstract, left-right, encoded sensory-perceptual information is transmitted from the left posterior cortex via the right posterior area to the left hand.

However, for sinistrals learning with the dominant left hand, the cortical mediation that occurs during both acquisition and transfer is envisioned to be quite different and simpler. These subjects are thought not to employ the abstract, left-right cues but the more body-oriented, lateral-medial cues mediated by the right, not left, posterior cortex. In this case, these subjects' right anterior "maze dominant" cortical area is in direct control of their dominant left hand movement. Thus, it is hypothesized that learning takes place entirely within the right hemisphere (IIIa). The exclusively intrahemispheric nature of this mediation may explain the dramatic left-handed learning superiority demonstrated by these sinistrals. During transfer testing (IIIb), only the transcallosal mediation of right hand motor activity by the right anterior cortex is added, with L-M cue information transmitted from the right posterior cortical area via the right anterior cortex to the left anterior cortex and eventually expressed by the right hand.

In discussing the cortical functioning outlined in this expanded model, it was presumed that the intact dextral and sinistral subjects used in the study were left hemisphere dominant for speech, since this has been found to be the case for a majority of individuals, with even most sinistrals having either all or some speech in the left hemisphere (Rasmussen & Milner, 1977). As presented here, the model is intended to account for tactuo-spatial finger maze learning in nearly all dextrals and most sinistrals. However, it would be simple to account for true right hemisphere speech dominance in sinistrals by assuming a left anterior locus for tactuo-spatial learning. The same reversal would apply to those relatively rare cases of right hemisphere speech dominant dextrals. Persons with bilateral speech and manual ambidexterity are not considered in the currently presented model.

Again, applying the expanded model to the patient with anterior callosotomy, it is postulated that when the anterior corpus callosum is not available to mediate the normal right frontal control over the left frontal motor areas, the lesser ability of the left frontal cortex to mediate the "maze learning" is shown in less efficient right hand acquisition performance (Ia). However, the L-R cue encoding information that is learned by the right hand during acquisition can be transferred from sensory-perceptual areas in the left posterior cortex to the right posterior cortex across the intact posterior corpus callosum. That information is then available to the homolateral right frontal area which mediates left hand activity during transfer testing (Ib). This results in the observed relatively good transfer of maze learning from the right to the left hand. In the case of left hand acquisition, the maze information learned by the left hand is mediated by the right frontal lobe, with left posterior cortex encoding of sensory-perceptual cue cues now transmitted via the right posterior cortex in the case of this dextral patient (IIa). But during right hand transfer testing (IIb), the right motor area's normal coordination of the motor and sensory expression of prior learning via the anterior callosal fibers is now disrupted. And while left posterior cortically mediated sensory-perceptual cue encoding can still be utilized by less efficient alternate hemispheric pathways, the lack of right frontal motor area assistance is expressed in diminished transfer of learning.

To summarize briefly, this model was developed to account for observations of superior nondominant left hand finger maze learning and asymmetry in intermanual transfer of learning in a dextral anterior callosotomy patient. It was suggested that the absence of the anterior callosal pathways may have interfered with the right anterior transcallosal mediation of the patients' dominant right hand maze acquisition performance and transfer to the right hand after left-handed acquisition. Following a discussion of supportive studies, a right anterior locus model for the mediation of nonvisual, tactuo-spatial motor learning on a finger maze task was postulated. An expansion of the model was then undertaken to accommodate apparent differences between intact dextrals and sinistrals in use of either left or right hemisphere strategies for encoding sensory-perceptual cues. The result is a model that retains the right anterior locus for the cortical mediation of nonvisual, tactuo-spatial motor learning, but that also postulates a concurrent intra- and/or interhemispheric interaction in which salient spatial reference cues can be mediated by the left posterior cortex for all dextrals and for sinistrals learning with the right hand. Maze learning for these subjects is hypothesized as bihemispheric in nature and dependent upon transcallosal interhemispheric communication, either anteriorly or posteriorly. However, for sinistrals learning with the left hand, both the sensory-perceptual and the motor components of maze learning are postulated to take place entirely within the right hemisphere, with the right hand activity mediated across the anterior corpus callosum during a test of learning transfer. Unlike all other conditions, the model for sinistrals' left-handed learning suggests that their posterior corpus callosum may not be necessary for efficient maze acquisition and transfer.

The authors consider it important that the stability of the results obtained from the anterior callosotomy patient and the model his performance suggests is demonstrated by findings in the performances of normal subjects; this strengthens the suggestion of a possibly unique function of the right anterior cortex, particularly the right frontal motor and premotor areas, in nonvisually guided movements in space. Furthermore, these findings supply a rare demonstration of a task for which the left hand appears to be better suited then the right, even when the latter is considered dominant, as in dextrals. Only some reports of left-handed superiority for motor tasks are available (e.g. Guiard, Diaz, & Beaubaton, 1983), although more cases have been described for a left-handed tactile-sensory superiority (Gardner et. al., 1977; Harriman & Castell, 1979; VanBlerkom, 1985; Young & Ellis, 1979). It is also interesting to speculate upon the implications of the use of a non-left-right cue encoding strategy that apparently is right hemisphere mediated. Is nonvisually guided motor movement influenced by the right parieto-tempero-occipital area dependent on an "older" or more primitive tactuo-spatial system, one that may precede a "newer" more abstract left posterior system both ontologically and phylogenetically? It is hoped that future work will aid in answering this question. Such research also appears of value in allowing exploration of possible applications and use of tactuo-spatial motor tasks such as fingermazes in clinical settings, since there are at present few clinical tests sensitive to right anterior cortical damage (Lezak, 1983).

References

Corkin, S. (1965). Tactually-guided maze learning in man: Effects of unilateral cortical excisions and bilateral hippocampal lesions. *Neuropsychologia, 3*, 339-351.

Gardner, E.B., English, A.G., Flannery, B.M., Hartnett, M.B., McCormick, J.K., & Wilhelmy, B.D. (1977). Shape recognition accuracy and response latency in a bilateral tactile task. *Neuropsychologia, 15*, 607-616.

Giuard, Y., Diaz, G., & Beaubaton, D. (1983). Left hand advantage in right handers for spatial constant error. Preliminary evidence in a unimanual ballistic armed movement. *Neuropsychologia, 21*, 11-115.

Harriman, J., & Castell, L. (1979). Manual asymmetry for tactile discrimination. *Perceptual & Motor Skills, 48*, 290.

Hecaen, H. & deAjuriaguerra, J. (1964). *Left-handedness*. Grune & Stratton, New York.

Kimura, D., & Archibald, Y. (1974). Motor functions of the hemisphere. *Brain, 97*, 337-350.

Lezak, M.D. (1983). *Neuropsychological assessment.* New York: Oxford University Press.

Mountcastle, V.B., Lyndh, J.C., Gerogopoulis, A., Sakata, G. & Acuna, C. (1975). Posterior parietal association cortex of the monkey: command functions for operation within extrapersonal space. *Journal of Neurophysiology, 38,* 871-908.

Rasmussen, T., & Milner B. (1977). The role of early left-brain in determining lateralization of cerebral speech functions. In S.J. Dimomd & D.A. Blizard (Eds.) *Evolution and lateralization of the brain.* New York: The New York Academy of Sciences.

Van Blerkom, M.L. (1985). Developmental trends in dichaptic lateralization. *Perceptual and Motor Skills, 60,* 951-959.

Ward, J.P., Alvis, G.R., Sanford, C.G., Dodson, D.L., & Pusakulich, R. L. (1987). Qualitative differences in tactile learning by left-handers. Submitted manuscript.

Young, A.W., & Ellis, A.W. (1979). Perception of numerical stimuli felt by fingers of the left and right hands. *Quarterly Journal of Experimental Psychology, 31,* 263-272.

17

The Neuropsychology of Autobiographical Memory

Walter F. Daniel

Memory deficits are among the most debilitating consequences of brain injury and disease. They affect many aspects of daily living and can seriously disrupt an individual's ability to function independently (Glisky, Schacter, & Tulving, 1986). Associated with a variety of neurological conditions, including closed-head injury, electroconvulsive therapy, Alzheimer's disease, Korsakoff's disease, encephalitis, anoxia, cerebral tumors, etc., memory disorders are as yet poorly understood and have proven largely resistant to remediation. In recent years, however, it has become increasingly evident that even severely amnesic patients can be taught perceptual, motor, and cognitive tasks (see reviews by Brooks & Baddeley, 1976; Baddeley, 1982; Parkin, 1982; Warrington & Weiskrantz, 1982: Cohen, 1984; Schacter, 1985, 1987a, 1987b; Shimamura, 1986; Squire, 1987; Booker & Schacter, this volume) (also see Table 1), in some cases comparable to that by control subjects (e.g., Cohen & Squire, 1980).

However, the hallmark of the human organic amnesic syndrome is that, while severely amnesic patients can be taught various tasks, they do not remember the autobiographical *experience* (autobiographical memory)[1] during which the learning took place (Wood, 1974; Kinsbourne & Wood, 1975; Rozin, 1976; Cohen & Squire; 1980; Zola-Morgan, Cohen, & Squire, 1983; Rubin, 1986; Butters, 1987).

All human beings exhibit decay of autobiographical memory (Crovitz & Schiffmann, 1974; Crovitz & Quina-Holland, 1976; Jenkins, Hurst, & Rose, 1979; Rubin, 1982, 1986; Winograd & Killinger, 1983). For example, many of us do not remember the exact episode during which we finally learned to tie our shoes, even though we still remember the actual skill of how to tie our

---

[1]In the neuropsychology and experimental psychology literature, various terms have been used to refer to the forgetting of an autobiographical episode. In addition to a *failure of autobiographical memory* (e.g., Jacoby & Dallas, 1981; Rubin, 1986; De Renzi, Liotti, & Nichelli, 1987), *source amnesia* (Evans & Thorne, 1966; Schacter, Harbluk & McLachlan, 1984), *lack of a feeling of me-ness* (Claparede, 1911/1951), *lack of declarative memory* (Cohen & Squire, 1980; Squire et al., 1988), *and lack of explicit memory* (Booker & Schacter, this volume) have all been used to refer to a forgotten autobiographical episode.

Daniel, W. F. (1988). The neuropsychology of autobiographical memory. In J. M. Williams and C. J. Long (Eds.), *Cognitive approaches to neuropsychology*, New York: Plenum.

331

shoes. Furthermore, one can hypnotize normal subjects and then, during the hypnotic trance, teach subjects new information (e.g., *"an amethyst crystal becomes _____ in color when heated;" correct answer = yellow*). If these same subjects are given the hypnotic suggestion that they will not remember having been hypnotized, they will, when asked for the answers to these questions in the posthypnotic state, answer them correctly (Evans & Thorne, 1966; Evans & Kihlstrom, 1976, 1980). However, when asked, *"How do you know that?"*, they will respond, *"I don't know"* or *"It only seems logical,"* or with a similar response devoid of autobiographical heritage.

One might ask why autobiographical amnesia is of interest if both normal and organic amnesic subjects forget autobiographical life episodes. Organic amnesics forget autobiographical memories at a much faster rate than do normal subjects (Wood, 1974; Kinsbourne & Wood, 1975), a rate which may be crippling to the patient in his or her everyday life. He or she may have difficulty remembering new autobiographical events (anterograde amnesia); in addition there can be a failure of autobiographical memory for life events from before the onset of the illness (retrograde amnesia). The duration of such retrograde amnesia can range from seconds (Crovitz & Daniel, 1987) to years (Milner, 1966; Gardner, 1974; Roman-Campos et al., 1980; Kritchevsky et al., 1988) to decades (Goldberg et al., 1981; Andrews, Poser, & Kessler, 1982; Rousseaux et al., 1984; Damasio et al., 1985; Sacks, 1985, p. 23; Baddeley & Wilson, 1986; Butters & Cermak, 1986).

It is important to state that organic amnesics who are aware of their premorbid memory capacity are not likely to be happy with their condition (cf. Baddeley & Wilson, 1986; Cockburn & Wilson, 1986). Gross autobiographical memory gaps, in fact, are likely to be disconcerting to the patient and the patient's family, because the patient's sense of continuity with his or her own past may be disrupted (cf. Merriam, 1980; Daniel et al., 1982; Prigatano, 1984; Powell, 1986). The neurologist Oliver Sacks (in his popular book entitled *The Man Who Mistook His Wife For A Hat* [1985]), when discussing an alcoholic Korsakoff amnesic (with a 30 year period of retrograde amnesia), asks the question, "...what sort of life (if any), what sort of a world, what sort of a self, can be preserved in a man who has lost the greater part of his memory and, with this, his past, and his moorings in time?" (p. 23). Furthermore, Baddeley & Wilson (1986, p. 250) state, "...there seems little doubt that autobiographical memory, by maintaining a record of the self, probably performs one of the most significant functions in human memory."

Table 1

Preserved Learning in Organic Amnesia

1. *Eyeblink Conditioning:* Talland (1965); Weiskrantz & Warrington (1979)
2. *Conditioned Avoidance*: Linskii (1954)
3. *Conditioning of Other Motor Responses:* Luria (1976).
4. *Pursuit Rotor*: Corkin (1965, 1968); Cermak et al. (1973); Brooks & Baddeley (1976); Butters (Alzheimer's Disease) (1987)
5. *Choice Reaction Time*: Knopman & Nissen (Alzheimer's Disease) (1987)
6. *Mirror Drawing*: Milner (1966); Damasio et al. (1985)
7. *Bimanual Tracking:* Corkin (1968)
8. *Visual Discrimination:* Sidman et al. (1968)
9. *Complex perceptual-motor skill*: Ostergaard (1984)
10. *Jigsaw Learning*: Brooks & Baddeley (1976)
11. *Maze Learning:* Talland (1965); Milner et al. (1968); Cermak et al. (1973); Cermak (1976); Starr & Phillips (1970); Meissner 1967); Martin (1984)
12. *Discrimination Learning*: Oscar-Berman, Sahakian, & Wikmark (1976); Oscar-Berman & Zola-Morgan (1980a, 1980b)
13. *Identification of stimuli on the basis of partial information*: Schneider (1912); Williams (1953); Milner et al. (1968); Warrington & Weiskrantz (1968, 1970, 1974); Weiskrantz & Warrington, (1970); Ostergaard (1984); Graft, Squire, & Mandler (1984)
14. *McGill Anomalies Test*: Warrington & Weiskrantz (1978); Baddeley (1982)
15. *Hidden Objects Test*: Crovitz, Harvey, & McClanahan (1981); Meudell & Mayes (1981); Daniel (this chapter)
16. *Mirror Writing & Reading Skill*: Cohen & Squire (1980)
17. *Picture Recognition:* Huppert & Piercy (1978); Johnson & Kim (1985)
18. *Complex Learning*: (see also Booker & Schacter, this volume)
    a. *Piano tunes:* Kohnstamm (1917); Starr & Phillips (1970)
    b. *Poetry*: Kohnstamm (1917)
    c. *Prose recall:* Payne & Butters (1982)
    d. *Paired-associates*: Winocur & Kinsbourne (1978)
    e. *Word lists*: Jaffe & Katz (1975); Crovitz (1979); Kovner, Mattis, & Pass (1985); Daniel (this volume)
    f. *Delayed nonmatching to sample:* Squire et al. (1988)
    g. *Mathematical concepts* (generation of the Fibonacci series): Wood (1974); Ostergaard (1984)
    h *Puzzle rule-learning* (Tower of Hanoi): Chuilli & Michaelis (1988)
    i. *Computer programming*: Glisky, Schacter & Tulving (1986); (see Booker & Schacter, this volume)

Note. Not all of the above studies determined whether autobiographical memory for the learning episode was or was not present. Instead, the above studies simply address the specific issue of what amnesics can learn. Furthermore, the above list is biased in that it only shows studies where amnesics demonstrated some learning; in some studies (e.g., Schacter & Graf, 1986), severely amnesic patients learned less than controls, whereas, in other studies (e.g. Squire et al., 1988), amnesics could not learn certain tasks at all. This table was modified after Parkin, 1982.

Unfortunately, only recently have investigators been directing their attention toward the study of autobiographical amnesia *per se* (Wood et al., 1982; Zola-Morgan et al., 1983; Baddeley & Wilson, 1986; Crovitz, 1986). Instead, a growing amount of research effort is being directed towards the study of preserved learning in amnesics (e.g., Table 1; Booker & Schacter, this volume). This research bias is unfortunate for two reasons. First, at a theoretical level, a more complete understanding of the human organic amnesic syndrome (and normal human memory functioning and failure, by extrapolation) will only occur after thorough investigations of autobiographical amnesia, preserved learning abilities in amnesics, and the study of the relationship between the two, take place.

Second, this research bias may result in few methods being developed to reinstate retrograde and/or anterograde autobiographical memory in organic amnesics. In fact, the present investigator knows of only one case study where a serious attempt was made to restore retrograde autobiographical memory in a person who had suffered a severe head-injury (Crovitz, 1986). (This attempt was successful.) This study aside, the rest of the studies have attempted to teach organic amnesics non-autobiographical memory skills and information (e.g., Jaffe & Katz, 1975; Godfrey & Knight, 1985; Schacter, Rich, & Stampp, 1985). However, it must be reiterated that, while teaching amnesics non-autobiographical memory skills and information is of course very important in helping them to regain control over their lives, the amnesics are still going to be left with a deficiency in the past retrieval and future encoding of autobiographical events - a deficit which may bother amnesics the most (Sunderland, Harris, & Baddeley, 1983; Crovitz, 1986).

Why has so little research been conducted into the study and restoration of autobiographical memory in organic amnesics? First, the study of autobiographical memory in normal subjects is still at a relatively early stage of development (Rubin, 1986). Second, the attempt to restore forgotten autobiographical memories in amnesics is a very difficult undertaking, one which some researchers may feel is not only difficult, but impossible for two reasons. First, it can at times prove difficult to delineate one neighboring autobiographical episode from the background of other neighboring autobiographical episodes in any person (Neisser, 1986). Second, with respect to retrograde autobiographical memories, it is difficult to unequivocally corroborate the occurrence of past autobiographical memories in all humans, whether organic amnesics (Baddeley & Wilson, 1986; Butters & Cermak, 1986; Crovitz, 1986), or normal research subjects (Rubin, 1986).

However, these difficulties do not let researchers off the hook with respect to failing to devote much attention to autobiographical amnesia, because organic amnesics can also have anterograde autobiographical amnesia (cf. Crovitz et al., 1984), which can be systematically studied.

There are two purposes to this chapter. The first purpose is to report results from two experiments in which autobiographical amnesia was prospectively studied. In this regard, as close as was possible, a standardized autobiographical event in the lives of patients undergoing electroconvulsive therapy (ECT) for depressive illness was created before patients' fifth or sixth ECT. In the creation of these autobiographical episodes, the examiner was part-and-parcel of that autobiographical episode, and therefore knew that the episode did indeed occur. Furthermore, as will be seen in both experiments, ECT served as a highly controlled means of producing autobiographical amnesia in patients despite the presence of preserved learning in the same patients of verbal stimuli (Experiment One) and of perceptual stimuli (Experiment Two).

The second purpose of this chapter is to discuss theoretical and practical issues related to the production of autobiographical amnesia in these patients. In particular, the following five questions will be asked: 1) Can autobiographical memory be broken-down into more basic component parts (e.g., temporal and spatial)? 2) If autobiographical memory cannot be broken down into component parts, does it have to be treated as a single entity? 3) If it can't be broken down into component parts, what implications does this have for reinstating autobiographical memory in organic amnesics? 4) Can autobiographical memory be cued in amnesics at all? 5) How is autobiographical amnesia related to preserved learning? In particular, is it possible that autobiographical memory might "spring into existence" if a certain critical threshold level of preserved learning is present?

Experiment One

Material and Methods

Subjects and ECT Technique. Sixteen male inpatients receiving a course of ECT for depression were studied. No patient was tested who had any evidence or history of neurological dysfunction. Further details concerning patient selection procedures and ECT technique can be found elsewhere (Daniel et al., 1982, 1985).

<u>Memory Testing.</u> Patients were tested 45 minutes before their sixth ECT. The sixth ECT treatment was selected because a substantial remission in depressive symptomatology is usually achieved by the fifth or sixth treatment (Fink, 1979). (We wanted to avoid the contaminating effects of depression that might have occurred earlier in the series of ECT treatments.) Thus, approximately 45 minutes before their sixth ECT, each patient was read the "Airplane List" (Crovitz, 1979) three times (see Table 2). This story contains ten target words structured in a bizarre imagery chain-mnemonic format to encourage deep and elaborate encoding (Crovitz, 1979). After each reading, free-recall memory was tested. A free-recall score was calculated by counting the total number of words recalled from the three readings. No single word was counted more than once in this score.

Following the third free-recall testing, multiple-choice recognition memory was tested. The correct word was randomly interspersed with four distractor words. The patient was shown all five choices printed on paper, while the examiner read all the choices to the patient and asked, "*Which of those words was in the story?*" If the patient said he did not know, he was told to guess.

Table 2

The Airplane List

The first word is ***Airplane.*** Remember that however you like. The next word is ***Giraffe,*** because the Airplane is filled with Giraffes sitting in the seats. The next word is ***Bologna,*** because each of the Giraffes is holding a Bologna and taking bites out of it. The next word is ***Moon,*** because the Moon is is really made out of Bologna, not green cheese. The next word is ***Elephant,*** because there is an Elephant on the Moon, not a man in the Moon. The next word is ***Ball,*** because the Elephant is hitting a Ball with his trunk. The next word is ***Grass,*** because the Ball is covered with Grass, not leather. The next word is ***Wall,*** because the Grass is growing all the way to the Great Wall of China. The next word is ***Cabinet,*** because the President's Cabinet is having a meeting inside the Wall. The last word is ***Street,*** because the Cabinet gets fired and goes off down the Street looking for work (from Crovitz, 1979).

The patient was then read each sentence of the story one at a time. Each sentence was printed on paper, with the same target and four distractor words printed below each sentence. As in the multiple-choice format, patients were instructed to pick-out the correct word. Following each response, the patient was corrected if he missed the word, because the correct word was always in the next sentence.

Twenty-four hours after the sixth ECT, each patient was first asked, *"Do you remember being told a story containing ten words yesterday morning before your treatment?"* The patient's "yes" or "no" response was accepted on face value as indicating the presence or absence of autobiographical memory for having heard the Airplane List. Each patient was told that he *was* told a story before his treatment, and was asked to free-recall words from the story. If the patient did not remember having heard the story, he was asked to guess some words that might have been in this story. Multiple-choice and story cued recognition testing were then performed exactly as was done before ECT. After story-cued recognition, each patient was asked, *"Do you now remember being told that story before yesterday's treatment?"* This question was asked to see if autobiographical memory was reinstated or cued by the various testing procedures (Schacter & Tulving, 1982).

Results

Autobiographical Memory

When patients were first asked whether or not they remembered hearing the story before their treatment, 7 of the 16 patients responded in the affirmative, indicating the presence of autobiographical memory. Furthermore, all seven of these patients could free-recall words (mean = 3.9 words) from the story, thus lending support to their claim of intact autobiographical memory (cf. Booker & Schacter, this volume). These seven patients will serve as the control group in Experiment One. When the remaining nine patients were asked the same question, they all responded in the negative, indicating the absence of autobiographical memory. Furthermore, none of the latter patients could free-recall words from the story.

Only two patients who initially had no autobiographical memory claimed to have autobiographical memory when asked whether they now remembered hearing the story after story-cued testing. One of these patients said, *"Yeah, about halfway through there it seemed like maybe I heard something about a crocodile and giraffe riding an airplane or something, but that's the first time it come to me.*" (This claim was judged not to be very convincing.) The other patient, after missing, and then being corrected with respect to the correct word in the first sentence during the story-cued testing, exclaimed, "*I remember the story now! It popped back in!*" Thus this person missed the first word, but remembered all of the rest of the words during story-cued testing, and claimed to have autobiographical memory after story-cued testing. (This claim was judged to be convincing.)

With respect to the reinstatement of autobiographical memory during cueing, however, the change with just these two patients is statistically non-significant by a McNemar Test for the significance of change ($T = 2.0$; $df = 1$; $p > .50$) (Conover, 1980). However, this investigator feels that this effect of cueing in at least the latter patient may be clinically significant, because it may indicate that autobiographical memory can be reinstated if enough cueing is performed (cf. Crovitz, 1986). More will said about this issue in the Discussion.

Verbal Memory in Relation to Autobiographical Memory

Figure 1 illustrates the percent forgetting of words as a function of the presence or absence of autobiographical memory on the first autobiographical memory question. Patients who had autobiographical memory tended to do better on all three levels of memory testing than patients without autobiographical memory. A 2 by 3 ANOVA revealed that more words were correctly identified as the patients went from free-recall to multiple-choice to story-cued recognition ($F = 17.7$; $df = 2, 28$; $p < .0001$), and that more words were remembered by patients with autobiographical memory than by patients without autobiographical memory ($F = 20.0$; $df = 1, 14$; $p < .00005$). There was no interaction between presence versus absence of autobiographical memory and level of testing ($F = 0.4$; $df = 2, 28$; $p > .20$).

Pairwise Tukey HSD tests revealed that patients without autobiographical memory forgot significantly more words than did patients with autobiographical memory on free-recall and multiple-choice testing ($p<.05$), but not on story-cued testing ($p>.05$). Nevertheless, patients without autobiographical memory demonstrated greater than chance word recognition (> 2.0 words) on multiple-choice testing (mean = 3.9 words, $t = 2.6$; $p <.025$, one-tailed) and story-cued testing (mean = 6.2 words, $t = 5.4$; $p <.0005$, one-tailed) after ECT. This finding that patients with autobiographical amnesia nevertheless demonstrated verbal learning is consistent with other reports of preserved learning in amnesics (see Table 1; Booker & Schacter, this volume).

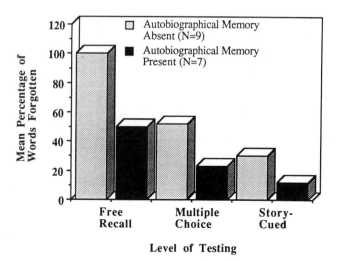

Figure 1. Mean percentage of words forgotten versus level of testing in patients with versus without autobiographical memory on the first autobiographical memory question.

Experiment Two

Material and Methods

Subjects. Fifty-six inpatients (1 female, 55 male) who were also receiving ECT for depression were studied. The same patient selection procedures and ECT techniques that were used in Experiment One were used in this experiment; exact details of these procedures and techniques can be found elsewhere (Daniel et al., 1983). Patients with any evidence of opthalmological disease were not tested, and, if a patient wore glasses, he or she was required to use them throughout all testing.

Memory Testing. In Experiment One, each patient's "yes" or "no" response to the presence versus absence of autobiographical memory was taken at face value as indicating the presence or absence of autobiographical memory. However, in the present experiment, two objectively verifiable autobiographical memory questions were incorporated into the experimental design.

Thirty to sixty minutes (mean = 51.6 minutes, SD = 35.9 minutes) before their fifth ECT, patients were asked to find a hidden figure of a cow in a

Figure 2. Hidden figure of a cow in the right photograph (Dallenbach, 1951). In the left figure, one sees a hand-traced copy of the cow stripped of extraneous background detail. The photograph is reprinted by permission of the University of Illinois Press.

photograph by one of two randomly selected examiners (see Figure 2 - right). A stopwatch was pressed immediately after the examiner said, *"I want you to tell me when you see a cow in this photograph."* If the patient did not perceive the hidden cow in two minutes, he or she was shown a hand-traced copy of the cow stripped of extraneous background detail   (see Figure 2 - left). He or she was told to find the cow first in the stripped figure, and then in the original photograph. When the patient indicated he or she saw the cow, he or she was asked three corroborative questions (*"Where are its eyes? Where is its mouth? What is the direction of its head?"*). Time was stopped (mean = 2.3 minutes, SD = 1.5 minutes) at the end of these questions only if they were correctly answered, and when it was clear that the patient saw the cow.

Twenty-four hours after their fifth ECT, each patient was approached by two examiners, one of whom had shown him the cow photograph the previous day. One of the examiners, who did all of the autobiographical memory questioning (randomly determined), asked the patient, *"Do you remember being shown a black-and-white photograph yesterday morning before your treatment?"* The patient's response was scored either "yes" or "no", and this response was taken as a global measure of autobiographical memory for having seen the photograph the day before.

The patient was then shown four hidden figure photographs, including the cow photograph, one at a time (All four of these hidden figure photographs can be found in Crovitz, Harvey, & McClanahan, 1981.) The order of presentation of these four photographs was randomly determined. With each hidden figure, a stripped figure was presented after two minutes if hidden figure perception had not occurred (in a similar fashion as with the cow photograph), and three corroborative questions were asked when the patient claimed perception of each figure. A perceptual learning score was calculated by counting the decline in seconds required to see the hidden cow after ECT compared to before ECT.

Following presentation of each photograph, the patient was shown all four photographs simultaneously (as in the photograph in Crovitz et al., 1981), and was asked, *"Which of these four photographs did you see before your treatment yesterday?"* If the patient did not know, he or she was told to guess anyway. This multiple-choice testing was performed to objectively verify the presence versus absence of autobiographical memory. After the multiple-choice testing, the patient was informed that he or she was shown the cow photograph before his or her treatment. He or she was then asked, *"Do you have any memory **now** of having seen the cow picture before your last treatment?"* Responses were scored "yes" or "no". This question was asked to see if *global* autobiographical memory was reinstated or cued by the repeated exposure to the cow photograph (Schacter and Tulving, 1982).

The patient was then asked, *"Which one of us showed you the cow photograph yesterday morning before your last treatment? "* The patient was advised that the correct person was not necessarily the one doing the talking. This procedure allowed us to further objectively verify the presence or absence of autobiographical memory by randomly varying the examiner before and after ECT, thereby using the examiner as a multiple-choice recognition stimulus after ECT.

Results

Autobiographical Memory

Thirty-three of the 56 patients claimed to have autobiographical memory when asked the first question *("Do you remember being shown a black-and-white photograph yesterday morning before your treatment?").* Eighteen of these 33 patients spontaneously volunteered information that unequivocally corroborated this positive response (e.g., *"It was a cow."*), while one of the 33 patients gave information (*"Seemed like it was a color photograph"*) that made us skeptical of his "yes" response (this patient displayed no evidence of autobiographical memory on the remaining three questions).

Six of the 56 patients changed their "yes" or "no" response from the first to the third question (third question = "*Do you have any memory **now** of having seen the cow picture before your last treatment?*"). This change is statistically nonsignificant (p >.50) (Conover, 1980). Furthermore, of the six patients who did change their global "yes" or "no" response, five patients changed from "yes" to "no", and only one patient changed from "no" to "yes". (This latter patient replied, to question three, "*I don't know where, but I remember seeing it before.*") The fact that five out of six patients changed their response from "yes" to "no" on questions one and three, respectively, indicates that, in all likelihood, the patients were trying to be honest during the autobiographical memory testing.

Figure 3 illustrates a histogram of the number of patients in relation to the number of questions indicating the presence of autobiographical memory. It is clear from Figure 3 that this frequency distribution is radically bimodal. In other words, evidence of autobiographical memory tended to be either completely present or completely absent (binomial randomization test: p < .0001; Quade, personal communication, September, 1981). It therefore might be concluded that, in the present experiment, the presence versus absence of autobiographical memory followed an "all-or-none" principle.

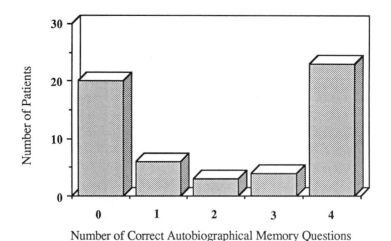

Number of Correct Autobiographical Memory Questions

Figure 3. Autobiographical memory frequency distribution.

It should be noted that neither the time required before ECT to perceive the hidden figure of the cow (p = .47) nor the actual time of presentation of the cow photograph before ECT (p = .38) were related to the patients' autobiographical memory scores. Therefore, neither the consolidation interval (i.e., the duration of the testing session) nor the length of time before ECT had any bearing on the autobiographical memory scores (cf. Ribot, 1882; McGaugh & Hertz, 1972; Weingartner & Parker, 1984).

Perceptual Learning in Relation to Autobiographical Memory

Forty-eight of the 56 patients were able to perceive the hidden figure of the cow before and after ECT. The 48 patients who did perceive the hidden cow on both occasions demonstrated perceptual learning by a pre-post savings in time required to see the hidden cow (means: pre-ECT = 139.5 seconds, post-ECT = 52.6 seconds; t = 6.75; p <.0005, one-tailed).

To test the hypothesis that patients with autobiographical memory would demonstrate greater perceptual learning than patients without autobiographical memory, only the perceptual learning scores by the patients with either complete evidence (i.e., all autobiographical memory questions indicated the presence of autobiographical memory) or no evidence (i.e., all autobiographical memory questions indicated the absence of autobiographical memory) were analyzed. This limitation was imposed to gain a certain degree of experimental purity. Thus the perceptual learning scores from the 24 patients who had intact autobiographical memory (these patients will serve as the control group) and the 19 patients with no evidence of autobiographical memory were compared.

The pre-post ECT savings in time was converted into a percentage savings score. Following arcsine transformation of these percent scores, statistical analysis revealed that patients with autobiographical memory demonstrated more perceptual savings than did patients without autobiographical memory (t = 4.04; p < .0005, one-tailed). Nevertheless, patients without autobiographical memory demonstrated, as expected, a pre-post savings in perceptual time required to see the hidden cow (t = 4.13; p < .005, one-tailed). Figure 4 illustrates these results.

The results displayed in Figure 4 indicate that autobiographical memory may somehow be related to perceptual learning. To investigate this result further, a Spearman rank-order correlational analysis revealed that, the greater the amount of perceptual learning, the higher was the autobiographical

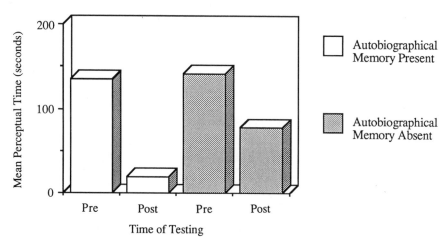

Figure 4. Perceptual learning in relation to presence or absence of autobiographical memory.

memory score (the number of questions indicating the presence of autobiographical memory) in all 48 patients (r = +.465; p = .001).

Discussion

In Experiments One and Two, a verbal learning task and a perceptual learning task were respectively nested within the experimentally created autobiographical episode. Despite the interpolated ECT treatment between the initial learning episode and the 24 hour delayed retention interval in both experiments, all patients, including those without autobiographical memory, demonstrated verbal or perceptual learning, respectively. This latter result with respect to preserved learning despite amnesia for having undergone the learning episode (autobiographical amnesia) is consistent with a growing body of research evidence indicating that amnesics can learn despite being unaware of having learned (see Table 1; Parkin, 1982; Booker & Schacter this volume).

Additionally, results from Experiments One and Two (see Figures 1 & 4, respectively) indicate that patients without autobiographical memory demonstrated less verbal and perceptual learning, respectively, than did patients with completely intact autobiographical memory. Furthermore, in Experiment Two, there was a positive rank-order correlation between the number of questions indicating the presence of autobiographical memory and the amount of perceptual learning. What do these results suggest with respect to understanding the relationship between autobiographical memory and preserved learning?

One might hypothesize that there is a complete dissociation between autobiographical memory and preserved learning systems (Parkin, 1982; Wood et al., 1982). At first glance, this hypothesis appears to be supported by results from the present two experiments, because the presence of autobiographical memory was distributed in such a radically bimodal fashion (e.g., see Figure 3). However, it has been suggested that the acquisition and retention of information in amnesics is impaired compared to normal controls (Cermak, 1984; Butters & Cermak, 1986; Squire et al., 1988). The results displayed in Figures 1 & 4 certainly support this suggestion; patients without autobiographical memory demonstrated less preserved learning than did patients with autobiographical memory.

What does this suggestion mean with respect to the hypothesis that there is a complete dissociation between autobiographical memory and preserved learning systems?. If these two systems were completely separable, one would not expect to see a lower level of preserved learning in patients without autobiographical memory compared to patients with autobiographical memory, which occurred in the present study (see Figures 1 & 4); one would expect to see equal levels of preserved learning. The fact that patients without autobiographical memory demonstrated less preserved learning than patients with autobiographical memory in fact suggests that preserved learning cannot be completely separated from autobiographical amnesia. This notion is further supported by the positive correlation between the number of questions indicating the presence of autobiographical memory and the amount of preserved learning in Experiment Two. It appears that autobiographical memory and preserved learning are inextricably intertwined. How might they be intertwined?

There are two ways in which autobiographical memory might be related to preserved learning. First, let us assume that autobiographical memory is composed of separable component parts (e.g., temporal, spatial). If one were able to construct an autobiographical memory questionnaire that objectively assessed these component parts (this could be done by creating an objectively verifiable autobiographical episode in patients' lives in which one systematically varies these component parts), one might find that autobiographical memory is directly related (maybe even linearly) to the amount of preserved learning. If this hypothetical relationship is true, one might conclude that diseases that cause an amnestic syndrome impair autobiographical memory and preserved learning to the same degree.

In order to discuss the second possible way in which autobiographical memory might be related to preserved learning, it is necessary to discuss the notion that autobiographical memory may exist as a single whole (cf. Rubin, 1986). In diametric opposition to the first reductionistic position, one might hypothesize that autobiographical memory is an "emergent" phenomenon in which the whole is greater than the sum of its component parts (cf. Merleau-Ponty, 1962, 1963, 1964; Polanyi, 1964, 1966, 1968; Sperry, 1969, 1970; Robinson, 1982; Neisser, 1986). By contrast, the previous reductionistic position states that autobiographical memory is simply equal to the sum of its component parts. The position that autobiographical memory is a completely emergent phenomenon appears to have been embraced by some investigators of autobiographical memory (e.g., Rubin, 1986).

However, the present investigator thinks that the finding (see Figures 1 & 4) that patients without autobiographical memory demonstrated less preserved learning than did patients with autobiographical memory invalidates the position that autobiographical memory is a completely emergent phenomenon that is separable from other cognitive processes, such as preserved learning. Furthermore, the finding of a significant correlation between autobiographical memory and preserved learning and the fact that one patient who had autobiographical memory reinstated both go against the position that autobiographical memory is a completely emergent phenomenon.

If autobiographical memory is neither the sum of its component parts nor a completely emergent phenomenon that is irreducible to component parts and/or preserved learning, what is left? The remaining possibility is that autobiographical memory is a partially emergent nested phenomenon (cf. Neisser, 1986), one which, while partially emergent, can nevertheless be measured. If one could measure the different components (e.g., temporal, spatial) of autobiographical memory with a fairly comprehensive test battery, one might find that autobiographical memory is related to preserved learning in a fashion like that illustrated in Figure 5. This hypothetical distribution of autobiographical memory scores in relation to preserved learning suggests a curvilinear relationship between the two up to a critical threshold level between "A" and "B", after which an asymptotic "ceiling effect" of complete (i.e., 100%) autobiographical memory is reached. Before this critical threshold is reached, however, one would expect incomplete autobiographical memory. In this region ("A"), patients might experience varying degrees of vague feelings of uncon-

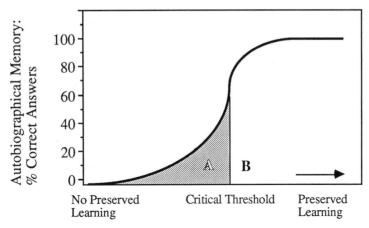

Figure 5. Hypothetical relationship of autobiographical memory to the amount of preserved learning. After the critical threshold of preserved learning is reached, complete autobiographical memory is present.

solidated familiarity with respect to having undergone the original autobiographical episode.

An example of the critical threshold of preserved learning being reached, followed by complete restoration of autobiographical memory, might be the patient in Experiment One who at first did not remember hearing the Airplane List before ECT, but, after hearing the first sentence during story-cued testing, then guessing the missing word (which was followed by the investigator telling him that he was wrong, and that the correct word was actually "Airplane"), exclaimed, *"I remember the story now! It popped back in!"* Because this patient then missed no more words during story-cued testing, and then claimed to have autobiographical memory after story-cued testing, one might surmise that this patient was close to the critical threshold of preserved learning at which time the experimenter-supplied correction pushed him over the threshold, thus allowing the emergence of complete autobiographical memory.

Obviously, however, one cannot conclude from just one patient that this hypothesis of partial emergence is unequivocally corroborated. Future studies need to systematically test this hypothesis. In this regard, for example, future studies could teach amnesic and/or normal subjects tasks in which the spatial context is varied (e.g., one could test patients in different rooms on different floors of a hospital), the temporal context is varied (e.g., one could test patients in the morning, afternoon, or evening), the examiner is varied, and various background stimuli are varied (e.g., background music versus no music, background smells versus no smells.). After a process that produces autobiographical amnesia, one could then re-test the subjects' autobiographical memory and preserved learning to see how they are inter-related. (The amnesia-inducing process could be the mere passage of time in organic amnesics who have ongoing anterograde autobiographical amnesia. With normal subjects, one could administer amnesia-inducing benzodiazepines [Clarke et al., 1970; Gregg et al., 1974; Gelfman et al., 1978; Bixler et al., 1979; Linnoila et al., 1981; Brown et al., 1982; Nissen et al., 1987; Wolkowitz et al., 1987]. With severely depressed individuals, ECT would produce the amnesia.).

From such studies, science would perhaps gain valuable theoretical information concerning the human organic amnestic syndrome. Furthermore, from a clinical standpoint, it might be possible to figure-out how to help organic amnesics to encode ongoing autobiographical episodes more deeply (perhaps by overlearning life tasks or rehearsing life episodes), so that a patient can have more of a sense of continuity with his or her own past.

Acknowledgements

This work was supported by funds from the Center for Applied Psychological Research made available through the Centers of Excellence Program of the State of Tennessee, and by the Medical Research Service of the Durham, North Carolina Veterans Administration Medical Center. I wish to thank David Power, Dennis Boyles, and Gary Strong for serving as alternate examiners, Andy Dattel for statistical assistance, and the staff of the Durham VA Psychiatry Service, for their full cooperation throughout this study. Finally, I would like to thank Herb Crovitz, Mike Williams, and Bob Vidulich for many lively discussions on autobiographical memory.

References

Andrews, E., Poser, C.M. & Kessler, M. (1982). Retrograde amnesia for forty years. *Cortex, 18*, 441-442.

Baddeley, A.D. (1982). Domains of recollection. *Psychological Review, 89,* 708-729.

Baddeley, A. & Wilson, B. (1986). Amnesia, autobiographical memory, and confabulation. In D.C. Rubin (Ed.) *Autobiographical memory*, Chapter 13, pp. 225-252, Cambridge: Oxford University Press.

Bixler, E.O., Scharf, M.D., Soldatos, C.R., Mitsky, D.J. & Kales, A. (1979). Effects of hypnotic drugs on memory. *Life Sciences, 25,* 1379-1388.

Booker & Schacter, D.L. (1988). Toward a cognitive neuropsychology of complex learning. In J.M. Williams and C.J.Long (Eds.), *Cognitive Approaches to Neuropsychology,* New York: Plenum.

Brooks, D.N. & Baddeley, A.D. (1976). What can amnesic patients learn? *Neuropsychologia, 14,* 111-122.

Brown, J., Lewis, V., Brown, M. Horn, G. & Bowes, J.B. (1982). A comparison between transient amnesias induced by two drugs (Diazepam or Lorazepam) and amnesia of organic origin. *Neuropsychologia, 20,* 55-70.

Butters, N. & Cermak, L.S. (1986). A case study of the forgetting of autobiographical knowledge: Implications for the study of retrograde amnesia. In D.C. Rubin (Ed.) *Autobiographical memory,* chapter 14, pp. 253-272, Cambridge: Oxford University Press.

Butters, N. (1987). Procedural learning in dementia: A double dissociation between Alzheimer and Huntington's disease patients in verbal priming and motor skill learning. *Journal of Clinical and Experimental Neuropsychology, 9,* 68-69.

Cermak, L.S. (1976). The encoding capacity of a patient with amnesia due to encephalitis. *Neuropsychologia, 14,* 311-326.

Cermak, L.S. (1984). The episodic/semantic distinction in amnesia. In N. Butters & L.R. Squire (eds.), *The Neuropsychology of memory* pp. 55-62). New York: Guilford Press.

Cermak, L.S., Lewis, R., Butters, N. & Goodglass, H. (1973). Role of verbal mediation in the performance of motor skills by Korsakoff patients. *Perceptual and Motor Skills, 37,* 259-262.

Chuilli, S.J. & Michaelis, J.F. (1988). Evidence for strategy use in procedural learning. *Journal of Clinical and Experimental Neuropsychology, 10,* 85-86.

Claparede, E. (1951) Recognition and 'me-ness' In D. Rapaport (Ed. & Trans.), *Organization and Pathology of Thought.* New York: Columbia University Press. (Reprinted from *Archives de Psychologie,* 1911, *11,* 79-90).

Clarke, P.R.F., Eccersley, P.S., Frisby, J.P. & Thornton, J.A. (1970). The amnesic effect of Diazepam (Valium). *British Journal of Anaesthesiology, 42,* 690-697.

Cockburn, J. & Wilson, B. (1986). How well do people with memory problems recognize their difficulties? *Journal of Clinical and Experimental Neuropsychology, 8,* p. 130.

Cohen, N.J. (1984). Preserved learning capacity in amnesia: evidence for multiple memory systems. In L.R. Squire & N. Butters (Eds.), *Neuropsychology of memory.* New York: Guilford Press.

Cohen, N.J. & Squire, L.R. (1980). Preserved learning and retention of pattern-analyzing skill in amnesia: dissociation of knowing how and knowing that. *Science, 210,* 207-210.

Conover, W.J. (1980). *Practical nonparametric statistics* (second edition). New York: John Wiley.

Corkin, S. (1965). Tactually-guided maze learning in man: Effects of unilateral cortical excisions and bilateral hippocampal lesions. *Neuropsychologia, 3,* 339-351.

Corkin, S. (1968). Acquisition of motor skill after bilateral medial temporal-lobe excision. *Neuropsychologia, 6,* 255-265.

Crovitz, H.F. (1979). Memory retraining in brain-damaged patients: The airplane list. *Cortex, 15,* 131-134.

Crovitz, H.F. (1986). Loss and recovery of autobiographical memory after head injury. In Rubin, D. (Ed.): *Autobiographical memory.* Cambridge: Oxford University Press.

Crovitz, H.F., Cordoni, C.N., Daniel, W.F. & Perlman, J. (1984). Everyday forgetting experiences: Real-time investigations with implications for the study of memory management in brain-damaged patients. *Cortex, 20,* 349-359.

Crovitz, H.F. & Daniel, W.F. (1987). Length of retrograde amnesia after head injury: A revised formula. *Cortex, 23,* 695-698.

Crovitz, H.F., Harvey, M.T., & McClanahan, S. (1981). Hidden memory: a rapid method for the study of amnesia using perceptual learning. *Cortex, 17,* 273-278.

Crovitz, H.F., & Schiffman, H. (1974). Frequency of episodic memories as a function of their age. *Bulletin of the Psychonomic Society, 4,* 517-518.

Crovitz, H.F. & Quina-Holland, K. (1976). Proportion of episodic memories from early childhood by years of age. *Bulletin of the Psychonomic Society, 7,* 61-62.

Dallenback, K. M. (1951). A picture puzzle with a new principle of concealment. *American Journal of Psychology, 64,* 431-433.

Damasio, A.R., Eslinger, P.J., Damasio, H., Van Hoesen, G.W. & Cornell, S. (1985). Multimodal amnesic syndrome following bilateral temporal and basal forebrain damage. *Archives of Neurology, 42,* 252-259.

Daniel, W.F., Crovitz, H.F., Weiner, R.D., & Rogers, H.J. (1982). The effects of ECT modifications on autobiographical and verbal memory. *Biological Psychiatry, 17,* 919-924.

Daniel, W.F., Weiner, R.D., & Crovitz, H.F. (1983). Autobiographical amnesia with ECT: An analysis of the roles of stimulus waveform, electrode placement, stimulus energy, and seizure length. *Biological Psychiatry, 18,* 121-126.

Daniel, W.F., Weiner, R.D., Crovitz, H.F., Swartzwelder, H.S., & Kahn, E.M. (1985). ECT-induced amnesia and postictal EEG suppression. *Biological Psychiatry, 20,* 520-531.

De Renzi, E., Liotti, M. & Nichelli, P. (1987). Semantic amnesia with preservation of autobiographical memory: A case report. *Cortex, 23,* 575-597.

Evans, F.J. & Kihlstrom, J.F. (1976). Recovery of memory after posthypnotic amnesia. *Journal of Abnormal Psychology, 85,* 564-569.

Evans, F.J. & Kihlstrom, J.F. (1980). Residual effect of suggestions for posthypnotic amnesia: a re-examination. *Journal of Abnormal Psychology, 86,* 327-333.

Evans, F.J. & Thorn, W.A.A. (1966). Two types of posthypnotic amnesia: recall amnesia and source amnesia. *International Journal of Clinical and Experimental Hypnosis, 14,* 162-179.

Fink, M. (1979). *Convulsive therapy: Theory and practice.* New York: Raven Press.

Gardner, H. (1974). *The shattered mind.* New York: Random House (see pp. 176 - 219).

Gelfman, S.S., Gracely, R.H., Driscoll, E.J., Wirdzek, P.R., Sweet, J.B. & Butler, D.P. (1978). Conscious sedation with intravenous drugs: A study of amnesia. *Journal of Oral Surgery, 36,* 191-197.

Glisky, E.L., Schacter, D.L., & Tulving, E. (1986). Learning and retention of computer-related vocabulary in amnesic patients: Method of vanishing cues. *Journal of Clinical and Experimental Neuropsychology, 8,* 292-312.

Godfrey, H.P.D. & Knight, R.G. (1985). Cognitive rehabilitation of memory functioning in amnesiac alcoholics. *Journal of Consulting and Clinical Psychology, 53,* 555-557.

Goldberg, E., Antin, S.A., Bilder, R.M., Gerstman, L.J., Hughes, J.E.O. & Mattis, S. (1981). Retrograde amnesia: Possible role of mesencephalic reticular activation in long-term memory. *Science, 213,* 1392-1394.

Graf, P., Squire, L.R. & Mandler, G. (1984). The information that amnesic patients do not forget. *Journal of Experimental Psychology: Learning, Memory and Cognition, 10,* 164-178.

Gregg, J.M., Ryan, D.E. & Levin, K.H. (1974). The amnesic actions of diazepam. *Journal of Oral Surgery, 32,* 651-663.

Huppert, F.A. & Piercy, M. (1978). Dissociation between learning and remembering in organic amnesia. *Nature, 275,* 317-318.

Jacoby, L.L. & Dallas, M. (1981). On the relationship between autobiographical memory and perceptual learning. *Journal of Experimental Psychology: General, 110,* 306-340.

Jaffe, P.G. & Katz, A.N. (1975). Attenuating anterograde amnesia in Korsakoff's psychosis. *Journal of Abnormal Psychology, 84,* 559-562.

Jenkins, C.D., Hurst, M.W. & Rose, R.M. (1979). Life changes: Do people really remember? *Archives of General Psychiatry, 36,* 379-384.

Johnson, M.K. & Kim, J.K. (1985). Recognition of pictures by alcoholic Korsakoff patients. *Bulletin of the Psychonomic Society, 23,* 456-458.

Kinsbourne, M. & Wood, F. (1975). Short-term memory processes and the amnesic syndrome. In D.A. Deutsch (Ed.) *Short-Term Memory,* New York: Academic Press.

Knopman, D.S. & Nissen, M.J. (1987). Implicit learning in patients with probable Alzheimer's Disease. *Neurology, 37,* 784-788.

Kohnstamm, O. (1917). Uber das Krankheitsbild der retro-graden amnesie und die unterscheidung des spontanen und des lernenden. *Merkens, Msch. Psychiatk. Neurol., 41,* 373-382.

Kovner, R., Mattis, S. & Pass, R. (1985). Some amnesics can freely recall large amounts of information in new contexts. *Journal of Clinical and Experimental Neuropsychology, 7,* 395-411.

Kritchevsky, Squire, L.R. & Zouzounis, J.A. (1988). Transient global amnesia: Characterization of anterograde and retrograde amnesia. *Neurology, 38,* 213-219.

Linnoila, M., Erwin, C.W., Brendle, A. & Logue, P.E. (1981). Effects of alcohol and flunitrazepam on mood and performance in healthy young men. *Journal of Clinical Pharmacology, 21,* 430-435.

Linskii, V.P. (1954). On the formation of conditioned reflexes in patients exhibiting Korsakoff's syndrome. *Zh. Vyssh. Nerv. Deiat. Pavlov, 4,* 791-798.

Luria, A.R. (1976). *The neuropsychology of memory.* New York: John Wiley.

Martin, A.J. (1984). Preserved memory in patients with Alzheimer's Disease. *The INS Bulletin* (November), 63-64.

McGaugh, J.L. & Hertz, M.M. (1972). *Memory consolidation.* San Francisco: Albion.

Meissner, W.W. (1967). Memory function in the Korsakoff syndrome. *Journal of Nervous and Mental Disease, 145,* 106-122.

Merleau-Ponty, M. (1962). *Phenomenology of perception.* London: Routledge & Kegan Paul.

Merleau-Ponty, M. (1963). *The Structure of behavior.* Boston: Beacon Press.

Merleau-Ponty, M. (1964). *The primacy of perception.* Chicago: Northwestern Press.

Merriam, S. (1980). The concept and function of reminiscence: A review of the research. *Gerontologist, 20,* 604-608.

Meudell, P. & Mayes, A. (1981). The Claparede phenomenon: A further example in amnesics, a demonstration of a similar effect in normal people with attenuated memory, and a reinterpretation. *Current Psychological Research, 1,* 75-88.

Milner, B. (1966). Amnesia following operation on the temporal lobes. In C.W.M. Whitty & O.L. Zangwill (Eds.) *Amnesia* (First edition), London: Butterworth, pp. 109-133.

Milner, B., Corkin, S. & Teuber, H.L. (1968). Further analysis of the hippocampal amanesic syndrome: 14-year follow up study of H.M. *Neuropsychologia, 6,* 215-234.

Neisser, U. (1986). Nested structure in autobiographical memory. In D.C. Rubin (Ed.) *Autobiographical memory,* chapter 5, pp. 71-81. Cambridge: Oxford University Press.

Nissen, M.J., Knopman, D.S. & Schacter, D.L. (1987). Neurochemical dissociation of memory systems. *Neurology, 37,* 789-794.

Oscar-Berman, M., Sahakian, B.J. & Wikmark, G. (1976). Spatial probability learning by alcoholic Korsakoff patients. *Journal of Experimental Psychology: Human Learning and Memory, 2,* 215-222.

Oscar-Berman, M. & Zola-Morgan, S.M. (1980a). Comparative neuropsychology and Korsakoff's syndrome. I.-Spatial and visual reversal learning. *Neuropsychologia, 18,* 513-525.

Oscar-Berman, M. & Zola-Morgan, S.M. (1980b). Comparative neuropsychology and Korsakoff's syndrome. II.-Two-choice visual discrimination learning, *Neuropsychologia, 18,* 513-525.

Ostergaard, A.L. (1984). Episodic, semantic and procedural memory in a case of amnesia at an early age. *The INS Bulletin* (November), p. 30.

Parkin, A.J. (1982). Residual learning capability inorganic amnesia. *Cortex, 18,* 417-440.

Payne, M.A. & Butters, N. (1982). Motivational factors affecting immediate recall for prose: A comparison of amnesic and dementing patients. *The INS Bulletin* (September), p. 31.

Polanyi, M. (1964). *Personal knowledge: Towards a post-critical philosophy.* Chicago: University of Chicago Press.

Polanyi, M. (1966). *The tacit dimension.* Garden City, N.Y.: Doubleday.

Polanyi, M. (1968). Life's irreducible structure. *Science, 160,* 1308-1312.

Powell, G.E. (1986). The self after brain-injury: Theory, research and rehabilitation. *Journal of Clinical and Experimental Neuropsychology, 8,* p. 115.

Prigatano, G.P. (1984). The problem of self-awareness after brain-injury: Methodological and clinical considerations. *The INS Bulletin* (November), p. 48.

Ribot, T. (1882). *Diseases of memory: An essay in the positive psychology.* New York: Appleton.

Robinson, D.N. (1982). Cerebral plurality and the unity of self. *American Psychologist, 37,* 904-910.

Roman-Campos, G., Poser, C.M. & Wood, R.B. (1980). Persistent retrograde memory deficit after transient global amnesia. *Cortex, 16,* 509-518.

Rousseaux, M., Delafosse, A., Cabaret, M., Lesoni, F. & Jomin, M. (1984). Amnesie retrograde post traumatique. *Cortex, 20,* 575-583.

Rozin, P. (1976). The psychobiological approach to human memory. In M.R. Rosensweig & E.L. Bennett (Eds.), *Neural mechanisms of learning and memory,* Cambridge: MIT Press.

Rubin, D.C. (1982). On the retention function for autobiographical memory. *Journal of Verbal Learning and Verbal Behavior, 21,* 21-38.

Rubin, D.C. (1986). *Autobiographical memory.* Cambridge: Oxford University Press.

Sacks, O. (1985). *The man who mistook his wife for a hat.* New York: Harper & Row (see pp 23-42).

Schacter, D.L. (1985). Priming of old and new knowledge in amnesic patients and normal subjects. *Annals of the New York Academy of Sciences, 444,* 41-53.

Schacter, D.L. (1987a). Implicit expressions of memory in organic amnesia: Learning of new facts and associations. *Human Neurobiology, 6,* 107-118.

Schacter, D.L. (1987b). Implicit Memory: History and current status. *Journal of Experimental Psychology: Learning, Memory, and Cognition, 13,* 501-518.

Schacter, D. L. & Graf, P. (1986). Preserved learning in amnesic patients: Perspectives from research on direct priming. Journal of Clinical and Experimental *Neuropsychology, 8,* 727-743.

Schacter, D.L., Harbluk, J.L., & McLachlan, D.R. (1984). Retrieval without recollection: an experimental analysis of source amnesia. *Journal of Verbal Learning and Verbal Behavior, 23,* 593-611.

Schacter, D.L., Rich, S.A. & Stampp, M.S. (1985). Remediation of memory disorders: Experimental evaluation of the spaced-retrieval technique. *Journal of Clinical and Experimental Neuropsychology, 7,* 79-96.

Schacter, D.L. & Tulving, E. (1982). Amnesia and memory research. In L.S. Cermak (Ed.), *Human memory and amnesia,* Hillsdale: Erlbaum.

Schneider, K. (1912). Uber einige klinisch-pathologische untersuchungsmethoden und ihre ergebnisse. Ergebnisse zugleich ein beitrag zur psychopathologie der Korsakowschen psychose. *Z. Neurol. Psychiat., 8,* 553-616.

Shimamura, A.P. (1986). Priming effects in amnesia: Evidence for a dissociable memory function. *Quarterly Journal of Experimental Psychology, 384,* 619-644.

Sidman, M., Stoddard, L.T. & Mohr, J.P. (1968). Some additional quantitative observations of immediate memory in a patient with bilateral hippocampal lesions. *Neuropsychologia, 6,* 245-254.

Sperry, R.W. (1969). A modified concept of consciousness. *Psychological Review, 76,* 532-536.

Sperry, R.W. (1970). An objective approach to subjective experience: Further explanation of a hypothesis. *Psychological Review, 77,* 585-590.

Squire, L.R. (1987). *Memory and brain.* New York: Oxford University Press.

Squire, L.R., Zola-Morgan, S. & Chen, K.S. (1988). Human amnesia and animal models of amnesia: Performance of amnesic patients on tests designed for the monkey. *Behavioral Neuroscience, 102,* 210-221.

Starr, A. & Phillips, L. (1970). Verbal and motor memory in the amnesic syndrome. *Neuropsychologia, 8,* 75-88.

Sunderland, A., Harris, J.E. & Baddeley, A.D. (1983). Do laboratory tests predict everyday memory? A neuropsychological study. *Journal of Verbal Learning and Verbal Behavior, 22,* 341-357.

Talland, G.A. (1965a). *Deranged memory: A psychonomic study of the amnesic syndrome.* New York: Academic Press.

Talland, G.A. (1956b). An amnesic patient's disavowal of his own recall performance, and its attribution to the interviewer. *Psychiatry and Neurology, 149,* 67-76.

Warrington, E.K. & Weiskrantz, L. (1968). A new method of testing long term retention with special reference to amnesic patients. *Nature, 217,* 972-974.

Warrington, E.K. & Weiskrantz, L. (1970). Amnesic syndrome: Consolidation or retrieval? *Nature, 228,* 628-630.

Warrington, E.K. & Weiskrantz, L. (1974). The effect of prior learning on subsequent retention in amnesic patients. *Neuropsychologia, 12,* 419-428.

Warrington, E.K. & Weiskrantz, L. (1978). Further analysis of the prior learning effect in
amnesic patients. *Neuropsychologia, 16,* 169-177.

Warrington, E.K. & Weiskrantz, L. (1982). Amnesia: A disconnection syndrome? *Neuropsychologia, 20,* 233-248.

Weingartner, H. & Parker, E.S. (1984). *Memory consolidation: Psychobiology of cognition.* Hillsdale: Erlbaum.

Weiskrantz, L. & Warrington, E.K. (1970). Verbal learning and retention by amnesic patients using partial information. *Psychonomic Science, 20,* 210-214.

Weiskrantz, L. & Warrington, E.K. (1979). Conditioning in amnesic patients. *Neuropsychologia, 17,* 187-194.

Williams, M. (1953). Investigations of amnesic defects by progressive prompting. *Journal
of Neurology, Neurosurgery and Psychiatry, 16,* 14-20.

Winocur, G. & Kinsbourne, M. (1978). Contextual cueing as an aid to Korsakoff amnesics.
Neuropsychologia, 16, 671-682.

Winograd, E. & Killinger, W.A. (1983). Relating encoding in early childhood to adult recall: Development of flashbulb memories. *Journal of Experimental Psychology:
General, 112,* 413-422.

Wolkowitz, O.M., Weingartner, H., Thompson, K., Pickar, D., Paul, S.M. & Hommer,
D.N. (1987). Diazepam-induced amnesia: A neuropharmacological model of an
"organic amnestic syndrome." *American Journal of Psychiatry, 144,* 25-29.

Wood, F.B. (1974). The amnesic syndrome as a defect in retrieval from episodic memory.
Duke University. Unpublished doctoral dissertation, 86 pp.

Wood, F., Ebert, V. & Kinsbourne, M. (1982). The episodic-semantic distinction in memory and amnesia: Clinical and experimental observations. In L.S. Cermak (Ed.):
Human memory and amnesia, pp. 167-193, Hillsdale, N.J.: Erlbaum.

Zola-Morgan, S., Cohen, N.J. & Squire, L.R. (1983). Recall of remote episodic memory in
amnesia. *Neuropsychologia, 21,* 487-500.

Subject Index

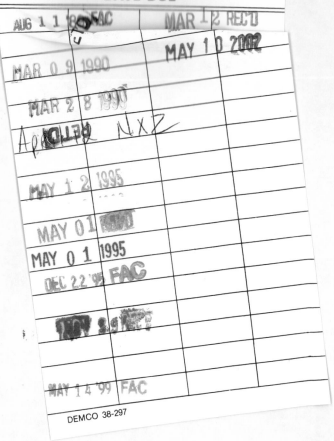